Greyfriars, Reading:
From Prison to Parish Church

Edited by Malcolm Summers

Berkshire Record Society
Volume 31
2024

Published by the Berkshire Record Society
c/o Royal Berkshire Archives
9 Coley Avenue, Reading
Berkshire
RG1 6AF

Printed and bound by
Short Run Press Limited
25 Bittern Road
Sowton Industrial Estate
Exeter, EX2 7LW

ISBN 978-1-7394930-2-8

© Berkshire Record Society
2024

Contents

Plans, photographs and other illustrations		ix
Note on the name of the church		x
Author's Acknowledgments		x

Introduction
- (i) The disposal and use of the friary church from its dissolution in 1538 — xi
- (ii) The purchase of the Bridewell, the Bridewell Keeper's house and Pigeons public house by Rev. William Whitmarsh Phelps — xxii
- (iii) The trustees of the new church — xxxiii
- (iv) Transfer of ownership to the Ecclesiastical Commissioners — xxxiv
- (v) The restoration and reconsecration of the church — xxxv
- (vi) The early years of the parish church of Greyfriars — xli

I. The disposal and use of the friary church from its dissolution in 1538

- (i) Charter of 34 Henry VIII (1542) clauses 5 and 6 — 1
- (ii) Charter of 2 Elizabeth I (1560), clauses 49 and 50 — 2
- (iii) Regulations concerning the reception of prisoners at, and the management of, the Houses of Correction at Speenhamland and Reading (1620) — 3
- (iv) Categories of 'disorderly persons' who should, upon conviction at the Quarter Sessions of the Peace, be sent to the House of Correction (1620) — 8
- (v) Complaint against various inhabitants of the town, including John Ballard, the Keeper of the House of Correction (1620/1) — 9
- (vi) Subsistence bill for prisoners (1743–5) — 10
- (vii) Nomination of Justices of the Peace to examine into the conditions of the Houses of Correction at Abingdon and Reading (1782) — 11
- (viii) Berkshire Quarter Session order book (1783–4) — 12
- (ix) Calendar of Bridewell prisoners (1778, 1783–4) — 13
- (x) Bill for various works, including at the Bridewell (1811–2) — 16
- (xi) Bill for work done at the Bridewell (1817–8) — 17
- (xii) Receipt for bill (above) for work done at the Bridewell (1819) — 19
- (xiii) Bill for Subsistence and other Expenses for the Prisoners in the Bridewell (1816–7) — 20
- (xiv) Bill for medicines at the Bridewell (1817) — 22
- (xv) Petition to the Crown for Grant of Separate Court of Quarter Sessions for the Borough of Reading (1836) — 23

II.	**The purchase of the Bridewell, Bridewell Keeper's House and 'Pigeons' public house by Reverend William Whitmarsh Phelps**	
(i)	Borough of Reading minutes of Council meetings from 9 November 1857 to 22 April 1863	29
(ii)	Abstract of the title of the Mayor, Aldermen and Burgesses of the Borough of Reading to certain properties called the Bridewell and 'Pigeons' public house contracted to be sold to Revd W. W. Phelps (1861)	46
(iii)	Requisitions and observations on title and responses (1861)	65
(iv)	Further abstract of the title of the Mayor, Aldermen and Burgesses of the Borough of Reading in the County of Berks. to the freehold property called the Bridewell and the 'Pigeons' public house agreed to be sold to the Reverend W. W. Phelps (1861)	70
(v)	Draft articles for the agreement for the sale and purchase of the Bridewell and 'Pigeons' Public House, Reading (1861)	74
(vi)	Certificate as to non-payment of knight's fee (1861)	77
(vii)	Abstract of contract for redemption of land tax (1861)	77
(viii)	Release of a piece of land, messuage and hereditaments called the Bridewell and 'Pigeons' in Friar Street Reading from mortgage of 31 March 1854 (1861)	78
(ix)	Statutory declaration of John Readings in proof of the identity of portions of the Bridewell property (1862)	80
(x)	Statutory declaration of John Jackson Blandy, Town Clerk, in proof of the identity of portions of the Bridewell and 'Pigeons' properties (1862)	81
(xi)	Correspondence with the Corporation regarding the lease of the 'Pigeons' (1835)	83
(xii)	Town Clerk's bill re the lease of the 'Pigeons' public house (1835)	84
(xiii)	Lease of the 'Pigeons' public house in Friar Street St Lawrence Reading, for eighty years from Michaelmas 1789 at a rent of £5 (1835)	85
(xiv)	Abstract of the title of Thomas Hawkins Esquire to a messuage, tenement or public house, called 'The Pigeons' situate in Friar Street in Reading in the County of Berks. for the residue of a term of 80 years from Michaelmas 1789 (1862)	89
(xv)	Supplemental abstract of the title of Thomas Hawkins Esquire to a messuage, tenement or public house called 'The Pigeons' situate in Friar Street in Reading in the County of Berks. for the residue of a term of 80 years from Michaelmas 1789 (1863)	95
(xvi)	Further supplemental abstract of the title of Thomas Hawkins Esquire to a messuage, tenement or public house called 'The Pigeons', situate in Friar Street in Reading in	99

	the County of Berks. for the residue of a term of 80 years from Michaelmas 1789 (1863)	
(xvii)	Assignment of the 'Pigeons' public house in Friar Street to the Venerable Archdeacon Phelps (1863)	105
(xviii)	Correspondence: from J. J. Blandy, Town Clerk, on behalf of Reading Corporation, to John Neale, purchaser's solicitor, concerning the payment of £350 for the 'Pigeons' public house (1861–2)	111
(xix)	Conveyance of the site of the late Greyfriars church and other hereditaments situate in Friar Street Reading in the County of Berks. (23 April 1862)	118
(xx)	Covenant for the production of title deeds: the Mayor, Aldermen and Burgesses of the Borough of Reading to the Reverend W. W. Phelps (23 April 1862)	128
(xxi)	Abstract of the title of Mr John Weedon to a freehold estate on the north side of Friar Street in the parish of St Lawrence Reading (1849)	130
(xxii)	Abstract of the title of Mr Francis Morgan Slocombe to a freehold piece of land part of the Greyfriars Estate in the parish of St Lawrence Reading (1862)	139
(xxiii)	Conveyance of pieces of land part of the Greyfriars Estate in the parish of St Lawrence Reading (1862)	146
(xxiv)	Draft deed of agreement between the bishop, patron and incumbent as to the patronage of a church intended to be built on the north side of Friar Street in the parish of St Lawrence Reading in the County of Berks. (1862)	152
(xxv)	Correspondence respecting the conveyancing of the Greyfriars property from Rev. W. W. Phelps to the Ecclesiastical Commissioners (1862–3)	156
(xxvi)	Draft conveyance of a church Site in Reading St Lawrence Parish church, County of Berks., Diocese Oxford, Rev. W. W. Phelps to the Ecclesiastical Commissioners for England (1862)	162

III.	**The restoration and reconsecration of the church**	
(i)	Greyfriars church, Reading. Circulars and appeals relative to the restoration, together with a list of subscribers, balance sheet &c. (1861–6)	164
(ii)	Correspondence by the Rev. W.W. Phelps to the earl of Radnor re the restoration of Greyfriars church, Reading (1861–3)	182
(iii)	Contract for mason's work required in the restoration of the Greyfriars church Saint Lawrence Reading (1862)	190
(iv)	Bond for performance of contract for mason's work required in the restoration of the Greyfriars church Reading (1862)	193
(v)	Plans for the Greyfriars church chancel (*c.*1910)	194

(vi)	Sentence of consecration of Greyfriars church (1863)	196
IV.	**The early years of the parish church of Greyfriars**	
(i)	Churchwardens of Greyfriars church pew rent accounts (1864–70)	198
(ii)	Rented and free seats in Greyfriars church (c1880)	205
(iii)	Extract from an Order in Council stating the boundaries of the to be created District of Greyfriars church. (1864)	206
(iv)	Plan of proposed District of Greyfriars (1864)	207
(v)	Log Book of Greyfriars Infant School (1865–9)	208
(vi)	Log Book of Greyfriars Junior Infant School (1867–9)	264
(vii)	Annual letter addressed to the congregation and parishioners of Greyfriars, Reading, by their pastor (1868)	290
(viii)	'Son, Remember. A sermon preached at Greyfriars church on 21 May 1865	306
(ix)	Permission for the solemnization of marriages at Greyfriars church (1866)	314
(x)	Greyfriars church minutes of Vestry Meetings from April 1869	314
(xi)	Licence of non-residence for 1869	315
(xii)	Correspondence and accounts for moving the pulpit and reading desk (1872)	316

Appendices

1. List of the Reading Borough Bridewell keepers from the late 18th century until the closure of the Bridewell in March 1862 — 320
2. Greyfriars church personnel during the first vicar's incumbency, from December 1863 to October 1874 — 320

Index 322

Plans, photographs and other illustrations

1	Interior of the Borough Bridewell	xvii
2	West Window, Greyfriars church. Drawn by John Billing, 1845	xxi
3	The Bridewell c1860	xxii
4	Portrait of the Venerable Archdeacon Phelps, archdeacon of Carlisle, painted c1865	xxiii
5	Land purchased by Phelps from the Weedon estate	xxiv
6	Plan of the 'Pigeons'	xxx
7	Strip of land to the north of the church building purchased by Rev. W. W. Phelps from Mr F. M. Slocombe	xxxii
8	Plan of land conveyed to the Ecclesiastical Commissioners by Rev. W. W. Phelps in 1862	xxxiv
9	Drawing of the proposed completely restored church	xxxvii
10	The restored Greyfriars church	xxxix
11	Rev. Shadwell Morley Barkworth	xli
12	Greyfriars Schools and Greyfriars church	xliii
13	Reredos, east end, Greyfriars church. Erected in 1894	xlix
14	The Barkworth Memorial, Greyfriars church. Erected in 1895	l
15	Plan of the Greyfriars site to be conveyed	59
16	Interior view of the west end of Greyfriars church before restoration	185
17	Proposed plan of the chancel of Greyfriars church c1910	194
18	Proposed chancel – external view of the east end	195
19	Rented and free Seats in Greyfriars church c1880	205
20	District of Greyfriars church 1864	207

Note on the name of the church

Not including old spellings (such as Fryers), throughout its history 'Greyfriars' has been known by slight variations that can be summarised as: Should the name be one word or two? And is there an apostrophe, and, if so, where should it go? These give rise to the following six variations, all of which occur in past records and newspapers:

Grey Friars church
Grey Friar's church
Grey Friars' church
Greyfriars church
Greyfriar's church
Greyfriars' church

    The form most frequently used in and around the time of the restoration and consecration of the church was Grey Friars church. Then, over the next twenty years, gradually the form Greyfriars' church became the most used. It took until the years after the First World War before the modern usage, one word without any apostrophe, came to be the favoured format.
    This format, Greyfriars church, will be used in the introduction whenever the church's name is mentioned, except in phrases such as 'the church of the Grey Friars'. Within transcribed documents, however, I shall give the format of the name used in the original.

Author's Acknowledgments

For permission to publish transcripts of documents in their keeping, and to reproduce the Greyfriars District map on p. 207, thanks to the Royal Berkshire Archives.

The Greyfriars Church Archive material transcribed in this volume is in the personal collection of the author. The Archive has been collected over many years by several people, and I gratefully acknowledge the part played by these fellow members of Greyfriars Church in saving so much for posterity.

Throughout the process of creating this book, I have greatly appreciated the assistance and expertise of Anne Curry as General Editor, not least for the part she played in originating the idea for the volume. I would like to thank the Council of Berkshire Record Society for their interest and support of this project. My thanks go also to the staff at the Royal Berkshire Archives, who have been unfailingly helpful.

Introduction

(i). The disposal and use of the friary church from its dissolution in 1538

The Franciscan friary in Reading flourished from its foundation on land granted by Reading Abbey in 1233,[1] until its closure and confiscation in 1538 as part of Henry VIII's suppression of religious houses in England and Wales.[2] The friary initially occupied the land beside Caversham Road from what is now the railway to Vachel Road, an area that was prone to occasional flooding. The abbey granted the friary an additional adjacent piece of land higher up the hill towards the town in May 1285[3] and the friary, previously built of wood, was then rebuilt using flint and stone. Of the range of buildings – cloister, chapter house, dormitory, refectory, infirmary, kitchens, warden's house, etc – nothing remains. Of the friary church, just the nave stands, dating from around 1300, and is now Greyfriars Church.[4]

The nave of the friary church survived because it was granted, in the town's charter of 34 Henry VIII (April 1542), to the therein incorporated 'Borough of Redynge' for use as their Guildhall.[5] From thenceforth the building remained in the hands of the Corporation until its sale in 1862, and although it experienced a variety of uses and was not always well maintained, it was continually occupied. The Mayor and Burgesses of Reading had moved into Greyfriars Church as their new Guildhall by 1543 as the old Guildhall, or Yield Hall, was rented out to former Mayor Richard Turner that year.[6] The Mayor and Burgesses held their full meetings quarterly, and a court meeting each Wednesday 'for hearing and settling…pleas and plaints'.[7]

By the 1560 charter of Queen Elizabeth[8] the Mayor and Burgesses were enabled to 'give grant alienate convey in fee or exchange or yield up' the church building and its access from Friar Street if they so desired. This paved the way some years later for a change of use of the old friary church when, in 1578, the Corporation decided to move their Hall again, this time to a specially

---

1 *Calendar of Charter Rolls, vol. 1: Henry III 1226–1257* (London, 1903), p. 187.
2 For the Act of Surrender of the 'House of Gray-friers in Reding', dated 13 September 1538, see Charles Coates, *The History and Antiquities of Reading* (London, 1802), 303–4, taken from a copy in Lambeth Palace Library cited by Coates as MSS. Wharton, f. 129 in Biblioth. MSS. Lambeth No. 594).
3 *Calendar of Close Rolls. Edward I, volume 2 (1279–1288)* (London, 1902), pp. 428–9.
4 For an account of the Franciscan Friary from 1233 to 1538 see Malcolm Summers, *Reading's Grey Friars* (Reading, 2020).
5 See 34 Henry VIII (24 April 1542), Clauses 5 and 6 (Document I (i)).
6 Royal Berkshire Archives, R/AT3/25/10 (1543) Counterpart of a lease for 40 years to Richard Turner, burgess of Reading, of a house and appurtenances called the old 'Yield Hall' and another house adjoining it to the west end called the Corkhouse.
7 34 Henry VIII (24 April 1542), Clause 13. See C. Fleetwood Pritchard, *Reading Charters, Acts and Orders 1253–1911* (London, 1913), 12.
8 See 2 Elizabeth (23 September 1560) Clauses 49 and 50 (Document I (ii)).

built upper floor in the old Abbey Hospitium building next to St Laurence's Church.[1]

Having moved their Guildhall, the Mayor and Burgesses of Reading used their powers under the charter of 2 Elizabeth to adapt the vacated former friary church building to be a hospital for the town. This was an early type of workhouse, caring for the 'impotent' (that is, powerless) poor, namely orphaned children and the incapacitated elderly. In its first year, 1578, the Hospital housed 21 children and 14 elderly people.[2] In return for room and board, the inmates had to work, and the income from their produce, supplemented by charitable gifts received, enabled the Hospital's costs to be paid. From 1601 the Hospital was maintained through a compulsory poor rate levied on each parish. The accounts for the Hospital continue until 1648, although the last record of anyone in the Hospital was 'Goody Bailey', who left on 23 May 1644.[3]

From 1614, the hospital had to share its accommodation with a House of Correction, a prison for the 'undeserving poor' – those that could but would not work. This had first been mooted by the Corporation in 1590,[4] but it was not until April 1614 that the necessary action was taken 'for the settinge to worke of suche rogues, vagabondes, sturdye and unruly persones as from tyme to tyme should arise and be within the said boroughe'.[5] Two documents from 1620, hereafter transcribed, give the regulations for the running of the House, and a description of those to be incarcerated there.[6]

The management of the House of Correction was initially entrusted to 'six honest men', two from each of the parishes of the town. These appointments were made annually, and the men were generally chosen from among the secondary burgesses of the Corporation. In the first year, the 'Governors of the House of Correccion' were Robert Bent, Roger Knight, Jerome Pococke, John Symes, George Thorne and Richard Winche, of whom only John Symes was not a secondary burgess.[7] From 1617 those appointed by the Corporation to be Cofferers and Constables (four men in all, two senior, two junior in each category) took on the roles of overseers and governors of the House of Correction and Hospital.

The day-to-day work at the House of Correction was carried out by a Keeper, the first of whom was John Dawson.[8] He had had control of the Hospital from 1610 and so extended his area of responsibility in 1614 to

---

1 The modern spelling of the name of this church, St Laurence's, is used throughout this introduction, while the older spelling, St Lawrence, is left whenever it appears with this spelling in the transcribed documents.
2 Coates, *History and Antiquities of Reading*, 307.
3 Royal Berkshire Archives, R/FZ2/24/4.
4 J. M. Guilding, ed., *Records of the Borough of Reading: Diary of the Corporation*, 4 vols (London, 1892-6), i, 403.
5 Ibid., ii, 59.
6 Document I (iii) and (iv).
7 Guilding, *Records,* ii, 62–3.
8 Ibid., ii, 39.

include the House of Correction. Dawson was replaced as Keeper by John Ballard by late 1620 or early 1621. Ballard was the subject of a complaint made to the Corporation,[1] which may have subsequently led to his employment being terminated as he was soon replaced by John Remnant.

The Keeper was assisted by a Matron, often the Keeper's wife or daughter, who looked after the females in the Hospital and House of Correction. A house was provided for the Keeper, built between the south wall of the church and Friar Street. Beside it, where the south transept of the church is now, in time there was an alehouse, later known as the Pigeons public house.

The House of Correction, as shown by the charter of 2 Elizabeth quoted above, belonged to the Borough of Reading and so was, throughout its existence, a Borough prison. However, by arrangement with the Justices of the Peace of the County, from 1615 until the County built its own House of Correction/Bridewell in the Forbury in 1786, some County prisoners were housed in the town's House of Correction, for which the County paid an annual sum towards the maintenance of the building and the salary of the Keeper, and a subsistence payment for each inmate.[2]

On 28 March 1625, William Clayton became the Keeper of the House of Correction and Hospital, together with his wife Margaret as Matron, at a salary of £4 per annum; they remained in post until March 1634. During the nine years that the Claytons were in charge, the Corporation Diary records the committal of 52 people to the House of Correction. Although this is not an exhaustive list (as it does not, for example, include any County prisoners), it is likely to be fairly representative of the committals at the time. The vast majority (43) were male, and almost half of the prisoners (25) were charged with vagrancy and/or begging. The next most common charge was of theft (12). Unfortunately, very few of the entries make any mention of length of time to be served in the House of Correction.

In March 1634, William Clayton was 'called in question for divers misdemeanours whereof he was accused' before the Mayor and Corporation. However, Clayton 'could not finde sufficient sureties for his good behaviour, [and] was therefore committed to the Gaole'.[3] This marked the end of his tenure as House of Correction Keeper, although it took many months to dislodge his wife from the Keeper's house! The fall from grace of the Claytons did not stop there. William and Margaret's son, Edward, was committed to the House of Correction for allegedly fathering an illegitimate child on Suzan Dan, while she was a prisoner in the House of Correction.[4]

Henry Tubb was appointed on 9 September 1634 to succeed William Clayton as Keeper on a salary of £18 per annum. Tubb had been an assistant to both John Remnant and William Clayton, and so he was already very

---

1 Document I (v).
2 Document I (iii).
3 Guilding, *Records*, iii, 222.
4 Ibid., iii, 257.

experienced in the role. A lengthy contractual agreement was drawn up between the Corporation and Tubb the following day.[1]

Local builder, Robert Westmerland, was contracted to keep the House of Correction in good repair and was recorded as being paid several sums about this time:[2]

13 December 1637	£11 15s. 1¼d.
1 September 1640	£10
21 October 1640	£15 19s. 10d.
14 January 1641	£15

The former friary church continued as a Hospital and House of Correction until the Civil War and the occupation of Reading by the Royalist army under Sir Arthur Aston in late 1642. Greyfriars Church formed part of the town's fortifications and doubled as a barracks for soldiers, both Royalist and subsequently Parliamentarian. Although externally the church did not suffer damage during the siege of Reading in April 1643, internally it seems that the soldiers housed there for the duration of the War left it much in need of repair.

In July 1646 the Corporation resolved that the House of Correction be 'repaired and some new particions made therein for the safe keeping and punishing of disorderly persons'. The work was not actually undertaken by anyone, as on 21 October, the Corporation decided that 'Henry Tubb is apointed, with the assistance of some carpenters, to view and consider what convenient roomes are needfull to be made againe in the House of Correccion, and to bring an accompte thereof to the Company att two of the clocke in this afternoone'.[3]

By the following year the building was restored to use, but only as a House of Correction and no longer as a Hospital as well. With the change of status of the building came a change of the arrangements regarding its Keeper. Henry Tubb continued in the role he had held since 1634 but was joined by William Woodes as an equal partner. They even shared the Keeper's House ('Henry Tubb is appointed to have one chamber in the said House for his owne private use and Willyam Woodes to have two chambers' – perhaps Woodes was married and needed more rooms for his family).[4] Tubb and Woodes appear as petitioners to the Justices of the Peace of the County on a document dated 11 January 1648 where they request the County to make good several missing payments over the previous five years that were due from the County to the Borough for the upkeep of the House of Correction. The County compromised and paid for the last two years, which was undoubtedly a fair response, given

---

1 Guilding, *Records*, ii, 288; Royal Berkshire Archives, R/Z8/5.
2 Guilding, *Records*, iii, 398, 508; iv, 2. Royal Berkshire Archives, R/FZ2/23/8. Westmerland's earliest recorded work was to rebuild a chimney at the House of Correction to make it stop smoking, for £3 10s., in October 1624: see Guilding, *Records,* ii, 201–2.
3 Guilding, *Records*, iv, 200, 218.
4 Ibid., iv, 246–7.

that the building had not been usable as a House of Correction when occupied by soldiers during the Civil War years![1]

During the early part of the 18th century Reading's House of Correction started to be referred to as the Town or Borough Bridewell, although the former name continued to be in occasional use well into the nineteenth century. Calling Houses of Correction by the name of Bridewell derived from London's Bridewell Prison, which is thought to have been the first House of Correction in England.

Among the various documents that survive in the Royal Berkshire Archives from the Bridewell, there are seventeen 'Subsistence Bills'.[2] The earliest is from September 1745, in which the Bridewell Keeper, Henry Dunt, itemised amounts owing to him for running the Bridewell. The bill was mainly a list of those committed to the Bridewell by the Borough with the details of the duration of each stay. This latter information was vital for his bill, as he was claiming back from the Corporation the 3d. subsistence per day he had paid to each prisoner for them to pay for their food. His total claim was for £17.1s.6d., which covered all that was owed to him since December 1742, including the town's contribution to his salary for the last three years.[3]

From time to time, escapes from the Bridewell were reported in the *Reading Mercury* newspaper, often by means of advertisements by the Keeper offering a reward for information leading to the recapture of the culprits. In January 1778, the Keeper, Joseph Clack, reported that four prisoners had made a daring escape by breaking through the Bridewell wall.[4] There was no subsequent report of their capture, so they probably evaded justice.

In the late 18th century, the Bridewell was visited several times by philanthropist and prison reformer, John Howard. After his fourth visit in 1782, his report stated:

> [The Town Bridewell] was formerly a church, and is a spacious room, with four dark suffocating huts on one side for night-rooms, one for men 16 feet by 10½ and 6½ high: aperture in the door 8 inches by 5: straw worn to dust, not changed for four months; one for women 15 feet 8 inches by 10 feet 9 inches: aperture in the door 7 inches by 5: the two other rooms less. The county pays rent to the corporation. It is dirty, and out of repair. Men and women are together in the day-time. No court: no water: allowance to felons, three pence a day; and to petty offenders, two pint loaves each, every Sunday, and one every week-day. Keeper's salary, £18 from the county, £2 from the town: fees, 4s. 4d. no table: licence for beer: half the profit of the prisoners' work: £2 a year to find them straw. Clauses against spirituous liquors hung up: and there were on a board, some orders

---

1 Royal Berkshire Archives, R/Z8/7.
2 These are all within R/FZ2. They are documents 31/21, 31/41, 37/1, 37/14, 40/18, 41/8, 43/6 (Document I (xiii) below) 46/25, 46/40, 47/3, 48/10, 48/13, 50/7, 55/1, 55/13, 56/45, 57/23.
3 Royal Berkshire Archives, R/FZ2/31/21, transcribed as Document I (vi).
4 *Reading Mercury* 26 January 1778, 3.

to be observed, approved by J. P. Andrews and Ferd. Collins, justices, April 28, 1778.

1776,	Jan. 1,	Prisoners 6.
1776,	Nov 1,	Prisoners 6.
1779,	April 21,	Prisoners 7.
1782,	March 5,	Prisoners 13.[1]

Later that year, at the summer Berkshire Quarter Sessions of the Peace at Abingdon, in response to new requirements for Houses of Correction contained in an Act of Parliament, a committee of three Justices of the Peace was appointed to 'Examine into the state and Condition of the House of Correction at Reading in this County and they or any two of them are also requested to make their report thereon at the next Quarter Sessions'.[2] They reported back at the Sessions in January and April 1783. Their overall conclusion can be read into the sentence: 'in its present state of building [the Borough Bridewell] is by no means calculated to fulfil the purposes of the Act of Parliament, but that the same must be greatly enlarged and rebuilt'.[3]

A set of 'Calendars of Bridewell Prisoners' of various dates from 1778 to 1784 illustrate some of the reasons for incarceration in the Bridewell by the County Justices of the Peace.[4] The majority of those imprisoned were awaiting the next opportunity to be tried, either before Reading Magistrates or at the County Quarter Sessions of the Peace. Remarkably, sixteen of the twenty individuals mentioned were arrested for theft. If found guilty, the individuals could find themselves back in the Bridewell or in the County Gaol. One prisoner, Joseph Packer, for example, having been committed to the Bridewell on 24 May 1783 on suspicion of stealing a saddle, was found guilty at the Quarter Sessions in July. His sentence was to be imprisoned in the Bridewell for a further fortnight, then whipped 'from the Bridewell to High Bridge, and discharged'.[5]

In 1786, a newly built County Bridewell was opened in the Forbury in Reading. This replaced the need for the County Justices of the Peace to use the Borough Bridewell, and so from this point the Bridewell at Greyfriars was used solely for town prisoners. Also from this point, there were, of course, two buildings in Reading called the Bridewell, and it is not always easy to distinguish between them.

The County replaced its Gaol on Castle Street in 1793 with a new Gaol built alongside the County Bridewell in the Forbury. In the course of time, with the County Gaol and Bridewell being on the same site and being run by a single

---

1 John Howard, *The State of the Prisons in England and Wales* (London 1792), 339.
2 The document appointing the committee is transcribed below as Document I (vii).
3 Document I (viii).
4 Document I (ix).
5 *Reading Mercury* 21 July 1783, 3.

Governor, the combined building came to be called by just the name of the County Gaol.

In September 1786 the Borough Bridewell gained an open-air exercise yard as the nave roof had to be removed because it had become unsafe during high winds.[1] The prisoners had to be moved temporarily to the newly built County Bridewell while the work was done. In addition to creating an open exercise yard, the removal of the roof opened up a new way of escape from the prison by climbing up and out. The first reported such escape was at the end of March 1791, when Robert Beesley, who had been convicted, along with an accomplice, of stealing 28 fowls belonging to Michael Blount, Esq., of Mapledurham, used an iron hook and rope that had probably been smuggled in for him, to scale the walls. John Shaylor, the Keeper, offered a five-guinea reward for his re-capture.[2]

In May 1789, the Corporation 'agreed that the Bridewell be repaired and improved according to the plan and estimate (amounting to £381) now produced by Mr Collier'.[3] This substantial amount of money may also have been sufficient to rebuild the Keeper's House, as it was described as 'the new Bridewell House' in the minutes of the Corporation on 2 April 1790.[4]

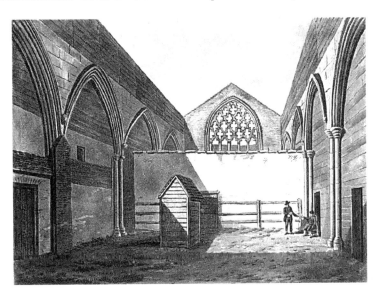

1. Interior of the Borough Bridewell.[5]

---

1 *Reading Mercury* 2 October 1786, 3.
2 *Reading Mercury* 19 January 1791, 3; 4 April 1791, 2 and 3.
3 Royal Berkshire Archives, R/AC1/1/24, Minutes of the Corporation 1786–1809.
4 Ibid.
5 John Man, *The History and Antiquities, Ancient and Modern, of the Borough of Reading in the County of Berks* (Reading, 1816), opp. 288.

Another prison reformer, James Neild, visited the Bridewell in 1801 and again in 1806. After the latter visit, he wrote the following report on the state of the prison:

> READING, Berkshire. The Town Bridewell. Keeper, John Shailor. Salary, 10*l*. No fees. Divine Service never performed here. Surgeon: Mr Bulley; makes a Bill. Number of Prisoners, 1801, Dec. 13th, three; 1806, Oct. 16th, three. Allowance, was sixpence each; now only fourpence each per day.
> REMARKS.
>
> This Prison was built out of the ruins of an ancient Church. Here is a court-yard for the Men, 48 feet by 27, and under an arcade are two hemp-blocks. They have no day-room, but four sleeping cells, of 15 feet by 9, and 8 feet high, which open into a small courtyard, 6 feet 9 inches square, and are lighted by a little iron-grating over each door. In one of these was the Male-Prisoner confined. No firing or candle allowed by the Corporation: Straw only for bedding on the floors.
>
> Opposite to those cells is another court-yard, 17 feet by 9; in which is a fifth sleeping-cell, of 9 feet by 7 feet 6 inches, entirely dark, except what light is occasionally thrown in through a pot-hole, or small aperture in the door, of 8 inches by 5. Over this cell is an ascent by a fifteen-step ladder, to another room of 9 feet 6 by 6 feet 6, and 8 feet high, lighted by a small iron-barred window.
>
> The Women's court-yard is 27 feet square; with a draw-well in the centre, and a sewer. Their day-room, 12 feet by 10 feet 6 inches, has a bricked floor, a glazed window, and a fire-place, but no grate. Their sleeping-room adjoining is 16 feet by 10, and 6 feet 4 inches high, with straw on the floor, but no light, except as admitted by a small iron-grating in the door, of 13 inches by 11. The two Women Prisoners were lodged here.
>
> Water, heretofore inaccessible to the Prisoners, is now properly supplied. Whatever be their employment, they have the produce of their earnings.[1]

A carpentry bill from around 1812 and a whitesmith's bill from 1818 illustrate the type of maintenance work required at the Bridewell, the latter notably including many charges of sixpence to put irons on a prisoner or to take them off.[2]

It is interesting to consider the 'Subsistence Bill for Prisoners' for the period 22 December 1816 to 25 March 1817.[3] Since by this date County prisoners were no longer housed in the Borough Bridewell these subsistence bills make it possible to build a picture of how many prisoners were

---

1 James Neild, *State of the Prisons in England, Scotland, and Wales etc.* (London, 1812), 500.
2 Document I (x).
3 Document I (xiii).

incarcerated at the same time. In the first quarter of 1817, there were 23 individuals (17 male, 6 female) imprisoned during the quarter. The maximum number of inmates at one time was 12 (9 male, 3 female), occurring for seven days, from 26 December 1816 to 1 January 1817. The minimum was 3 prisoners, occurring on 25 and 26 January, and again on 20 to 22 March. There was not a day in the quarter when the Bridewell was empty. The mean number of prisoners in the Bridewell over the period was 6.5 (4.6 male, 1.9 female). Four were imprisoned for a week or less, six for two to three weeks, nine for four to five weeks, three for seven to eight weeks and one for 82 days.[1]

Overlapping with the information about the inmates of the Bridewell is a document that shows the various medicines that were prescribed for the inmates in 1817.[2] Although simply a list of 'Powders' and 'Pills' it adds a dimension to what we know of the life under the open roof of the Bridewell.

According to an official return in 1819, the Bridewell's maximum occupancy was 20, and a total of 89 individuals had spent some time there in the previous year.[3] By 1821 a further four cells had been added, bringing its maximum capacity to 24.[4] Two years later, however, after the annual visit to the Bridewell by the Committee of the Society for the Improvement of Prison Discipline, a damning report was issued, which said in part:

> The floor ... is laid out into three small yards, and the vaulted aisles have been fitted up as cells, but they are unaccountably small and low, the ceilings being scarcely six feet high. These cells, of which there are seven on the ground floor, are very badly ventilated having only one small aperture, about nine inches square, to admit air: one of these cells appeared about seven feet square, others about twelve feet; but in consequence of their having no other vent hole to afford a circulation of air, they are offensively close, particularly on unlocking them in the morning. The walls have not been whitewashed for nearly two years. No bedding is allowed; straw only, with a ragged coverlet, is laid on the floor; the straw was, at the period of this visit, in an offensive state; it is changed once a month, or less often, but without any fixed regulation. These cells, which are used day and night, appeared altogether in a very bad state...
>
> Water is not accessible to the prisoners but is brought to them when wanted by the keeper; a trifling expense would remedy this grievous evil, as water is laid on, from the town waterworks, within a few feet from the

---

1 This last was Jane Richerson, and since she was in prison at the start of the period, she may well have been incarcerated for longer as the count is just within the quarter.
2 Document I (xiv).
3 *Account of Gaols, Houses of Correction or Penitentiaries in the United Kingdom*, Parliamentary Papers 1819, XVII.371, 2.
4 *The Third Report of the Committee of the Society for the Improvement of Prison Discipline and for the Reformation of Juvenile Offenders* (London, 1821), 90, and Appendix, 5.

prisoners' quarters.[1] The yards, with the exception of one, require paving; in wet weather they are generally in a muddy state.

The whole of the interior of the prison is out of the keeper's view, not a window of his house looks into it… There were at the time of this visit nine men and one woman in the prison; there have been as many as 24 in confinement at once, and dangerously thronged together… There is but one privy, which is in the men's yard…[2]

The Corporation took advantage of an unusual situation in the summer of 1829. There were just two men in the Bridewell, both imprisoned for debt until they could pay the amounts off. A 'humane gentleman' cleared their debts, enabling them to go free – and consequently leaving the Bridewell temporarily empty. The Corporation promptly ordered that the whole building be thoroughly cleansed and ventilated, and sent in various workmen (bricklayers, carpenters, plumbers, glaziers and painters) to effect repairs and improvements. Six years after the above report made its recommendation, water was finally laid on to the building.[3]

In 1832, a widower, John Readings, by trade a shoemaker, successfully applied for the post of Bridewell Keeper, and took up residence in the Keeper's House next to the Bridewell, with his daughter Elizabeth, who took on the role of Matron looking after the female prisoners. This was the start of a twenty-seven-year tenure for Readings as Keeper.

The Borough Bridewell was an important element in the Corporation's 1836 'Petition to the Crown for Grant of Separate Court of Quarter Sessions for the Borough of Reading'. The Petition gave the Bridewell's maximum occupancy as 'at least' 26, with separate wards for felons and debtors. At that time, the Bridewell catered for three categories of prisoner: debtors, those committed for further examination, and those committed for a short period of imprisonment without hard labour.[4]

In September 1845, John Billing read a paper before the Architectural Section of the British Archaeological Association at Winchester entitled 'On the History and Remains of the Franciscan Friery, Reading'.[5] Accompanied by drawings, the paper gives a good description of the building. The west window is singled out as 'by far the finest part of the whole edifice, and even now, worn and dilapidated as it is, presents a beautiful appearance'. In Billing's drawing

---

1 In Neild's report from 1806, cited above, it stated that water was supplied, probably by pump from the well mentioned in Neild's report. Whatever arrangements had been put in place, it seems they had fallen into disrepair or removed by 1823.
2 *The Fifth Report of the Committee of the Society for the Improvement of Prison Discipline and for the Reformation of Juvenile Offenders* (London, 1823) Appendix, 4.
3 *Reading Mercury* 6 July 1829, 3.
4 This petition, together with a report into the state of the Bridewell and correspondence with Lord John Russell, Secretary of State, is transcribed below as Document I (xv).
5 *Reading Mercury* 20 September 1845, 3. The paper was published in *The Archaeological Journal* III (June 1846), 141–8.

of the window (see below), one can clearly see that it is bricked up to the base of the tracery.

Billing concluded his architectural description of the church by stating that:

> It is to be lamented that this fine relic of ancient art is devoted to no better purpose than that of a prison. The present scanty church accommodation would be ample reason for restoring it to a somewhat more decent state, and as the walls and arches are undisturbed, a small expenditure would render it at once fit for worship and an ornament to the town.

The old friary church was visited by members of the British Archaeological Association on 16 September 1859 as part of a flying visit that took in the sights of St Laurence's Church, the Abbey ruins, and St Mary's Church as well. One of their number 'urged the duty devolving on the authorities of a rising town like Reading to preserve ancient buildings which remained within it, and deploring that there was no museum in the town, suggested that the Friary should be restored, and so appropriated, if a church were not needed'.[1]

2. West Window, Greyfriars Church.
Drawn by John Billing, 1845.

---

1 *The Builder* 24 September 1859, 627.

(ii). The purchase of the Bridewell, the Bridewell Keeper's House and Pigeons public house by Rev. William Whitmarsh Phelps

3. The Bridewell c.1860.
The entrance is immediately behind the standing figures on the right.
The building on the extreme right is the Keeper's House.

    The Corporation had been uncertain about what to do to improve what, for the sake of convenience, they called the Police Buildings. At a Council meeting in May 1858, it was agreed to appoint a committee, chaired by the Mayor, George Palmer, to identify a suitable building that could be altered and set up as a Police Station, with Lock-ups, and Magistrates' Offices within a budget of £4,000.[1] One of the aims of this accommodation was to replace the Town Bridewell.

    The committee considered and rejected several sites, including the Bear Inn on Bridge Street and a property on Middle Row, a triangle of houses that split the southerly part of St Mary's Butts into two narrow roads. Their recommendation was to purchase High Bridge House from Mr William Blandy, a member of the Council, for the sum of £1,600. This large property, which still stands, lies between the River Kennet and Star Lane, just south of what is now called Duke Street Bridge, but was then known as High Bridge.

    The Council, however, rejected this proposal, which led to a series of fruitless attempts to resolve the problem. In May 1859, the decision about the

---

1 See the transcribed Borough of Reading Minutes of Council Meetings, Document II (i).

purchase of a building, or site upon which to erect new buildings, was postponed and instead it was agreed to carry out remedial works at a cost of £422 at the Borough Bridewell to bring its accommodation up to the standard required by the Government Inspector. The majority of the work consisted of paving the floor with bricks, as prior to this only the women's day room had been paved, and to 'erect new cells' which possibly meant putting in new wooden partitions and doors to create more cells.

4. Portrait of the Venerable Archdeacon Phelps, Archdeacon of Carlisle, painted c.1865[1]

With this temporary expedient, the Council's consideration of what to do about the Police Buildings stalled. Then, on 10 August 1860, local clergyman William Whitmarsh Phelps, Incumbent of Trinity Church, Oxford Road, in Reading, noted in his journal that he 'Thought out a scheme for a new district church', namely the purchase and restoration of Greyfriars Church by public subscription. Knowing that what was in his mind would probably cost in the region of £10,000, he sought the encouragement of Rev. Peter French, who had been born in Reading and still owned property there although he was now Vicar of Holy Trinity, Burton upon Trent.[2] French promptly wrote back with his full support and pledged £100 if Phelps could find nine others to match that sum.[3]

The Rev. William Whitmarsh Phelps[4] had lived in or near Reading since taking up the curacy of St Laurence's in 1840 at the invitation of the vicar, John Ball. Curacies at Sonning (September 1841 to May 1842) and

---

1 Charles Hole, *The Life of the Reverend and Venerable William Whitmarsh Phelps M.A.*, 2 vols (London 1873), ii, frontispiece.
2 Rev. Peter French (1799–1878) was Vicar of Holy Trinity, Burton upon Trent from 1824 to 1871. In 1823, he married Penelope Valpy, youngest daughter of the Rev. Dr. Richard Valpy who was Head Master of Reading School for 49 years. French retired back to Reading, living in Russell Street for the last seven years of his life. His son, Rev. Thomas Valpy French, became the Bishop of Lahore in 1877.
3 Hole, *The Life of the Reverend and Venerable William Whitmarsh Phelps M.A.*, ii, 213.
4 Phelps was born on 1 October 1797 in Wilton, Wiltshire. He attended Corpus Christi College, Oxford, from 1815–22 and took up his first curacy at Hindon, Wiltshire, on leaving university. From 1826 to 1839 he was a Master at Harrow School.

Sulhamstead (May 1842 to May 1845) followed, before he was invited to be perpetual curate of Trinity Church, Oxford Road, Reading. Trinity Church was a proprietary chapel,[1] built 1825-7 by Rev. George Hulme, and Phelps ministered there from 1845 to 1864. In August 1860 he accepted a post as Chaplain in the Carlisle Diocese, becoming Archdeacon of Carlisle in February 1863 and thereafter styled the Venerable Archdeacon Phelps. He resigned from his incumbency at Reading a year later.

Phelps had chosen this particular moment to act because some land immediately to the west of the Bridewell had come onto the market. He believed this area to be a vital part of any restoration of the church. Phelps paid £696 to Sarah Weedon for the land, which covered the area from the west wall of the church and around the corner of Friar Street with Caversham Road.[2]

While the availability of the land to the west of the church was a catalyst, it was not the reason that Phelps had decided to act. He felt that there was a need for 'a greater supply of accommodation for religious worship' in the area due to a great increase in population to the north and west of the church, with many of the inhabitants being amongst the poorest of the town.

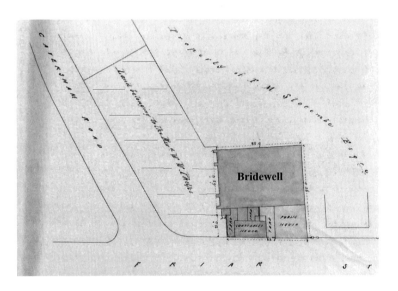

5. Land purchased by Phelps from the Weedon estate (hatched area).

---

1 That is, built by a private individual and open to the public.
2 See Phelps's first circular letter, transcribed below, Document III (i).

This increase in population can be quantified by comparing the census data from 1851 and 1861. In the area that became the parish of Greyfriars,[1] the population grew from 1,864 in 1851 to 2,503 ten years later.[2] This represents a 34% increase in population, which was slightly more than twice the 16% growth of the town between those two dates.

The number of houses in what was to become Greyfriars parish grew over the same period from 360 to 465, a 29% increase. This growth can be seen from the relevant sheets of the 1853 Board of Health Maps, where the 1853 houses are shaded in pink and the later houses (up to about 1865) are shaded in red.[3] The censuses enable the housing growth in each road to be quantified. Most roads had an additional house or two built during the ten years, but more substantial development had taken place in some roads, as shown below:

	Number of Houses	
	In 1851	In 1861
Chatham Place	0	20
Great Knollys Street	6	24
Lower Thorn Street	9	25
North Street	4	10
Vachel Road	4	14
Weldale Street	81	93

The house building continued into the 1860s. To the north of the Bridewell, the land in the area from Vachel Road to Tudor Road, which was still generally known as part of the Greyfriars Estate, was mostly owned by Sarah Weedon, and she gradually sold plots off to local builders for development. Development of Stanshawe Road began in 1862, initially with houses on the south side.[4]

Many of the houses in the area were quite substantial, for example those in Regent Place, a row of six houses built in 1847 and still standing today. These are on the west side of Caversham Road, between Great Knollys Street and the railway bridge. However, in eleven Courts and Places[5] in the parish there were, in 1861, a total of 119 houses that had no garden or surrounding land except a paved court with shared toilet and washing facilities. Many

---

1 See the description of the first Greyfriars parish area and plan, Document IV (iii).
2 The details given here are from an analysis of the 1851 and 1861 censuses, including only those houses in what became the first parish of Greyfriars Church. Note that The National Archives of the UK have confirmed that, for the 1861 census, only the summary numbers exist for Great Knollys Street, and the individual pages (RG9/745 f151 to f155, pages 45 to 51) containing the household schedules for 161 individuals no longer exist.
3 The Board of Health Maps are in the Royal Berkshire Archives and can be viewed on their website. The maps covering the Greyfriars parish area are R/AS2/4/2, 3, 16 and 17.
4 See for example Royal Berkshire Archives, R/D142/3/18, Deeds of 7 Stanshawe Road. See *Reading Mercury* 14 January 1865, 3 for the newly erected set of three houses on sale. The development of Sackville Street did not begin until the early 1880s.
5 These were: Ball Court, Chatham Court, Chatham Place, Ebenezer Place, Hope Place, North Court, Oxford Court, Somerset Place, Thorn Court, Warren Place and York Place.

would now be described by the term back-to-back housing, where each house had one room on the ground floor and one above, and a thin partition at the back to an identical house behind it facing the other way. There was a whole row of 18 pairs of terraced back-to-back houses called Somerset Place (south side) and Warren Place (north) between Chatham Street and Weldale Street.

Reading has always attracted people to come to live and work there – I am a 20th century example! In 1861, just under half (46%) of the population in the future parish of Greyfriars were born in Reading, although a substantial number of these were the children of adults who had migrated there. Only 28% of the adults living in the area had been born in Reading. About 62% of the adults in the parish had been born in Berkshire. The next most popular counties were Oxfordshire (8.5%), Middlesex (5.3%), Wiltshire (4.6%) and Hampshire (4.2%). In total, 84% of the population of the area came from Berkshire or one of its immediate neighbours, and so 1 in 6 had come from further afield.

The people followed a wide variety of occupations. Almost one in five of the adult males described themselves as labourers, and one in six worked on the railway in some capacity. Almost a third of the adult males were engaged in a skilled trade, of which the most popular were boot and shoemakers (48 men), carpenters and joiners (43), bakers (26), tailors (22), and stone masons (17). There were a small number of professional males: 6 teachers, 3 accountants, 3 attorneys, 2 architects, a surgeon, a dentist, and the Governor of St Laurence's Workhouse.

About half of the adult females in the 1861 census for the area have an occupation assigned to them. The most popular occupations were: domestic servant of various kinds (74), dress maker (49), laundress (40), charwoman (17) and needlewoman (17). One woman had the wonderful occupation of 'mangling trousers', which seems a very specific part of the operations of a washerwoman, but perhaps it was an especially skilled job. Eight females were involved in teaching.

Many of the children were identified in the 1861 census as 'Scholars'. It is possible that where children were not identified as such, they may still actually have attended school. However, if we take the data at its face value, many children in the parish started attending school at age 3 and left after the age of 13 – though 13% of 14- to 16-year-olds were identified as scholars. In all 69% of the 3- to 13-year-olds in the parish area went to school, with little difference between boys (70%) and girls (68%). Attendance after the age of 11 dropped to just over half of the children. There were almost 200 children (aged 3 to 13) in the parish not attending a school.

The proposed parish contained St Laurence's Workhouse. This was situated on the corner of Friar Street and Thorn Street, in the area now covered (perhaps appropriately) by the Reading Jobcentre, from Cheapside to the slip road to the Inner Distribution Road. In 1861 there were 37 adult male inmates, 26 adult female inmates, and 14 children, all under 5 years of age.

The area proposed as the new Greyfriars parish would reduce St Mary's parish by 1,659 people (out of the whole parish of 10,853 people), and St Laurence's by 844 (out of the whole parish of 4,729). Although the total new parish size would be comparatively small – it would become only about two thirds of the size of the reduced St Laurence's parish, and just over a quarter of the reduced St Mary's – the expectation was that it would be an area of continued population growth and need.

In summary, the population of the future parish was mixed, but with the majority of people being unskilled workers. About a quarter of the population were living in poor accommodation in the various Courts and Places. While there was some high-class housing, and some professional people, the numbers of these were comparatively small. In the middle of the social scale between these two were the skilled workers (about a third of the adult males), though very few shopkeepers or shop owners.

Following the reply received from Rev. Peter French, Phelps sought the necessary pledges of £100 from nine others to his proposal. Although it is not certain who made these donations, since the first subscription list was published several months later and had almost twenty donations of £100 or more listed, it is a reasonable supposition from their later involvement that these first subscribers included John Neale,[1] John Simonds,[2] and Martin Hope Sutton.[3] Having received these initial pledges of support, Phelps wrote to the Mayor and Corporation of Reading on 12 December 1860 offering to purchase the Bridewell, the Bridewell Keeper's House and the Pigeons public house 'with a view to restoring the [church] building and applying it to the purpose of a district church, which we purpose to build and endow for the use of that part of the town, should it be competent for us to do so'. The letter was read at a Council meeting on 22 December, where it received unanimous support.[4]

By the end of January 1861, the Council had set the sale price of the Bridewell site and buildings at £1,250 and it had been agreed by Phelps. The Council had also finally decided in favour of High Bridge House, as the only eligible property for the new Police Buildings. William Blandy, the property's owner, had become reluctant to sell after the former difficulties but he was persuaded to change his mind and accepted the proposed £1,600 sale price.

---

1 John Neale (1799/1800–1865), of 13 Friar Street, Reading, acted as Phelps's solicitor throughout the process of the purchase and restoration of Greyfriars.
2 John Simonds (1807–76) was a Reading Banker, of John & Charles Simonds Bank, 3 King Street, Reading.
3 Martin Hope Sutton (1815–1901) of Sutton & Sons seed merchants, is probably the most notable Reading resident to have been a member in Greyfriars Church's early years. He attended Greyfriars from 1863 until his death in 1901. He became the second vicar's father-in-law when his daughter Laura married Rev. Seymour Henry Soole in 1876. When he died in 1901, his children arranged for a memorial to be erected in the church's south transept, and Laura Soole successfully spearheaded an appeal to build the Martin Hope Sutton Memorial Hall, which opened in 1902, and which is still in use. Thus, Greyfriars has the only two memorials in Reading to Martin Hope Sutton.
4 Document II (i).

Although there were still challenges ahead, both the purchase of High Bridge House and its conversion to the requisite Police Building and Magistrates' Offices moved forward to a satisfactory conclusion.

Phelps had set himself to buy three properties from the Corporation and each of them had issues to be solved before the transfer of Title could be achieved.[1] The simplest of the three was the purchase of the Bridewell itself. The Corporation could cite the charter of Henry VIII to prove their ownership of the land and building of the former church of the Grey Friars, together with the passageway access from Friar Street. However, there remained four issues to solve before the Bridewell could be said to be unencumbered by any potential costs, rents, mortgage or liabilities.

The first issue was that, in both the charters of Henry VIII and of Elizabeth I, the Corporation were charged with paying an annual rent for the Greyfriars building to the Crown of one hundredth part of one knight's fee and a half-penny at Michaelmas. Although this had fallen into abeyance, the Corporation had to prove that the charge was no longer payable by the new owner of the building. In order to do this, the Corporation applied to the Keeper of the Records at the Office of Land Revenue Records and Inrolments for a certificate of its non-payment by the Borough of Reading since time immemorial (that is, at least a period of sixty years), which was duly received in October 1861.[2] The legal implication was therefore that this payment could no longer be required by the Crown, and that the charge was null and void.

In the same way that the charter of Elizabeth I had imposed an annual rental charge on the Greyfriars building, it also imposed a general annual rent of £22 on all the property received by the Corporation by this grant. The ownership of this annual £22 rent had passed from the Crown through many hands but had finally been bought by the Corporation in 1845 from Thomas Bros junior so that 'the same annual rent might thenceforth sink into and be absolutely extinguished in the lands tenements tolls profits and other the premises out of which the same was issuing and payable'. Therefore, all that was needed was a legal document to show that this was indeed the case.[3]

The next potential charge on the building was Land Tax. At the end of the 18th century this amounted to an annual charge of £2 on the Bridewell. However, following an Act of Parliament that allowed Corporations to redeem the Land Tax on their properties on payment of a capital sum, the Borough of Reading had done so in 1801. Consequently, the Corporation only needed to

---

1 See 'Abstract of the Title of the Mayor Aldermen and Burgesses of the Borough of Reading to certain properties called the Bridewell and 'Pigeons' Public House contracted to be sold to Revd W.W. Phelps', Document II (ii). Also see Document II (iii).
2 Document II (vi).
3 See 'Further Abstract of the Title of the Mayor Aldermen and Burgesses of the Borough of Reading in the County of Berks to the Freehold property called the Bridewell and the Pigeons Public House agreed to be sold to the Reverend W. W. Phelps', Document II (iv).

supply Phelps with certification that the Bridewell was one of the properties upon which the Land Tax had been redeemed.[1]

The final potential encumbrance (which related to all three of the properties that Phelps was seeking to purchase) was that the Council had, several years before, mortgaged its whole Corporate Estate to Richard Fellowes (who since inheriting the Englefield Estate had changed his name to Richard Benyon). Happily, Benyon was content freely to release the three properties from being part of the mortgage arrangements, being satisfied that enough Corporate Estate remained to secure his £7,000 loan to the Council.[2]

With no encumbrances left to worry about, the Bridewell property Title was established and only the approval of the Lords Commissioners of Her Majesty's Treasury was needed before it could go ahead. This approval was received by the Corporation in July 1861.[3]

There was a fundamental problem with the purchase of the Bridewell Keeper's House. The Corporation could not actually prove its Title to the property. Initially it tried to maintain that it was given to the Borough under the charter of Henry VIII, but it became clear that this would not hold water. All of the Greyfriars' Estate had been granted by Henry VIII to Robert Stanshawe, a Groom of his Chamber, for an initial payment of £30 and an annual rent of 6s 8d,[4] with the only exception being the nave of the church and some ground for access to the building from the road. The implication was that, in fact, the land upon which the Bridewell Keeper's House was built was part of the grant to Robert Stanshawe, and not to the Corporation.

However, there was no doubt that the land and the Keeper's House upon it had been in the undisputed possession of the Council for a substantial time. All parties agreed that the way forward would be for the Vendor (the Council) to provide Statutory Declarations of their long-term possession. These were provided by John Readings,[5] who had lived in Reading all his long life and had moreover been the Bridewell Keeper, and so had been resident in the Keeper's House, for 27 years, and by John Jackson Blandy, the Town Clerk, who searched the Town Records for proof of the Council's ownership of the Bridewell Keeper's House.[6] These Statutory Declarations were adequate to show that the Bridewell House had been in the Corporation's possession from time immemorial.

The purchase of the public house next door to the Bridewell Keeper's House was perhaps unexpectedly complicated. The premises were owned by the Corporation of the Borough of Reading, although, as with the Bridewell Keeper's House, it was not possible to identify the origin of the Corporation's ownership. The land had not been part of either the grant by Henry VIII or of

---

1 Document II (vii).
2 See the Indenture of Release from Mortgage, Document II (viii).
3 Document II (i), entry dated 25 July 1861.
4 The grant to Robert Stanshawe was made by letters patent in 31 Henry VIII (5 February 1540).
5 Document II (ix).
6 Document II (x).

Elizabeth I. When the Town Clerk, John Jackson Blandy, wished to show the Corporation's ownership by references to the property in the Diaries of the Corporation the earliest mention he could find was on 6 May 1789:

> [The Corporation] Agreed to grant a Lease of the Alehouse adjoining to the Bridewell as now marked out in Collier's plan to Mr Matthias Deane for 4 score years from Michaelmas at £5 per annum he having agreed to repair and improve the same.[1]

Deane decided not simply to repair the public house, but to rebuild it. This was carried out in 1790, as shown by another entry in the Corporation's Diaries that gave leave to John Shaylor, who at that time ran the pub,[2] to live temporarily in the newly rebuilt Bridewell Keeper's house while the works went on.

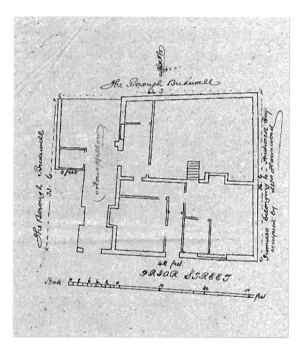

6. Plan of the 'Pigeons'.

---

1 This can be found in Royal Berkshire Archives, R/AC1/1/24 Minutes of the Corporation 1786–1809. 'Collier's plan' was a plan and estimate for repair and improvement of the Bridewell, amounting to £381.
2 He was appointed Bridewell Keeper on 3 October 1791 on a salary of £10 per year.

By 1835 the Lease of the 'Pigeons'[1] had passed to the joint ownership of Thomas Rickford and Charles Curry Bickham of the Castle Street Brewery. Rickford and Bickham applied to the Corporation for award of the Lease that had been promised, and on 11 December 1835 they were successful. This Lease, having been initially granted for 80 years in 1789, was to last therefore until 1869, at the same rent of £5 per annum payable by them to the Corporation.[2]

In 1846, Charles Curry Bickham left Castle Street Brewery and sold his half share in the various businesses (which included the Pigeons public house) to Thomas Hawkins, who therefore entered into partnership with Thomas Rickford in Bickham's place. When Rickford died in February 1855, he bequeathed his real estate to his wife Hannah Maria Rickford and son Thomas Parker Rickford. In the following year, Thomas Hawkins bought Rickford's half share in the business, and so Hawkins now owned the whole, including the Leasehold on the Pigeons. In order to afford the purchase of Rickford's 'moiety', or half share, Hawkins mortgaged the properties (the Lease of the Pigeons included) for £4,000 with Hannah Maria Rickford and Thomas Parker Rickford.[3]

When Phelps wanted to purchase the Pigeons public house, he therefore not only had to purchase the land and building, but also had to purchase the remaining lease from Thomas Hawkins. The purchase of the lease, for £210,[4] was completed on 31 December 1863.[5]

In 1839, Parliament had passed an Act 'to enable the Mayor Aldermen and Burgesses of the Borough of Reading in the County of Berks to sell certain real Estate discharged from certain liabilities and to invest the purchase moneys arising from such sales in the purchase of other real estate to be charged with such liabilities'.[6] The Act aimed to make it possible for Corporations to sell properties that had come to them under the charter of Elizabeth I. Attached to the Act was a Schedule of buildings to which it applied and this list included the Pigeons public house, in spite of the fact that the Corporation did not gain the land on which the public house was later built from Elizabeth's grant. The Act decreed that any purchase money from the

---

1 The public house was at times called the 'Three Pigeons', but the simpler name of 'Pigeons' was the more frequent appellation.
2 'Lease of the Pigeons Public House in Friar Street St Lawrence Reading – For Eighty Years from Michaelmas 1789 Rent £5', Documents II (xi–xiii).
3 See 'Abstract of the Title of Thomas Hawkins Esquire to ... the Pigeons'; 'Supplemental Abstract of the Title of Thomas Hawkins...', and 'Further Supplemental Abstract of the Title of Thomas Hawkins...', Documents II (xiv–xvi).
4 Strangely, this amount is given as £210 in the relevant legal documents, but in the accounts is given as £220. See 'Greyfriars Church, Reading. Circulars and Appeals Relative to the Restoration, together with a List of Subscribers, Balance Sheet &c', Final Accounts, Document III (i).
5 See 'Assignment of Pigeons to The Venerable William Whitmarsh Phelps', Document II (xvii).
6 2 & 3 Victoria Cap. 40 (Local).

sales of the Scheduled buildings had to be paid into the Bank of England and kept there until re-invested in land.

Therefore, of the £1,250 purchase price paid by Phelps for the Bridewell, the Keeper's House and the Pigeons public house, £350 (representing the cost of the Pigeons) had to be paid into the Bank of England and could not be used by the Corporation for the works at High Bridge House. This was a problem for the Corporation who had counted on the purchase money as part of the capital they were going to use to refurbish the new Police Buildings. The Town Clerk endeavoured to persuade Mr Phelps's solicitor, John Neale, that it was unnecessary to have this arrangement, but legal opinion went against him.[1]

Phelps was able to complete the purchase of the Bridewell, the Keeper's House and the Pigeons from the Corporation on 23 April 1862, even though it was sometime later that Phelps completed the purchase of the Pigeons' lease.[2] The cost of the Pigeons was £560 in total, comprised of £210 for the purchase of the Lease and £350 for the land and building.

As will be mentioned below, early in the restoration works it was decided to build transepts to the church, and this necessitated a further purchase of land by Phelps. This consisted of a strip of land to the north of the building, shown in the plan below, to the outline of the north transept to the east, and an access way along the north side of the church that enabled a vestry to be built with access from the north transept. The land was part of the large garden of Francis Morgan Slocombe, who owned the neighbouring property, known as Greyfriars House. Phelps paid Slocombe £300 for the land.[3]

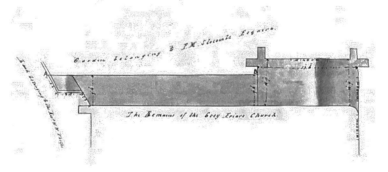

7. Strip of land to the north of the church building purchased by Rev. W. W. Phelps from Mr F. M. Slocombe.

---

1 See the correspondence between John Neale (solicitor for the purchaser, Rev. W. W. Phelps) and John Jackson Blandy (Town Clerk), Document II (xviii). Also see the transcribed Borough of Reading Minutes of Council Meetings, Document II (i), entry dated 7 February 1862.
2 See 'Conveyance of the Site of the late Greyfriars Church and other hereditaments', Document II (xix). Also see the transcribed Borough of Reading Minutes of Council Meetings, Document II (i), entry dated 23 April 1862.
3 See 'Abstract of the Title of Mr John Weedon to a Freehold Estate on the North side of Friar Street', 'Abstract of the Title of Mr F. M. Slocombe to a Freehold piece of Land part of the Greyfriars Estate' and 'Conveyance of pieces of land part of the Greyfriars Estate', Document II (xxi–xxiii).

In summary, Phelps paid the following capital sums for the buildings and the land required for the restoration of the church:

Purchase prices of Buildings and Land paid by Phelps:

	£
Land to the west of the church belonging to Sarah Weedon	696
Purchase price of the Bridewell and Keeper's House	900
Purchase price of the Pigeons public House	350
Purchase price of the Lease of the Pigeons	210
Land to the north of the church belonging to F. M. Slocombe	300
Total	2,456

(iii). The Trustees of the new church

The patronage of Anglican churches was and is a complicated subject. The key point is that whoever holds the role of patron, whether an individual or group or organisation, that patron has the power of choosing who the incumbent of the parish will be whenever there is a vacancy. The patronage arrangements can be changed, but only with the agreement of the parties concerned.

Of equal importance to Phelps as the restoration of the Greyfriars building to ecclesiastical use was the intention that the ministry in the new church would be evangelical, or low church. Phelps had seen the patronage of the three parishes of Reading being gathered into the hands of the Bishop of Oxford, the Rt. Rev. Samuel Wilberforce.[1] Wilberforce was no friend to evangelicals and had already started to place high churchmen in the town. Phelps believed that, by establishing and maintaining Greyfriars in an evangelical tradition, the people of Reading would have the option of whichever tradition they wished to worship in. Phelps therefore proposed that the patronage of Greyfriars would be vested in a group of five men whose churchmanship was soundly evangelical. He named them in his first Circular to the Reading public in June 1861, by which he announced the project and sought the town's financial support.[2] These Trustees were: Phelps himself, Rev. Peter French, Rev. John Ball,[3] John Neale and John Simonds. This proposal was formally agreed by the Bishop of Oxford just over a year later.[4]

---

1 See Phelps's comments to the Earl of Radnor in his letter of 10 June 1861 in 'Correspondence by the Rev W.W. Phelps to the Earl of Radnor re the restoration of Greyfriars Church, Reading', Documents III (ii).
2 See Phelps's first circular letter, Document III (i).
3 Vicar of St Laurence's Church from 1833 to 1865, in whose parish the Greyfriars church stood. Phelps had been curate to Ball at St Laurence's in 1840–1.
4 See 'Draft Deed of Agreement between the Bishop Patron and Incumbent as to the Patronage of a Church intended to be built on the North side of Friar Street the parish of St Lawrence Reading in the County of Berks', dated 8 August 1862, Document II (xxiv).

(iv). Transfer of ownership to the Ecclesiastical Commissioners

Not long after Phelps became the owner of the Greyfriars buildings and land, he sought to transfer them to the Board of the Ecclesiastical Commissioners, giving ownership of the church and lands to the Church of England. The process is described in a set of letters from the Ecclesiastical Commissioners to Phelps, via his solicitor John Neale, which are transcribed below.[1] The process was completed by the application of the Ecclesiastical Commissioners seal on 21 August 1862.[2]

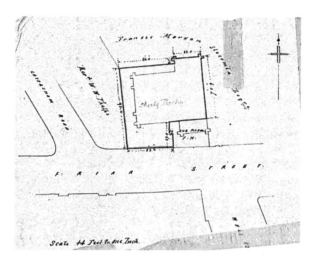

8. Plan of land conveyed to the Ecclesiastical Commissioners by Rev. W. W. Phelps in 1862 (outlined in a slightly darker line).

At this stage, Phelps had not yet completed purchasing the Lease to the Pigeons public house, and so, since that part of the Church and land remained under an encumbrance, it could not be conveyed to the Ecclesiastical Commissioners. Phelps did not at this stage convey all of the first piece of land he had purchased to the west of the church, as no doubt there were already thoughts to build some schools there. Consequently, the plan of the area conveyed was as above, omitting the south transept (where the Pigeons had stood) and including only some of the land to the west.

The south transept and the land to Friar Street were conveyed to the Ecclesiastical Commissioners after Phelps bought the Lease of the Pigeons for £210 on 31 December 1863.

---

1 See 'Correspondence respecting the conveyancing of the Greyfriars property from the Rev W. W. Phelps to the Ecclesiastical Commissioners', Document II (xxv).
2 See 'Draft Conveyance of a Church Site in Reading St Lawrence Parish Church County Berks Diocese Oxford. The Revd. W. W. Phelps to The Ecclesiastical Commissioners for England', Document II (xxvi).

(v). The restoration and reconsecration of the church

On 4 June 1861, Phelps wrote his first circular letter, appealing to the 'townsmen' of Reading for financial support for the project to purchase the various buildings and land and for the works needed to restore the Greyfriars Church to ecclesiastical use. He estimated the cost to be about £7,000 plus a sum of at least £3,000 for the endowment, to be invested so that the incumbent could receive an annual income. In the event he was not far off the final cost of £8,887, to which was added £2,860 for the endowment.[1]

When Phelps wrote this first circular a total sum just in excess of £3,500 had already been subscribed – although this included four gifts, each of £500, from those named as Trustees. Phelps was very active in canvassing support. Although a number of individual letters and replies exist, the best illustration is given by Phelps's correspondence with the Earl of Radnor.[2] Phelps had invited the Earl to become one of the Trustees of the new church, but the latter had declined. Phelps then engaged the Earl in correspondence about the project, culminating ultimately in the Earl giving £100 to the Restoration Fund.

As we have seen above, the conveyance of the Bridewell, the Keeper's House and the Pigeons, from the Corporation to Phelps, was signed, sealed and delivered on 23 April 1862. Earlier that month, the Reading newspapers carried the following advertisement:

> RESTORATION OF THE GREYFRIARS' CHURCH
> *TO CARPENTERS AND OTHERS.*
> PARTIES desirous of submitting TENDERS for the Carpenter's and Tiler's Work to the Roof of the Church, and for the Plumber's Work, Gutters, Water Pipes, and for the Drainage, can see the Drawings and Specifications at our Offices, on and after Wednesday next, April 2nd.
> Tenders to be delivered to us on Monday, April 14th, at 12 o'clock. The lowest Tenders will not necessarily be accepted.
> POULTON & WOODMAN, Architects.
> *1, Greyfriars' Road, Reading.*[3]

In due course various contracts were settled by Poulton & Woodman. The main contract was placed with Messrs. Wheeler for the stone mason's work.

---

[1] See 'Greyfriars Church, Reading. Circulars and Appeals Relative to the Restoration, together with a List of Subscribers, Balance Sheet &c', Document III (i). The letter appeared in the *Reading Mercury* 8 June 1861, 5, and 15 June 1861,7, and in the *Berkshire Chronicle* 8 June 1861, 4, and 15 June 1861,3.
[2] See 'Correspondence by the Rev W.W. Phelps to the Earl of Radnor re the restoration of Greyfriars Church, Reading', Document III (ii). The documents in the Royal Berkshire Archives have the Earl's scribbled notes to his secretary to enable him to write replies to Phelps, but these are largely indecipherable.
[3] *Reading Mercury* 5 April 1862, 1; *Berkshire Chronicle* 5 April 1862, 4.

This firm had been in Reading since about 1818, when John Wheeler, a statuary mason, moved from his home village of Broughton Poggs in Oxfordshire to set up a Mason's Yard, first in Gun Street, then at 55 St Mary's Butts, in Reading. In the 1840s his sons Samuel[1] and John had joined the business. The contract was signed on 16 June 1862 for the sum of £1,885,[2] and Messrs. Wheeler signed a Bond for performance of contract on the same day.[3] By the end of the work, with the additions needed that had not been planned for initially, the total cost of the building work had risen to £3,250.

The contract for the carpentry work, laying the roof, and the tiler's work went to Mr Sheppard[4] for £899, which rose to £2,073 by the end of the restoration. Of the other contracts, only details of two others are known. The bells were cast by John Warner & Sons of London (who had cast Big Ben a few years previously), and the hot air heating apparatus was installed by Haden of Trowbridge.[5]

William Woodman, the architect for the restoration, carefully excavated around the church building and discovered what he imagined to be footings for a north transept of the church. He then incorporated transepts into his design. However, since only one known Franciscan church in England had transepts,[6] it was much more likely that he had found evidence of the cloister.

Woodman's plans included reinstating a chancel, although of somewhat shorter length than the original had been. Since, however, the land beyond the east wall of the nave was not for sale,[7] the plans could not be carried out beyond the line of the east wall, giving the church a T shape instead of a cross. The intention, however, was in the course of time to purchase the land if possible and carry out the extension to include a chancel. This explains why the east wall, when viewed from the exterior, has a brick section while around it the rest of the church is faced in flint.[8]

---

1 Samuel Wheeler (1819–1902) attended Greyfriars Church from its consecration and the Wheeler family connection continued (becoming Williams by marriage – a family notable for the number who served as Greyfriars' missionaries) without interruption until 2020.
2 See 'Contract for Mason's Work required in the Restoration of the Greyfriars Church St Lawrence Reading', Document III (iii).
3 See 'Bond for performance of Contract for Masons Work required in the Restoration of the Greyfriars Church Reading', Document III (iv).
4 Most probably Ambrose Sheppard, of Friars Place, Caversham Road, and later of Greyfriars Road.
5 The final accounts are transcribed in Document III (i).
6 A. R. Martin, *Franciscan Architecture in England* (Manchester, 1937), 78. Writing about the Coventry friary he stated 'The evidence, in fact, seems to be sufficiently clear to justify the conclusion that the church had a two-armed transept and was thus in this respect, so far as surviving evidence can show, unique among Franciscan churches in this country'.
7 The house and land belonged to Francis Morgan Slocombe, with Charles Andrewes as tenant.
8 Later architect's plans for the chancel are given below in Document III (v).

9. Drawing of the proposed completely restored church.
The actual restored building ends in the line including the belfry.

The work of restoration began on Monday 21 April 1862. Many local people took the opportunity of visiting the site and seeing inside the former Bridewell building, as it had not been accessible to the public before. When the old wooden partitions had been removed it was possible to inspect the state of the interior stonework. Much of the original late thirteenth/early fourteenth century stonework was in a good enough condition to leave in place, including most of the pillars and arches, although the west window needed careful restoration. The exterior flint work was in a remarkably good state, requiring only re-mortaring. Within a few weeks the Bridewell Keeper's House had been demolished and its remnants cleared away.

Phelps was able to report by the end of November 1862 that over £6,000 had been donated.[1] There was a concern that the rate of donations was slowing down, especially since several other appeals, both local and national, had been made. The rate of contributions did indeed fall: over the following six months Phelps received only just over half the amount that had been raised in the previous six months.

On 18 December 1862 there was a serious accident at the site. While working on scaffolding, about 15 feet above the ground, one of Wheeler's stonemasons, John Aust, slipped and fell, and the stone he was working on then fell on his right leg. His leg had to be amputated at the Royal Berkshire Hospital later that day. Happily, he recovered well.

---

1 See 'Greyfriars Church, Reading. Circulars and Appeals Relative to the Restoration, together with a List of Subscribers, Balance Sheet &c', Document III (i). The letter appeared in the *Reading Mercury* 29 November 1862, 3, and in the *Berkshire Chronicle* 29 November 1862, 4.

Aust had been taking down part of the chancel arch on the east wall in preparation for the partial rebuilding of that wall. A complete skeleton had been found buried beneath the foundation of the east wall, by the chancel arch, which had rendered the wall unsafe. The newspapers reported that the body must have been buried before the wall was first built, but in fact that is unlikely. It was a greatly desirable thing to be buried in friary churches, with new space becoming difficult to find before long. It became common practice for burials to take place even under the walls of churches to solve this problem.

As well as extending the footprint of the church to include transepts, the architect increased the height of the roof, as can be seen from comparing drawings and photographs of the church from just before the restoration, where the roof line is only just above the apex of the west window, with later photographs. The roof itself was in place by mid-summer 1863. By that date, a bell turret had been added above the east wall, in an unusual arrangement of three bells in a line. The turret is surmounted by a weathercock, taking the overall height to 88 feet (27 metres).

Inside the church, the pews were of dark oak, as were the communion rails and reading desk. The window glass was mostly clear (although of 'church glass' and so not transparent), but with some colour in places. The pulpit and font were carved from Caen stone. Initially a harmonium was installed to accompany hymns, replaced in August 1864 by the church's first organ.

Phelps, by February 1863 elevated to be the Venerable Archdeacon Phelps of Carlisle and soon no longer a Reading resident, nevertheless ensured that he saw the work of restoration through. One of the last things to do was to convince the Corporation of the need to lower the footpaths and roads around the church in order that the floor level of the church would be the same as of the footpath outside. It took the offer of a £50 contribution to the works from Phelps before the alteration was made, lowering the footpaths and roads by between 15 and 18 inches in the area.

The new church was consecrated in December 1863. However, it was not until 21 December 1866 that the 'subscription list' for the contributions to the restoration of the church was closed. In a letter of that date, Phelps wrote that:

> It only remains that to the ascription of praise to Him, by whose blessing I am thus enabled – within five years and a half from the commencement of the undertaking, and three years from the consecration of the church, – to record the fact that the subscriptions have overtaken the outlay, I add my grateful thanks to every individual who has contributed to the work.[1]

---

1 See 'Greyfriars Church, Reading. Circulars and Appeals Relative to the Restoration, together with a List of Subscribers, Balance Sheet &c', in Document III (i). The letter appeared in the *Reading Mercury* 29 December 1866, 2; *Berkshire Chronicle* 22 December 1866, 2.

The analysis of monetary donations to the building fund showed that there were 390 individuals who contributed to the restoration (apart from those who gave in kind or to the endowment fund). The largest contribution was by Rev. Peter French (£921 3s. 8d.) who had the added distinction of being the first and the last contributor to the fund. About three quarters of the building cost had been given by the 28 people who gave £100 or more.[1] It had clearly proved harder to attract people to give to the endowment fund: in the end, Phelps nearly reached his £3,000 target, with £2860 5s. given by a total of just five people.

10. The restored Greyfriars Church.

The reconsecration of Greyfriars Church took place on Wednesday 2 December 1863 at 10am. It began at the south door where Rev. John Ball, Vicar of St Laurence's Church, presented the 'petition for the consecration of Greyfriars Church' to the Bishop of Oxford, the Right Reverend Samuel Wilberforce.

A congregation of over 700 had filled the Church and watched as the Mayor of Reading, Lewis Cooper, and members of the Corporation entered behind mace-bearers, followed by the Bishop and a large number of local clergy. The Bishop, the Venerable Archdeacon Randall, the Revs A. P. Cust (the Rural Dean, and vicar of St Mary's), T. V. Fosbery (Vicar of St Giles) and

---

1 See 'Greyfriars Church, Reading. Circulars and Appeals Relative to the Restoration, together with a List of Subscribers, Balance Sheet &c', Document III (i), for the accounts and full list of subscribers.

J. R. Woodford (Vice-Principal of Cuddesdon College) all sat within the 'altar rail', with the Rev. John Ball at the reading desk. The rest of the clergy, including Rev. W. W. Phelps, sat in a number of front pews.

Mr Ball read the Morning Service, with lessons read by Mr Fosbery, Mr Cust, the Ven Archdeacon Randall and the Rev. J. R. Woodford. Miss Binfield, a well-known local musician, conducted the choral parts of the service. There were two hymns: *Come, Holy Ghost, our souls inspire* and *All people that on earth do dwell*.

The Bishop preached from Matthew chapter 14 verse 16: 'And he said unto them they need not depart; give ye them to eat' from the story of Jesus feeding the 5,000. Explaining his choice of text, the Bishop said: 'You know that in this great and growing population there has been hitherto very little accommodation for the poor for Christian worship in our churches. This is an attempt, by rebuilding and restoring one in which of old time God has been worshipped, to provide for this necessity. It is the providing for these people the bread of heaven which connects the object today with the passage of scripture which I have selected for our consideration'.

After the sermon, the 'sentence of consecration' was read by the Chancellor.[1] The Bishop then ordered the signed document to be enrolled and preserved in the Registry of the Diocese.

A collection for the church building fund was taken, amounting to £108 14s, and then most of the congregation left, leaving the clergy and a few others to take communion.

After the service, the Ven. Archdeacon Phelps presided over a lunch for about thirty guests at the Great Western Hotel, although unfortunately the Bishop had to catch a train to a further engagement in London and so could not stay for the meal. Various speeches were made, and proceedings were concluded by the Mayor:

> The Mayor on behalf of himself and the Corporation thanked the Ven. Archdeacon Phelps for kindly inviting them to the ceremony of opening the new Church, and that handsome spread, and he could assure the Archdeacon that ever since he took the initiative for the restoration of the Church, the Corporation had taken the most lively interest in it. Had it not been for the great efforts and the liberality of the Archdeacon Phelps, Greyfriars' Church would still have been 'a den of thieves'. (Applause.)[2]

---

[1] See 'Sentence of Consecration of Greyfriars Church', Document III (vi).
[2] *Reading Mercury* 5 December 1863, 6.

(*vi*). *The early years of the parish church of Greyfriars*

11. Rev. Shadwell Morley Barkworth.

The Trustees appointed 44-year-old Rev. Shadwell Morley Barkworth as the first incumbent of Greyfriars Church. He was designated its Perpetual Curate until his title officially became Vicar in August 1868, after a change in the law allowed incumbents of new parishes, if carrying out the duties of a vicar in their parish, to be so called.

Barkworth had been born in Hull on 6 November 1819. His father, John, was a man of standing in the town, who had been Mayor of Hull in 1832. Having graduated from Worcester College, Oxford, in 1842, Barkworth entered the Church. Before arriving in Reading, he held several posts including at St Peter-le-Bailey in Oxford and St Jude's in Chelsea. His living before his move to Greyfriars was as Perpetual Curate of Southwold, on the Suffolk coast.

In April 1854, Barkworth had married Ellen Jansen while he was Perpetual Curate at Walthamstow. Their first child, Alfred William, was born in February the following year. He was classified, in the terms of the time, as an 'imbecile', and probably had what is now known as Down's Syndrome. He was cared for in the family until just after his 16th birthday in 1871, at which point he was admitted as a private patient to the then recently opened Normansfield Hospital in Teddington. This hospital had been founded and was run by Dr John Haydon Langdon-Down, who was the first doctor to identify Down's Syndrome. Alfred lived at Normansfield until he died in 1932.

Sadly, their second and third children died soon after birth.[1] By the time that the Barkworths arrived in Reading in December 1863, their young family consisted of Alfred (aged 8), Walter (4), and two daughters, Emma (2) and Edith (1). Two more daughters were born to the Barkworths during their time in Reading.[2]

---

[1] Ellen Gertrude Barkworth b. 26 November 1856 d. 25 December 1856; Reginald Edward Barkworth b. 24 February 1858, d. April 1858.
[2] Walter Theodore Barkworth b. 22 November 1859; Emma Louisa Barkworth b. 19 March 1861; Edith Marion Barkworth b. 27 August 1862; Constance Helena Barkworth b. 23 January 1866; Adela Catherine Barkworth b. 30 August 1868.

As the incumbent of Greyfriars Church, Barkworth's income came from two sources. The first was the capital sum that had been invested with the Office of Queen Anne's Bounty, which dealt with paying out the 3% annual dividend in two half yearly sums. The initial sum raised for the endowment was £2,860, which yielded an annual salary of £85 16s. This compares poorly with the vicars of St Laurence's (£250 and a house), of St Giles's (£600 and a house) and of St Mary's (£706 and a house).[1] Although Greyfriars did not have a vicarage to accommodate the incumbent, Phelps had loaned Barkworth the use of Trinity Lodge (now Carlisle House), off Trinity Place, next to Trinity Church.

The second source of income was pew rent. This was a payment by a member of the congregation to secure a specific seat in the church. The Churchwardens' Pew Rent Accounts[2] from March 1864 show three payments that year to the vicar of £50 (April), £60 (July) and £100 (October).

In 1864, Barkworth therefore received an income in total of just under £300, of which pew rent represented about 70%. Since pew rent was uncertain, Barkworth's income was subject to fluctuation, although in reality the pew rent was generally about £200 per year.[3]

Being the first vicar of a new church must be an especially onerous task, as very many things need to be done all at once. Barkworth was a noted speaker, and so his sermons and the pattern of services would have been the first priority. High on his agenda, however, was the establishment of Sunday Schools for the very many children in the area (although Greyfriars did not yet have its District assigned). With no parish rooms attached to the church to accommodate Sunday School classes, Barkworth rented a room in nearby West Street Hall and before long about 200 children were attending regularly.

By mid-June 1864, plans had been drawn up by William Woodman and tenders invited from contractors to build boys', girls', and infants' schools in a single building on the land to the west of the church which had been bought by Phelps in 1860. Barkworth launched a public appeal for funds in mid-July, expecting to need about £1,100. On 26 July 1864, the cornerstone of the building was laid.

In August 1864, a district, or parish, was assigned to Greyfriars.[4] Applications for children from families in the parish were invited for enrolment at the new schools in October. The subsequent demand for places (over 100 boys, about 100 girls, and 129 infants) meant that the accommodation being

---

1 See the entries in *Crockford's Clerical Directory for 1868* Fourth Issue (London 1868) for Revs Lewin George Maine (St Laurence), Arthur Cust (St Mary) and Thomas Fosbery (St Giles).
2 See 'Churchwardens of Greyfriars Church Pew Rent Accounts book (1864–70)', Document IV (i).
3 An undated plan (probably from the 1870s) of seats taken by holders shows 395 seats allocated by number, with a further 172 'free'. See 'Rented and Free seats in Greyfriars Church', Document IV (ii).
4 'Extract from an Order in Council stating the boundaries of the to be created District of Greyfriars Church' and 'Plan of Proposed District of Greyfriars', Document IV (iii).

built was inadequate, and so a further room was immediately planned to house an additional Infant School. This extension also included a 'soup kitchen'. These plans entailed an additional cost of £400.

12. Greyfriars Schools and Greyfriars Church.

On Thursday 29 December 1864, the Schools were officially opened. Three days later, the Sunday Schools met in the new school rooms for the first time, and the day schools were opened on Monday 9 January 1865. Initially there were three Schools: Infant (for ages about 3 to 7), and a Boys' and a Girls' School (both up to about 11). The latter two were known as the National Schools.[1] The cost of attending was initially set at 2d. per week for the first child in a family, and 1d. for each child thereafter.

When the Schools opened, the Infant School occupied just a single room which was divided into four classes by age. It took until March before the number attending reached 129, the number that had initially registered, but the admittances did not stop there, with attendance reaching almost 160 by the end of April. On 28 April the Infant School Head Teacher (and only Certified Teacher), Miss Caroline Willcox, wrote 'We have managed to make a 5th class near the door, but it is very crowded'. In early May, the Infants expanded into the new additional Infants' room, even though it was not quite completed, because their number had risen to 174. This new room had the added advantage of a gallery, which increased the available floor space considerably.

Miss Willcox was assisted by 'Monitresses', girls who had recently finished school themselves. The first was Rose Evans, a 12-year-old, who stayed for just under three months from January to April 1865. She was joined

---

[1] See 'Log Book of Greyfriars Infant School (1865–9)' and 'Log Book of Greyfriars Junior Infant School (1867–9)', Document IV (v) and (vi).

by Caroline Cray, aged 14, in February 1865, who managed only slightly longer before leaving with no prior notice in May, 'the work being considered too much for her brain'. A number of the later assistants went on to take examinations to become Pupil Teachers.

The Infant School's attendance continued to increase, the highest recorded being 230 on 11 June 1866 and again on 25 February 1867. With such large numbers it was decided to split the Infant School into the Junior Infants and the Senior Infants, from 6 May 1867. Caroline Willcox continued as Head Teacher of the Senior Infants, and Amelia Moody, a probationary teacher, took over the Junior Infants.

The curriculum of the Infant Schools included reading, writing and arithmetic, singing, needlework, knitting, 'object lessons' on natural history subjects (for example, the elephant) and science (for example, salt), and 'marching' and drill. These latter two were the physical education of the day. Being Church Schools, the children also had scripture lessons, the learning and reciting of 'texts', and catechism.

There are occasional insights into the state of the parish in the log books of the Infant Schools. Every winter, for example, sickness increased, with outbreaks of Hooping (sic) cough, scarlet fever, consumption (tuberculosis) and measles, with the occasional death of a pupil recorded.[1] The collection of the 'school pence' was not always straightforward, with pupils sent home to fetch the money and either not returning or returning without it. A number of the children were taken away from school at times to 'go into the country', which would be to do seasonal work in the fields, such as 'hopping'.

Another interesting feature of the log books is the occasional reference to wider events in Reading, such as the annual fairs and visits of various circuses. On 1 May 1865, for example, many parents kept their children at home: Miss Willcox wrote 'Only 105 and 90 present, respectively [morning/afternoon], owing to the May 'Cattle Fair'. People afraid to send their little ones'. Whereas at other times, the fairs clearly entice many children away, as on the day following the one cited above: 'The Pleasure Fair drew away a great many children this afternoon'.

Unfortunately, the early log books from the Boys' and Girls' schools are missing. These ran as separate schools until the end of 1895, opening as a Mixed Junior School in January 1896. William Moore was Head of the Boys' School from when it opened, until it became Mixed, and then was Head of the Mixed Junior School until 1908. Miss Agnes Missen was Head of the Girls' School when it opened.

---

[1] Seventeen deaths were recorded in five years. Three deaths were recorded in each of 1865 and 1866, none in 1867, one in 1868, and ten in 1869. Seven deaths were from scarlet fever, or fever; two from measles; one each from diphtheria, consumption, inflammation, and by being burned to death. The causes of the other four were not given.

By 1867, the accommodation was again overstretched, this time needing additional accommodation for the Boys' and Girls' schools. Dr Barkworth[1] purchased land adjoining the Schools' site on Caversham Road from George Simmonds Strong for £275 to build another large classroom. There was a further appeal to the public for £350 to cover the building costs.[2]

The average attendances at the Greyfriars Schools, during the week and on a Sunday, were given in the Church's Annual Report for 1867:

DAY SCHOOLS.

SCHOOL	NO. ON REGISTER	AVERAGE ATTENDANCE
Boys	175	156
Girls	148	107
Senior Infants	123	106
Junior Infants	114	102
Total	560	471

SUNDAY SCHOOLS.

SCHOOL	NO. ON REGISTER	AVERAGE ATTENDANCE	
		Morning	Afternoon
Boys	210	122	128
Girls	165	105	122
Infants	168	123	131
Total	543	350	381

By 1867 the church had divided the parish into twenty areas and assigned District Visitors to each from among the women in the congregation. Although no description is given of their role, it would have included bringing relief to the poorest,[3] as well as information about the church and its activities to all. The ladies of the congregation also formed the Dorcas Society and, of course, the Mothers' Meetings. The former of these was a gathering to make clothes for the poor. The idea was that at weekly Dorcas Sales families from the parish could purchase items cheaply.

At the Schools, a Boot Club was created, where families could deposit money on any Monday afternoon to save towards a pair of boots for their child. The church promised to add 25% to whatever was saved. In 1867, 198 pairs of boots for the children were bought by this method, with the church actually adding just over 90% to the amount saved, and so nearly halving the cost of the boots to the family. In addition, almost £110 worth of clothing was distributed by the church to the members of the Sunday School and through the Mothers' Meetings.

---

1 Rev. S. M. Barkworth had become D.D. in November 1866.
2 See 'Annual Letter addressed to the Congregation and Parishioners of Greyfriars, Reading, by their Pastor', Document IV (vii).
3 The account within Document IV (vii) showing 'sacramental alms' in the 'Annual Letter &c', totals over £65 for the year (1867) distributed among the poor of the parish.

In terms of the church's spiritual mission to its parish, the church was very active. There were three Church services a week, two on Sundays and one on Wednesday evening. There were several Bible Classes for young men and for young women, and various services per week in the Mission Room.

Weekly Greyfriars Church Activities in 1868

Sunday	8am	Holy Communion (3rd Sunday in the month)	Church
	9.30am	Bible Class for Young Men	Mission Room
	11am	Morning Service	Church
		Morning Sunday School	Schools
	2.30pm	Bible Class for Young Men	Mission Room
		Afternoon Sunday School	Schools
	3pm	Baptisms (Last Sunday in the month)	Church
	3.30pm	Bible Class for Servants and Young Women	Infant School
	6.30pm	Evening Service	Church
Monday	2.30pm	Mothers' Meeting	Mission Room
	4pm	Dorcas Sale	Infant School
	7.30pm	Mothers' Meeting	Girls' School
Tuesday	4pm	Working Party for the Poor (Last Tuesday in the month)	
Wednesday	7pm	Service	Church
Thursday	2.30pm	Juvenile Missionary Gathering (1st Thursday in the month)	
	8pm	Teachers' Meetings (Alternate weeks)	Schools
Saturday	7.30pm	Prayer Meeting	

The Mission Room was in the home of Charles Collins, who was salaried by the church as a 'Scripture reader' and whom the 1871 census called a 'missionary'. The house was at 84 (later renumbered to be no. 28) Chatham Street, which until as recently as 1865 had been the Pine Apple public house. It was then bought by Miss Mary Neale,[1] a member of Greyfriars Church, and

---

1 Mary Neale, of 12 Friar Street, Reading, was a younger sister of John Neale, who acted as Purchaser's Solicitor for Rev W. W. Phelps and was one of the first Trustees of Greyfriars Church.

rented to the church for use as the Mission Room and the home of the Collins family for £16 per annum.[1] The location of the house was chosen to be 'in the poorest part of [the] district'[2] and was next to a footpath through to the back-to-back houses in Somerset Place and Warren Place.

One of the reasons that the Trustees had chosen Mr Barkworth as incumbent was that he was a noted preacher. From time to time, members of the congregation managed to persuade him to allow a specific sermon to be published. The sermon then appeared in a small booklet, printed by T. Barcham of 89 Broad Street, Reading. Later, a number of his sermons were collected into a volume called 'Occasional Sermons', but this seems no longer to be in existence. The earliest of Mr Barkworth's sermons at Greyfriars that I have been able to find is transcribed later.[3]

Greyfriars was soon established as the local people's parish church. The first baptism that occurred was of Harry Frank Marlow, son of Thomas (a baker) and Emma, of 6 Caversham Road, which took place on Sunday 24 July 1864. In total, 27 children were baptised by the end of the year, with 51 in 1865, and 79 in 1866.[4] The church was granted permission by the Bishop of Oxford for marriages to take place there in January 1866.[5] There were just five marriages that year, the first being on 19 March between John Allum, a carpenter, and Mary Neal, a farmer's daughter. In 1867 there were 22 marriages, and 14 in 1868.[6]

The first Vestry Meeting to appoint churchwardens was reported in the *Reading Mercury* in November 1864:

> GREYFRIARS CHURCH. At a meeting of the members of the congregation of Greyfriars Church, held at the Schoolroom[7] on Monday night, Mr. Hodges, Oxford-street, nominated by the Incumbent, and Mr. Willson, West-street, nominated by the meeting, were appointed Churchwardens of the new district.[8]

Dr Henry Moses and William Woodman had acted as Churchwardens from the consecration in December 1863 to this time. The next record of a Vestry Meeting is the first entry in a Minute Book whose intention was to contain the annual meetings' minutes, but in the event only the meetings of

---

1 In 1901, following Miss Neale's death, the property was bought outright by Greyfriars for £100, and was then used as the home of the church caretaker, Thomas Searle and his family.
2 *Reading Mercury* 23 December 1865, 5; *Berkshire Chronicle* 23 December 1865, 5.
3 See "Son, Remember.' A Sermon preached at Greyfriars Church on 21 May 1865', Document IV (viii).
4 Royal Berkshire Archives, D/P163/1/1, Reading Greyfriars Baptisms 1864–75.
5 See 'Permission for the Solemnization of Marriages at Greyfriars Church', Document IV (ix).
6 Royal Berkshire Archives, D/P163/1/5, Reading Greyfriars Marriages 1866–96.
7 The Schools were not officially opened until the following month, but must have been sufficiently completed and furnished for this meeting to take place.
8 *Reading Mercury* 5 November 1864, 5.

April 1869 and April 1871 were actually entered from Dr Barkworth's incumbency,[1] and regular entries do not begin until 1885.

In November 1866, two alterations were made to the restored church. At the south door (which leads to Friar Street) an internal porch was built, and at the end of the strip of ground that Phelps had purchased so that a north transept could be built, a vestry was constructed that opened into the transept. A note from John Davenport, Oxford Diocesan Secretary, to Dr Barkworth stated that although strictly a Faculty[2] was needed, if there was no opposition from anyone in the church he could go ahead without incurring the usual £9 charge.

Unfortunately, after five years as Incumbent of Greyfriars, the vicar began to suffer significant ill health, even though he was not yet fifty years old. He applied for, and was granted, a leave of absence throughout 1869, though he actually only spent just over seven months away from his duties. The family left Reading on 6 April and returned about 20 November.[3] Rev. Colin Campbell deputised for him during his absence. Dr Barkworth was able to resume his duties on his return, but he continued to suffer ill health.

In 1872, Dr Barkworth sought further alterations to the church building. He felt that both the pulpit and the reading desk had been placed badly, and he was labouring under the adverse effects of the situation. He wrote to one of the churchwardens that he had 'suffered more than anyone can possibly conceive'. There is a record of the issue because Dr Barkworth was away on his annual holiday at the time that everything came to a head, and so letters were written that have been preserved.[4] One wonders whether part of the problem was due to the vicar's ill health, or whether it was the other way round, and his ill health was made worse by the issue. The outcome was an agreement to move both the pulpit and the reading desk forward into the body of the church by a couple of feet, and at the same time to reduce the height of the pulpit. No doubt Dr Barkworth was pleased with the outcome.

Unfortunately, Dr Barkworth continued to suffer ill health, and in June 1874 he tendered his resignation to the Bishop. On hearing of his resignation, the *Berkshire Chronicle* told its readers:

> ... it is with regret that we... announce that the Rev. Dr Barkworth has resigned the living of Greyfriars' Church, which he has occupied for eleven years. Dr Barkworth was the means of erecting large and handsome schools which a few years ago were considerably enlarged; he bore no inconsiderable portion of the expense as well as contributed the land, and had he remained the schools would no doubt have been still further enlarged, as they are quite full at the present time. Through his

---

1 See 'Greyfriars Church Minutes of Vestry Meetings from April 1869', Document IV (x). See also Appendix 2 for a list of the early churchwardens.
2 A Faculty is the mechanism by which a church receives permission from its Diocese to carry out building works.
3 See the 'Licence of non-residence for 1869', Document IV (xi).
4 See 'Correspondence and Accounts for moving the Pulpit and Reading Desk', Document IV (xii).

instrumentality also an organ was erected in the church, and a short time ago was enlarged. Dr Barkworth and Mrs Barkworth have been very assiduous in their attention to the wants and welfare of the parishioners; and Mrs Barkworth especially will be missed by the poor people. We may also mention that during his occupation of the living the Rev. gentleman received the degree of Doctor of Divinity. Both Dr and Mrs Barkworth have been in failing health for some time, and at length he has been compelled to resign.[1]

Dr Barkworth preached his last sermon at Greyfriars at the evening service on Sunday 25 October 1874. The next day, there was a farewell gathering in the Schools where the vicar received a clock and a cheque for £50. Dr Barkworth died in 1891. In August 1894, a stone reredos was erected at the east end of Greyfriars in his memory. Mrs Barkworth died in early 1895, and subsequently a memorial tablet was erected on the south wall of the church to both Dr and Mrs Barkworth. Both these memorials are still in the church.

13. Reredos, East end, Greyfriars Church
Erected in 1894.

---

1 *Berkshire Chronicle* 20 June 1874, 5.

14. The Barkworth Memorial, Greyfriars Church.
Erected in 1895.

I. The disposal and use of the friary church from its dissolution in 1538

(i)   Charter of 34 Henry VIII (1542). Royal Berkshire Archives R/IC1/6.[1]

This Charter granted to the Mayor and Burgesses of Reading part of the former Franciscan friary for their use as a guildhall, or town hall, on payment to the Crown of an annual hundredth part of a knight's fee and one halfpenny.

CLAUSE 5
And Whereas also we through other our letters patent bearing date the fifth day of February in the thirty-first year of our reign have given and granted to our well beloved servant Robert Stanshawe Groom of our Chamber his heirs and assigns forever all that house and site of a house once belonging to the Minor Brothers commonly called les Grey Freres of Redyng in our county of Berk then dissolved And all the Burial places and all houses buildings orchards orts gardens lands tenements trees woods pools vineyards and all other our hereditaments whatsoever with all and singular the appurtenances thereof within the site enclosure and precinct and walls and ditches of the said house of the said formerly existing Minor Brothers And all walls ditches waters pools and enclosures of the said site enclosure and precincts of the said house of the said former Minor Brothers and lying around them and adjacent to the same and the site enclosure and precinct of that house including and containing in all by estimation six acres so fully and completely as the late Warden or Minister and Body of the said house of the former Minor Brothers or any of their predecessors in right of that house at any time before the dissolution of the same house had held or enjoyed or ought to have held enjoyed all and singular the same premises or any parcel of them and as fully and completely and in so full manner and form as they all and singular devolved or ought to have devolved into our hands by reason and pretext of the dissolution of the said house of the former Minor Brothers or by reason and pretext of any act of parliament or in any manner whatever and then were or ought to have been in our hands the body and the side aisles of the church of the said house together with a competent and sufficient road to the same being excepted and entirely reserved to us our heirs and successors as in the same our letters patent made to the said Robert Stanshawe more fully appears and is contained which body and side aisles of the same church together with a competent and sufficient road to the same are of the clear annual value of five pence and no more Know ye that we of our special grace have granted and by these presents for us our heirs and successors grant to the said Mayor and Burgesses of Redyng aforesaid and their successors for ever aforesaid the body and the side aisles of the said church and one competent and sufficient road to the same.

---

1 This English translation of the original Latin charter is taken from C. Fleetwood Pritchard, *Reading Charters, Acts and Orders 1253–1911* (Reading and London, 1911), 8–9.

CLAUSE 6

And Whereas the body and the side aisles together with the road aforesaid by the said our other letters patent made as is set forth above to the said Robert Stanshawe were excepted and reserved to us our heirs to have possess enjoy and use the body and the side aisles of the said church and the said competent and sufficient road the same by the said Mayor and Burgesses and their Successors for ever to be held of us our heirs and successors for ever for the hundredth part of one knight's fee and by giving and paying to us our heirs and successors yearly at the feast of St. Michael the Archangel at the Court for the Augmentation of the revenues of our Crown one halfpenny for all services exactions and demands whatsoever with the intent that the Mayor and Burgesses of Redyng aforesaid at their own expense should therefrom make and construct or cause to be made and constructed from the same a sufficient house there commonly called Le Gyldhawle for the said town to be and remain for ever.

(ii)   Charter of 2 Elizabeth I (1560). Royal Berkshire Archives R/IC1/8.[1]

This charter confirmed Henry VIII's grant to the Mayor and Burgesses of Reading of the 'body and side aisles' of the nave of the former Franciscan friary church at the rent set by Henry's charter. In that charter, the building was directed to be used as the town's guildhall, but Elizabeth released the Corporation from that limitation, allowing the building to be used for any purpose the Mayor and Burgesses wished, or even for them to sell it.

CLAUSE 49

Whereas our most dearly beloved Father Henry the Eighth King of England by his letters patent bearing date at Westminster the twenty-fourth day of April in the thirty-fourth Year of his reign among other things gave and granted for himself his heirs and successors to the then Mayor and Burgesses of the said Borough of Reding and their successors in future the body and syde Iles of the church of the late house of minor Friars commonly called the gray fryers of Reding in his county of Berk lately dissolved And to have possess use and enjoy a competent and sufficient way to the same bodye and syde Iles of the late church aforesaid and for the aforesaid then the Mayor and Burgesses and their successors in future to hold the competent and sufficient way aforesaid to the same from our father aforesaid and his successors in future rendering and paying to our said father His heirs and successors yearly on the feast of Saint Michael the Archangel the Hundredth part of one knights fee and one half penny into the revenue of the late Augmentation Court of the Crown of our said father for all services levies or demands whatsoever to the intent that the Mayor and Burgesses of Reding aforesaid might at their own proper costs thereof make and build and cause to be made and built out of the same one

---

[1] This English translation of the original Latin charter is from Pritchard, *Reading Charters, Acts and Orders 1253–1911*, 33–34.

sufficient house there commonly called the Guild Hall to be and continue in the Borough aforesaid in future as it more fully is evident and appears among other things by the same letters patent aforesaid of our father

CLAUSE 50
Know ye that we of our especial grace and certain knowledge and mere motion have granted and given licence and do for ourselves our Heirs and successors as much as in us lies by these presents grant and give licence and free leave power and authority to the aforesaid Mayor and Burgesses of the Borough aforesaid and their successors by feoffment or otherwise to give grant alienate convey in fee or exchange or yield up the aforesaid body and syde Iles of the said late church and the way aforesaid belonging to the same to any person or persons whatever according to their own will and pleasure or to convert alter and dispose of them to any other use the aforesaid letters patent of our Father aforesaid or any condition specified in the same or any other thing cause or matter whatever to the contrary in any wise notwithstanding

(iii)   Regulations concerning the reception of prisoners at, and the management of, the Houses of Correction at Speenhamland and Reading (1620). Royal Berkshire Archives R/Z8/1.

This document agreed an increase to the fee paid by the County of Berkshire to the Borough of Reading for its use of the Reading House of Correction (in the Greyfriars building) for county prisoners from Cookham, Bray, Theale and Reading. It then gave instructions for the management of the House of Correction, including weekly whipping on a Friday afternoon for 'every Rogue, vagabond idler wandring and disorderlie person in… Custodie'.

At the Quarter Sessions of the Peace at Newbury … in April in 18 James I [1620]
Whereas by an amercyent[1] order made at Wantage on Tuesday after the translacon of Thomas the Martire in the Nyneth yere of the raigne of our Soveraigne Lord James[2] by the grace of God Kinge of England &c. It was ordered that one house of Correction should be erected at Speenehamland to serve for this whole Countie of Berk, and Giles Hinde Constituted and appoynted the M[ast]er and governour thereof allowing him for his sallarie or stipend for the execution of his said place and for the use of his house Fortie pounds yerelie, such order was to indure during the terme of Seaven yeres, As by Indentures made betweene divers of the Justices and the said Giles Hinde more playnlie appeareth, And whereas also since that tyme by another order made at the generall Sessions holden at Newbery the weeke after the Clause[3]

---

1 Probable reading of the word.
2 1611.
3 Close.

of Easter in the Thirteenth yere of our said Soveraigne Lord James[1] &c. upon the request of the Maior and Corporation of the Borough of Reading and with the consent of the whole bench and alsoe of the said Giles Hinde it was ordered that that house of Correction at Reading w[hi]ch the Maior and Corporation had prepared and made fit for the use of the Borough onlie should also be a house of Correction for the Countie, Twentie pounds out of the said Fortie pounds ordered unto the said Giles Hinde should from henceforth bee ymployed

[p.2]
towards the maynitenance of the said house of Correction at Reading, and that all such Rogues and sturdie beggars as should be apprehended or taken w[i]thin the seaven hundreds of Cookeham and Bray and the hundreds of Reading and Theale should bee sent to the house of Correction at Reading aforesaid, such said order was to Contynew for longe as it please the Justices and the Maior and Corporation of the Borough of Reading, And whereas alsoe at this Sessions Nicholas Gunter then Maior of Readinge being present in open Court desired some larger allowance towards the maynitenance of the said house of Correction at Readinge, and made it alsoe appeare unto the Court, that the said yearlie allowance of Twentie pounds p[er] ann[um] was not a sufficyent maynitenance for the said house of Correction at Readinge being soe apt and convenient for the punishm[en]t of Rogues and disorderly persons as they had nowe made it at their owne great charge, Whereupon the Justices nowe at this Sessions assembled gave orders that there shalbee allowed levied and paid to the Maior and burgesses of the Borough of Reading the further some of Ten pounds yerely for the better maynitenance of the said house of Correction over and above the saide Twentie pounds formerlie allowed, w[hi]ch said some of Ten pounds shalbe taxed by the Justices at the next Sessions in open Court and

[p. 3]
anew Contract is to bee made w[i]th Giles Hinde for the Contynewance of a house of Correction in the dwelling house at Speenehamland. This order to contynew for longe as the Justices, the Maior and Corporation of the Borough of Readinge and the said Giles Hinde can agree And for asmuch alsoe as for the better governem[en]t of the Country and apprehendinge and punishinge of Rogues and disorderlie persons and bringing them to the house of Correction it seemeth needfull to the said Justices that there should bee in every devision of the said Five devisions of this Countie one Marshall It is ordered at this Sessions that the Justices in every devision shall under their hands and seales assigne and appoynt one Marshall for the same devision w[hi]ch shall wholie ymploy himself in the apprehendinge of Rogues and vagabonds and the Court have alsoe thought it meet that they should bee allowers of as Informers for

---

1 1615.

sundry offences as the Justices have agreed upon at this Sessions As by a declaration made at this Sessions of such things it doth and may more at large appeare every of w[hi]ch Marshall is to have a stipend or wages of Five pounds p[er] ann[um] to be rated and levied by the Justices of every severall devision of every parish and townshipp w[i]thin their devision and to be Collected by the high Connstables to be paid unto them quarterly for longe as they contynew in the said place, And forasmuch as it seemeth meet unto the

[p.4]
Justices to alter the orders of the house of Correction formerlie made in some points Therefore it is at this Sessions ord[e]red that hereafter the orders of the said house of Correction shalbe as followeth.
1. Imprimis the M[aste]r and Governor shall take and receave men into their custodie but such onelie as shalbe sent unto them by warrant under the hand and seale of some one or more Justices of peace of this Countie and the Maiors of Reading and Newberry and the Justices in the same Townes.
2. Item that none be admitted into the said houses or receaved into them or either of them that is under Twelve yeres of age or above Threescore, nor any woman aparantlie with Child, nor any that is mayhemed[1] in his her or their hand or hands soe as they cannot worke, nor any that have any apparent sickness or disease.
3. Item the said M[aste]r or Governor shall not exact or require any monie or other things whatsoever of such as shall bringe the Rogues and vagabonds to the house of Correction nor shall take any monie at all of the Rogues or any on their behalf by [*illegible*] of any fee for Irons or otherwise whatsoever nor shall take any monie or reward whatsoever directlie or indirectlie of the Rogue or his friends for lodginge or Chamber roome or for sparing their worke or punishment.
4. Item the M[aste]r or governor shall not require or have of the Countie any allowance at all for any meat drinke or lodginge to be given to any Rogue

[p. 5]
vagabond sturdy beggar or disorderly person that shalbe comitted to his custody except onelie two loads of straw apeece to every Governor yerely for the lodging of such as shalbe comitted to the said house of Correction, to bee delivered unto them by the County by the provision of the Treasurers.
5. Item such Rogues vagabonds wandring idle and disorderly persons as being able to worke shalbe sent and comitted to the house of Correction the said M[aste]r or Governor shall not provide to or for them any other or more dyes drinke victuals or apparell then shall or may be bought had or provided w[i]th such monie as from tyme to tyme during their aboade in the said house of Correction they shall gett and earne by their worke and labour And if any man comitted earne above Fower pence a day, or woman above Three pence a day or boy or gerle above two pence the day, the overplus shall goe to the M[aste]r or governor of the house of Correction.

---

1 maimed.

6. Item the M[aste]r or governor shall provide and prepare w[i]thin the houses of Correction severall and distinct Roomes for men by themselves and weomen by themselves to lodge in and worke in having dores w[i]th locks and bolts to keepe them asunder.

7. Item they shall have in a readynes from tyme to tyme severall and distinct Tooles and instrum[en]ts to worke w[i]th and severall stuffes and things to worke both for men and weomen that shalbe comitted to them as namely for

[p. 6]
men stockcards and woll, hempe from threed quernes to grinde corne, wedges beetles, hatchetts and axes to cleave wood and the like, For weomen needles, Cards, wheeles, reeles, wooll, hempe, yarne and the like or suche or soe many of them as shalbe needful in such sort that noe Rogue vagabond idle and disorderlie person that shalbe sent and Comitted to the said house of Correction shall or may want such worke as he or she can doe or be able or fitt to doe having regard to their sexe strength and skill.

8. Item the M[aste]rs and governors of the said houses of Correction shall once ev[er]y weeke punish and correct by whipping every Rogue, vagabond idler wandring and disorderlie person in his Custodie, That is to saie, every Friday in the afternoone, at the whipping poste in Reading and Speenehamland, such Correction shalbe donne in the presence of the vicar or mynister, Connstables Bayliffe or Tithingman of the p[ar]ish of St Laurence, in Reading, And the vicar or mynister Connstable Bayliffe and tythingman of the said libertie of Speenehamland, or Connstable or Bayliffe of the towne of Newberry or some of them for the tyme beinge, And the said vicars or mynisters Connstables Bayliffs and tythingmen aforesaid are desired to give their assistance accordinglie, and they or any two of them upon their owne view or Credible information of others or relacion of the said M[aste]rs or Governors may by their discretions cause to be increased the punishment

[p. 7]
of sturdie and notorious roagues, and to be mittigated the punishm[en]t of others more milde, penitent and Conformable as they shall finde them to alter from tyme to tyme.

9. Item the said M[aste]rs or governors shall not upon any warrant at all deliver out of the said houses of Correction any Rogues, vagabonds, sturdy beggars except disorderlie persons onelie sent and comitted to them before the same person shall or hath been twice whipped at the tymes and places aforesaid And after such twice whipping then by warrant from the said Justices of peace that comitted him or any two other Justices, the said M[aste]rs or governors may deliver him, soe as he be not w[i]thin the degree of an Incorrigible Rogue And soe as the said M[aste]rs or Governors doe in his deliverance observe the Course hereafter followinge viz that they make a certificate under their hands and seales to be alsoe subscribers by the mynister or Curates of the parish of St ~~Giles~~ Laurence aforesaid and Connstables or Bayliffs of the said Borough and the minister or curate of Speenehamland, and Connstables or Bayliffs of the said libertie or one of them directors to the overseers of the poore of the parish where such Rogues alledgeth that he was borne, testefying that he was

comited to the house of Correction here at R[eading] or N[ewbury] in Bark upon such a day, and there remayned soe longe, and hath been corrected soe often. And upon his

[p. 8]
conformitie and promise to leave his Roguish life and his desire and since to bee sent to the place where he was borne there to be sett on worke he hath been delivered and is now sent to the parish of A being the place where he was borne as he alleged to be conveyed from parish to parish until he come thether. And if it fall out that he were not there borne then he is in case of an Incorrigible Rogue.

10. Item if the Rogue vagabond or wandring person hath been whipped for Roguish Life in any place whatsoever and doe wander, and is apprehended for the same offence againe, or if any doe name and declare the p[ar]ish where he was borne untrulie, or doe refuse to tell the name of the p[a]rish where he was borne or being comitted to the house of Correction shall there attempt to breake prison to the end to escape or shall conspire to beat the governor or M[aste]r of the house or to fire his house, or to make the prisoners there to mutiny against the Governor or such as shalbe appointed to looke to his safe keepinge or sett him on worke, or shall make escape out of the house of Correction against the will of the said Governors or Keepers or if any once burnt in the hand for fellony shalbe comitted afterwards to the house of Correction for Roguish life, Or if any one sent to the house of Correction and delivered shalbe sent thether agayne for Roguish life Or if any one sent to the house of Correction and delivered shalbe sent

[p. 9]
thether agayne by another name, In all their cases every such person is an Incorrigible rogue, and therefore the M[aste]rs or governors of the said house of Correccon shall soe soone as he conveniently can give notice to the Justices of peace that sent in the said person, of the circumstances aforesaid to the end every such incorrigible Rogue may be forthwith sent and comitted to the common gaole of the Countie, there to remayne untill the next generall quarter Sessions of the peace for that Countie, and then to be brought before the Justices at the said Sessions to the end he may be dealt w[i]thall as an Incorrigible Rogue, that is to say, to be indicted, convicted and burnt w[i]th the l[ette]re R in the left shoulder and then delivered, And if any one soe burned [*16cm gap*][1] shall wander and Rogue agayne and shalbe sent to the house of Correction or be otherwise apprehended, the same p[er]son is eftsoones[2] to be comitted by some Justice of peace where he shalbe apprehended to the comon gaole of the said Countie There to remayne untill the next generall Quarter Sessions of the peace of the same Countie or gaole delivery then and there to be indicted, tried, adiudged and executed as a fellon.

11. Item that the Justices of peace that shall comitt any offender to the house of Correction shall thereuppon make warrant under his hand and seale to the

---

1 This is due to a crease and a tear in the document with part missing.
2 A second time, or again.

Connstables of the hundred to pay unto the conductors of the saide persons comitted after the rate of ijd. the mile, And the said constables at the next quarter Sessions to be allowed that uppon his accompt given up to the Tre[asure]rs'.

(iv)   Categories of 'disorderly persons' who should, upon conviction at the Quarter Sessions of the Peace, be sent to the House of Correction (1620). Royal Berkshire Archives R/Z8/2.

For the avoidance of any doubt, the Justices of the Peace in 1620 produced this document to describe the meaning of the category of 'disorderly persons' who were to be committed to the House of Correction. It is interesting that among others the label was to be used for the 'reported fathers of Bastard children'. Evidently, rogues, sturdy beggars, vagabonds, and idlers needed no similar clarification.

At the Quarter Sessions of the Peace at Newbury … in April in 18 James I

Forasmuch as some question hath been made what persons shalbe said disorderly persons to be Comited to the House of Correction as comprehended within the words, disorderly persons, although they be not wanderers, The Justices at this Sessions have thus farr agreed, That the reported fathers of Bastard children, persons usually drunke, in Alehouses or ells where, Such as sett drinkinge in Alehouses or Tavernes in the tyme of Divine service or sermons, or in that tyme play at unlawfull games, and such as being no subsedy men,[1] (in respect they be not able to answer the penaltie of the Lawe) doe use Buckstalls,[2] setting doggs, netts or Engins[3] to take deere, partridges or phesants, or that being not subsedy men shoot with guns at pidgeons upon dovehouses or pidgeons in the feild or other places, or being not subsedy men keepe and use netts and tramills[4] to ketch fish in Rivers or ponds And such as be subsedy men or not and use hunting in warrens by night or upon the Saboth Daies, Such as are great swearers and Blasphemers of the word of god, Servants or apprentices that purloyne their M[aste]rs goods if it bee not fellony, or Consort and Conspire to Cosenage or deceipt, whereby their M[aste]rs are defrauded of their goods, Such as assault beat or strike their M[aste]r mistres or dame, Such as breake and teare hedges and Carry away the wood, Such as robb orchards of Fruite, Such as beat assault or ill use Constables or other officers in Executinge their offices, may be sent to the House of Correction there to bee once whipped and discharged without pasport.

---

1 A subsidy man was a person liable to pay subsidy, or tax, and so a man of means or substance.
2 A buck-stall was a large net for catching deer.
3 An engin, or engine or gin, was a mechanical contrivance for catching game, e.g., a snare or a trap.
4 A trammel is a fishing or fowling net with three layers of mesh.

(v)   Complaint against various inhabitants of the town, including John Ballard, the Keeper of the House of Correction (1620/1). Royal Berkshire Archives R/Z3/13.

William Hill was Constable of the Borough from 2 October 1620 to 1 October 1621, which enables this otherwise undated document to be dated at least within that year.[1]

To the right wor[shipfu]ll Mr Maior, and the Capitall Burgesses of the Towne and burrough of Readinge and to Will[ia]m Hill Constable of the same

Theis may be in all loving duetye to certifye yo[u]r good wor[shi]ps that there are divers disordered persons that lyve within the lymitts and precincts of ye Towne and Burrough of Readinge whoe are verye dissolute in their lyves, very obstinate, stubborne, and disobedient to their parents and governors, and suche as are not onelye Gadders and spinners of Streete webbs in the daye time, but very unruly in the Evenings, ordinarye nightwalkers, and suche as have their comon assemblies and meetings in the nighte tyme w[i]th their Companyons, by meanes whereof, unlesse there may be some Readye redress taken therein, by yo[u]r diligent name, and provident cicumspeccon, manye sundrye inconveniences maye growe, and (p[er]adventure) a greater chardge may aryse to the Inhabitants of ye Corporation than is yet manifestly known or suspected. May yt please you to be further advertized that the Keeper of the house of Correccon (Ballard by name) intertayneth poore mens Children, other mens servaunts, both by daye and by nighte, suffering them to be there typling and spending their money untill they be druncken, w[hi]ch was not soe in John Dawsons tyme the names of some of theis disordered p[er]sons are hereunder written (vizt)

>The two Daughters of William Glover whose wyfe doth maineteyne them against her owne husband, their Father
>Johan Barfoote,
>Wydow Robinsons daughter,
>William Dolmans daughter,
>Wydow Farrowes daughter
>Thomas Brownes Daughter
>Johan Nashe

---

1 J. M. Guilding, ed., *Records of the Borough of Reading: Diary of the Corporation*, 4 vols (London, 1892-6), ii, 93.

(vi)   Subsistence Bill for Prisoners (1743–5). Royal Berkshire Archives R/FZ2/31/21.

Berks The Corporation of Reading Dr to Henry Dunt

		li.	s	d
Barba Fulker	From the 5th of Decemr Exclusive to the 15th of Janry Inclu being 41 Days at 3d p day	-	10	3
John Casky	From the 9th of Decemr 1742 Exclu to the 22 of Janry Inclu being 44 Days	-	11	0
John Over	From the 2d of March 1742 to the 13th of April 1743 42 Days	-	10	6
Wm May	From the 4th of April 1743 to the 14th of the Same being 10 Days	-	2	6
Peter Morse	From the 30th of June 1743 to the 9th of July being 9 Days	-	2	3
Wm Pain	From the 12th of Augt 1743 to the 13th	-	-	3
James Munvile	From the 12th of Augt 2 11th of Octor 1743 60 Days	-	15	-
James Underwood	From the 17th of Octor 1743 to the 13th of Janry following 88 Days	1	2	-
Joseph Janaway	From the 18th of October 1743 to the 14th of Janry 88 Days	1	2	-
Barnard Pryor	From the 4th of Novemr 1743 to the 14th of Janry 71 Days	-	17	9
Sarah Scotford	From the 19th of Decr 1743 to the 14th of Janry following 26 Days	-	6	6
John Bowes	From the 7th of May 1744 to the 30th of June following 54 Day	-	13	6
Han. Saunders	From the 6th of July 1744 to the 10th of October 96 Day	1	4	-
Han Pinnork	From the 24th July to the 10th of Octor 78 Days	-	19	6
	Carried Over	8	17	0

[p. 2]

		li.	s	d
	Brot Over	8	17	-
	For 2 Years Sallery due at Lady Day 1744	4	0	-
		12	17	0
Sarah Piggott	From the 29th of Octor 1744 Exclu to the 2d of Janry following being 65 Days	0	16	3
Mary Pink	From the 28th of Feb to the 11th of March following Inclu being 11 days	0	2	9
Sarah Peircy	From the 22d of Feb Exclusive to the 26th of April Inclu being 63 Days	0	15	9

Jane Cooper	From the 14th of April Exclu to the 26th of Ditto Inclu being 12 Days	0	3	-
Alce Ravenscraft	From the 22d of June Exclu to the 19th of July Inclu being 27 Days	0	6	9
	One Years Sallary due at Lady Day 1745	2	0	0
		17	1	6

September 28 1745
Reced of Richd Tilleard Chamberlayn for the Hall Revenues for the Corporation of Reading the full Contents of this Bill
per me [Signed] Henry Dunt

(vii)   Nomination of Justices of the Peace to examine into the conditions of the Houses of Correction at Abingdon and Reading (1782). Royal Berkshire Archives D/ELV/O17.

The state of local Houses of Correction had started to give great concern, especially as awareness began to be raised by the work of the prison reformer John Howard. A consequence was an Act of Parliament requiring the Justices of the Sessions of the Peace around the country to ensure their Houses of Correction were up to specification. This document, part pre-printed (given in italics below) and part handwritten, delegates to three of the Justices of the Peace in Berkshire the task of inspecting the Reading House of Correction and reporting back upon its condition.

Berkshire. To wit, At the General Quarter Sessions of the Peace of our Sovereign Lord the King holden at Abingdon *in and for the said County, on Tuesday in the first week after the* Translation of Saint Thomas the Martyr *(to wit) the* sixteenth *Day of* July *in the 22nd Year of the Reign of our Sovereign Lord GEORGE the Third, by the grace of GOD, of Great Britain, France and Ireland, King, Defender of the Faith and so forth, and in the year of our Lord One Thousand Seven Hundred and* Eighty-two *before* James Patey, Ferdinando Collins Esquires *and others of their Fellows, Keepers of the Peace, and Justices of our said Lord the King, assigned to preserve the Peace in the said County, and also to hear and determine divers Felonies, Trespasses and other Misdemeanours, committed in the said County, and so forth.*

In pursuance of an Act of Parliament made and passed in the said twenty-second year of his said Majesty's reign Intituled 'An Act for the amending and rendering more effectual the Laws in being relative to Houses of Correction' This court have nominate John Elwes, Henry James Pye, and Edward Loveden Loveden[1] Esquires three of his Majesty's Justices of the Peace for this County to Examine into the state and Condition of the House of Correction at

---

1 Edward Loveden Loveden is his correct name, not an accidental repetition in the text!

Abingdon in this County and they or any two of them are requested to make and deliver in their report in pursuance of the said Act at the next Quarter Sessions And have also nominated Penyston Powney and James Patey Esquires and the Reverend Henry Wilder Clerk to Examine into the state and Condition of the House of Correction at Reading in this County and they or any two of them are also requested to make their report thereon at the next Quarter Sessions.
By this Court
Payn, Dept Clerk of the Peace

(viii)   Berkshire Quarter Session Order Book (Extracts from 1783–4). Royal Berkshire Archives Q/SO/5.

Following the inspection of the Reading House of Correction, as authorised in midsummer 1782 (given in the previous document), the delegated group submitted their report to the following Quarter Sessions in January and April 1783. Unsurprisingly, it proved easier to identify the problems than to rectify them.

[p. 117]
14 January 1783 Houses of Correction: The Committee appointed at the last Midsummer Quarter Sessions of the Peace holden at Abingdon in and for this County to examine into the State and Condition of the House of Correction at Reading in the said County and to make and deliver in their Report thereon pursuant to an Act of Parliament made and passed in the Twenty second Year of his present Majesty's Reign, Intituled, 'an Act for the amending and rendering more effectual the Laws in being relative to Houses of Correction' having delivered in their Report stating that they have examined and inspected the said House of Correction at Reading, and that the same in its present state of Building is by no means calculated to fulfil the purposes of the Act of Parliament, but that the same must be greatly enlarged and rebuilt. It is now ordered that the said Report be filed with the Records of this Court the same having been received and approved of, and it is ordered that the same be taken into further Consideration at the next Sessions.

[p. 141]
29 April 1783 House of Correction: The Committee appointed to Examine into the State and Condition of the House of Correction at Reading in the said County having delivered in their Report at this Sessions stating that a place of closer confinement is absolutely necessary for Refractory Prisoners and that a Division should be made to keep the Male and Female Prisoners separate and apart from each other, and that they have ordered Estimates to be made of such Alterations and an Inquiry for Persons who will contract to furnish Materials for employing the Prisoners in the said House of Correction It is ordered by the Court that the said Report be carried into Execution and that the said Committee be continued to see the same done in a proper manner.

[p. 208]
20 April 1784 House of Correction: It having been represented that the present House of Correction at Reading in the said County, is in a very ruinous State; It is ordered by the Court that George Vansittart, Penyston Powney, John Grant, Francis Page, Alexander Cobham, Henry Deane and John Deane Esquires, and the Reverend James Morgan Clerk, be a Committee assisted by any other Justices of the Peace for the said County, to treat with the Corporation of Reading relative to the repairing and improving thereof, or building a new one, and to settle the Rent that shall in future be paid for the same; And that three or more of the said Committee and Justices, do form a competent Meeting to do Business, and that they report their Proceedings at the next General Quarter Sessions.

(ix) Calendar of Bridewell Prisoners (1778, 1783–4). Royal Berkshire Archives R/JQ1/10A/1-4.

This set of four 'calendars of prisoners' illustrate the varied reasons for imprisonment in the Bridewell in the latter part of the 18th century, at the time of the inspections referred to in the previous two documents.

RBA R/JQ1/10A/1
Borough of Reading to Wit: A Calendar of Prisoners in Reading Bridewell January 16th 1778

William Taylor – Committed by Edward Skeate White Gent., Mayor, October 17th 1777 for stealing one Shift the property of William Willis.

Daniel Eales – Committed by the above December 24th 1777 on Suspicion of Stealing and Carrying away some Chips the Property of Thomas Watson.
                                                            Joseph Clack, Keeper

RBA R/JQ1/10A/2
Borough of Reading in the County of Berks: A Calendar of the Prisoners in the Bridewell in the said Borough April 30th 1783

John Handcock (out on bail) – Committed February 3rd, 1783 by Henry Deane Esquire Mayor charged on the Oaths of Robert Poore and Richard Clement on suspicion of having stolen several pieces of Plank Slabs and Oak Tops in the Parish of Saint Giles in the said Borough the Property of the said Robert Poore

Francis Woodley Labourer 27 years of Age – Committed February 7th, 1783 by the same Gentleman charged on the Oaths of Joseph Thorp and others on suspicion of stealing a saddle and Bridle the Property of David Berkley Esquire

Charles Simmons Labourer 51 – Committed February 11th 1783 by the same Gentleman charged on the Oaths of John Mansfield and John Harris on suspicion of having stolen a silver Spoon the Property of the said John Mansfield of the Parish of Saint Lawrence in the said Borough

Alice Stewart Servant 23 – Committed March 1st 1783 by the same Gentleman charged on the Oath of John Fillensor on suspicion of stealing a Sheet the Property of John and Ralph Fillensor of the Parish of St Mary in the said Borough

John Worthy Gundry Shoemaker aged 32 years – Committed March 13th 1783 by the same Gentleman charged on the Oaths of William Ducket and Japhet Batho on a strong suspicion of having stolen three Shirts in the Parish of St Giles in the said Borough the property of the said William Ducket

Bathsheba Johnson Tramper 16 and Mary White Tramper 14 –Committed March 14th 1783 by the same Gentleman charged on the Oath of John Glover on suspicion of having feloniously stolen a silver Punch Ladle in the Parish of Saint Mary in the said Borough the Property of his Brother Jacob Glover

Robert Lewis (out on Bail) – Committed March 15th 1783 by the same Gentleman charged on the Oaths of Sarah Fuller Samuel Williams James Clayton and Thomas Skye with assaulting them the Night before in the said Borough

Elizabeth Jones Tramper 24 – Committed April 16th 1783 by the same Gentleman charged on the Oaths of Mary the Wife of Thomas Newbury and Richard Shaile on suspicion of having stolen a Shoe in the Parish of St Lawrence in the said Borough the Property of the said Thomas Newbury

John Edgar Shoemaker 28 – Committed April 17th 1783 by the same Gentleman charged on the Oaths of Thomas Fletcher and John Parry with having behaved in a most indecent Manner to the Great Terror of the Female Inhabitants of this Borough

Joseph Clack Keeper

Thomas Haines alias Jumper – Convicted January 16th 1783 of an Assault was fined five Guineas and ordered to be imprisoned till it was paid which was paid the 19th and he was discharged

RBA R/JQ1/10A/3
Borough of Reading in the County of Berks
A Calendar of the Prisoners in the Bridewell in the said Borough
July 17th 1783
Alice Stewart – Ordered at the last Sessions to be imprisoned 12 months and twice privately whipped

Robert Lewis – Ordered at the same Sessions to pay a fine of £10 or be imprisoned 6 months

Mary Boyle – Committed May 2nd by Henry Deane Esquire Mayor on the Oaths of John Neale and Jacob Walter on suspicion of stealing a Shirt and other Things the Property of the said John Neale[1]

Joseph Packer and John Perry – Committed May 24th 1783 by Henry Deane Esquire on the Oaths of Thomas Chamberlain and Thomas Haines on suspicion of stealing a Saddle the Property of the said Thomas Chamberlain of the Parish of St Giles in this Borough[2]

James Nokes – Committed May 27th by Henry Deane Esquire he having about 8 years and ½ ago got Martha Wild with Child and refused to indemnify the Parish of St Giles for the Maintenance of the same

John Wallace – Committed June 9th by William Blandy Gentleman on the Confession of John Barnes with being an Accessory before the Fact to the stealing six Sacks of Bran with the Sacks in the Parish of St Giles aforesaid the property of William East the sacks being found concealed in John Wallaces Outhouse[3]

Joseph Clack Keeper

RBA R/JQ1/10A/4
Borough of Reading in the County of Berks
A Calendar of the Prisoners in the Bridewell in the said Borough
October 7th 1784

Ann King Aged 40 Years – Guilty[4] – Committed August 2nd 1784 by Mr Annesley Esquire Mayor charged on the Oath of James Swallow on suspicion of stealing a Linen Shirt in the Parish of St Lawrence in the said Borough the Property of the said James Swallow

Sampson Brewer – not Guilty – and William Farley – Guilty – aged 13 years each – Committed August 5th 1784 by Henry Deane Esquire charged on the Oaths of Francis Hedges John Copeland and William Blake on suspicion of having feloniously stolen taken and carried away in the Parish of St Lawrence in the said Borough a Hat which had been left to the Care of the said Francis Hedges to be turned and dyed

Joseph Wallington aged 60 years – Guilty – Committed August 9th 1784 by Henry Deane Esquire charged on the Oaths of James Bushnell and Mr Thomas Warner on suspicion of having feloniously stolen taken and carried away in

---

1 Boyle was sentenced on 20 July 1783 to be privately whipped and then discharged. *Reading Mercury* 21 July 1783, 3.
2 Packer was sentenced on 20 July 1783 to be imprisoned for a fortnight and then whipped from the Bridewell to High Bridge, and there discharged. *Reading Mercury* 21 July 1783, 3.
3 Barnes was sentenced on 20 July 1783 to be privately whipped and imprisoned for a month. Wallace (or Wallis) was committed to the county gaol, to be tried at the next county assizes as an accomplice before the fact. *Reading Mercury* 21 July 1783, 3.
4 Annotations of guilt in this document have been added later, probably at the subsequent Assizes.

the Parish of St Lawrence in the said Borough amongst many other Things a Pair of Shoes the Property of the said Mr Warner

Thomas Houlton Aged 21 years – Guilty – Committed September 15th 1784 by Martin Annesley Esquire Mayor charged on the Oath of Hannah Stamp and Grace Webb with having feloniously in his Possession a Linen Frock which was stolen out of the House of John Webb Husband to the said Grace Webb and which is his property

Joseph Clack Keeper

(x) Bill for various works, including at the Bridewell (1811–2, extract). Royal Berkshire Archives R/FZ2/38/6.

This is a carpenter's bill for works at the Bridewell in 1811–2. Unfortunately, the abbreviations make it difficult to be certain of the meaning of many of the entries, but nevertheless the document gives an idea of the scope of the work carried out over the year. These lines are extracted from a larger document which includes work for the Corporation on a number of other sites.

The Corporation of Reading
To R. Billing & Son

		£	s	d
1812[1]				
Nov 5	To Altering roof of Old Bridewell			
to 7	¼ @ 12d. ¼ @ 20d. ¼ @ 30d hs Carp^r 3 days		13	3½
1812				
May 7	To rep^g doorcases &c. at the Old Bridewell			
& 8	1'4 cube Oak @ 6/6 3'0 sup^r ½ deal @ 4		9	8
	½ @ 6d. ¼ @ 12d hs Carp^r 1¼ day		5	6
June 17	To Altering Doorways at the Bridewell			
to 19	5¼ ft Spikes ¼ @ 6d. 2 @ 20d hs		7	4¼
	Carp^r 4 days		16	0
June 22	To Bridewell			
to 26	4'9 cube Timber in Shoring @ 9d		3	6¾
	9'6 sup^r In deal @ 7 6'0 sup^r ¾ Elm @ 5½		8	3½
	5'0 run Eaves board 1 P^r 16in x Gamus 1 @ 6d–10d & 20d hs		6	2½
	Carp^r 6¾ days	1	7	0
Oct 1	To the Old Bridewell			
	17'8 sup^r 1½ deal 4 Pan^l door lead butt & Sq^l	1	6	6

1 This seems to be an error for 1811.

18'8 sup^r 1¼ Shutters lead butt & Sq^l 4 Pan^l	1	9	6½
7'9 sup^r ¾ ledg^d Shutter wrot & bead^d		7	1¼
1'10 sup^r 1½ deal hanging Stile wrot		1	9
-'6 cube Oak @ 6/6 7'0 sup^r ¾ deal @ 5/2		6	5½
1'9 sup^r In deal. 1'9 @ 7 In Oak @ 7		2	0½
1'6 sup^r 1¼ deal. 2 P^r 10in H hinges		6	1½
3 d In Screws 1 @ 4d. 1½ @ 6d ½ @ 12 hs		2	7
Carp^r 2¾ days		11	0
Old Bridewell	9	9	11¾

(xi)   Bill for work done at the Bridewell (1817–8). Royal Berkshire Archives R/FZ2/45/7.

The main interest in this whitesmith's bill is that it shows that inmates of the Bridewell were not necessarily free to move around inside the building. It is probable that only some were 'ironed', as, for example, no women are included in this list but would have been present at times in the Bridewell.

1817 The Gentlemen of the Corporation. Work done at the Bridewell &c.
To John Havell[1]

		£	s	d
Oct 18th	New bridge and wards to a lock a [*tear*] mending the key		2	
	Taking Iron of[f] a Man			6
Nov 5	Ironing a Man			6
1818				
Janry 15	Ironing a Man			6
16	Taking the Irons of a Man			6
27	Taking the Irons of a Man			6
	Mending a Latch			6
Febry 25	Ironing 3 Men		1	6
March 18	Ironing a Man			6
April 1	Ironing a Man			6
3	Taking the Irons of five Men and Ironing 3 Men		4	
17	Taking Irons of a Man			6
27	Ironing a Man			6
29	Ironing a Man			6
May 6	Ironing a Man			6
30	Ironing a Man			6
	Mending a key and mending a Staple to lock and puting in		1	6
June 1	Taking the Irons of a Man			6

---

1 John Havell's Whitesmith shop was on Fisher Row, Reading.

	20	Taking Irons of a Man		6
July 17		Ironing two Men	1	
	23	a Bar to window and putting up	3	6
	25	Mending a lock and mending the key	2	
		Ironing a Man		6
Augst 4		Ironing a Man		6
	5	Taking Irons of a Man		6
		Mending a tether	1	
		New lock and pins and nutts and putting on	5	
		Six [*Illegible*] rivits and burs	1	
	13	Taking Irons of a Man		6
	29	Ironing a Man		6
Sept 1		Taking Irons of Two Men	1	
		Taking a lock of and rivits and nails and mending the lock and putting on	2	4
	9	Two chimney bars 29½ lb	12	3½
		Three Clamps and nails to hold a Chimney 32½ lb	13	6½
	17	Four Strong holdfasts and nails	3	
		a New eye and lengthening the fastening and lengthening a bar to door	2	
	21	Two new S fitted keys and cleaning two lock	5	
		Mending a large lock	1	
		Four pins and nuts	1	4
	24	Two Water Grates	2	6
		Two holdfasts and 12 nails		10
			£3 17	4

[p.2]
1818

			£	s	d
		Brought forward	3	17	4
Sept 25		a Strong plate Staple and 32 Strong nails for a lock		2	
	28	Mending and cleaning a lock and a plate and screws		1	9
		Six bars to Windows 14¾ lb		6	1½
		Twelve screws and 12 nails			8
Oct 8th		a New Lock		4	9
		Two nuts and mending 4 screw pins to lock			8
		Two holdfast and nails			8
	9	New Spikes and repareing same Do. for the Wall and making of holes and nails		10	
		Four Clamps and round pins and nails 33¼ lb		16	7½
	10	Pointing some Spikes		1	4

	Key to Stock Lock			9
	Two Staples			4
13	Ironing a Man			6
23	New Key to Large Lock		2	6
		6	5	11
30	Recvd Old Iron 1c 2qr 1½ lb	1	4	1½
	Old Cast Iron 2qr 0 lb		1	6
		1	5	7½
		5	0	3½

(xii)   Receipt for Bill (above) for work done at the Bridewell (1819). Royal Berkshire Archives R/FZ2/45/6.

It is slightly perplexing that while Havell's bill included an odd ½ d., this receipt does not. Havell presented his bill at the end of October 1818, but was not paid by the Corporation until August 1819.

Reading August 19 1819
Received of Mr B Simonds Esquire Chamberlain for the Hall Revenues Five Pounds and three pence for the Annexed Bill for work done at the Town Bridewell for the Corporation
£5. 0. 3.
John Havell

(xiii)   Bill for Subsistence and other Expenses for the Prisoners in the Bridewell (1816–7). Royal Berkshire Archives R/FZ2/43/6.

The Corporation of Reading to William Simpson[1] Keeper of the House of Correction for the Borough of Reading

Subsistence	£.	s.	d.
For Mary Else from the 22nd of December 1816 to the 19th January 1817 29 days at 5½ per day		13	3½
Ann Powell from the 22nd of December 1816 to the 18th January 1817 28 days at 5½ per day		12	10
William Leaver from the 22nd of December 1816 to the 18th January 1817 28 days at 5½ per day		12	10
Thomas Turner from the 22nd of December 1816 to the 18th January 1817 28 days at 5½ per day		12	10
James Reade from the 22nd of December 1816 to the 13th February 1817 54 days at 5½ per day	1	4	9
Benjamin Howard from the 22nd of December 1816 to the 17th January 1817 27 days at 5½ per day		12	4½
Charles Walker from the 22nd of December 1816 to the 24th January 1817 34 days at 5½ per day		15	7
John Pope from the 22nd of December 1816 to the 17th February 1817 58 days at 5½ per day	1	6	7
Jane Richerson from the 22nd of December 1816 to the 13th March 1817 82 days at 5½ per day	1	17	7
James Spokes Senior from the 26th of December 1816 to the 8th January 1817 14 days at 5½ per day		6	5
James Spokes Junior from the 26th of December 1816 to the 1st January 1817 7 days at 5½ per day		3	2½
James Blunnon from the 26th of December 1816 to the 23rd January 1817 29 days at 5½ per day		13	3½
James Chesterman from the 17th of January 1817 to the 18th January 1817 2 days at 5½ per day			11
John Dunn from the 22nd of December 1816 to the 24th January 1817 34 days at 5½ per day		15	7
Ann Grover from the 27th of January 1817 to the 12th February 1817 17 days at 5½ per day		7	9½
William Bonney from the 31st of January 1817 to the 5th February 1817 6 days at 5½ per day		2	9
Sarah Ironmonger from the 31st of January 1817 to the 19th February 1817 20 days at 5½ per day		9	2

---

1 According to the Corporation records Henry Simpson was the Keeper of the House of Correction/Bridewell from 1810 to 1818 (Royal Berkshire Archives R/AC1/1/25 Minutes of the Corporation) and this is the only instance during that time that I have found the name William Simpson. Perhaps he was Henry's brother and assisted in the role. Whoever he was, one has to admire his arithmetical ability to correctly multiply by 5½ and covert to £ s d.

Thomas Tucker from the 5th of February 1817 to the 25th March 1817 49 days at 5½ per day	1	2	5½
William Young from the 17th of February 1817 to the 12th March 1817 24 days at 5½ per day		11	
Ann Lackley from the 27 of February 1817 1 day at 5½ per day			5½
Samuel Lovejoy from the 1st of March 1817 to the 19th March 1817 19 days at 5½ per day		8	8½
Thomas Day from the 12 of March 1817 to the 25 March 1817 14 days at 5½ per day		6	5
William White from the 13 of March 1817 to the 25 March 1817 13 days at 5½ per day		5	11½
James White from the 23 of March 1817 to the 25 March 1817 3 days at 5½ per day		1	4½
Paid at Mr Blandys Shop for a pair of handcuffs for the use of prison		2	6
Paid Hewlings for sweeping all the chimneys		3	
Paid Jane Richerson when discharged by order of the Mayor		2	
Paid for coals for James Read when sick by order of the surgeon		4	
Extra Prison allowance for Ann Grover when sick by order of the Surgeon 8 days at 6d per day		4	
Paid for Oil for the use of Locks in Prison			6
Paid Day the Carpenter for a new handle in one of the [illegible – looks like bitels]			8
Mr Havells Bill whitesmith mending a Lock and Key to one of the Prison doors		2	
For Punishing John Pope twice Publickly		5	
For Punishing William Leaver Privately twice		5	
For Punishing Charles Walker		5	
Straw for the use of the Prisoners		8	
Paid for Six Calenders for the use of last Sessions		4	
Paid Kingston for assistance last Sessions		3	
For Brooms and a Mop		3	4
	16	6	2

[p. 2]

Brot over	16	16	2
Stamp		1	
Also one Quarters Salary from the 22nd December 1816 to the 25 March 1817	3	15	
£	20	12	2

Recd 26 March 1817
[Signed] W Simpson

(xiv)   Bill for Medicines at the Bridewell (1817). Royal Berkshire Archives R/FZ2/43/32.

This is a list of medicines given to the inmates of the Bridewell in 1817.

1817 The Corporation of Reading, For Prisoners in the Town Bridewell
To Ring, Bulley & Co.

		s.	d.
Jan	8 Powders	2	
	Opening Ditto	1	
	11 Ditto --- 25 Ditto --- 29 Ditto	6	
Feb	3 A Blister & Cerate[1]	1	6
	Powders --- 4 Ditto --- 6 Ditto --- 7 Ditto	8	
	13 Ditto --- 27 Ditto	3	
March	3 Ditto --- 24 Ditto --- 26 Ditto & Cerate	6	6
	27 Ditto --- 31 Ditto & Cerate	4	6
Apr	3 Ditto, Cerate & Salts	3	
	4 Pot of Cerate --- 7 Ditto	4	
	Powders 10 Pills	4	
	11 Cerate ---12 Powders --- 22 Cerate	4	
	30 Powders, Blister & Cerate	3	6
May	4 Ditto Pills --- 6 Powders ---13 Ditto	7	6
	22 Pills --- 23 Powders --- 24 Pills	5	
	27 Cerate --- 30 Pills	2	6
June	4 Powders --- 8 Pills --- 11 Powders	5	6
	12 Cerate --- 17 Pills & Cerate --- 21 Pills	5	6
	22 Cerate --- 27 Powders & Pills	4	6
July	1 Ditto Ditto --- 6 Ditto Ditto	6	6
	9 Pills --- 13 Powders	4	
	17 Powders --- 19 Cerate --- 22 Pills	4	6
	30 Pills & Powders	4	
Aug	3 A Powder --- 5A Blister --- 6 Powders	3	6
	8 Pills --- 15 Powders --- 18 Pills	6	
	22 Powders --- 28 Ditto --- 29 Pills	6	
	31 Cerate and Powders	2	6
Sept	Pills – Cerate --- 9 Pills & Powders	6	6
	12 Pills --- 16 Ditto --- 18 Powders --- 22 Ditto	8	
	24 Ditto --- 28 Cerate --- 29 Pills	5	
Oct	2 Ditto --- 8 Ditto --- 14 Ditto --- 16 Ditto	8	
	29 Cerate	1	
Nov	5 Ditto --- 9 Ditto	4	
	14 Ditto --- 15 Powders	3	
Dec	1 Powders --- 15 Ditto	4	
	14 Pills and Cerate	2	
		£8 0 0	

---

1 A stiff ointment composed of wax, lard or oil and other ingredients.

(xv)   Petition to the Crown for Grant of Separate Court of Quarter Sessions for the Borough of Reading (1836). Royal Berkshire Archives R/JQ1/19

This set of papers begins with a report on the condition of the Bridewell with a view to submitting a petition to the Government requesting that Reading have its own permanent Quarter Sessions of the Peace. Perhaps it is not too surprising that in the circumstances the Bridewell is found to be in a clean and wholesome state. If true, this was the only time for which that was the case. Reading was successful in its bid to have its own Quarter Sessions, as these papers show, but it was only because of the arrangement with the County to have use of its gaol when necessary, as the Bridewell was not considered sufficient for the town's purposes. Although it was a long road from this to the ultimate sale of the Bridewell in 1862, this must have provided impetus in that direction.

1.   Report of Committee of the Borough of Reading as to the state of the Borough Bridewell and Petition to the King[1]

10th February 1836

> Report of the Committee appointed to view the state of the Borough Bridewell and also to Settle and approve a Petition to His Majesty in Council for a separate Court of Quarter Sessions to be continued to this Borough.

Your Committee report that they have viewed the Bridewell and they find that it contains a Dwelling for the Keeper with two Court Yards and sufficient Cells for the confinement of at least fourteen Prisoners charged with Felony or Misdemeanor, that it also contains a Court Yard with five rooms for the confinement of Prisoners for Debt which are capable of containing twelve persons – that at the present time there is only one person confined for Debt within the said Prison and he is detained under a Writ of Capias ad Satisfaciendum for a debt of ten Shillings which notwithstanding Judgement has been recovered he still disputes and therefore though a Prisoner he refuses to make any arrangement for his liberation.

That your Committee find that in the month of November 1824 a Contract was entered into between the Justices of the County thro' the medium of a Committee, of whom the late J. B. Monck Esq. was the Chairman, and the Magistrates of this Borough for the Maintenance and Custody of the Borough Prisoners in the County Gaol and House of Correction, and that such Contract was approved by the late Corporation and is recorded upon the Minutes of their Diary, and that it has ever since been acted upon, and the Prisoners for this Borough as well before Trial as after Conviction

---

1 Also see Royal Berkshire Archives R/AC1/2/1 Minutes of the Corporation 1835–40.

[p. 2]
are confined in the County Gaol or House of Correction by which means Safe Custody, proper Classification, due punishment, and strict prison discipline are obtained, with at the same time the advantage of Moral Improvement, and these in a much superior degree and at much less Cost, than could possibly be derived in the Borough Bridewell.

That the Borough Bridewell is therefore only used for the confinement of Prisoners under Examination and those who are committed for short periods of Imprisonment, where hard labour is not inflicted.

Your Committee have much Satisfaction in reporting that they found the whole of the Bridewell in a clean and wholesome state.

Your Committee are of Opinion that although considerable Sums appear to have been from time to time expended upon the Bridewell to add to its Security – yet that in their Opinion it is not capable of being made so Strong and Secure as a Prison in their Judgement ought to be without incurring a very heavy expence and from its peculiar situation they could not recommend any such Alterations to be made, and therefore in their Opinion it appears most desirable that the existing Arrangement with the County should still be continued.

Your Committee have perused and approved a Petition framed by the Town Clerk to the King for a separate Court of Quarter Sessions of the Peace for this Borough and which accompanies this Report.
[Signed] Hy Hawkes Mayor

2.   Petition to the Crown for Grant of Separate Court of Quarter Sessions for the Borough of Reading

12 February 1836
To the King's Most Excellent Majesty in Council

Most Gracious Sovereign,
We your Majesty's most dutiful and faithful subjects the Council of the Borough of Reading in the County of Berks humbly represent to your Majesty that under the authority of a Charter which in the first year of your Majesty's auspicious Reign your Majesty was most graciously pleased to grant to the said Borough and of various Charters of divers of your Majesty's Royal predecessors Sovereigns of England the Justices of the Peace acting in and for the said Borough were empowered to hold a separate Court of Quarter Sessions of the Peace within the said Borough its Liberties and precincts and to enquire of hear and determine all such matters and things as in and by the said Charters respectively are mentioned and granted with jurisdiction exclusive of Justices of the Peace of the County of Berks who were not in any manner to intromit themselves therein And we further represent to your Majesty that we are desirous such separate Court of Quarter Sessions shall still be continued to be holden in and for the said Borough its Liberties and precincts.

And we further represent to your Majesty that the privilege of having a separate Court of Quarter Sessions in and for the said Borough has been attended with much advantage and convenience to the Inhabitants thereof has promoted the speedy and due administration of the laws and has been a saving of much time and expense to your Majesty's subjects Inhabitants of the said Borough.

That the said Borough has of late years very greatly increased in extent and population and is still increasing that only one General Quarter Sessions of the Peace is now holden for the County of Berks within the said Borough the other Courts of Quarter Session for the said County of Berks being held at Abingdon and Newbury and therefore should a separate Court of Quarter Sessions not be continued to the said Borough the inhabitants thereof would experience much inconvenience and loss of time and the expense which would be occasioned by the trial of offences committed within the said Borough at Abingdon or Newbury which places are distant the one 26 miles and the other 17 miles from the said Borough would tend greatly to increase the public Burdens.

[p. 2]
And we further represent to your Majesty,

That there is within the said Borough a Gaol or Bridewell which is of extent sufficient to contain in the felons Wards at least 14 prisoners and in the debtors wards at least 12 prisoners but that it is used now only for prisoners confined for debt for persons committed for further examination or for short periods of imprisonment in cases when hard labour is not inflicted the Justices of the Peace of the said Borough having in the year 1824 made an arrangement with the Justices of the Peace for the County of Berks in pursuance of which the Justices for the Borough are enabled to send all prisoners charged with offences within the said Borough as well before trial as after conviction to the Gaol or house of correction for the said County the said Borough contributing a fair and rateable proportion for the clothing subsistence and other expenses of the said prisoners and by this means the Borough prisoners committed to hard labour are properly employed and all are subject to the same classification punishment and discipline and have the advantage of the same moral improvement as prisoners committed by Justices of the Peace of the said County of Berks.

And we further represent to your Majesty

That the present Recorder of this Borough is Henry Alworth Merewether Esquire Serjeant at Law who has been such Recorder since the year 1830 and that we your Majesty's petitioners as the Council of this Borough have agreed and are willing to pay to the said Recorder a Salary of 40 Guineas for the discharge of the duties which will devolve upon him if a separate Court of Quarter Sessions shall by your Majesty be still continued to this Borough.

And we further represent to your Majesty

That we have within the said Borough a fit and suitable Building called the public or police office in which are suitable rooms and offices for the transaction of the business of the Justices of this Borough in which such business has for many years past and still continues to be transacted and that no part of such building is licensed as a Victualling House or Alehouse.

Your Petitioners therefore humbly pray that your Majesty will be graciously pleased to grant that a separate Court of Quarter Sessions of the Peace shall be henceforth holden in and for our said Borough with such powers

[p. 3]

and jurisdiction to try offences as your Majesty in your Royal wisdom should see fit to grant And your petitioners shall ever pray &c.

(Signed by the Mayor, 6 Aldermen and 14 Councillors)

3.　　On His Majesty's Service: To the Town Clerk of Reading from the Secretary of State's Office

Whitehall 30th April 1836

Sir,

I am directed by Lord John Russell to acquaint you, for the information of the Council of the Borough of Reading, that His Majesty has been pleased to grant that a separate Court of Quarter Sessions shall be henceforward holden in and for the Borough of Reading.

But in making this communication I am directed by Lord John Russell at the same time to desire you to inform the Council that they

[p. 2]
are to consider the grant of separate Quarter Sessions as made upon condition, and so to be accepted, that they will put the Borough Gaol into a fit and proper state for the confinement of Prisoners and for the due maintenance of prison discipline, or, if the existing Gaol will not admit of this, that they will either build a new Gaol, or contract with the County for the reception of the Borough Prisoners in the County Gaol,

I am, Sir, Your obedient Servant,
[Signed] J. M. Phillips

4.　　Extract from the Diary of the Corporation of Reading 13 May 1836

Upon the motion of the Mayor, Seconded by Mr Cottrell – It is Ordered that the Grant of a separate Court of Quarter Sessions for this Borough be accepted – that the Contract entered into by the late Corporation of this Borough with the Justices of the Peace for the County of Berks for the reception of the Borough Prisoners in the County Gaol be confirmed, and that the Town Clerk do forthwith communicate this Minute to the Secretary of State.

5.   From the Town Clerk, Reading, to the Secretary of State, Lord John Russell, Whitehall

Reading May 13th 1836

My Lord,

I have the Honour to inform your Lordship that I have this day laid before a Meeting of the Council of this Borough your Lordship's communication of the 30th ultimo directing me to inform the Council that they are to consider the Grant of a separate Quarter Sessions to this Borough as made upon condition and so to be accepted that they will put the Borough Gaol into a fit and proper state for the confinement of Prisoners and for the due maintenance of Prison discipline or if the existing Gaol will not admit of this they will either build a new Gaol or contract with the County for the reception of the Borough Prisoners in the County Gaol, and with reference to your Lordship's communication the Council of this Borough have ordered that His Majesty's Grant that a separate Court of Quarter Sessions shall be in future holden in and for this Borough be accepted and that the contract entered into by the late Corporation of this Borough with the Justices of the Peace for the County of Berks for the reception of the Borough Prisoners in the County Gaol be confirmed.

I have therefore to request that your Lordship will please to order that His Majesty's grant may be transmitted to me that the necessary proceedings under it may be had within the time prescribed by law.

I have the honour to be &c.

J.J. Blandy, Town Clerk

6.   On His Majesty's Service: To the Town Clerk of Reading from the Secretary of State's Office

Whitehall 14th May 1836

Sir,

I am directed by Lord John Russell to acknowledge the receipt of your letter of the 13th inst. stating that the Council of Reading accept the Grant of separate Quarter Sessions on the Condition mentioned in my Letter of the 30th April, and will continue to contract with the Justices of the County of Berks for the reception of the Borough Prisoners in the County Gaol.

Lord John Russell desires me to inform you, that if at any time

[p.2]
Prisoners shall be committed to the Borough Gaol on summary conviction or otherwise, the Council will be required to make the Gaol in every respect fit for the confinement of Prisoners and for the maintenance of Prison discipline.

I am, Sir, Your obedient Servant,

[Signed] J.M. Phillips

7.   Extract from the Diary of the Corporation of Reading

Friday 20th May 1836

The Town Clerk laid before this meeting a Copy of the Letter written by him to the Secretary of State in pursuance of the Minute made at the last Meeting of the Council, and also a Letter he had received from the Under Secretary of State in reply dated the 14th instant and the same having been read and the Subject debated It was moved by Mr Garrard seconded by Mr Alderman Barrett and carried in the Affirmative that the Council bind themselves to make application to the Justices of this County at their next Quarter Sessions to enter into Contract for the reception of all Prisoners committed by the Justices of the Peace for this Borough whether on Summary Conviction or otherwise and in the event of the County Justices being unwilling so to extend the existing Contract (which the Council do not anticipate) then the Council bind themselves to make the Borough Gaol in every respect fit for the Confinement of Prisoners and for the maintenance of Prison discipline. And that a Copy of this Minute be forthwith transmitted by the Town Clerk to the Secretary of State with a request that the Grant of the separate Quarter Sessions may be transmitted to prevent the difficulty which otherwise may arise in committing Prisoners charged with offences within this Borough for Trial.

8.   From the Town Clerk, Reading, to the Secretary of State, Lord John Russell, Whitehall

20th May 1836

My Lord,
    I have the honour to transmit to your Lordship the Copy of a Resolution passed at a Meeting of the Town Council of this Borough this Morning and I have in pursuance of their instructions to request that your Lordship will be pleased to direct that the Grant of the Separate Quarter Sessions may be transmitted as early as is consistent with your Lordship's convenience in order that the difficulty alluded to in the latter part of that Resolution may be avoided.
    I am &c.
    [Signed] J.J. Blandy, Town Clerk

9.   On His Majesty's Service: To the Town Clerk of Reading from the Secretary of State's Office

Whitehall May 21 1836

Sir,
    I am directed by Lord John Russell to acknowledge receipt of your letter of the 20th inst., with its Inclosure, and to acquaint you for the information of the Town Council, that the Grant of a separate Quarter Sessions for Reading will be completed with the least possible delay and that it will be ready in about a Week.
    I am, Sir, Your obedient Servant,
    [Signed] J. Maule

II. The purchase of the Bridewell, Bridewell Keeper's House and 'Pigeons' public house by Reverend William Whitmarsh Phelps

(i)   Borough of Reading Minutes of Council Meetings from 9 November 1857 to 22 April 1863 (Extracts). Royal Berkshire Archives R/AC1/2/4.

The following extracts from the Council Minutes are those parts that refer to the Borough Bridewell or to the plans for a new Police Building.

[p. 53]
At a meeting of the Council of the Borough of Reading on 6 May 1858.
The following Report of the Finance and Watch Committee pursuant to the Minute of the Council of the 30th November last was presented and read.

Report to the Council of the Borough of Reading by the Finance and Watch Committee to whom it was referred on the 30th day of November 1857 'to consider whether by any and what means the Finances of the Borough may be brought into a better state and the expenses reduced within reasonable limits, regard being had to the necessity of securing better and more commodious premises for the administration of Justice and the detention of Prisoners' …

[p. 54]
The report ends:
In directing their attention to the above mentioned subjects your Committee have not been unmindful of that

[p. 55]
part of the minute of reference to them which alludes to 'the necessity of securing better and more commodious premises for the administration of Justice and the detention of Prisoners'. They cannot, and they believe the Council will not, deny that there is a great necessity for better accommodation for the administration of Justice in this Borough and that it is imperatively needful to make better provision for the detention of prisoners before Commitment. They have therefore spent much time in deliberation upon these matters with a view to offer to the Council some recommendation which might commend itself to their unanimous adopted [sic] but a difference of opinion between them prevents this and they therefore beg to recommend that nothing more be done at present than that which is necessary to secure the Government allowance of one fourth of the expenses of pay and Clothing to the Police viz. to provide better Lock-ups in accordance with the suggestion of the Government Inspector.

George Palmer, Mayor

It was moved by Councillor Dr Wells, and seconded by Mr Councillor Monck That such Report be received and the question having been put was carried unanimously.

Mr Alderman Darter having moved and Mr Alderman Brown seconded the Motion 'That a sum not exceeding £4000 be appropriated for the erection of Lock-ups, Police Station and Magistrates' Offices, also that a Committee consisting of Messrs Darter, Brown, Cooper, Taylor, Boorne, and the Mayor be appointed for the purpose of selecting a suitable site and to obtain a Plan for the same and that they report the result to a Committee of the Whole Council' An amendment was moved by Councillor Dr Wells seconded by Mr Councillor Monck 'That a Committee be formed to provide proper Lock-ups and to report thereon to the Council, the Committee to consist of the following Members:- The Mayor, Mr Alderman Darter, Mr Alderman Brown, Mr Councillor Boorne, Mr Councillor Cooper and Mr Councillor Taylor'. The amendment was put but lost on a division and the original motion was then put and carried.

[p. 61]
At a meeting of the Council of the Borough of Reading on 22 June 1858.
Public Buildings and Magistrates Offices:
The following report having been presented and read It was moved by Mr Alderman Darter and seconded by Mr Councillor Cooper That the same be received and the site adopted Whereupon an amendment was moved by Mr Councillor Simonds and seconded by Mr Alderman Harris That the Report be received but not adopted and that it be referred back to the Committee to reconsider the subject and to suggest another site, and the amendment having been put and carried on a division by a majority of 4 votes the original motion was lost.

> Report of the Committee appointed by the Council of the Borough of Reading on the sixth day of May 1858 'for the purpose of selecting a suitable site for the erection of Lock-ups, Police Station and Magistrates' Office, and to obtain a plan for the same'.

Your committee beg to report that they have met several times since the date of their appointment and used every endeavour to perform the task assigned them which they have found far more difficult of accomplishment than they had reason to anticipate it would have been. They are glad

[p. 62]
however to state that they have at length been enabled to make a selection of a site which appears to them admirably adapted for all the purposes required, and they have therefore had a plan prepared by the Borough Surveyor in accordance with the Minute of their appointment.

Without troubling the Council with the particulars of all their proceedings the Committee desire to state that after looking out for properties themselves and desiring the Borough Surveyor to do the same, several were brought under their notice but only one of which was considered in all respects eligible, and this could not be purchased except under compulsory powers. They then advertised in the newspapers for sites, but failed of obtaining any offer worthy of being recommended to the Council. They however feel great confidence in recommending the site they have last had under consideration which consists of the premises called High Bridge House in the occupation of Mr Granville Sharp. This property belongs to Mr William Blandy who is not unwilling to sell if the Corporation should decide to purchase, and your Committee have ascertained that he would accept £1600 for the property including Fixtures.

Your Committee therefore recommend this site and the accompanying plans for adoption by the Council.

George Palmer, Mayor. 21st June 1858

[p. 67]
At a meeting of the Council of the Borough of Reading on 5th August 1858.
The following Report of the Committee of the whole Council was presented and read and upon the motion of Mr Alderman Harris seconded by Mr Councillor Leach ordered to be received and entered upon the Minutes.

[p. 68]
    Report of the Committee of the whole Council to the Council of the Borough of Reading

Your Committee beg to report that on the 19th ult. they met and received the accompanying Report from the Committee appointed on the 6th May last but that they did not deem it expedient to adopt it.

5th August 1858

George Palmer, Mayor

    Report of the Committee of the whole Council by the Committee appointed on the 6th May 1858 for the purpose of selecting a suitable site for the erection of Lock-ups Police Station and Magistrates' Offices and to obtain a plan for the same.

Your Committee beg to report that in compliance with the resolution of the Council on the 23rd June[1] last they met and reconsidered the subject of their former Report when after much deliberation they came to the conviction that they cannot suggest a more eligible site. They had previously to presenting their last Report well considered the eligibility of many sites and of the Bear Inn among them. They came to the conclusion then, and they are still of the same opinion that this property is not eligible, either in point of situation or in the practicability of adapting the existing Buildings to the purposes required, even if it could be purchased for such an amount as they could afford out of the sum placed at their disposal, by the Council to give. They have also considered a site offered to them in Middle Row, viz. the house and premises occupied by Mr Poole. To this also there are many objections and not the least is that of the situation which together with the narrowness of the frontage, the confined nature of the buildings on either side, and the price required, viz. £1600 for the Landlord's interest alone, have led the Committee to look in another direction. They then had their attention drawn to the property in the Market Place occupied by Mr J. G. Hawkes but the area of this was found to be insufficient besides which it was deemed objectionable on account of the confined character of the spot except to the northern frontage.

---

1 The meeting took place on 22nd June 1858, not 23rd.

[p. 69]
Under all circumstances your Committee feel that they cannot do better than again recommend the site at High Bridge to the serious consideration and adoption of the Council, and in the event of its not being adopted can only suggest one alternative, viz. to apply to the Court of Chancery for an order to enable the Council to purchase the piece of land in the Forbury held by Mr Fulkes or some other portion of the Blagrave property, that being in their opinion the only means left of obtaining a suitable site otherwise than by applying to parliament as pointed out in the Report presented to the Council in the month of August 1856.
George Palmer, Mayor. 5th July 1858

It having been moved by Mr Alderman Darter seconded by Mr Councillor Boorne 'That the Resolution of the Council of the 6th day of May last on the subject of Police Buildings be referred to a Committee of the whole Council for the purpose of selecting a site and approving of a plan subject to confirmation by the Council and that the Committee be requested to report thereon as early as practicable'. An amendment was moved by Councillor Dr Wells and seconded by Mr Alderman Harris 'That the Resolution of this Council of the 6th day of May last in the following words 'That a sum of £4000 be appropriated for the erection of Lock-ups, Police Station and Magistrates' Offices, also that a Committee consisting of Messrs Darter, Brown, Cooper, Taylor, Boorne and the Mayor be appointed for selecting a suitable site and to obtain a plan for the same and that they report the result to a Committee of the whole Council' be now rescinded, and that the whole subject be referred to a Committee of the whole Council who shall report thereon to the Council'. And a further amendment having been moved by Mr Councillor Simonds and seconded by Mr Councillor Phillips 'That the Committee of the whole Council be authorised to take all proceedings

[p. 70]
necessary for the immediate erection of Courts &c. at an expense not exceeding £4000' such further amendment was put but lost on a division when the amendment moved by Dr Wells was put and also lost on a division. Whereupon the original motion was put and carried.

[p. 122]
At a meeting of the Council of the Borough of Reading on 5 May 1859.
Police Buildings
Councillor Dr Wells having moved and the late Mayor seconded the motion 'That the powers given to a Committee of the whole Board to erect Police Buildings at a cost not exceeding £4000 to be rescinded, and that the same Committee be empowered to spend a sum not exceeding £200 in the repair of the Borough Bridewell to meet the requirements of the Government Inspector', an amendment was moved by Mr Councillor Taylor and seconded by Mr Councillor Simonds 'That a sub Committee do examine, and the Surveyor prepare a plan for the alteration of the Town Hall with a view to convert the same into Police Buildings in accordance with the requirements of the

Government Inspector' and a further amendment having been moved by Mr Alderman Walford, and seconded by Mr Councillor Monck 'That the Police Buildings Committee be requested to consider the question of putting into a satisfactory state the existing Lock-ups at a moderate expense' the question was debated and considered when the motion proposed by Councillor Dr Wells and the amendment proposed by Mr Councillor Taylor were withdrawn, and the amendment moved by Mr Alderman Walford was thereupon put and carried unanimously.

[p. 137]
At a meeting of the Council of the Borough of Reading on 4 August 1859.
Report of Police Buildings Committee
The following Report of the Police Buildings Committee was presented and read.
    Report of the Police Buildings Committee to the Council of the Borough of Reading.
Your Committee beg to report that in accordance with the resolution of the Council on the 5th day of May last they have taken into consideration 'the question of putting into a satisfactory state the existing lock-ups at a moderate expense' and that having regard to the difficulty of procuring a suitable site for the erection of Police Buildings of a permanent nature, they are of opinion that it is desirable as a temporary measure to put the Lock-ups at the Borough Bridewell into such a state as will meet the requirements of the Government Inspector. They accordingly directed the Borough Surveyor to prepare a plan for that

[p. 138]
purpose which he has done and upon which your Committee have had the benefit of the Government Inspector's opinion and they are happy to report that with a few additions which he has suggested such plan will be satisfactory to him. The cost of carrying it into effect will probably be about £400 and as this outlay will ensure to the Town the Government allowance of one fourth of the annual costs of the pay and clothing of the police which at the present time exceeds £400 your Committee have no hesitation in recommending the Council to adopt the plan now submitted with the additions recommended by the Government Inspector and that a sub Committee consisting of the Mayor, Mr Alderman Darter, Mr Councillor Steward and Mr Councillor Clark be appointed for the purpose of carrying it into effect.
Charles J Andrewes, Mayor. Public Office. July 29th 1859.

Cells at Borough Bridewell to be fitted up &c.
Resolved unanimously on the motion of the Mayor seconded by the late Mayor That the Report of the Police Buildings Committee be received and adopted and that it be referred to a Sub Committee consisting of The Mayor, Mr Alderman Darter, Councillor Dr Wells, Mr Councillor Steward and Mr Councillor Clark to carry out the works referred to in such Report, that such Sub Committee be requested to consult and report to the Committee of the whole Council as they may have occasion, and that the last mentioned

Committee be empowered to give all such directions and take all such measures as shall be requisite for carrying their recommendations into effect.

[p. 154]
At a meeting of the Council of the Borough of Reading on 9 November 1859.
Report of Police Buildings Committee
The Police Buildings Sub Committee presented the following Report and the same having been read it

[p. 155]
was moved by Councillor Dr Wells and seconded by Mr Councillor Brain That the same be received and adopted and that an order be issued to the Borough Treasurer in accordance with the recommendation of the Committee.

    Report of the Police Buildings Sub Committee to the Council of the Borough of Reading

Your Committee have to report that pursuant to the powers given to them by the Council at the last quarterly meeting they approved of the Surveyor's plans and specifications and advertised for tenders for the work. That four tenders were sent in, the highest of which amounted to £510 and the lowest to £422 being a Tender of Mr John Wells which your Committee accepted and the works are now in progress.

    Your Committee recommend that an Order be issued to the Treasurer of the Borough Fund for payment from time to time to Mr Wells of such sums not exceeding £75 per cent upon the value of the work performed as shall be recommended by the Certificate of the Borough Surveyor and authorised by an Order from three members of your Committee countersigned by the Town Clerk.

Charles J. Andrewes, Mayor. Public Office. November 4th 1859.

[p. 194]
At a meeting of the Council of the Borough of Reading on 10 May 1860.
Report of the Police Buildings Committee
The following Report of the Police Buildings Committee was presented and read.

    Report of the Police Buildings Committee to the Council of the Borough of Reading

Your Committee have to report that the new Cells at the Borough Bridewell have been completed, and will be ready for use as soon as they have been furnished with bedding and other necessary articles. Also, that the new charge-room has been constructed, and when furnished will be ready for use.

    Your Committee have taken into consideration the arrangements it is expedient to make for the future care and management of the Bridewell and are unanimously of opinion that it is essential to place it under the control of the police and having well

[p. 195]
considered the suggestions of the Chief Superintendent as contained in the accompanying Report which he prepared at the request of your Committee they unanimously recommend that Inspector Charles Hardiman be appointed to reside and take charge of the Bridewell under such regulations the Watch Committee shall deem expedient, at the salary of £1.2.0 per week besides the usual police Clothing and the allowance of Coals and Gas and that his wife be appointed to discharge the duties of Matron at salary of £5 per annum.

As the adoption of this resolution will occasion the removal of John Readings the present Bridewell keeper from his Office your Committee have taken into consideration the subject of the Compensation to which he will be entitled under the 66th section of the Municipal Corporations Act and the Mayor and Town Clerk having had an interview with him and found that he is willing to accept it in the form of an annuity of £35 for life which sum is to include any compensation to which his daughter might think herself entitled for being removed from the Office of Matron your Committee consider it advisable that the above arrangement should be carried into effect and they recommend that an Order be made accordingly.

H.A. Simonds, Mayor. Public Office. April 25th 1860

> To the Police Buildings Committee of the Borough of Reading
> Borough Police Office
> Reading 19th March 1860

Gentlemen,
Having been requested by the Deputy Mayor C.J. Andrewes Esquire to report to him for your information my views respecting the future management of the Borough Lock-ups I beg most respectfully to do so.

I have in the first place to state that upon the occasion of the Government Inspector's last visit to Reading, he intimated to me that he considered a Police Officer was the proper person to take charge of the Bridewell, and in reply to a question I put to him he stated that the appointment of an Officer to that duty ought not to lessen the number of the Force, and therefore that an additional policeman should be appointed.

[p. 196]
I therefore beg respectfully to say that after full consideration of the subject I am of opinion that it is advisable that a Police Officer should be appointed to reside at and take charge of the Bridewell…

John Peck, Chief Superintendent

[p. 197]
Resolved unanimously on the motion of the late Mayor seconded by Mr Alderman Harris That the Report of the Police Buildings Committee be received and adopted, That it be referred to the Watch Committee to make such regulations as they shall deem expedient for the future management of the Bridewell and that they be authorised to purchase such furniture for the Cells and Charge Room and for the Bridewell generally as they think necessary.

[p. 319]

At a meeting of the Council of the Borough of Reading on 17 December 1860.
The following letter received by the Mayor was presented to this meeting and read by the Town Clerk.
To the Worshipful the Mayor and Corporation of the Borough of Reading.
              Reading, Dec. 12, 1860.
Gentlemen, May I permitted to enquire if you would be

[p. 320]

disposed to part with the site occupied at present by the Borough Bridewell with the buildings adjoining viz. the Governor's House and the Pigeons Public House.

 I make this application on the part of myself and friends who would be glad to purchase, with a view to restoring the building and applying it to the purpose of a District Church, which we purpose to build and endow for the use of that part of the town, should it be competent for us to do so.
I have the honour to remain, Gentlemen, Your obedient humble servant,
W. W. Phelps.

It having been moved by Mr Councillor Blandy and seconded by Mr Alderman Darter That this Council do now resolve to enter into treaty with the Revd. W.W. Phelps and those in whose behalf he has addressed the Council for the sale (subject to the approbation of the Lords Commissioners of Her Majesty's Treasury) of the properties comprising the Bridewell, the Governor's House and the Pigeons Public House at such price and subject to such conditions and stipulations as shall be determined by the Borough Surveyor under the direction of a Committee of the whole Council provided that Mr Phelps and his friends will give an undertaking in writing that such Buildings shall be restored and adapted to the purposes of a Church. The question was put and carried unanimously.

 It having been moved by Mr Councillor Blandy and seconded by Mr Alderman Walford That it be referred to a Committee of the whole Council to consider and report upon the arrangements which it may be deemed necessary to make with a view to the Sale of the Borough Bridewell and adjoining properties, and that such Committee be requested to instruct the Borough Surveyor with reference to his valuation and Report and that they also consider and report upon the terms and conditions which they may deem it advisable should be embodied in any provisional agreement the Council may enter into with Mr Phelps. The question was put and carried unanimously.

[p. 327]

At a meeting of the Council of the Borough of Reading on 23 January 1861.
The Committee of the whole Council appointed on the 17th December last presented the following Report and the same having been read It was moved by Mr Councillor Steward and seconded by Mr Councillor Butler That the same be received and the question having been put was carried unanimously.

    Report to the Council of the Borough of Reading by the Committee of the whole Council appointed on the seventeenth day of December 1860.

Your Committee have to report with reference to the arrangements necessary to be made with a view to the sale of the Bridewell and adjoining properties that the contract entered into by the Council with the Justices of the Peace for Berkshire for the reception and maintenance of Borough prisoners in the County Gaol makes provision for the reception of all prisoners except persons in custody previous to examination; and therefore that it is only needful for the Council to make provision

[p. 328]

for the latter class, before entering into a contract for the sale of the Borough Bridewell. Assuming however that whenever such provision is permanently made it will be in connection with the Police Station and Magistrates' offices, your Committee deemed it desirable previously to entertaining the question of recommending any temporary measure, to take into consideration the broader question of the practicability of embracing this opportunity for providing appropriate Police Buildings the want of which has so generally and so long been felt.

With these views your Committee appointed a Sub Committee, who have made the accompanying Report, in which your Committee fully concur as well as in the recommendation that the site and plans proposed should be adopted.

Your Committee present herewith a Report which has been made to them by the Borough Surveyor and recommend that the property be offered the Revd. W. W. Phelps (subject to the approval of the Lords of the Treasury) at the sum of £1250, the Council being at liberty to remove the Cells and reconstruct them elsewhere at their own cost.

James Boorne, Mayor, Public Office. 15th January 1861.

> Report of the Sub Committee appointed by the Committee of the whole Council on the eighth day of January 1861 to select and report upon suitable sites for the erection of police cells in connexion with the Magistrates offices and provision for Fire Engines

Your Committee beg to report that they have met upon the subject referred to them and having regard to the Reports of former Committees and to all that has taken place since the year 1856 with reference to the procuration of a site for the erection of Police Buildings the difficulties which have presented themselves and the necessity that now exists for the adoption of some immediate measure, they have carefully considered the whole question, with a view to recommend

[p. 329]

some course of action which the Committee of the whole Council may report upon with confidence of its practicability and with reasonable expectations of its being adopted by the Council.

With this object, your Sub Committee have directed their attention to the selection of a site which should combine the merits of eligibility for situation, adequate extent, capability of adaptation, reasonableness of price, simplicity of title, facility of acquisition and of which immediate or early possession could be obtained.

It is needless and would be only futile for your Committee to refer to many sites which have already been under consideration and which did not possess the merit of eligibility. It would equally so to advert to other sites, eligible in situation, but which can only be obtained by a large expenditure of money in preliminary expenses, and perhaps only at an extravagant cost, owing to the peculiarities of the title, the terms upon which they are held, the plurality of interest affecting them, or other similar circumstances. They deem it sufficient for this Report to say, that after the most attentive consideration they can give to the subject they have come to the conclusion, that the best, and, indeed the only site possessing the various merits to which they have referred is the property called High Bridge House, the particulars and circumstances relating to which were two years and a half ago fully reported upon by the Borough Surveyor, and twice recommended by Committees to the adoption of the Council. The circumstances then stated in favor of this site remain the same only strengthened by the subsequent experience the Council and successive Committees have gained of the extreme difficulty there is in obtaining any equally inexpensive and eligible site; and it is with a full persuasion that they cannot do better, that your Sub Committee repeat the recommendation of former Committees, that the property called High Bridge House should be purchased and adapted to the purposes required.

James Boorne, Mayor, Public Office. 11th January 1861.

[p. 330]
To the Committee of the whole Council for the sale of the Bridewell
                                                    Reading 14th January 1861
Mr Mayor and Gentlemen,
In accordance with your instructions I have examined the Bridewell, first, to ascertain what materials in the present cells could be retained and removed with advantage, and secondly to estimate the value of the Bridewell and Residence, and the 'Pigeons' Public House.

First. I think all the materials in the cells can be retained and I consider they could be taken down, removed, and re-erected on another site for the sum of £150.

Secondly. I have prepared a plan shewing the extent and dimensions of the Buildings as proposed to be bought by the Revd. W. W. Phelps. The whole is in hand except the 'Pigeons' and small yard adjoining, which is let on lease for 80 years from Michaelmas 1789, at the yearly rent of £5.

I estimate the outside value of the site and buildings irrespective of the new cells at the sum of £1100.0.0

Should the Council determine to sell the Buildings I consider the cost of reconstructing the cells should be added to the price of £1100.0.0.

I am, Your obedient Servant, W. H. Woodman, Borough Surveyor

Mr Alderman Brown having moved and Mr Alderman Exall seconded the motion That the recommendation contained in the Report of the Committee of the whole Council relative to the offer of the Bridewell and adjoining properties at the sum of £1250 be adopted the question was put and carried unanimously.

The Mayor read the following letter he had received from Mr W. Blandy.

Mill Lane, January 21st, 1861.

My dear Mr Mayor,

Since the last meeting of the Bridewell Committee I have thought much on the proposition, then adopted, to recommend to the Council the purchase the High Bridge

[p. 331]
House and premises. I am not desirous to sell that portion of my property apart from other portions held with it, but the strong approval of the Sub Committee, coupled with my wish not to put any obstacle in the way of the sale of the Grey Friars' Church to Mr Phelps, disposed me at first to accede it. I cannot however but feel that a question so important as the choice of a site for new Police and Justice Buildings can only be settled satisfactorily with the concurrence of a large majority of the Council, and as that of High Bridge is not likely to obtain such a preference, I am justified in requesting you to inform the Council that I decline selling that property as proposed by the Committee.

Believe me, my dear Mr Mayor, with sincere respect,
Yours most faithfully, William Blandy.

It having been moved by Mr Alderman Brown and seconded by the late Mayor 'That the committee be requested to consider and report upon the question of erecting Police Buildings &c. in connexion with an extension of the Corn Exchange' an amendment was moved by the Mayor and seconded by Mr Councillor Clark 'That the recommendation contained in the Report of the Committee of the whole Council relative to the purchase of High Bridge House and premises for the purpose of Magistrates rooms, police cells &c. be adopted' and such amendment having been put was carried the votes (which were required to be taken in writing) being on a division as follows: [There follows a list of 13 names for the amendment and 4 against].

It having been moved by the Mayor and seconded by Mr Councillor Cooper 'That the letter of Mr William Blandy addressed to the Mayor be entered on the Minutes, but this Council would express its hope that in consideration of the foregoing resolution by so large a majority of the Council he will reconsider his determination and dispose of the High Bridge property to the Corporation', the question was put and carried.

[p. 344]
At a meeting of the Council of the Borough of Reading on 7 February 1861.
The following Report of the Committee of the whole Council appointed on the 17th of December last was presented and read.

Report to the Council of the Borough of Reading by the Committee of the whole Council appointed on the 17th day of December 1860.

Your committee have to report that the Town Clerk forwarded to The Revd. W. W. Phelps and Mr William Blandy copies of the resolutions passed by the Council at its last meeting, and has since received from those Gentlemen the accompanying letters:

In consequence of the acceptance by Mr Phelps of the offer of the Bridewell and adjoining properties and of the acquiescence of Mr W. Blandy in the wish of the Council that he should sell to them his property at High Bridge your Committee have considered what measures it will now be necessary to adopt for the purpose of giving effect to

[p. 345]
these different objects, and they beg to make the following recommendations.

That provisional agreements be at once entered into with Mr Phelps and Mr W. Blandy in accordance with the terms already arranged with them. That application be made to the Court of Chancery for an order for the appropriation of the money now invested in Exchequer Bills or such part thereof as the Court shall see fit, to the payment of the purchase money and adaptation of the High Bridge property to the purposes required and that a memorial be presented to the Lords of the Treasury for permission to sell the Bridewell property and 'Pigeons' Public House to Mr Phelps and to apply so much of the purchase money as does not relate to the 'Pigeons' to the further alteration and completion of the Buildings at High Bridge House.

The proportion of the purchase money which relates to the 'Pigeons' cannot be so applied, that property being Scheduled in the Local Act of 2 and 3 Vic, c. 40, and a mode of investment of the purchase moneys of all such properties being prescribed by such Act which deprives the Lords of the Treasury of the power of dealing with them as they may do with the Bridewell property which is not so Scheduled.

Your committee entertain no doubt that the Court of Chancery will at least order the payment of the purchase money for the High Bridge property out of the Exchequer Bills and think it not improbable that the whole £2,800 so invested may be ordered to be applied in effecting and carrying out the alterations proposed to made; and if this should be the case and the Lords of the Treasury should sanction the appropriation of the purchase money of the Bridewell property to the same object (of which your Committee entertain no doubt) they estimate that these sums will sufficient to accomplish all that is desired and that it will not be necessary that any money should be borrowed. If, however, the Court of Chancery should decline to do more than order the purchase money of the High Bridge property to be paid out of the Exchequer Bills, and the Lords of the Treasury should allow the money to be received for the Bridewell to be applied as proposed, your Committee estimate that £1,000 will be all that will be necessary for the Council to borrow which may

[p. 346]
be done by mortgage of the Corporate estates and Borough Fund or by Bond as may considered most advisable.

Anticipating the probability of these preliminary matters being brought to an early termination, and being mindful of the importance of taking advantage of the summer months for the prosecution of the works proposed, your Committee have taken into consideration the arrangements it may be advisable to make for the detention of Borough Prisoners during the time the alterations are progress, and they recommend that the Justices should be requested to commit all prisoners (whether upon remand or otherwise) to the County Gaol, and that such temporary accommodation as may be needful for prisoners previous to examination be provided when the necessity for it shall arise.

James Boorne, Mayor, Public Office. 11th January 1861.

[To] J. J. Blandy, Esq., Town Clerk.

Trinity Parsonage, January 31, 1861

Dear Sir,

In reply to your letter of yesterday informing me of the Report presented to the Town Council on the 23rd inst. and their Resolution thereon, I beg to say, that I hereby agree to purchase the Bridewell and adjoining properties for the sum of £1250, subject to the approval of the Lords of the Treasury, the Council being at liberty to remove the cells and reconstruct them elsewhere at their own cost.

I request you will do me the favour of expressing to the Town Council that I consider the price they have set on the premises quite satisfactory; and the manner which it was arrived at such as to lay me under a great obligation to their consideration and courtesy.

I am, dear Sir, yours faithfully, W. W. Phelps

Mill Lane, January 31, 1861

Dear Mr Town Clerk,

I beg to acknowledge the receipt of the copy of the Resolutions adopted at the meeting of the Council, on the 23rd inst and request you to inform the Council

[p. 347

that in compliance with the wish expressed by so large a majority of the Body, I place the High Bridge House and premises, as proposed, at their disposal, at the price, £1600, as before agreed on.

I am, my dear Mr Town Clerk, Yours most truly, Wm. Blandy.

Resolved unanimously on the motion of Mr Councillor Blackwell seconded by the late Mayor That the Report of the Committee of the whole Council be received and adopted, and that it be referred to such committee to settle the terms of the agreements necessary to be entered into with the Revd. W. W. Phelps and Mr William Blandy to direct the necessary petition to be presented to the Court of Chancery to settle and approve of a suitable Memorial to the Lords of the Treasury and generally to direct and perform all matters and things necessary to be done for the purpose of giving effect to the proposed sale of the Bridewell and adjoining properties and the purchase of the High Bridge property and the construction thereon of Police Buildings and Magistrates Offices as proposed.

[p. 361]
At a meeting of the Council of the Borough of Reading on 9 May 1861.
The following Report was presented and read when it was moved by Mr Councillor Hewett seconded by Mr Councillor Cooper and carried unanimously That the same be received that the proceedings of the Committee

be approved and that such Committee be requested to continue their labours until the matters referred to them be fully carried into effect.

> Report of the Police Buildings and Bridewell Committee to the Council of the Borough of Reading

Your Committee report that immediately after the last quarterly meeting they settled the terms of the agreement with Mr William Blandy for the purchase of High Bridge House, which was executed by that Gentleman and by the Mayor on behalf of the Council. That they then directed a Petition to be presented to the Court of Chancery for an order for the appropriation of the money invested in Exchequer Bills to the purchase, and adaptation of the property to Police purposes and the accompanying order has been made thereon. It will be seen that the Court has only authorised the payment of the purchase money from that source it being found that the Act does not authorise the application of the money in the Accountant General's hands to any other purpose than the purchase of real estate.

Your Committee have also settled the terms of an agreement for the sale of the Bridewell property to the Revd. W. W. Phelps which has been sent to that Gentleman for approval.

Your Committee have deemed it advisable to direct notice to be given to Mr F. M. Slocombe of the intention of the Council to quit the Police Station at Michaelmas next, and to Mr Henry Simonds of their intention to quit the

[p. 362]
Fire Engine House at the same time.

The tenant of High Bridge House having consented to the Council taking immediate possession of the Garden and entering upon the premises for the purpose of examining and doing anything that may be requisite to the Campsiding[1] when the water is drawn off at Whitsuntide and for the purpose of erecting the cells which are to be removed from the Bridewell in consideration of the Council allowing him to retain possession of the dwelling house and shop until the 31st July next, your Committee deem it advisable that measures should be immediately taken for the examination and repair or otherwise of the Campsiding and for the removal of the cells from the Bridewell and their re-erection at High Bridge House, and they have accordingly appointed a Sub Committee to obtain Tenders and enter into Contracts for those purposes and for the performance of any other works that may be immediately necessary or thought advisable.

James Boorne, Mayor, Public Office. 9th May 1861.

[p. 363]
The Town Clerk laid before the meeting the Draft Agreement with the Revd. W. W. Phelps (referred to in the above Report) and explained the form in which Mr Phelps was willing that the same should be finally settled, which being approved It was on the motion of the late Mayor seconded by Mr Councillor

---

1 Campsiding (sometimes campshotting): A facing of piles and boarding along the bank of a river, or at the side of an embankment, to protect the bank from the action of the current, or to resist the out-thrust of the embankment (Oxford English Dictionary).

Blandy resolved unanimously That the Agreement be altered in the terms now stated by the Town Clerk and then engrossed and that the Mayor be authorised to affix the common seal thereto.

[p. 385]
At a meeting of the Council of the Borough of Reading on 24 June 1861.
The following Report of the Police Buildings and Bridewell Committee was presented and read.
> Report of the Police Buildings and Bridewell Committee to the whole Council of the Borough of Reading

Your committee have the pleasure to report that the Conveyancer of the Court of Chancery has approved of the Title to the High Bridge House property and that the purchase is progressing to completion…

James Boorne, Mayor. 21st June 1861.

[p. 397]
At a meeting of the Council of the Borough of Reading on 8 August 1861.
The Police Buildings and Bridewell Committee presented the following Report
> Report of the Police Buildings and Bridewell Committee of the whole Council to the Council of the Borough of Reading

Your committee have much pleasure in presenting the accompanying very satisfactory reply which the Mayor has received to the Memorial presented by the Council to the Lords Commissioners of Her Majesty's Treasury whereby it will be seen that the sum of £800 is all that it is requisite for the Council to borrow for the purpose of carrying into effect their Agreement for the purchase of High Bridge House and the erection of Police Buildings.

Your Committee recommend that as soon as the purchase has been completed steps be taken to raise this sum by Mortgage of the High Bridge House property in accordance with the directions contained in the above mentioned letter, and your Committee purpose taking immediate measures to obtain Tenders for the completion of the Buildings.

James Boorne, Mayor. Public Office. 2nd August 1861.

To The Mayor of Reading
Treasury Chambers, 25th July 1861.
Sir,
The Lords Commissioners of Her Majesty's Treasury have had before them the Memorial from the Town Council of Reading requesting their Lordships' approval of the alienation of certain Corporate property therein referred to and of the application of the proceeds thereof to the improvement of the property of the Corporation called High Bridge House and I am directed by my Lords to signify their approval of the sale of the properties called the Bridewell and 'Pigeons' Public House to the Revd. William Whitmarsh Phelps for the sum of £1250 and of the application of the said purchase money in the manner set forth in the Memorial viz. towards the cost of the works proposed to be done at the premises called 'High Bridge Works' (sic). I am also directed to signify the approval by my Lords of a Mortgage of the Corporation property for £800 either by a second charge on the whole property or by a separate Mortgage on

the property referred to in the Memorial as agreed to be purchased for the purpose of Police Offices on condition that the money so raised be

[p. 398]
applied to the purposes of the proposed works and buildings and that either provision be made for the repayment of the same by instalments within a term of 30 years or that a Sinking Fund be maintained for the repayment thereof within the same period, under the terms of the 1st Section of the Municipal Corporations Mortgages Act of 1860.

The formal sanction of this Board will be obtained by two of my Lords being made parties to the Conveyances and the Mortgage drafts of which must be sent to their Solicitor at this office for perusal.

I am, Sir, Your obedient Servant, Geo. A. Hamilton

Resolved unanimously on the motion of Mr Councillor Taylor seconded by Mr Councillor Hewett That the Report of the Police Buildings Committee be received and adopted and that it be referred to the same Committee to obtain the Loan of £800 therein referred to, and to take all necessary measures for the completion of the Buildings and for carrying into effect the arrangements entered into by the Council.

[p. 440]
At a meeting of the Council of the Borough of Reading on 7 February 1862.
The Police Buildings Committee presented the following report.
… It being found impracticable to act upon the authority given by the Lords of the Treasury for the sale of the Bridewell property to the Revd. W. W. Phelps, in consequence of their Lordships having directed the payment of the purchase money to the Borough Treasurer to be applied towards the cost of the works at High Bridge House while the Local Act of 2 & 3 Vic. cap 40 makes it incumbent on the purchaser to pay so much of the purchase money as relates to the Pigeons Premises into the Bank of England to the account of the Accountant General of the Court of Chancery the Town Clerk under the direction of your Committee has been in correspondence with the Lords of the Treasury thereon with a view to obtain an amended authority in accordance with the necessities of the case, but their Lordships decline to entertain the subject except upon a new Memorial. The letter received from them expressing that determination is presented herewith together with a new Memorial to which your Committee recommend that the Common Seal should be affixed.[1]

Robert Hewett, Mayor. Council Chamber. 7th February 1862.

---

1 See Document II (xviii).

[p. 441]
To the Mayor of Reading

Treasury Chambers, 24th January 1862

Sir,

The Lords Commissioners of Her Majesty's Treasury have had before them the letter from the Town Clerk of Reading dated the 16th inst. and its enclosure (herewith returned) further relative to the Sale of certain Corporate property sanctioned by this Board, and the investment of the proceeds, and I am directed by their Lordships to acquaint you that as the arrangement now proposed differs both in regard to the amount to be raised by Mortgage and as to the application of the proceeds of the sale from that contained in the prayer of the Memorial forwarded to this Board in June last, My Lords cannot entertain the proposal until it has been submitted to them in a fresh Memorial after due Notice has been given.

I am, Sir, Your obedient servant F. Peel

[p. 442]
The Common Seal was affixed to a Memorial to the Lords Commissioners of Her Majesty's Treasury for their Lordships' approbation to the sale of the Bridewell, Bridewell Keeper's House and Pigeons property to the Revd. W. W. Phelps for the sum of £1250 and to the appropriation of £900 part thereof towards the cost of the works at High Bridge House and to the borrowing on Mortgage of the sum of £1100 being the further amount to defray the cost of such works.

[p. 452]
At a meeting of the Council of the Borough of Reading on 23 April 1862.
The Town Clerk reported that the Lords of the Treasury had approved of the Sale of the Bridewell and Pigeons properties to Mr Phelps and had sanctioned the appropriation of £900 of the purchase money towards the cost of the Works at High Bridge House and the borrowing of £1100 on Mortgage as stated in the following letter.
To The Mayor of Reading

Treasury Chambers, 17th March 1862

Sir,

The Lords Commissioners of Her Majesty's Treasury have had before them the Memorial dated the 11th ult. from the Mayor and Town Council of Reading, and their Lordships have directed me to signify to you their approval of, as requested in the Memorial,

1st   The Sale of the property called Bridewell and 'Pigeons' public house shown on the plan attached to the Memorial to the Revd. W. W. Phelps for the sum of £1250.

2nd   The application of £900 of the proceeds of the above mentioned sale to the improvement of the property called High Bridge House, and

3rd   ly   a sum of £1100 being borrowed on Mortgage of the property of the Corporation and the Borough Fund to be applied towards the expense of the proposed improvement of High Bridge House.

I am, Sir, Your obedient Servant, George A Hamilton

[p. 453]
The Common Seal was by unanimous consent on the motion of Mr Councillor Fearnley seconded by Mr Councillor Butler affixed to a Deed of Conveyance from this Corporation to the Revd William Whitmarsh Phelps of the properties called the Bridewell and the 'Pigeons' public house in consideration of £350 paid into the Bank of England to the Account of the Accountant General of the Court of Chancery Exparte this Corporation and of £900 to be paid to the Treasurer of the Borough Fund for the purpose of being applied towards payment of the Costs of the Works at High Bridge House pursuant to the authority of the Lords of the Treasury above set out.[1]

The Common Seal was also by unanimous consent on the motion of Mr Councillor Fearnley seconded by Mr Councillor Butler affixed to a Deed of Covenant from this Corporation to the Revd. W. W. Phelps for the production of certain Deeds and Evidences of Title relating to the Bridewell and 'Pigeons' property this day conveyed to him.[2]

(ii)   Abstract of the Title of the Mayor Aldermen and Burgesses of the Borough of Reading to certain properties called the Bridewell and 'Pigeons' Public House contracted to be sold to Revd W.W. Phelps (1861). Original in the Greyfriars Church Archive

August 1861

[p. 1]
Abstract of Title of the Mayor Aldermen and Burgesses of the Borough of Reading in the County of Berks to certain Freehold hereditaments called the Bridewell and the 'Pigeons' situate in Friar Street Reading

23rd September 2nd Elizabeth.
Letters Patent granted by Queen Elizabeth to the Mayor and Burgesses of Reading contain the following clauses:
[Transcribed above: see Document I (ii).]

[p. 2]
6th May 1789
The following entry is found in the Corporation Diary of this date:
> 'Agreed to grant a Lease of the Alehouse adjoining to Bridewell as now marked out in Collier's Plan to Mr Matthias Deane for four score years from Michaelmas next at £5 per annum: he having agreed to repair and improve the same'.

---

[1] See Document II (xix).
[2] See Document II (xx).

11th December 1835[1]

Indenture of this date made between said Mayor Aldermen and Burgesses of the one part and Thomas Rickford and Charles Curry Bickham of Reading aforesaid Common Brewers and Copartners of the other part.

Reciting the last abstracted minute dated 6th May 1789 and reciting that by another minute of said Mayor Aldermen and Burgesses made and entered on their Journal or Diary and dated 2nd April 1790 leave was given for John Shaylor to inhabit the new Bridewell House until Michaelmas then next that the Public House might be rebuilt.

And reciting that in pursuance of said first mentioned minute the said Public House was rebuilt and afterwards occupied by said Lessee or his undertenant for several years but no lease thereof was ever granted by said Mayor Aldermen and Burgesses.

And reciting that by virtue of divers measures assignments and other acts of the law the equitable and beneficial right and intitlement of and in said

[p. 3]

Public House and premises had become vested in the said Thomas Rickford and Charles Curry Bickham for a valuable consideration and they had accordingly applied to and requested said Mayor Aldermen and Burgesses to grant them a Lease of said Public House and premises for the residue of said term of four score years according to said minutes of Hall of 6th May 1789 which they said Mayor Aldermen and Burgesses had consented and agreed to do.

It was witnessed that in consideration of the premises and of the rent covenants and agreements thereinafter reserved and continued on the part of said Thomas Rickford and Charles Curry Bickham their executors administrators and assigns to be paid observed and performed they said Mayor Aldermen and Burgesses by now abstracted presents did demise and lease unto said Thomas Rickford and Charles Curry Bickham their executors administrators and assigns:

All that Messuage tenement or Public House and premises commonly called or known by the name or sign of the Pigeons situated lying and being in the parish of Saint Lawrence in Reading aforesaid on the north side of a certain street called Friar Street formerly in the occupation of Robert Wilson and then George Williams.

Together with all outhouses and a plan or ground plot whereof was drawn in margin of now abstracted presents.[2]

To hold unto said Thomas Rickford and Charles Curry Bickham their executors administrators and assigns from the 29th September 1789 for the term of four score years from thence next ensuing and fully to be complete and ended at the yearly rent of £5 by equal half yearly payments on the 25th March and 29th September in every year without any deduction the first payment to be considered as having commenced on the 25th March 1790 and the next of such payments which became due and payable on the 25th March 1836.

---

1 See Document II (xiii).
2 See Figure 6.

Covenant by said Thomas Rickford and Charles Curry Bickham to pay said yearly rent of £5 on the days and times and in manner aforesaid And also to pay all taxes and outgoings whatever payable in respect of said premises And also to substantially repair said messuage and premises and so leave same at the end or other sooner determination of said term And also that said Mayor Aldermen and Burgesses should be at liberty at all reasonable times during the term to enter into said demised premises and view state and condition thereof and of all defects or wants of reparation then

[p. 4]

found to give notice to said Thomas Rickford and Charles Curry Bickham who should within 3 Calendar months after such notice repair same accordingly And further that said Thomas Rickford and Charles Curry Bickham should insure said premises in 2/3rds of the value thereof at least in the 'Sun' or some other Public Fire Insurance Office in London or Westminster which said Mayor Aldermen and Burgesses should by their Town Clerk or Surveyor approve and appoint and should at their or his request produce the Policy and receipts for the premium of such Insurance for the current year And in case of destruction or damage by fire that they said Thomas Rickford and Charles Curry Bickham should reinstate same under the direction of said Mayor Aldermen and Burgesses or their Surveyor and should apply all moneys received under such Insurance towards reinstating said premises And should pay said rent thereby reserved in the same manner as if no such accident by fire had happened.

Covenant by said Thomas Rickford and Charles Curry Bickham not to lease or otherwise part with the possession of said premises to any person for any greater term than 21 years without the license in writing of said Mayor Aldermen and Burgesses under their Common Seal which license should (unless otherwise expressed) extend only to the underlease therein licensed to be made and should not be absolute so as to exonerate said Thomas Rickford and Charles Curry Bickham or the person taking any such underlease from the necessity of obtaining a similar license on every future occasion Provided that such license should not be unreasonably withheld nor should said Mayor Aldermen and Burgesses be entitled to demand any sum of money for giving or granting the same (except the necessary expenses and usual fees)

Proviso for re-entry by said Mayor Aldermen and Burgesses after default made by said Thomas Rickford and Charles Curry Bickham.

Covenant by said Mayor Aldermen and Burgesses with said Thomas Rickford and Charles Curry Bickham for quiet enjoyment until default.

Duly Executed and attested

There being no further documentary evidence of the title of the Corporation to this property it is proposed to furnish a Statutory Declaration by the Town Clerk that from time immemorial it has been in the possession of the Corporation and used as a Borough Bridewell.[1]

---

1 See Documents II (ix) and (x).

[p. 5]
1835 5 & 6 William IV Cap 76 sec 94:
By this Act it is enacted that it shall not be lawful for the Council of any Body Corporate to be elected under that Act to sell mortgage or alienate the lands tenements and hereditaments of the said Body Corporate or any part thereof except in pursuance of some Covenant contract or agreement bona fide made or entered into on or before the 5th June in that present year by or on behalf of the Body Corporate of any Borough or of some resolution duly entered in the Corporate Books of such Body Corporate on or before the said 5th day of June Provided nevertheless that in every case in which such Council shall deem it expedient to sell and alienate any of the said lands tenements or hereditaments it shall be lawful for such Council to represent the circumstances of the case to the Lords Commissioners of Her Majesty's Treasury and that it shall be lawful for such Council with the approbation of any three of the Lords Commissioners to sell and alienate any of the lands tenements and hereditaments of the said Body Corporate in such manner and on such terms and conditions as should have been approved by the said Lords Commissioners Provided always that notice of the intention of the Council to make such application as aforesaid shall be fixed on the outer door of the Town Hall or in some public and conspicuous place within the Borough one Calendar month at least before such application and a copy of the Memorial intended to be sent to the said Lords Commissioners shall be kept in the Town Clerk's Office during such Calendar month and shall be freely open to the inspection of every Burgess at all reasonable times during the same.

1839 2 & 3 Victoria C. 40 (local)
By this Act intituled 'An Act to enable the Mayor Aldermen and Burgesses of the Borough of Reading in the County of Berks to sell certain real Estate discharged from certain liabilities and to invest the purchase moneys arising from such sales in the purchase of other real estate to be charged with such liabilities' It is (amongst other things) enacted 'that from and after the passing thereof it shall and may be lawful for the Council for the time being of the Borough of Reading aforesaid with the approbation of any three of the Lords Commissioners of Her Majesty's Treasury at such time or times as the said Council shall deem expedient absolutely to sell alienate dispose of and convey all and every or any of the messuages lands tenements hereditaments and premises comprised in the Schedule to that Act subject and without prejudice nevertheless to the subsisting leases thereof for the time being whether granted previously to the passing of that Act or subsequently to the passing and under the authority of the same Act and to make every such sale alienation

[p. 6]
disposition and conveyance of said messuages lands tenements hereditaments and premises freed and absolutely and for ever exonerated and discharged of and from a certain annual sum of £10 payable to the Schoolmaster of the Free School within the said Borough as his Stipend and Salary and of and from all liability thereto or to the payment thereof and from all remedies claims and demands in respect thereof and also freed and absolutely and for ever

exonerated and discharged of and from all repairs of the Bridges way roads streets and places therein referred to or any other Bridges way roads streets and places whatsoever to the repairs whereof the said Mayor Aldermen and Burgesses or the Lessees tenants or occupiers of any of their lands or hereditaments were previously to and at the time of the passing of that Act or would have been in case that Act had not been passed subject or liable either under or by virtue or means of certain Letters Patent thereinbefore recited or any clause matter or thing therein contained or implied or by usage custom prescription tenure or other legal ways means or obligations whatsoever and from all costs charges and expenses of repairing sustaining rebuilding and making all and every or any such Bridges ways roads streets and places respectively and all liability thereto or to contribution of the same and from all remedy claims and demands whatsoever by the Queen's most Excellent Majesty her heirs and successors and all and every other Bodies and Body Politic or Corporate and person and persons whomsoever in respect or by reason of any such liability as aforesaid and of and from all other burdens duties charges and liabilities whatsoever to which such messuages lands tenements and hereditaments or the rents and profits thereof or any part thereof were subject or liable at the time of the passing of that Act under or by virtue or means of the said recited Letters Patent either expressly or in construction of Law (save and except only a certain annual rent of £22 reserved to the Crown by the said Letters Patent until such time as the same annual rent should have been purchased or acquired by the said Mayor Aldermen and Burgesses under the power for that purpose thereinafter contained and the Council for the time being of the said Borough should and were thereby authorised to make such sale alienations and dispositions as aforesaid either by Public Auction or Private Contract or partly in each mode and in such manner and on such terms and conditions as should be approved by any three of the Lords Commissioners of Her Majesty's Treasury. By the said last mentioned Act it is further enacted that the purchasers of all or any of the said hereditaments should pay his her or their purchase money into the Bank of England in the name and with the privity of the Accountant General of the Court of Chancery to be placed to his account there 'exparte the Mayor Aldermen and Burgesses of the Borough of Reading' pursuant to the method in the said Act prescribed or preferred to

[p. 7]
17th April 1845
By Indenture of this date expressed to be made between Thomas Bros the younger of the Inner Temple London Esquire Barrister at Law of the first part Arthur Lennox Esquire (commonly called Lord Arthur Lennox) and Alexander Pringle and Henry Baring Esquire three of the Lords Commissioners of Her Majesty's Treasury of the 2nd part and The Mayor Aldermen and Burgesses of the Borough of Reading in the County of Berks of the 3rd part.

> Reciting that by an Act of Parliament passed in the Session held in the 2nd and 3rd years of the reign of Her then present Majesty intituled 'An Act to enable The Mayor Aldermen and Burgesses of the Borough of Reading aforesaid to sell certain real Estates discharged from certain liabilities and to invest the purchase moneys arising from such sales in the purchase of

other real estate to be charged with such liabilities – After reciting that Her then late Majesty Queen Elizabeth by her letters patent under her Great Seal of England dated in the 2nd year of her reign.

After reciting amongst other things that her late Majesty Mary then late Queen of England by Her Letters Patent under Her Great Seal of England dated at Westminster in the first year of Her reign did give grant and to farm let to Sir Francis Englefield Knight amongst other things her lands called the Little Orte and Orte lands in Reading and a Chapel and site of the Chapel at Caversham Bridge in the County of Berks and a rood of Meadow of the said Chapel adjoining them late in the tenure or occupation of William Penyson Knight and William Marquis of Northampton then late of High Treason attainted or of either of them and all the tolls and profits of Two Fairs yearly holden in the outer Court called the Forbury in the Monastery of Reading then lately in the tenure of the said William Penyson and the said William Marquis of Northampton or either of them and the reversion and reversions of all and singular the premises aforesaid and the rents and annual profits thereof except as therein excepted To hold to the aforesaid Sir Francis Englefield his executors and assigns from the feast of Saint Michael the Archangel then last past until the end of the

[p. 8]
term of 21 years then next following under the rents thereby reserved Her said then late Majesty Queen Elizabeth for the considerations in the Letters Patent now in recital mentioned did give and grant to the Mayor and Burgesses of the Borough of Reading aforesaid the reversion of the aforesaid premises by the aforesaid Letters Patent of Queen Mary to the said Sir Francis Englefield Knight demised and the rents by the same Letters Patent reserved and divers other messuages or tenements lands grounds sites rents emoluments and other hereditaments in the Letters Patent now in recital particularly mentioned and described To hold of her said then late Majesty Queen Elizabeth her heirs and successors as therein mentioned and rendering therefore yearly to her said then late Majesty her heirs and successors at the receipt of the Exchequer of her said then late Majesty her heirs and successors £22 at the feast of Saint Michael the Archangel in every year to be paid for all other rents services and demands whatsoever therefore to her said then late Majesty her heirs and successors in anywise to be rendered paid or made.

And reciting an Act of Parliament passed in the 6th year of the reign of His then late Majesty King William the 4th intituled 'An Act to provide for the regulation of Municipal Corporations in England and Wales' under which the style or title of the said Body Corporate had been changed to that of the Mayor Aldermen and Burgesses of the Borough of Reading in the County of Berks.

And reciting that the said Mayor Aldermen and Burgesses of the said Borough of Reading were then by virtue of the said last mentioned Act seized and possessed of the property theretofore granted by the said Letters Patent respectively and of the messuages lands and hereditaments therein particularly mentioned subject to certain liabilities in the said Act mentioned or referred to.

And reciting that it would be greatly to the advantage of the Mayor Aldermen and Burgesses and Inhabitants of the said Borough of Reading and tend greatly to the improvement of the said Borough and also greatly increase the funds and revenue of the Mayor Aldermen and Burgesses of the said Borough if the said Mayor Aldermen and Burgesses were enabled to purchase

[p. 9]
the said fee farm rent of £22 reserved and charged upon the said messuages lands and hereditaments under and by virtue of the said letters patent of Her then late Majesty Queen Elizabeth and also to grant leases upon or absolutely to sell and dispose of the messuages lands and hereditaments of or belonging to them other than and except the tolls and profits therein mentioned exonerated and discharged from all such liabilities therein mentioned so that the monies to arise from such sale or sales should be invested in the purchase of the said fee farm rent of £22 charged upon the said messuages lands and hereditaments and also in the purchase of other lands hereditaments and real Estate as therein mentioned It was by the said Act of Parliament now in recital enacted that from and after the passing of the said Act it should and might be lawful for the Council for the time being of the Borough of Reading aforesaid with the approbation of the Lords Commissioners of Her Majesty's Treasury or any three of them at such time or times as the said Council should deem expedient absolutely to sell alienate dispose of and convey all and every or any of the messuages lands tenements hereditaments and premises comprised in the Schedule to the Act now in recital annexed subject to the subsisting Leases thereof for the time being and to make every such sale alienation disposition and conveyance freed and discharged from the several claims and liabilities in the said Act mentioned or referred to and from all other burthens duties charges and liabilities whatsoever to which such messuages lands tenements hereditaments or the rents and profits thereof or any part thereof were subject or liable at the time of the passing of the said Act by virtue or means of the letters patent therein recited either expressly or in construction of law save and except only the said annual rent of £22 reserved to the Crown by the said letters until such time as the same annual rent should have been purchased or acquired by the said Mayor Aldermen and Burgesses Under the power for that purpose thereinafter contained And it was by the said Act now in recital further enacted that the purchaser or purchasers of all or any of the said messuages lands tenements and hereditaments which should be sold under the powers and authorities in the said Act contained should pay his her or their purchase money or monies into the Bank of England in the name and with the privity of the Accountant General of the Court of Chancery to be placed to his Account there 'Exparte the Mayor Aldermen and Burgesses of

[p. 10]
the Borough of Reading' pursuant to the method prescribed by the Act of the 12th year of the reign of King George the 1st Cap 32 and the general orders of the said Court.

And it was further enacted that out of the moneys said to be paid into the Bank of England as aforesaid certain costs charges and expenses in the said Act mentioned and generally all other costs charges and expenses attending the execution of the powers and provisions of the said Act should in the first place be paid and satisfied and that a sufficient part of the surplus of the said moneys shall be laid out and invested under and subject to the directions of the said Court in pursuance of an Order or Orders for that purpose to be obtained upon petition in a summary way to be preferred by the said Mayor Aldermen and Burgesses in the purchase of the said annual rent of £22 reserved to the Crown by the said therein and hereinbefore recited letters patent in case the same annual rent should be purchased by the said Mayor Aldermen and Burgesses under the power in that behalf thereinafter contained And by the Act now in recital it was further enacted that it should be lawful for the said Mayor Aldermen and Burgesses of the said Borough of Reading by the Council for the time being with the approbation of the said Lords Commissioners of Her Majesty's Treasury or any three of them at any time or times after the passing of the said Act to contract for and purchase the said annual rent of £22 reserved to the Crown by the therein and thereinbefore recited letters patent and to take a conveyance or conveyances of the same annual rent or of the Estate or Interest therein which should be purchased as aforesaid to the said Mayor Aldermen and Burgesses their successors and assigns without any license or Writ of ad quod damnum the Statutes of Mortmain or any other law usage statute or custom to the contrary notwithstanding and that when and so soon as the said annual rent of £22 should have been purchased by and conveyed to or otherwise vested in the said Mayor Aldermen and Burgesses the same rent should sink into and be absolutely extinguished in the lands tenements hereditaments tolls profits and other the premises out of which the same should be issuing and payable or which should be or which (but for such extinguishment) would have been charged with or liable to the payment thereof and the same rent should not nor should any part thereof be thereafter payable or recoverable And power

[p. 11]
was by the said Act given to all incapacitated bodies and persons to sell and convey the said annual rent of £22 to the said Aldermen and Burgesses and their successors and assigns And by the Act of Parliament now in recital it was further enacted that the like notice of the intention of the Council of the said Borough of Reading to make application to the Lords Commissioners of Her Majesty's Treasury for and in relation to any Act matter or thing whatsoever to the doing making executing effecting or authorizing of which the approbation of the said Lords Commissioners or any three of them was by that Act made necessary and the like means and opportunities for the inspection of a copy of the Memorial intended to be

sent to the said Lords Commissioners should be given and afforded as in the thereinbefore mentioned Act of the 6th year of the reign of his then late Majesty King William 4th was provided or required with respect to the obtaining such approbation of the said Lords Commissioners to any sale alienation demise or lease proposed to be made under the authority of the said last mentioned Act and to the making of which such approbation was by the same Act made necessary.

And reciting that under and by virtue of divers mesne acts conveyances and other assurances in the law and ultimately under and by virtue of an Indenture bearing date on or about the 1st day of July 1835[1] expressed to be made between Thomas Bros herein described (the Father of the said Thomas Bros the younger party thereto) of the first part John Alliston therein also described of the 2nd part and the said Thomas Bros the younger of the 3rd part the said annual rent of £22 reserved and made payable by the thereinbefore recited letters patent of her said then late Majesty Queen Elizabeth was by the description of all that annual rent of £22 reserved and issuing out of and for the rent of all and all manner of lands tenements rents and hereditaments goods and chattels forfeitures waifs and strays within the Borough of Reading paid by the Mayor and Burgesses of Reading and their successors granted and assured to and became vested in the said Thomas Bros the younger his heirs and assigns for ever.

And reciting that certain portions of the lands and hereditaments comprised in the Schedule to the said recited Act of the second

[p. 12]
and third years of the reign of Her then present Majesty and by such Act authorised to be sold and disposed of have since the passing of that Act been sold and disposed of under the provisions thereof with the approbation of the Lords Commissioners of Her Majesty's Treasury and conveyed by the said Mayor Aldermen and Burgesses to the respective purchasers thereof and such purchasers had paid their respective purchase monies into the Bank of England in the name and with the privity of the Accountant General of the Court of Chancery pursuant to directions in that behalf contained in the said last mentioned Act and out of such purchase monies the costs charges and expenses by the same Act directed to be paid had been paid and satisfied accordingly and after such payments there remained in the Bank of England in the name of the Accountant General to the Account 'Exparte the Mayor Aldermen and Burgesses of the Borough of Reading' a sum more than sufficient to effect the purchase of the said annual rent of £22 by the said recited Act of the 2nd and 3rd years of the Reign of Her then present Majesty authorised to be purchased and extinguished as aforesaid.

And reciting that the said Mayor Aldermen and Burgesses having by the Council of the said Borough proposed to purchase under the power in that behalf contained in the said last mentioned Act the said annual rent of £22 made application by Memorial to the Lords Commissioners of Her

---

1 See Document II (iv).

Majesty's Treasury for their approbation of such purchase and the provisions of the said last mentioned Act as respected notice of the intention of the Council of the said Borough to make application to the Lords Commissioners of Her Majesty's Treasury and keeping in the Town Clerks Office a copy of the Memorial to the said Lords Commissioners freely open to the inspection of every Burgess of the said Borough of Reading were duly complied with.

And reciting that the said Mayor Aldermen and Burgesses had by the Council of the said Borough under the authority of the power in that behalf contained in the said last mentioned Act and with the approbation of the Lords Commissioners of Her Majesty's Treasury testified &c contracted and agreed with the said Thomas Bros the younger for the absolute purchase of the said annual rent of £22 and the fee

[p. 13]

simple and inheritance therein free from incumbrances at or for the price or sum of £770.

And reciting that by an Order of the High Court of Chancery made by his Honour the Vice Chancellor of England on the 6th December 1844 on the Petition of the Mayor Aldermen and Burgesses of the said Borough of Reading after setting forth the matters of the said Petition It was Ordered that out of the sum of £1904.13.3 Cash then in the Bank to the Credit of 'Exparte the Mayor Aldermen and Burgesses of the Borough of Reading' the sum of £770 the amount of the purchase money of the annual rent of £22 in the said Act of Parliament and in the Petition mentioned be paid to Thomas Grint Curties as the Treasurer of the Borough of Reading to be by him applied in discharge of such purchase money upon the execution of a proper Conveyance of the said annual rent by Thomas Bros Junior the person in whom the same was then vested to the Mayor Aldermen and Burgesses of the Borough of Reading And it was ordered that it be referred to the taxing Master of that Court in rotation to tax the Costs Charges and expenses of the Petitioners of this application or incident thereto and also incident to the applying for and obtaining the approbation of the Lords Commissioners of Her Majesty's Treasury and of and incident to the purchase of the said fee farm rent and the said taxing master was to certify the total amount thereof and it was ordered that out of the sum of £1134.13.3 which would be the residue of the said sum of £1904.13.4 after the payment aforesaid the amount of such costs charges and expenses when so taxed to be paid to Mr Swarbreck Gregory the Solicitor of the Petitioners.

It is witnessed that in consideration of £770 to the said Thomas Bros the younger to be paid forthwith after the execution of the abstracting presents out of the said sum of £1904.13.3 then in the Bank of England in the name of William Russell Esquire the Accountant General to his Account there 'Exparte the Mayor Aldermen and Burgesses of the Borough of Reading' pursuant to the thereinbefore recited order of the said Court Receipt &c the said Thomas Bros the younger did with the approbation of the Lords Commissioners of Her Majesty's Treasury (testified &c) grant bargain sell alien and confirm and also remise release and for ever quit claim and for ever discharge the Mayor Aldermen and Burgesses of the Borough of Reading their successors and assigns.

[p. 14]
>All that the annual rent of £22 reserved and made payable in and by the thereinbefore recited letters patent of Her said then late Majesty Queen Elizabeth howsoever the same might be or might theretofore have been called known distinguished or described and all arrears and future payments thereof and all powers remedies and authorities whatsoever vested in or appertaining to the said Thomas Bros the younger for recovering and compelling payment of the said annual rent. And all the Estate &c

To hold receive take and enjoy the said annual rent of £22 and all and singular other the premises.

>Unto and to the only proper use and behoof of the said Mayor Aldermen and Burgesses of the Borough of Reading aforesaid and their successors and assigns absolutely for ever and to the intent and so that as provided and enacted by the said recited Act of the 2nd and 3rd years of the Reign of Her then present Majesty the same annual rent might thenceforth sink into and be absolutely extinguished in the lands tenements and hereditaments tolls profits and other the premises out of which the same was or might be issuing and payable or which were or which (but for such extinguishment) would have been charged with or liable to the payment thereof and so as that the same rent should not nor should any part thereof be thereafter payable or recoverable.

>Covenant by the said Thomas Bros the younger for his heirs executors and administrators that he had good right to grant for quiet enjoyment free from incumbrances and for further assurance.

>Executed by the said Thomas Bros the younger Alexander Pringle Arthur Lennox and Henry Baring and attested as to the said Thomas Bros by two witnesses and as to the others by one – Receipt for £770 indorsed signed by the said Thomas Bros the younger and witnessed.

[p. 15]
1854 March 31st
By Deed Poll of this date under the Common Seal of the Mayor Aldermen and Burgesses of the Borough of Reading in the County of Berks and under the hand & seal of Richard Fellowes of Englefield House in the County of Berks Esquire By virtue of the Reading Corporation Markets Act 1853 They the said Mayor Aldermen and Burgesses in consideration of the several sums amounting in the whole to £7000 by the said Richard Fellowes paid to the Treasurer of the Borough at the several times appearing by the several receipts by the Treasurer thereon indorsed for the purposes of that Act did with the approval of the Lords Commissioners of Her Majesty's Treasury testified by the signature of two of the said Lords Commissioners whose names were written in the margin thereof grant and assign unto the said Richard Fellowes his executors administrators and assigns –

All the Corporate Estates of the Mayor Aldermen and Burgesses of the Borough Fund of the Borough

To hold to the said Richard Fellowes his executors administrators and assigns from that day until the said sum of £7000 with interest at £4 per cent per annum for the same such Interest to be calculated on the several sums so paid from the respective times of the payment thereof to the Treasurer should be fully paid and satisfied the principal sum to be repaid at the end of 30 years from the date thereof and the interest to be paid half yearly on the 24th day of June and the 25th day of December in every year in the meantime and the first payment of Interest to be made on the 24th day of June 1854.

And the said Richard Fellowes did thereby for himself his heirs executors and administrators Covenant with the Mayor Aldermen and Burgesses that he or his executors or administrators would on the day of the date thereof pay to the Treasurer of the Borough £2000 part of the £7000 to be advanced and would pay to him £5000 residue thereof in such sums and at

[p. 16]

such times as the Mayor Aldermen and Burgesses from time to time within 30 years from the date thereof by notice in writing under the hand of the Treasurer delivered to him (the said Richard Fellowes) or his executors or administrators or left for him or them at Englefield House aforesaid should require –

Receipt for the said sum of £7000 in three sums of £2000 £2000 and £3000 respectively indorsed and signed by Charles Stephens Treasurer of the Borough Fund and witnessed.

24th June 1861
Indenture of this date expressed to be made between the said Richard Fellowes (by his then name of Richard Benyon) of the one part and the said Mayor Aldermen and Burgesses of the Borough of Reading of the other part.

Reciting that the said Mayor Aldermen and Burgesses had requested the said Richard Benyon to enter into the Covenant therein aforesaid covenanted for the production to them and their assigns of the before abstracted Deed Poll of 31st March 1854 to enable them to produce same Deed Poll to purchasers of the hereditaments intended to be released therefrom and from the moneys thereby secured which said Richard Benyon had agreed to do in manner thereafter appearing.

It was witnessed that in pursuance of said agreement the said Richard Benyon did thereby so far only as related to his own acts and so as to bind himself and his representatives only while having the actual custody of said Deed Poll thereby (by now abstracting presents) covenanted to be produced and so far as practicable to bind such Deed Poll into whosesoever hands the same might come and not so as to bind himself or his representatives or to incur any liability in relation thereto further or otherwise did thereby for himself his heirs executors and administrators covenant with said Mayor Aldermen and Burgesses and their assigns that said Richard Benyon his heirs executors administrators and assigns would upon every reasonable request in writing by the said Mayor Aldermen and Burgesses or their assigns or any person lawfully or equitably claiming any estate right title or interest in or to the said hereditaments at the cost of the person or persons requiring the same produced and shew to them him or any of them or to such person or persons as they or he should require or at any trial hearing or examination in any Court of Law or other judicature or in the examination of any Commission or elsewhere as occasion should require the said abstracted Deed Poll of 31st March 1854 for the

[p. 17]
manifestation defence and support of the established title and possession of said Mayor Aldermen and Burgesses or their assigns and every or any such other person as aforesaid And would at all times at the cost of said Mayor Aldermen and Burgesses or their assigns or any such other person as aforesaid make and furnish to them or him such true copies attested or unattested extracts and abstracts of the same Deed Poll as they or he might require And would in the meantime keep same Deed Poll safe whole uncancelled and undefaced unless prevented from so doing by fire or other inevitable accident.

Executed by said Richard Benyon and attested by one witness.
3rd August 1861
Indenture of this date made or expressed to be made between said Richard Benyon of the one part and said Mayor Aldermen and Burgesses of the Borough of Reading of the other part.

Reciting the before abstracted Deed Poll of 31st March 1854 And reciting that by an agreement dated 22nd May 1861 and made between said Mayor Aldermen and Burgesses of the one part and the Reverend William Whitmarsh Phelps Clerk of the other part said Mayor Aldermen and Burgesses for the considerations therein mentioned did agree to sell to said William Whitmarsh Phelps the fee simple and inheritance in possession free from incumbrance of all that piece of land situated on the north side of Friar Street in Reading aforesaid with the Ruins of the Church of the Grey Friars and all other Buildings (except as therein mentioned) standing and being thereon some of which were used for the purposes of a Bridewell or House of Correction and for a residence and offices for the Keeper of the same except such portions of the said Buildings as had been recently erected for the better accommodation and detention of prisoners confined in said Bridewell which the said Mayor Aldermen and Burgesses were to be at liberty at any time within 2 years from the date of the said agreement to take down remove and carry away (doing no damage thereby) without making any compensation to said William Whitmarsh Phelps for the same which said piece of land was delineated on the plan annexed to said agreement and therein distinguished by a Red colour And also the fee simple and inheritance free from incumbrances (subject to the Lease thereof thereinafter mentioned) of all that messuage then used as a Public House.

[p. 18]
called the 'Pigeons' situate on the north side of Friar Street aforesaid and adjoining the piece of land thereinbefore described which said messuage called the 'Pigeons' was by an Indenture of Lease dated the 11th December 1835[1] demised by said Mayor Aldermen and Burgesses to Thomas Rickford and Charles Curry Bickham for the term of 80 years from 29th September 1789 at the yearly rent of £5 and was delineated on the said plan annexed to said agreement and then coloured Blue Together with the appurtenances to the said piece of land messuage and hereditaments respectively belonging all which said hereditaments contained the several dimensions and were bounded as stated or described on said plan.

And reciting that said Mayor Aldermen and Burgesses in order to carry into effect said agreement had requested said Richard Benyon to grant and release to them said piece of land messuage and hereditaments absolutely discharged from said Mortgage Debt and all Interest thereon which he had consented to do being satisfied that the residue of the Corporate Estates and Borough Fund was an ample security for his said Mortgage debt.

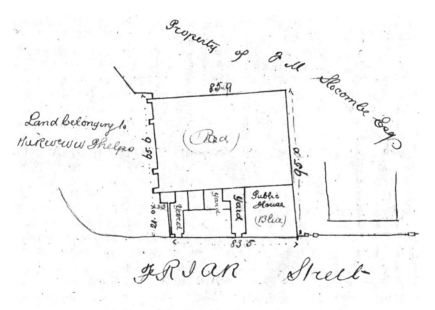

15. Plan of the Greyfriars' site to be conveyed

It was witnessed that in pursuance of said agreement said Richard Benyon did thereby grant and also remise release and quit claim unto said Mayor Aldermen and Burgesses[2] their successors and assigns

---

1 See Document II (xiii).
2 See Document II (viii).

All that piece of land with the Ruins of the Church of the Grey Friars and all other Buildings standing and being thereon as thereinbefore described And all that messuage or Public House called the 'Pigeons' with the yard and appurtenances to the same belonging All which said piece of land messuage and hereditaments were for the better identification thereof delineated on the plan drawn in the margin of now abstracted presents and therein distinguished by being coloured Red and Blue respectively.
Together with all ways &c.
And all the Estate &c.
To hold unto and to the use of said Mayor Aldermen and Burgesses their successors and assigns absolutely discharged from said Mortgage Debt of £7000 and all Interest and arrears of Interest in respect thereof and all liens claims and demands in respect or on account thereof.
Covenant by said Richard Benyon that he had done no act to incumber.
Duly executed by said Richard Benyon and attested.

[p. 19]
22nd May 1861
Memorial of the Council of the Borough of Reading in the County of Berks to the Lords Commissioners of Her Majesty's Treasury.
Stating (inter alia) the Municipal Corporations Act (5 & 6 William IV C 76) as hereinbefore abstracted.[1]
And stating the said Act of 2nd & 3rd Victoria intituled 'An Act to enable the Mayor Aldermen and Burgesses of the Borough of Reading in the County of Berks to sell certain real estate discharged from certain liabilities and to invest the purchase moneys arising from such sales in the purchase of other real Estate to be charged with such liabilities' as hereinbefore abstracted.
And stating that by said last mentioned Act it was enacted that it should be lawful for the Mayor Aldermen and Burgesses of the said Borough of Reading (with the approbation of three of the Lords Commissioners of the Treasury) at any time after the passing of that Act to contract for and purchase the said annual rent of £22 reserved to the Crown by the before abstracted Letters Patent and to take a conveyance or conveyances of the same Annual rent or of the Estate or Interest therein which should be purchased as aforesaid to said Mayor Aldermen and Burgesses their successors and assigns with any License or Writ of ad quod damnum the Statutes of Mortmain or any law usage or custom to the contrary notwithstanding and that when and so soon as said annual rent of £22 should have been purchased by and conveyed to or otherwise vested in the said Mayor Aldermen and Burgesses the same rent should sink into and be absolutely extinguished in the lands tenements and hereditaments tolls profits and other the premises out of which the same should be issuing and payable or which should be or which (but for such extinguishment) should have been charged with or liable to the payment thereof and the same rent should not nor should any part thereof be thereafter payable or recoverable.

---

1 See Document II (ii).

And stating that the Memorialists did deem it advisable and expedient that the said Annual rent of £22 reserved to the Crown by the said recited Letters Patent should be purchased by them said Mayor Aldermen and Burgesses under the powers contained in said last mentioned Act of Parliament and with the approbation of the Lords of the Treasury they entered into a Contract with Thomas Bros the younger Esquire the person then seized possessed of or interested in said annual rent for the sale thereof to said Mayor Aldermen and Burgesses for £770 Sterling and such annual rent was

[p. 20]

with the approbation of said Lords Commissioners conveyed by the before abstracted Indenture of the 17th April 1845 to said Mayor Aldermen and Burgesses their successors and assigns.

And stating that by said Act of 5 & 6 William IV C. 76 it is enacted that the Council of every Borough to which a separate Commission of the Peace should be granted under the provisions of the said Act should be authorized and required to provide and furnish one or more fit and suitable Office or Offices to be called 'The Police Office' or 'Offices' of the Borough for the purpose of transacting the business of the Justices of the said Borough and to pay from time to time out of the Borough Fund such sums as might be necessary for providing upholding and furnishing and for the necessary expenses of such Police Office or Offices.

And stating that the Borough of Reading had a separate Commission of the Peace. The then present Police Offices of the Borough consisted of a house rented on a yearly tenancy at £25 a year which was used for a Police Station and residence for the Superintendent and some of the Police Constables and of a room for the transaction of the business of the Justices in Petty Sessions in a house belonging to the Memorialists the other portion of which were used as a residence for one of the Serjeants-at-Mace. Those Offices were small confined inconvenient and extremely ill adapted to the purposes for which they were used and were situate at considerable distance from the Borough Bridewell portions of which were used as the Lock-ups or temporary detention cells for the confinement of prisoners previously to examination and irrespective of the insufficient accommodation of said Police Offices the then present arrangements involved the keeping a separate Officer and Matron at the Bridewell to receive charges and take care of Prisoners whereas if the buildings were concentrated the Superintendent and the Constables lodging at the Station would be sufficient for the purpose.

And stating that under these circumstances the Memorialists then lately entered into a Contract with Mr W. Blandy of Reading for the purchase of him for an estate of inheritance in fee simple in possession free from incumbrances of a dwelling house and premises called High Bridge House for the sum of £1600 with a view to

[p. 21]

of [sic] converting the same into Police Offices and by an Order of the Right Honourable the Master of the Rolls dated the 20th April 1861 the sanction of the Court of Chancery was given to such purchase (provided the title was found satisfactory) and the purchase money of £1600 was ordered to be paid out of the said sum so invested in Exchequer Bills as aforesaid pursuant to the said Act of the 2nd & 3rd Victoria C. 40.

And stating that plans and specifications for adapting the said property to the purpose of Police Offices had been prepared by the Surveyor to the Memorialists and it was estimated that the cost of carrying the same into effect would amount to £2000.

And stating the Clauses in the Letters Patent of Queen Elizabeth hereinbefore abstracted.

And stating that the said body and side aisles of the Church of the Grey Friars then belonged to the Memorialists as one of the Corporate properties of the Borough and had from time immemorial until a recent period been appropriated to the purposes of a Bridewell or House of Correction for Borough Prisoners but of late only a portion thereof had been used for the temporary detention of prisoners previous to examination. That no material alteration had been made in the Structure of the Grey Friars Church and the Building still retained all the Characteristics of an Ecclesiastical Edifice and was reported by competent authorities to be capable of restoration and adaptation to the purposes of a Church.

And stating that an application had been made to the Memorialists by the Reverend William Whitmarsh Phelps Incumbent of Trinity Church Reading for the purchase of said property together with a House which was used as a residence for the Bridewell Keeper and a small Public House adjoining thereto called the 'Pigeons' also belonging to the Memorialists which was held upon Lease by Messrs Blandy & Hawkins Brewers as the assignees of Messrs Rickford and Bickham at the rent of £5 per Annum for a term of 80 years which would expire at Michaelmas 1869 with a view to the restoration and endowment of same as a Church and the Memorialists deeming it very desirable that such an object should be carried into effect had had the properties surveyed and valued by their Surveyor who

[p. 22]

considered the remains of the said Grey Friars Church and the Bridewell Keepers House to be worth £900 and the said property called the 'Pigeons' (subject to the existing Lease upon the same) to be worth £350 making together £1250 and the Memorialists had entered into a Contract with Mr Phelps for the sale of the said properties to him (subject to the approbation of the Lords of the Treasury) at the sum of £1250 accordingly to deliver possession thereof at Michaelmas then next.

And stating that Memorialists would have no need to retain the said Bridewell or Lock-ups after Michaelmas then next as they had made arrangements for the erection of Lock-ups or Cells for the detention of prisoners until commitment in connection with the Police Offices and Magistrates Chambers which they had determined to construct at High Bridge House aforesaid and they had entered into a Contract in writing with Her Majesty's Justices of the Peace for Berks for the reception and maintenance in the County Gaol at Reading of all prisoners upon commitment whether for trial or in execution or under examination or upon summary conviction or otherwise for an indefinite term until said Contract should be put an end to by either party by one year notice in writing.

And stating that the portion of said property called the 'Pigeons' (and which was delineated on the plan annexed to the now abstracting Memorial by a Blue colour) was included in the Schedule to said Act of Parliament of 2 & 3 Victoria C. 40 by the following description.

Situation of property	Friar Street North
Lessee or Assignee	Messrs Rickford and Bickham
Present or Last known Occupier	George Williams
Description of Property	Messuage with the appurtenances called the Three Pigeons
Yearly Rent	£5
How Holden by the Tenant Lessee or Assignee	By Lease for 80 years from Michaelmas 1789

but the other portions of said property used as a Bridewell and Keepers

[p. 23]

House (and which were delineated on said plan by a red colour) were not Scheduled or in any way mentioned or referred to in the said Act.

And stating that by 'the Municipal Corporations Mortgages &c, Act 1860' their Lordships were authorised to give their approval to the sale of any hereditaments of any Body Corporate upon such conditions in relation to the investment of the proceeds of sale for the benefit of the Body Corporate as their Lordships might see fit and their Lordships are empowered to require as a condition of their consent to the application of the proceeds of such sale or any part thereof for the benefit of the Inhabitants of the Borough that provision should be made for raising and investing in Government Annuities a sum equivalent to the amount of money so paid to such Body Corporate or their Treasurer Provided that nothing in the said Act contained should be deemed to make it imperative on their Lordships to require such provision as aforesaid as a condition of their Lordships assent to the payment of any purchase money or compensation in respect of hereditaments of a Body Corporate to such Body Corporate or its Treasurer where by reason of the application of such moneys to improvement of the property of such Body Corporate or for the permanent benefit of the Borough or otherwise under the special circumstances of the case their Lordships in their discretion think fit to dispense with such provision.

And stating that the money proposed as aforesaid to be laid out on the premises called High Bridge House would be an improvement of the property of the Body Corporate of said Borough of Reading and would be for the permanent advantage of the Borough.

It was by the now abstracting Memorial prayed that their Lordships would be pleased to approve of the Sale by the Memorialists to The Reverend William Whitmarsh Phelps of the properties thereinbefore referred to and more particularly described in the plan thereto annexed for the sum of £1250 Also that their Lordships would be pleased to approve of the said purchase money (or so much thereof as they should see fit) being paid to the Treasurer of the Borough Fund for the purpose of being applied by Memorialists towards the costs of the works and buildings proposed to be done at the premises called High Bridge House as aforesaid And that their Lordships would be pleased to
[p. 24]
approve of Memorialists raising such further sum as would be required with the money so to be received of Mr Phelps (not exceeding together £2000) for the purpose of carrying into effect said works and buildings or that their Lordships would make such other order in the premises as to them should seem meet.

25th July 1861

The following Letter was received by the Mayor of Reading in reply to such Memorial.

Treasury Chambers 25th July 1861

Sir, The Lords Commissioners of Her Majesty's Treasury have had before them the Memorial from the Town Council of Reading requesting their Lordships approval of the alienation of certain Corporate property therein referred to and of the application of the proceeds thereof to the improvement of the property of the Corporation called High Bridge House and I am directed by my Lords to signify their approval of the sale of the properties called the Bridewell and 'Pigeons' Public House to the Reverend William Whitmarsh Phelps for the sum of £1250 and of the application of the said purchase money in the manner set forth in the Memorial viz. towards the cost of the works proposed to be done at the premises called 'High Bridge House'.

I am also directed to signify the approval by my Lords of a Mortgage of the Corporation property for £800 either by a second charge on the whole property or by a separate mortgage on the property referred to in the Memorial as agreed to be purchased for the purpose of Police Offices on condition that the money so raised be applied to the purposes of the proposed works and buildings and that either provision be made for the repayment of the same by instalments within a term of 30 years or that a Sinking Fund be maintained for the repayment thereof within the same period under the terms of the 1st section of the Municipal Corporations Mortgages Act of 1860.

The formal sanction of this Board will be obtained by two of my Lords being made parties to the Conveyances and the mortgage, drafts of which must be sent to their Solicitor at this Office for perusal.

I am, Sir, your obedient servant. George A. Hamilton

(iii) Requisitions and Observations on Title and Responses (1861). Compiled from four documents in the Greyfriars Church Archive.

The questions in this compilation were in response to the Abstract transcribed above (Document II (ii)) and page numbers mentioned here refer to that Abstract's document page numbers. The documents that this is compiled from are:

A. *'Requisitions and Observations on Title' by John Neale, Purchaser's Solicitor (19 August 1861)*
B. *'Requisitions and Observations on Title and Answers Thereto' by John Jackson Blandy, Town Clerk (20 September 1861)*
C. *'Observation on Answers to Requisitions on Title' by Alfred Hanbury Whitaker, for the Purchaser's Solicitor (26 September 1861)*
D. *'Further Observations and Requisitions on Title and Answers thereto' by John Jackson Blandy, Town Clerk (22 October 1861)*

1.
A. It would seem from the agreement between the Corporation and Mr Phelps for the purchase that three distinct properties have been contracted for. First 'The Body and side aisles of the Grey Friars Church'. Secondly 'A House which was used as the Bridewell Keeper's residence and Thirdly 'A Public House called the Pigeons'.
B. *This is so except the Bridewell Keeper's House is connected with and adjoins 'the Bridewell' which would appear to be the body and side aisles of the Greyfriars Church*

A. As to the Body and side aisles of the Church these appear to have belonged to the House of the Minor Friars and upon the dissolution of that House to have come into the hands of the Crown and were granted to the Corporation of Reading by Henry the Eighth and licensed to be aliened by the Letters Patent of Queen Elizabeth (see Abstract page 1).
B. *This is so.*
C. I have perused the Extract from the Letters Patent of King Henry 8th dated 24th April AR 34 [1542] from which it appears that the House and lands (estimated at 6 acres) belonging to the Grey Friars previously to the dissolution of their body, were by Letters Patent of his Majesty dated 5th February AR 30 [1539] granted to Robert Stanshawe his heirs and assigns for ever. The body and side aisles of the Church with a competent and sufficient way being excepted and reserved to his Majesty his heirs and successors. And that the body and side aisles of the Church and way so reserved out of the grant to Robert Stanshawe were by the first mentioned Letters Patent granted to the Mayor and Burgesses of the Borough of Reading.

I am of opinion that under this grant the Corporation only acquired the Body and side aisles of the Church with a sufficient way thereto, the adjoining land seeming to have passed under the Grant to Robert Stanshawe from the fact of a way to the Church having been reserved. The Title to the Church and side aisles or to the Bridewell founded on their site is clearly deducible from this Grant to the Corporation. But as regards the Bridewell Keeper's House and the Public House called the Pigeons the Title to these must be otherwise shown; and, excepting the Lease of the Pigeons abstracted at page 2 of the Abstract there appears to be no other Documentary Evidence of Title in the Vendor's possession.

'The Pigeons' seems to have been treated by the Legislature as having passed by the Grant of Queen Elizabeth to the Corporation being included in the Schedule to the Act 2nd & 3rd Victoria C.40 authorizing its Sale free from the charges of the said Annual Rent of £22. But this property nowhere appears to have been specifically named in the Grant and that it should have passed under the description of 'All the void ground of Her Majesty in the Borough of Reading' seems scarcely consistent with the prior grants by Her Father. As to the Bridewell Keeper's House the Purchaser may be content with the proposed Statutory Declaration by the Town Clerk as to the uninterrupted possession and enjoyment of the property by the Corporation.

D. *The Vendors cannot shew any other documentary evidence of Title besides that which has been abstracted and it is submitted that the purchaser ought to be satisfied with the Town Clerk's Statutory Declaration as to possession a draft of which is sent herewith for the perusal of the purchaser's Solicitor.*[1]

A. The original grant or at least a translation of it should have been abstracted, in chief a yearly rent of one hundredth part of one Knights fee and a farthing appears to have been reserved. Is this rent still payable or how has it been disposed of? It is presumed that the Bishop will not consecrate Land subject to a burthen.

B. *An extract from the original Grant is sent herewith. It is believed that this rent has not been paid from time immemorial. The Corporation accounts for upwards of 50 years last past have been examined and they contain no evidence of its payment and it is submitted that no claim can now be adduced by the Crown – see the Act of 9 Geo 3rd Cap 16.*

C. As to the yearly Rent of the one hundredth part of one Knight's fee and a farthing. Whether the Nullam Tempus Act operates as a bar to the claim of the Crown depends upon the fact whether or not within 60 years the Rent has been in charge with the Auditor or other proper Officer of the

---

1 See Document II (x).

Crown Revenues the receipt of this Rent would seem to be immaterial if the Rent was entered on the Revenue Roll – see Attorney General v. Lord Eardley 8 Price 41 and 74.

D. *This Rent has not been paid now in charge within the last sixty years as will be seen by the Certificate a copy of which is sent herewith.*[1]

A. As to the House used as 'the Bridewell Keepers residence' to this there appears to be no documentary evidence of Title but it is proposed that a Statutory Declaration of the Town Clerk shall be accepted as to the proprietorship of the Corporation. From the position and contiguity of this House to the other properties contracted for it seems probable that it formerly formed part of the Grey Friars Land and with the Church fell to the Crown any subsequent Grant from the Crown would have been enrolled and would probably be found among the Records of the Town.

B. *There is no subsequent Grant among the Records of the Town, and at this distance of time it must be presumed that the site of the Bridewell Keepers House is part of the property which came to the Corporation under the Grant of Henry 8th*

A. As to the Public House called the 'Pigeons' I infer this to have been granted to the Corporation by Queen Elizabeth from the fact of its having been comprised in the Schedule to the Act of the 2nd and 3rd Victoria C.40 (see Abstract page 22) authorizing the Sale thereof discharged from an Annual Rent of £22 reserved by the Letters Patent of Queen Elizabeth mentioned in Page 7. The Grant or a translation should have been abstracted.

B. *The Public House cannot be identified as one of the properties given to the Corporation by Queen Elizabeth although included in the Schedule to the Local Act. It must therefore be presumed to be part of the property granted to them by Henry 8th, or at least to be part of the ancient possessions of the Corporation, as evidence of uninterrupted possession for a period much exceeding 60 years can be given by receipt of Rent &c.*

2.
A. The 'Pigeons' I presume now to be sold under the provisions of the 2nd & 3rd Victoria C.40 (see Page 22) and 'the Body and side aisles of the Church' and the 'House late the Bridewell Keeper's residence' under the provisions of the Municipal Corporations Act.

B. *The Bridewell and the Bridewell Keeper's House are sold under the Municipal Corporations Act (the local Act of 2 & 3 Vic. C.40 having no reference to them) but the Public House may be considered as sold under both. It should not be considered as sold only under the powers of the Local Act, although that Act is of importance as releasing it from any*

---

1 See Document II (vii).

burdens, to which it was liable if it could be shewn to have been one of the properties acquired by the Corporation under the Charter of Queen Elizabeth

3.
- A. The properties, or some part as the 'Pigeons' appear to have been subject to an annual rent of £22 reserved to the Crown by the Letters Patent of Queen Elizabeth mentioned at Page 7 and 8 which appears ultimately to have vested in Mr Bros (see Page 7). The Grant from the Crown of this Rent and the subsequent Title thereto at least for the last 60 years anterior to the present time must be abstracted.
- B. *No portion of the property of which the Corporation became possessed under the Charter of Henry 8th, was subject to the rent of £22 and it cannot be shewn (though it may be supposed) that the 'Pigeons' was so subject. The Corporation have executed many Conveyances since 1845 of portions of their Corporate Estates, which were subject to this Rent, but in no instance has a purchaser required to see the title to it except as disclosed in the Conveyance from Mr Bros to the Corporation (which was approved and executed by the Lords of the Treasury) and it is submitted that the purchaser in this case ought to be satisfied with the same.*
- C. The Legislature as previously mentioned have treated the Pigeons Public House as having passed by the Grant of Queen Elizabeth and so subject to the burthens thereby created. The approbation of the Lords of the Treasury of the purchase by the Corporation cannot in any manner that I am aware of (but I am subject to correction) warrant the Title to the Annual Rent of £22 and as I feel that the Bishop's Secretary would require to satisfy himself of the Title to this Rent in order that the Land to be consecrated may be perfectly free of all claims, I think the purchaser must ask for an Abstract of the Title as expressed in the 3rd Requisition to be proved in the usual way.
- D. *An Abstract of the Conveyance of this Rent to Thomas Bros the younger (who sold to the Corporation) and of a Deed of Covenant from the persons of whom he purchased to produce the earlier documents of Title to the Corporation (being the only Documents in the possession of the Vendors, besides those of which an Abstract has already been furnished) is sent herewith[1] and as the Conveyance to Thomas Bros Junior is dated more than twenty years ago the recitals contained in it must be accepted by the purchaser under his Contract and if any further evidence of Title to this Rent is required it must be obtained at his expense.*

4.
- A. At Page 16 of the Abstract it appears that Mr Richard Fellowes has taken the name of 'Benyon'. I presume this was done under Her Majesty's

---
1 See Document II (iv).

License, notified in the Gazette. (A copy of the Gazette should be produced.)
  B. *The Vendors have not a copy of the Gazette in their custody and if the purchaser requires one to be produced it must be at his expense.*
  C. Probably the purchaser will dispense with this being a matter of notoriety.
5.
  A. It must be shewn that the requisitions in the latter part of section 94 of the 5th & 6th William 4th C.76 (abstracted at Page 5) have been complied with.
  B. *This has been sufficiently shewn by the copy Memorial and notice thereof with the endorsements on the same respectively which were produced to the purchaser's Solicitors for examination with the Abstract. If any confirmation of this is required it is found in the sanction given by the Treasury to the proposals contained in the Memorial.*
6.
  A. The Schedule referred to in the 2nd & 3rd Victoria C.40 (Page 5) seems only to comprise the 'Pigeons'.
  B. *No, because the other portions of the property not having been acquired under the Charter of Queen Elizabeth were not liable to the charges and incumbrances in the Act referred to.*
7.
  A. What are these Letters Patent referred to in the 2nd & 3rd Vic. C.40 (Page 6)?
  B. *The Letters Patent of Queen Elizabeth popularly called Queen Elizabeth's 'Charter' hereinbefore referred to.*
8.
  A. It must be shewn that the Requisitions in the latter part of the recital of the Act passed in the 6th William 4th (Page 11) have been complied with.
  B. *This is covered by the 5th Requisition.*
9.
  A. Are the Vendors Solicitors aware of any Incumbrances Judgements lis pendens or otherwise affecting the property.
  B. *No, except as disclosed in the Abstract.*
10.
  A. State what Documents of Title will be delivered to the Purchaser.
  B. *The Lease of 11th December 1835[1] and the Deed of 3rd August 1861[2]*

11.
  A. The Purchaser preserves to himself the right to make any further requisitions which may appear necessary on being supplied with the information sought for by these Requisitions.

---

1 See Document II (xiii).
2 See Document II (viii).

(iv) Further Abstract of the title of the Mayor, Aldermen and Burgesses of the Borough of Reading in the County of Berks. to the Freehold property called the Bridewell and the 'Pigeons' public house agreed to be sold to the Revd W. W. Phelps (1861). Original in the Greyfriars Church Archive.

This document traces the title to the annual rent of £22 that was initially to be paid to Queen Elizabeth I on the properties granted to the Corporation by her charter of 1560. The right to this rent subsequently passed through various hands (some mentioned here) until it was held by Thomas Bros the younger, from whom the Corporation purchased it in 1845. The Corporation's purpose in purchasing the annual rent of £22 was that the rent could then 'sink and be absolutely extinguished' and so not encumber any Corporation property thereafter.

As to the rent of £22 per annum reserved to the Crown by the Letters Patent of Queen Elizabeth to the said Mayor Aldermen and Burgesses.

1st July 1835
Indenture of this date made between Thomas Bros of Upper Clapton County of Middlesex Esquire of the first part John Alliston of Freemans Court in the City of London Esquire of the second part and Thomas Bros the younger of the Inner Temple in the City of London Esquire Barrister at Law (the only child of the said Thomas Bros) of the third part.

    Reciting that His Majesty King Charles the Second by his Letters Patent dated 11th November in the 22nd year of His reign [1670] granted to certain persons therein named their heirs and assigns among other rents All that annual rent of £22 reserved and issuing out of and for the rent of all and all manner of lands tenements rents and hereditaments goods and chattels forfeitures waifs and strays within the Borough of Reading in the County of Berks then or then late paid by the Mayor and Burgesses of the Borough of Reading and their successors nevertheless in trust for his said Majesty.

    And reciting that by divers mesne Conveyances and assurances in the Law and lastly by certain Indentures of Lease and Release dated respectively 6th and 7th November 1818 and a fine duly levied in pursuance of a Covenant contained in the said Indenture of Release and certain other Indentures of Lease and Release dated respectively 18th and 19th January 1821 and a Recovery duly suffered in pursuance of a Covenant contained in the said last mentioned Indenture of Release the said annual rent (among and together with other hereditaments and premises) was conveyed and assured as to one undivided moiety thereof to certain uses for the benefit of the said Thomas Bros and his assigns during his life with remainder To the

[p. 2]
    use of the heirs and assigns of the said Thomas Bros for ever and as to the other undivided moiety thereof to certain uses for the benefit of the said

John Alliston and his assigns during his life with remainder To the use of the heirs and assigns of the said John Alliston for ever.

And reciting that the said Thomas Bros in consideration of the natural love and affection which he had and bore towards his son said Thomas Bros the younger and the said John Alliston in consideration of the sum of £271.18s. paid by said Thomas Bros the younger as thereinafter mentioned had respectively contracted and agreed with said Thomas Bros the younger for the sale to him of the said annual rent of £22 thereinbefore described and intended to be thereby granted and conveyed and all their estate right and interest therein free from incumbrances.

It was witnessed that in pursuance of said agreement and in consideration of the natural love and affection which the said Thomas Bros had and bore for and towards his son the said Thomas Bros the younger and in consideration of £271.18s. paid to said John Alliston by said Thomas Bros the younger at &c. the receipt &c. they said Thomas Bros and John Alliston by now abstracting presents did and each of them did grant bargain sell and confirm unto said Thomas Bros the younger his heirs and assigns.

All that annual rent of £22 reserved and issuing out of and for the rent of all and all manner of lands tenements rents and hereditaments goods and chattels forfeitures waifs and strays within the Borough of Reading paid by the Mayor and Burgesses of Reading and their successors with all and every benefit and advantage of distress and entry and of all other powers and remedies whatsoever reserved to or vested in the said Thomas Bros and John Alliston their or either of their heirs and assigns or any other persons or person for them or either of them or on their or either of their behalf for recovering and receiving the same together with all and all manner of other rights privileges advantages and appurtenances whatsoever to the said yearly rent charge

[p. 3]
or annual sum belonging or in anywise appertaining.

And all the Estate &c.

To have hold receive and take said annual rent charge or yearly sum hereditaments and premises thereby granted and conveyed or intended so to be with their appurtenances from Michaelmas then last past (1834) unto and

To the use of said Thomas Bros the younger his heirs and assigns for ever.
Declaration to bar Dower

Covenants by said Thomas Bros for himself his heirs executors and administrators as to one undivided moiety only of said premises and for his own acts and defaults only and by said John Alliston for himself his heirs executors and administrators as to one undivided moiety only of said premises and as to his own acts and defaults only that they respectively were seized in fee.

Had good right to grant said premises
For quiet enjoyment
Free from incumbrances and
For further assurance

Duly executed by all said parties and attested Receipt for £271.18s. consideration money endorsed signed by said John Alliston and attested.

17th April 1845

Indenture of this date expressed to be made between said Thomas Bros the elder and John Alliston of the one part and the said Mayor Aldermen and Burgesses of the Borough of Reading in the County of Berks of the other part.

Reciting that by an Indenture of Grant or Conveyance bearing even date with and executed before the now abstracting presents and made or expressed to be made between said Thomas Bros the younger of the first part Arthur Lennox Esquire (commonly called Lord Arthur Lennox) and Alexander Pringle and Henry Baring Esquires three of the Lords Commissioners of Her Majesty's Treasury of the second part and said Mayor Aldermen and Burgesses of the third part In pursuance of a Contract for purchase therein recited and for the consideration therein expressed

[p. 4]

said Thomas Bros the younger granted bargained sold aliened and confirmed and also remised released and for ever quitted claim unto said Mayor Aldermen and Burgesses their successors and assigns the annual rent of £22 reserved and made payable in and by certain Letters Patent of Her late Majesty Queen Elizabeth under Her Great Seal of England dated in the 2nd year of her reign and issuing out of and for the rent of all and all manner of lands tenements rents and hereditaments goods and chattels forfeitures waifs and strays within said Borough of Reading paid by the said Mayor Aldermen and Burgesses of the Borough of Reading which said annual rent was by the before abstracted Indenture granted and conveyed unto and to the use of the said Thomas Bros the younger his heirs and assigns for ever To hold receive take and enjoy the same rent with all rights remedies and appurtenances thereto belonging or appertaining unto and to the only proper use and behoof of the said Mayor Aldermen and Burgesses and their successors and assigns absolutely and for ever and to the intent and so that as provided and enacted by an Act passed in the session held in the 2nd and 3rd years of the reign of Her present Majesty intituled 'An Act to enable the Mayor Aldermen and Burgesses of the Borough of Reading in the County of Berks to sell certain real Estate discharged from certain liabilities and to invest the purchase moneys arising from such sales in the purchase of other real estate to be charged with such liabilities' the same annual rent might thenceforth sink into and be absolutely extinguished in the lands tenements tolls profits and other the premises out of which the same was issuing and payable.

And reciting that in regard that the several title deeds and writings enumerated in the Schedule thereunder written related not only to said annual rent of £22 but also to other real Estate of the said Thomas Bros the elder and John Alliston of greater value the same were on the execution of the Conveyance to said Thomas Bros the younger as aforesaid retained by them as aforesaid and were then in their possession and on the treaty for the purchase of the said annual rent by said Mayor Aldermen and Burgesses said Thomas Bros the elder and John Alliston at the request of the said Thomas Bros the younger agreed to enter into a

[p. 5]
Covenant with the said Mayor Aldermen and Burgesses to produce the same several title Deeds and writings and to furnish attested or other copies thereof in manner thereinafter expressed.

It was witnessed that in pursuance of said Agreement said Thomas Bros the elder and John Alliston did by now abstracting presents for themselves jointly and severally and for their respective heirs executors administrators and assigns covenant and declare with and to said Mayor Aldermen and Burgesses and their successors and assigns that they said Thomas Bros the elder and John Alliston their heirs and assigns some or one of them should and would unless prevented by fire or some other inevitable accident from time to time and at all times thereafter upon every reasonable request and at the cost of said Mayor Aldermen and Burgesses their successors and assigns produce and shew forth or cause or procure to be produced and shewn forth in England and not elsewhere unto said Mayor Aldermen and Burgesses their successors or assigns or to their Counsel Town Clerk Attorneys Solicitors or Agents or to any person or persons whom they should in that behalf appoint or in or before any Court or Courts of Law or Equity or upon any trial or trials Commission or Commissions for the examination of witnesses or otherwise as occasion should require the several title Deeds and writings mentioned and enumerated in the Schedule thereunder written undefaced uncancelled and unobliterated for the manifestation support and defence of the Title of said Mayor Aldermen and Burgesses their successors or assigns to the said annual rent of £22 granted and released to them as aforesaid or any part thereof And also that they said Thomas Bros the elder and John Alliston their heirs and assigns or some or one of them should and would from time to time and at all times thereafter upon the request and at the costs of said Mayor Aldermen and Burgesses their successors or assigns deliver or cause to be furnished to said Mayor Aldermen and Burgesses their successors or assigns one or more true copy or extract copies or extracts attested or unattested as might be required of and from the same title deeds and writings or any of them an should and would permit the same respectively to be compared with the originals thereof either by said Mayor Aldermen and Burgesses their successors or assigns or by any person or persons whom they should appoint for that purpose.

The Schedule referred to.
1775 June 23
    Copy Will of Basil Bacon

[p. 6]

1818 January 23 & 24
> Indentures of Lease and Release between Charles Basil Bacon Lieutenant in the Royal East Middlesex Militia of the one part and said Thomas Bros and John Alliston of the other part

1818 November 6 & 7
> Indentures of Lease and Release the latter between said Charles Basil Bacon of the first part said Thomas Bros and John Alliston of the second part and John Howe Merchant of the third part

Michaelmas Term 59 George 3rd [1819]
> Indenture of fine between said Thomas Bros and John Alliston plaintiffs and said Charles Basil Bacon Defendant

1818 November 6 & 7
> Indenture of Lease and Release (the latter endorsed on the Indenture of Release of the 24th January 1818) between said Thomas Bros and John Alliston of the one part and the said Charles Basil Bacon of the other part

1819 January 29 & 30
> Indentures of Lease and Release (endorsed on the Indentures of the 23rd and 24th of January 1818) between said Charles Basil Bacon of the one part and said Thomas Bros and John Alliston of the other part

1821 January 18 & 19
> Indentures of Lease and Release the latter between said Thomas Bros and John Alliston of the first part the said John Howe of the second part said Charles Basil Bacon of the third part George Hundleby Gentleman of the fourth part and Nathan Atherton the younger Gentleman of the fifth part

Hilary Term 1st George 4th [1821]
> Exemplification of Recovery wherein said Nathan Atherton was demandant said George Hundleby Tenant and said Charles Basil Bacon Vouchee
>
>> Duly executed by said Thomas Bros and John Alliston and attested by two witnesses.

(v)   Draft Articles for the Agreement for the Sale and Purchase of the Bridewell and 'Pigeons' Public House Reading (1861). Original in the Greyfriars Church Archive.

Articles of Agreement made the [Blank] day of [Blank] 1861 Between the Mayor Aldermen and Burgesses of the Borough of Reading in the County of Berks (by the Council of the same Borough) hereinafter called the Vendors of the one part and The Reverend William Whitmarsh Phelps of Reading aforesaid Clerk (hereinafter called the Purchaser) of the other part

The Vendors and Purchaser so far as relates to the acts and deeds on their respective parts to be performed hereby agree with the other of them as follows The Vendors shall sell and the Purchaser shall purchase (subject to the approbation of her Majesty's Secretary of State and of the Lords Commissioners of Her Majesty's Treasury as hereinafter mentioned) at the price of £1250 Sterling to be paid to the Vendors on the 29th day of September next the fee simple and inheritance in possession free from Incumbrances of all that piece of Land situate on the North side of Friar Street in Reading aforesaid with the Ruins of the Church of the Grey Friars and all other Buildings (except as hereinafter mentioned) standing and being thereon some of which are used for the purposes of a Bridewell

[p. 2]
or House of Correction and for a Residence and Offices for the Keeper of the same (except such portions of the said Buildings as have been recently erected for the better accommodation and detention of Prisoners confined in the said Bridewell which the Vendors are to be at liberty at any time within 2 years from the date hereof to take down remove and carry away without doing any damage or making any compensation to the purchaser for the same) which said piece of Land is delineated in the Plan drawn in the Margin of these presents thereon distinguished by a Red Colour[1] And also the fee simple and inheritance free from Incumbrances (subject to the Lease thereof hereinafter mentioned) of All that messuage now used as a Public House called the 'Pigeons' situate on the North side of Friar Street aforesaid and adjoining the piece of Land hereinbefore described which said messuage called the 'Pigeons' was by an Indenture of Lease dated the 11th day of December 1835[2] demised by the said Mayor Aldermen and Burgesses to Thomas Rickford and Charles Curry Bickham for the Term of 80 years from the 29th day of September 1789 at the Yearly Rent of £5 and is also delineated on the Plan drawn in the Margin of these Presents and thereon coloured Blue together with the

[p. 3]
appurtenances to the said piece of Land messuage and hereditaments respectively belonging All which said hereditaments contain the several dimensions and are bounded as stated or described on the said Plan.
The Vendors will at their own expense deliver to the purchaser an abstract of their Title to the property and will deduce a good Title thereto. Every Deed and Document dated more than 20 years ago shall be conclusive evidence of everything recited stated noticed assumed or implied therein and the expense of the production examination and furnishing abstracts of all evidences and muniments of Title, if any, not in the Vendors possession and of obtaining all Office and other Copies of Registers Deeds and other Documents not in their possession where required for verifying the Title or otherwise shall be borne by the purchaser who shall also bear the expense of all searches enquiries and Journeys for the above purposes or any of them. Upon payment on the said 29th day of September next of the said sum of £1250 the Vendors and all other necessary parties (if any) will execute a proper Assurance of the Property to the Purchaser such assurance to be prepared by and at the expense of the Purchaser.
The Rents and possession will be received and retained

---

1 See Figure 15.
2 See Document II (xiii).

[p. 4]
by the Vendors up to the said 29th day of September next and as from that day the outgoings shall be discharged and the Rents and possession taken by the purchaser and such Rents and Outgoings shall if necessary be apportioned between the Vendors and purchaser for the purpose of this stipulation.

If from any cause whatever other than the refusal of the Vendors to make out their Title or convey the property the purchase shall not be completed on the 29th day of September next the purchaser shall pay Interest after the rate of £5 per cent per annum on the purchase Money from that day until the purchase shall be completed.

The Purchaser shall in his Conveyance covenant with the Vendors that the remains of the late Church of the Grey Friars now standing on the said piece of Land shall within [Blank] years after the date of the said Conveyance be restored and adapted to the purposes of Religious Worship according to the Rites and Doctrines of the Church of England or in case it shall be found impracticable to restore the same that the same shall be taken down and a decent and suitable Building shall be erected in lieu thereof for the purpose of being consecrated and used as a Church or Place for Religious

[p. 5]
Worship as aforesaid Provided always that the purchaser shall not be restrained from erecting Houses Schools or any other Buildings upon any portions of the said Land which shall not be required for a Church as aforesaid nor from selling and disposing of such portions of the said Land at his freewill and pleasure.

And whereas certain parts of the said Land and hereditaments are used as a Bridewell or House of Correction for the detention of Prisoners apprehended in the said Borough and it is doubtful whether or not the sanction of Her Majesty's Secretary of State is requisite to the Sale of that portion of the said Land and hereditaments

And Whereas Municipal Corporations are prohibited from selling any portion of their Corporate Estates without the approbation of the Lords Commissioners of Her Majesty's Treasury the Vendors hereby agree that they will as soon as practicable after the execution hereof at their own costs and charges make application to the Lords Commissioners of Her Majesty's Treasury for their approbation to the said Sale and will in like manner apply to Her Majesty's Secretary of State for his sanction thereto if the Vendors shall be advised that such last mentioned sanction is

[p. 6]
necessary.

And it is hereby expressly agreed that if the said Lords Commissioners or the said Secretary of State shall refuse to sanction the said sale this Contract shall upon such refusal being signified to the Purchaser became absolutely void and the parties hereto shall bear their own Costs charges and expenses of and incidental to the same and all matters and things relating thereunto.

In witness whereof the said Mayor Aldermen and Burgesses have hereunto affixed their Common Seal and the said W. W. Phelps hath set his hand the day and year first above written.

(vi)   Certificate as to non-payment of Knight's Fee (1861). Legal Copy in the Greyfriars Church Archive

These are to Certify That it does not appear that the Service of the 100th part of a Knight's fee and rent of one farthing as issuing out of premises in Reading and payable by the Corporation of Reading has been in Charge on the Crown Rental for the County of Berks for the last sixty years and upwards.

Office of Land Revenue Records and Inrolments
21st October 1861

T. R. Fearnside
Keeper of the Records

(vii)   Abstract of Contract for Redemption of Land Tax (1861). Original in the Greyfriars Church Archive.

Corporation of Reading to The Reverend W. W. Phelps
Blandy, Town Clerk

Abstract of Contract for Redemption of Land Tax

7th October 1801
Deed Poll of this date under the hands and seals of Sir Charles Marsh and Alexander Cobham Esquire two of the Commissioners appointed for the purposes of an Act intituled 'An Act for making perpetual subject to redemption and purchase in the manner therein stated the several sums of money now charged in Great Britain as a Land Tax for one year from the 25th March 1798' for the County of Berks whereby said Commissioners certified that they had contracted with the Mayor Aldermen and Burgesses of the Borough of Reading in the said County for the redemption by them of £71.3s Land Tax being the Land Tax charged upon the several Estates situate as therein mentioned and (inter alia)

> In the parish of Saint Lawrence in Reading aforesaid a messuage or tenement and the House of Correction in and for the said Borough to the same belonging with the appurtenances then in the occupation of John Shaylor which said messuage or tenement and premises were charged with Land Tax in the assessment made for the year 1800 as follows.

'Corporation – Bridewell and John Shaylor – £2 0s 0d'

Duly executed & Registered 24th March 1802

(viii) Release of a piece of land Messuage and Hereditaments called the Bridewell and 'Pigeons' in Friar Street Reading from Mortgage of 31st March 1854 (1861). Original indenture in the Greyfriars Church Archive.

In 1854, Richard Benyon (then Fellowes) loaned the Corporation £7,000 upon the security of the Corporation's property. In order for William Whitmarsh Phelps to purchase the Bridewell properties and Pigeons public house, these properties needed to be released from being included in that agreement. This indenture allows that release, as Benyon was content that the remainder of the Corporation's property was sufficient to secure his loan.

<u>Dated 3rd August 1861</u>

Richard Benyon Esquire -----to----- The Mayor Aldermen and Burgesses of the Borough of Reading in the County of Berks	Release of a piece of land Messuage and Hereditaments called the Bridewell and 'Pigeons' in Friar Street Reading from Mortgage of 31st March 1854.

This Indenture made the third day of August One thousand and sixty one Between Richard Benyon of Englefield House in the County of Berks Esquire of the one part and The Mayor Aldermen and Burgesses of the Borough of Reading in the County of Berks of the other part

Whereas by a Deed Poll dated the thirty first day of March One thousand eight hundred and fifty four under the Common Seal of the said Mayor Aldermen and Burgesses and under the hand and seal of the said Richard Benyon (then Richard Fellowes but who has since taken the surname of Benyon instead of Fellowes) the said Mayor Aldermen and Burgesses by virtue of 'The Reading Corporation Markets Act 1853' in consideration of the several sums amounting in the whole to Seven thousand pounds by the said Richard Benyon paid to the Treasurer of the Borough at the several times appearing by the several receipts of the Treasurer thereon endorsed for the purposes of the said Act Did with the approval of the Lords Commissioners of Her Majesty's Treasury testified by the signatures of two of the said Lords Commissioners whose names were written in the Margin thereof grant and assign unto the said Richard Benyon his executors administrators and assigns All the Corporate Estates of the Mayor Aldermen and Burgesses and the Borough Fund of the said Borough To hold to the said Richard Benyon his executors administrators and assigns from that day until the said sum of seven thousand pounds with Interest at Four pounds per Centum per Annum should be fully paid and satisfied the principal sum to be repaid at the end of thirty years from the date thereof and the Interest to be paid half yearly on the twenty fourth day of June and the twenty fifth day of December in every year in the meantime

And Whereas by an agreement dated the twenty second day of May One thousand eight hundred and sixty one and made between the said Mayor Aldermen and Burgesses of the one part and the Reverend William Whitmarsh

Phelps Clerk of the other part the said Mayor Aldermen and Burgesses for the considerations therein mentioned did agree to sell to the said William Whitmarsh Phelps the fee simple and inheritance in possession free from incumbrances of All that piece of land situate on the North side of Friar Street in Reading aforesaid with the ruins of the Church of the Grey Friars and all other Buildings (except as thereinafter mentioned) standing and being thereon some of which were used for the purposes of a Bridewell or House of Correction and for a residence and offices for the Keeper of the same except such portions of the said Buildings as had been recently created for the better accommodation and detention of prisoners confined in the said Bridewell which the said Mayor Aldermen and Burgesses were to be at liberty at any time within two years from the date of the said agreement to take down remove and carry away (doing no damage thereby) without making any compensation to the said William Whitmarsh Phelps for the same which said piece of land was delineated on the Plan annexed to the said agreement[1] and therein distinguished by a red colour And also the fee simple and inheritance free from incumbrances (subject to the Lease thereof thereinafter mentioned) of All that messuage then used as a Public House called the 'Pigeons' situate on the North side of Friar Street aforesaid and adjoining the piece of land thereinbefore described which said messuage called the 'Pigeons' was by an Indenture of Lease dated the eleventh day of December One thousand eight hundred and thirty five demised by the said Mayor Aldermen and Burgesses to Thomas Rickford and Charles Curry Bickham for the term of Eighty years from the twenty ninth day of September One thousand seven hundred and eighty nine at the yearly rent of Five pounds and was delineated on the said plan annexed to the said Agreement and thereon coloured Blue Together with the appurtenances to the said piece of land messuage and hereditaments respectively belonging All which said hereditaments contained the several dimensions and were bounded as stated or described on the said plan

And whereas the said Mayor Aldermen and Burgesses in order to carry into effect the said agreement have requested the said Richard Benyon to grant and release to them the said piece of land messuage and hereditaments absolutely discharged from the said Mortgage Debt and all Interest and arrears of Interest thereon which he hath consented to do being satisfied that the residue of the Corporate Estates and Borough Fund is an ample security for his said Mortgage Debt.

Now this Indenture witnesseth that in pursuance of the said agreement the said Richard Benyon doth hereby grant and also remise release and quit claim unto the said Mayor Aldermen and Burgesses their successors and assigns All that piece of land with the Ruins of the Church of the Grey Friars and all other Buildings standing and being thereon as hereinbefore described And all that messuage or Public House called the 'Pigeons' with the yard and appurtenances to the same belonging All which said piece of land messuage and hereditaments are for the better identification thereof delineated on the plan drawn in the margin of these presents and therein distinguished by being coloured red and blue respectively Together with all ways paths passages

---

1 See Figure 15.

easements waters watercourses commodities and appurtenances to the same belonging or in anywise appertaining And all the Estate right title claim and demand whatsoever both at law and in equity of the said Richard Benyon therein and thereto To have and to hold the said piece of land messuage and hereditaments and all other the premises intended to be hereby granted and released with the appurtenances unto and to the use of the said Mayor Aldermen and Burgesses their successors and assigns absolutely discharged from the said Mortgage Debt of seven thousand pounds and all Interest and arrears of Interest in respect thereof and all liens claims and demands in respect or on account thereof And the said Richard Benyon doth hereby for himself his heirs executors and administrators Covenant with the said Mayor Aldermen and Burgesses their successors and assigns that he the said Richard Benyon hath not done or knowingly suffered or been party or privy to anything whereby or by means whereof the said premises hereinbefore expressed to be hereby granted and released or any of them or any part thereof are is or may be charged incumbered or in anywise prejudicially affected in title Estate or otherwise howsoever

In witness whereof the said parties to these presents have hereunto set their hands and seals the day and year first above written.

[Seal in red wax]
[Signed] Richard Benyon

[On reverse]
Signed sealed and delivered by the within named Richard Benyon in the presence of
    [Signed] J. J. Blandy
    Town Clerk

(ix)   Statutory Declaration of John Readings in proof of the identity of portions of the Bridewell property (1862). Original in the Greyfriars Church Archive.

16th January 1862
The Corporation of Reading to The Reverend W. W. Phelps

I John Readings of Reading in the County of Berks do solemnly and sincerely declare as follows:-

That I am seventy eight years of age, am a Native of Reading and have resided in Reading all my life.

That I have known the properties in Friar Street Reading called the Bridewell the Bridewell Keeper's House and the 'Pigeons' Public House adjoining thereto ever since the time of my earliest recollection and can positively state that the main Buildings now standing upon the sites of those properties are the same that were standing there fifty years ago at the least and that they have not been materially altered in their elevations and structure during the last fifty years except two years ago when the new Cells were erected.

And I further declare that from the year One thousand eight hundred and thirty two until the year One thousand eight hundred and fifty nine I was the Keeper of the said Bridewell and resided in the said Bridewell Keeper's House.

And I make this solemn declaration conscientiously believing the same to be true and by virtue of the provisions of an Act of Parliament made and passed in the Session of the fifth and sixth years of the reign of His late Majesty King William the Fourth intituled 'An Act to repeal an Act of the present Session of Parliament intituled 'An Act for the more effectual abolition of Oaths and Affirmations taken and made in various Departments of the state and to substitute Declarations in lieu thereof and for the more entire suppression of voluntary and extra-judicial Oaths and affidavits' and to make other provisions for the abolition of unnecessary Oaths'.

[Signed] John Readings

The above declaration was made and subscribed at Reading in the County of Berks the sixteenth day of January One thousand eight hundred and sixty two.

Before me [Illegible signature]

A Commissioner to administer Oaths in Chancery in England

(x) Statutory Declaration of John Jackson Blandy, Town Clerk, in proof of the identity of portions of the Bridewell and 'Pigeons' properties (1862). Original in the Greyfriars Church Archive.

28th April 1862
The Corporation of Reading to The Reverend W. W. Phelps
I John Jackson Blandy of Reading in the County of Berks Gentleman do solemnly and sincerely declare as follows:-

That I am the Town Clerk of the Borough of Reading in the County of Berks and have been so ever since the year One thousand eight hundred and thirty three and as such Town Clerk I have the custody of the Diaries Records and Documents belonging to the Corporation of Reading.

That I have examined the Diaries of the said Corporation and find therein the following entries that is to say –

3rd May 1784 'on taking the proposed plan of improving Bridewell into consideration It is agreed that any sum not exceeding £200 be laid out in repairing and improving Bridewell and making the Dwelling house fit for the habitation of the Keeper on the County's paying the yearly Rent of £30 instead of £21 the present Rent and that the Mayor Mr Knapp Mr Thomas Deane Mr Henry Deane and Mr Poulton or any three of them be a Committee to treat with the Justices of the County'.

21st August 1786 'Agreed that in case the new County Bridewell be not fit for the prisoners at Michaelmas next the County may continue to use the present Bridewell and Keeper's House till the new Bridewell is fit'.

6th May 1789 'Agreed to grant a Lease of the Alehouse adjoining to the Bridewell as now marked out in Collier's plan to Mr Matthias Deane for 4 score years from Michaelmas at 5£ per annum he having agreed to repair and improve the same'.

2nd April 1790 'Leave is given to John Shaylor to inhabit the new Bridewell House until Michaelmas next that the public House may be rebuilt'.

3rd October 1791 'John Shaylor is appointed Bridewell Keeper with the occupancy of the new Keeper's House and Ten pounds a year from this Michaelmas and to be paid Ten pounds and forgiven all arrears of Rent due to this Corporation as a recompense for his trouble for the time past'.

That there are several other entries in the Diaries of the Corporation from the year One thousand seven hundred and eighty four to the year One thousand seven hundred and ninety one respecting the Bridewell which with the entries above set out tend to shew that about that period extensive repairs were done to it and that there were then in connexion with the Bridewell a house or place of residence for the Bridewell Keeper and also a public House which was let by the Corporation.

That among the Documents in my custody as such Town Clerk as aforesaid is a Bill of one William Collier against the Chamberlain of the Corporation amounting to the sum of One hundred and fifty three pounds fourteen shillings and four pence half penny for sundry works done in the year One thousand seven hundred and eighty nine 'to the Town Bridewell' and 'to the new Dwelling House' and which Bill was paid by the said Chamberlain to the said William Collier as appears by his receipt annexed thereto.

And I say that I verily believe that the properties at present known as the Borough Bridewell, the Bridewell Keeper's House and the Public House thereto adjoining called the 'Pigeons' and which by Articles of Agreement dated the twenty second day of May One thousand eight hundred and sixty one were contracted to be sold by the said Corporation to the Reverend William Whitmarsh Phelps are the same properties as those referred to in the entries in the Corporation Diaries above set out and referred to and that the freehold and inheritance of the same is legally vested in the Mayor Aldermen and Burgesses of the Borough of Reading in the County of Berks and has been so from beyond the time of the memory of any person now living.

And I make this solemn declaration conscientiously believing the same to be true and by virtue of the provisions of an Act of Parliament made and passed in the Session of the fifth and sixth years of the reign of His late Majesty King William the Fourth intituled 'An Act to repeal an Act of the present Session of Parliament intituled 'An Act for the more effectual abolition of Oaths and Affirmations taken and made in various Departments of the state and to substitute Declarations in lieu thereof and for the more entire suppression of voluntary and extra-judicial Oaths and affidavits' and to make other provisions for the abolition of unnecessary Oaths'.

[Signed] J. J. Blandy

The above declaration was made and subscribed at Reading in the County of Berks the twenty eighth day of April One thousand eight hundred and sixty two.

Before me [Signed] Robert C. Dryland

A Commissioner to administer Oaths in Chancery in England

(xi)   Correspondence with the Corporation regarding the Lease of the 'Pigeons' (1835). Royal Berkshire Archives R/AC1/1/26 Minutes of the Corporation (1827–35) (Extract)

[p. 300]
At a meeting of the Corporation on Tuesday 14th July 1835.

The following letter from Messrs Rickford and Bickham having been read – agreed to refer the same to the Committee of Leases.

Castle Street Brewery
22nd June 1835

To the Worshipful the Mayor and Corporation of the Borough of Reading

Gentlemen,
 Having become the purchasers of the Pigeons Public House in Friar Street held under the Corporation by Minute in their Books granted in the year 1789 for 80 years to Mr Matthias Deane in consideration of the rent and certain substantial repairs to be then done which having been fully perfected on the part of our Predecessors – We now respectfully solicit that you will be pleased to grant to us such Document as may ensure to us the peaceable possession for the remainder of such term.
         We have the honour to remain
             Gentlemen
                 Your obedient Servants
                     [Signed] T. Rickford   Chas. C. Bickham

[p. 321]
At a meeting of the Corporation on Friday 11th December 1835.

The Pigeons Public House
The Common Seal was affixed to an Indenture of Lease to Thomas Rickford and Charles Curry Bickham of Reading Berks Brewers and Copartners of All that Messuage Tenement or Public House and premises called or known by the name or sign of the 'Pigeons' situate in the parish of St Lawrence on the North side of Friar Street in

[p. 322]
Reading aforesaid now in the occupation of George Williams for the term of Four score years from Michaelmas 1789 in consideration of the yearly rent of £5 and for other considerations in the said Indenture of Lease mentioned.[1]

---

1 See Document II (xiii).

(xii)   Town Clerk's Bill re the Lease of the Pigeons Public House (1835). Royal Berkshire Archives R/FZ2/62/13

The Corporation of Reading To J. J. Blandy.

The Pigeons Public House.

1835			
July 14	Attending you on the subject of a Letter from Messrs Rickford & Bickham stating they were become the purchasers of this public House held under you, and requesting Lease might be granted in pursuance of an Agreement entered into in 1789 the Stipulation on the part of the Lessee having been fulfilled, when it was agreed that such Letter should be referred to the Committee of Leases.	6	8
October 28	Attending Meeting of Committee of Leases when this subject was considered and it was agreed that Messrs Rickford & Co. should be called on to deduce their Title to Mr Matth[ia]s Deane with whom the Original Agreement was entered into and on this being done that it be recommended to the Corporation to carry the Contract into effect.	6	8
	Writing Messrs Rickford & Co. to deduce their Title accordingly.	3	6
		16	10

9 November 1835 Recd. the above Bill by payment of the Chamberlain.
[Signed] J. J. Blandy

(xiii) Lease of the Pigeons Public House in Friar Street St Lawrence Reading for eighty years from Michaelmas 1789 Rent £5 (1835). Original lease and its counterpart lease both in the Greyfriars Church Archive.

11 December 1835
The Mayor Aldermen and Burgesses of the Borough of Reading County Berks to Messrs Rickford and Bickham

[First Sheet]
This Indenture made the Eleventh day of December in the year of our Lord One thousand eight hundred and thirty five Between The Mayor Aldermen and Burgesses of the Borough of Reading in the County of Berks of the one part and Thomas Rickford and Charles Curry Bickham of Reading aforesaid Common Brewers and Co-partners of the other part
Whereas by a Minute of Hall of the said Mayor Aldermen and Burgesses made and entered on their Journal or Diary and dated the sixth day of May in the year One thousand seven hundred and eighty nine It was amongst other things agreed to grant a lease of the Alehouse adjoining to Bridewell as marked out in Colliers Plan to Matthias Deane for Four score years from Michaelmas then next he having agreed to repair and improve the same
And Whereas by another Minute of Hall of the said Mayor Aldermen and Burgesses made and entered on their Journal or Diary and dated the second day of April in the year One thousand seven hundred and ninety leave was given for John Shaylor to inhabit the new Bridewell house until Michaelmas then next that the Public house might be rebuilt
And Whereas in pursuance of the said first mentioned Minute the said Public house was rebuilt and afterwards occupied by the said Lessee or his undertenant for several years but no lease thereof was ever granted by the said Mayor Aldermen and Burgesses
And Whereas by virtue of divers mesne assignments and other Acts of the law the equitable and beneficial right and interest of and in the said Public house and premises hath become vested in the said Thomas Rickford and Charles Curry Bickham for a valuable consideration and they have accordingly applied to and requested the said Mayor Aldermen and Burgesses to grant them a lease of the said Public house and premises for the residue of the said term of Four score years according to the said Minute of Hall of the sixth day of May One thousand seven hundred and eighty nine which they the said Mayor Alderman and Burgesses have consented and agreed to do
Now this Indenture Witnesseth that in consideration of the premises and of the rent Covenants and Agreements hereinafter reserved and contained on the part of the said Thomas Rickford and Charles Curry Bickham their executors administrators and assigns to be paid observed and performed They the said Mayor Aldermen and Burgesses Have demised and leased And by these presents Do demise and lease unto the said Thomas Rickford and Charles Curry Bickham their executors administrators and assigns All that messuage tenement or Public house and premises commonly called or known by the

name or sign of the Pigeons situate lying and being in the Parish of Saint Lawrence in Reading aforesaid on the north side of a certain Street called Friar Street formerly in the occupation of Robert Wilson and now of George Williams Together with all and singular outhouses buildings ways paths passages advantages and appurtenances whatsoever to the said messuage and premises hereby demised belonging or appertaining a Plan or ground plot whereof is drawn in the margin of these presents[1] To have and to hold the said messuage tenement or Public house and premises hereby demised and every part and parcel thereof with their and every of their appurtenances unto the said Thomas Rickford and Charles Curry Bickham their executors administrators and assigns from the twenty ninth day of September which was in the year one thousand seven hundred and eighty nine for and during and unto the full end and term of Four score years from thence next ensuing and fully to be complete and ended Yielding and Paying therefore yearly and every year during the said term unto the said Mayor Aldermen and Burgesses their successors and assigns the rent or sum of Five pounds of lawful money of Great Britain by equal half yearly payments at the two most usual feasts or days of payment in the year (that is to say) the Feast of the Annunciation of the Blessed Virgin Mary and Saint Michael the Archangel in every year without any deduction or abatement whatsoever for or in respect of any taxes charges rates assessments or outgoings whatsoever the first payment of the said yearly rent to be considered as having commenced and been made on the Feast day of the Annunciation of the Blessed Virgin Mary which was in the year One thousand seven hundred and ninety and the next of such payments which will become due and payable on the feast day of the Annunciation of the Blessed Virgin Mary which will be in the year One thousand eight hundred and thirty six And the said Thomas Rickford and Charles Curry Bickham do hereby for themselves their heirs executors and administrators Covenant and Agree with the said Mayor Aldermen and Burgesses their successors and assigns in manner following (that is to say) that they the said Thomas Rickford and Charles Curry Bickham their executors administrators or assigns shall and will during the continuance of the said term hereby granted well and truly pay or cause to be paid unto the said Mayor Aldermen and Burgesses their successors and assigns the said yearly rent or sum of Five pounds clear of all taxes and deductions as aforesaid on the days and times and in the manner and form on and in which the same is hereinbefore reserved and made payable And also shall and will during the said term hereby granted bear pay and discharge all and all manner of taxes rates assessments and outgoings whatsoever whether Parliamentary Parochial or otherwise which now are or which shall or may at any time or times hereafter during the said term hereby granted be assessed or imposed upon or payable in respect of the said premises hereby demised or any part thereof And also that they the said Thomas Rickford and Charles Curry Bickham their executors administrators and assigns shall and will at all times during the said term hereby granted well and sufficiently repair and keep in good and substantial repair order and condition the said messuage or tenement and Public house and premises hereby demised with their appurtenances And the said premises so

---

1 See Figure 6.

well and sufficiently repaired and kept in good and substantial repair order and condition shall and will at the end expiration or other sooner determination of the said term peaceably and quietly leave surrender and yield up to the said Mayor Aldermen and Burgesses their successors and assigns and also that it shall be lawful for the said Mayor Aldermen and Burgesses their successors and assigns and for any person or persons deputed by them with or without Workmen or others in his or their Company at reasonable and convenient times in the day from time to time during the continuance of the said term to enter into and upon the said hereby demised premises or any

[Second Sheet]

Part thereof to view the state and condition of the repairs thereof and of all defects or wants of reparation and amendment which upon any such view shall be found to give or leave notice in writing at or upon the said demised premises or any part thereof to or for the said Thomas Rickford and Charles Curry Bickham their executors administrators and assigns to repair and amend the same within the space of three Calendar months next after every or any such notice And that they the said Thomas Rickford and Charles Curry Bickham their executors administrators or assigns shall and will at their own expense well and sufficiently and substantially repair all and every the defects decays and wants of repairs whereof any such notice shall be given or left as aforesaid And further that they the said Thomas Rickford and Charles Curry Bickham their executors administrators or assigns shall and will at his and their own expense insure and keep insured all and every the said messuage or tenement and Public house and premises hereby demised in two thirds of the value thereof at the least in the Sun Fire Insurance Office or some other Public Fire insurance office in London or Westminster which the said Mayor Aldermen and Burgesses shall by their Town Clerk or Surveyor approve of and appoint And shall and will at the request of the said Mayor Aldermen and Burgesses their successors or assigns or their Town Clerk or Surveyor produce or cause to be produced to them or him the subsisting Policy or Policies and the receipts or vouchers for the premium for such insurance for the Current year And in case any of the said premises hereby demised or any part thereof shall at any time during the term hereby granted be destroyed or damaged by fire that they the said Thomas Rickford and Charles Curry Bickham their executors administrators or assigns shall and will with all convenient speed reinstate and rebuild the same under the direction of the said Mayor Aldermen and Burgesses their successors and assigns or their Surveyor and shall and will apply or cause to be applied all monies that may be received or obtained under or by virtue of such insurance as aforesaid in or towards rebuilding and reinstating the said premises And shall and will pay the said rent hereby reserved at the time and in the same manner as if no such accident by fire had happened And moreover that they the said Thomas Rickford and Charles Curry Bickham their executors administrators or assigns shall not nor will at any time during the said term hereby granted demise lease underlet assign or set over the said messuage and premises hereby demised or any part thereof or otherwise part with the possession thereof or his or their term Estate or interest therein to any person or persons whomsoever for any greater or more extensive term than twenty one years from the time of making any underlease or assignment without the licence and consent in writing of the said Mayor Aldermen and Burgesses their successors and assigns under their Common Seal being first had and obtained which Licence and consent shall (unless it be otherwise expressed) extend only to the Underlease or assignment therein licensed to be made and shall not be absolute so as to exonerate the said Thomas Rickford and Charles Curry Bickham their executors administrators or assigns or the person or persons taking any such underlease or assignment from the necessity of obtaining a similar licence and consent on every future occasion Provided nevertheless that such Licence and consent shall not be unreasonably withheld nor shall the said Mayor Aldermen and Burgesses their successors or assigns be entitled to demand any fine premium or sum of money for giving or granting the same save and except the necessary expenses and usual fees of or attending the preparing and perfecting the deed or Instrument by which such licence and consent shall be given

Provided always and these Presents are upon this express Condition that in case the said yearly rent of Five pounds hereinbefore reserved or any part thereof shall be in arrear and unpaid by the space of twenty one days next after any of the days hereinbefore appointed for payment thereof being first lawfully demanded and not paid when demanded or if the said Thomas Rickford and Charles Curry Bickham their executors administrators or assigns shall neglect or fail in the performance or observance of all or any of the Covenants Conditions or Agreements hereinbefore contained and which by him or them are or ought to be performed or observed then and in any of the said Cases it shall be lawful for the said Mayor Aldermen and Burgesses their successors and assigns to enter into and upon the said hereby demised premises or any part thereof in the name of the whole and the same to have again repossess and enjoy and the said Thomas Rickford and Charles Curry Bickham their executors administrators and assigns and all other Occupiers of the said premises or any part thereof to expel and remove therefrom and from the time of such entry this present lease and the term hereby granted shall cease determine and become absolutely void any thing herein contained to the contrary thereof in anywise notwithstanding And the said Mayor Aldermen and Burgesses for themselves their successors and assigns do Covenant and Agree with the said Thomas Rickford and Charles Curry Bickham their executors administrators and assigns that they the said Thomas Rickford and Charles Curry Bickham their executors administrators and assigns paying the said yearly rent hereby reserved and performing and fulfilling all and every the Covenants Clauses and Agreements hereinbefore contained within on his and their parts are or ought to be observed and performed shall and may peaceably and quietly hold use occupy possess and enjoy the said messuage or tenement and Public house and premises hereby demised and every part thereof with the appurtenances for and during all the rest residue and remainder of the said term of Four score years now to come and unexpired therein without any molestation or disturbance whatsoever from or by the said Mayor Aldermen and Burgesses their successors or assigns or from or by any person or persons whomsoever lawfully or equitably or rightfully claiming or to claim by from under or in trust for them

In witness whereof to one part of these presents remaining with the said Thomas Rickford and Charles Curry Bickham the said Mayor Aldermen and Burgesses have affixed their Common Seal and to the other parts of these presents remaining with the said Mayor Aldermen and Burgesses the said Thomas Rickford and Charles Curry Bickham have hereunto set their hands and seals the day and year first above written

[Below: the Common Seal of the Borough of Reading in red wax, with the written signature of Henry Hawkes, Mayor]

[Reverse of First Sheet]

The Common Seal of the within named Mayor Aldermen and Burgesses was affixed to the within written Indenture in the presence of
    [Signed] J. J. Blandy
    Town Clerk

(xiv)   Abstract of the Title of Thomas Hawkins Esquire to a Messuage Tenement or Public House, called 'The Pigeons' situate in Friar Street in Reading, in the County of Berks for the residue of a Term of 80 years from Michaelmas 1789 (1862). Original in the Greyfriars Church Archive.

When William Whitmarsh Phelps purchased the Lease of the Pigeons public house on 21 December 1863, it was in the possession of Thomas Hawkins. This document describes how the Lease had passed from the co-ownership of Charles Curry Bickham and Thomas Rickford (in the previous document) to Thomas Hawkins as a result of transactions that saw Hawkins take over first Bickham's half of the Castle Street Brewery business, and then Rickford's. It also notes the mortages Hawkins needed in order to achieve this.

    The involvement of Mary Gardner and James Agg Gardner is explained by the 'Supplemental Abstract' which follows this document, and that of Hannah Maria Rickford, Thomas Parker Rickford, Charles William Calvert and John Wills is explained in the 'Further Supplemental Abstract' that follows that one.

11th December 1835
[Abstracted as transcribed above, see Document II (ii), document pages 2 to 4; and for the full Lease see Document II (xiii).]

[p.3]
7th November 1846
Indenture of Conveyance and Assignment made between the said Charles Curry Bickham of the first part Mary Gardner of Cheltenham in the County of Gloucester Widow and James

[p. 4]

Agg Gardner of the same place Esquire of the second part Edith Agg of Cheltenham aforesaid Widow of the third part Thomas Hawkins late of Basildon in the said County of Berks but then of Link Saint Mary Bourne in the County of Southampton Gentleman of the fourth part and Grantham Robert Dodd of New Broad Street in the City of London Gentleman of the fifth part

> Reciting (inter alia) that the said Thomas Hawkins had contracted and agreed with the said Charles Curry Bickham for the absolute purchase of his the said Charles Curry Bickham's undivided moiety or equal half part or share of and in (inter alia) the Leasehold Premises comprised in the 4th 5th 6th and 8th Schedules to the now abstracting Indenture annexed for the sum of £11,118.10.0

It is witnessed that in pursuance of the said Contract and for the consideration therein mentioned They the said Mary Gardner and James Agg Gardner at the request of the said Charles Curry Bickham testified &c. Did and each of them Did bargain sell assign transfer and set over and the said Charles Curry Bickham Did grant bargain sell assign transfer and set over ratify and confirm unto the said Thomas Hawkins his executors administrators and assigns

>> All that one full and equal undivided Moiety half part or share (the whole into two Moieties or equal half parts or shares being considered as divided) of and in
>> All those Leasehold Messuages or Tenements Inns and Public Houses Lands and all and singular other the Leasehold Premises respectively described and comprised in the 4th 5th 6th and 8th Schedules to now abstracting Indenture annexed and the Appurtenances
>> And all the Estate &c.

To hold the same unto the said Thomas Hawkins his executors Administrators and assigns thenceforth for all the residue of the Term for years granted by the several Indentures of Lease thereof freed from the thereinbefore recited Mortgages and Charges thereon but subject to the payment of the rent and to the observance and performance of the covenants and agreements in the said several Indentures of Lease contained on the part of the Lessee
Covenants by the said Charles Curry Bickham that

[p. 5]

the said Lease was valid – had good right to assign – for quiet enjoyment – free from Incumbrances – and for further assurance

> The 6th Schedule
> All that Messuage Tenement Public House and Premises commonly called or known by the name or sign of 'The Pigeons' situate lying and being in the Parish of Saint Lawrence in Reading aforesaid on the North side of the said Street then called Friar Street in the occupation of Robert Wilson late of George Williams and then of Charles Hewitt
> Executed by all Parties and attested by two witnesses as to Charles Curry Bickham and James Agg Gardner and by one witness as to the others

> Receipts endorsed signed and witnessed

9th June 1852
Will of the said Thomas Rickford whereby after a Bequest of his Household Furniture &c. and a devise of a Public House called 'The Lodge' he devised unto and to the use of his Wife (Hannah Maria Rickford) his Son (Captain Thomas Parker Rickford) and to Edward Vines of Reading aforesaid Esquire their Heirs and Assigns
> The residue of his Real Estate

And bequeathed to them their executors administrators and assigns
> The residue of his Personal Estate

Upon Trust for Sale as therein mentioned
And the said Testator thereby appointed his said Wife and Son and the said Edward Vines Executrix and Executors of that his Will
Declaration that the receipt of the said Trustees should be good and sufficient discharges for all monies paid to them under the said Will
> Executed by the said Thomas Rickford and attested by two Witnesses

15th August 1854
Codicil to said Will, whereby the said Thomas Rickford revoked the appointment of the said Edward Vines as a Trustee and Executor of the said Will (but in no other respect revoked or altered the same)
> Executed by the said Thomas Rickford and attested by two witnesses

[p. 6]
The said Will and Codicil were duly proved by the said Hannah Maria Rickford and Thomas Parker Rickford in the Prerogative Court of Canterbury on the 9th day of March 1855

17th April 1856
Indenture of Conveyance and Assignment made between the said Hannah Maria Rickford of Bradenham in the County of Buckingham Widow and the said Thomas Parker Rickford of Hamilton House in the County of Southampton Esquire of the first part the said Thomas Hawkins of Reading aforesaid Common Brewer of the second part and William Hobbs of Reading aforesaid Gentleman of the third part
> Reciting that the said Thomas Rickford late of Reading aforesaid Esquire carried on the Business of a Brewer in Co-partnership with the said Thomas Hawkins
> And reciting that the said Thomas Rickford being (inter alia) possessed of and entitled to one Moiety or half part of and in the Leasehold Messuages and Hereditaments described in the 4th 5th 6th and 8th Schedules thereunto annexed for the residue of the several Terms of years created therein by the Leases under which the same were respectively holden duly made his last Will and Testament as hereinbefore abstracted
> And reciting the said Codicil to the said Will

And reciting that the said Thomas Rickford died on or about the 5th day of February 1855 without having revoked or altered his said Will (except as aforesaid) and without having revoked or altered his said Codicil

And reciting (inter alia) that the said Thomas Hawkins had contracted with the said Hannah Maria Rickford and Thomas Parker Rickford for the purchase of the said Moiety or half part late of the said Thomas Rickford of and in (inter alia) the said Leasehold Hereditaments free from Incumbrances for the sum of £12,166.8.11

It is witnessed that in pursuance of the said Contract and for the considerations therein mentioned They the said Hannah Maria Rickford and Thomas Parker Rickford Did and each of them Did assign and transfer unto the said Thomas Hawkins his executors administrators and assigns

>All that one full and undivided Moiety half part or share (the whole into two moieties or equal half parts

[p. 7]

>being considered as divided) of and in All those Leasehold messuages or tenements Inns and Public Houses lands and all and singular other the Leasehold Premises respectively described and comprised in the 4th 5th 6th and 8th Schedules to the now abstracting Indenture annexed and each and every of them and every part and parcel thereof respectively and of in their and each and every of their appurtenances

>And all the estate &c.

To hold the same unto the said Thomas Hawkins his executors administrators and assigns thenceforth for all the residue and remainder of the several and respective terms for years granted and agreed to be granted in and by the said several Indentures of Lease &c. in the 4th 5th 6th and 8th Schedules mentioned or referred to and as were then to come and unexpired in the same premises respectively subject to the payment of the several yearly and other rents and to the observance and performance of the covenants and agreements in and by the said several Leases &c. respectively reserved and contained and which ought to be thenceforth by and on the part and behalf of the several Lessees and Assignees of the said premises respectively paid observed performed and kept so far as concerned or related to the said moiety or half part of the said Premises.

Covenant by the said Hannah Maria Rickford and Thomas Parker Rickford against Incumbrances

>The 6th Schedule to which the said Abstracting Indenture referred
>
>All that messuage tenement or Public House and Premises commonly called or known by the name or sign of 'The Pigeons' situate lying and being in the Parish of Saint Lawrence in Reading aforesaid on the North side of the said Street then called Friar Street formerly in the occupation of Robert Wilson late of George Williams then of Charles Hewitt and then of James Davies which said messuage or tenement and premises were demised

[p. 8]

and leased to the said Thomas Rickford and Charles Curry Bickham by a certain Indenture dated the 7th day of November 1835[1] and made between the Mayor Aldermen and Burgesses of Reading of the one part and the said Thomas Rickford and Charles Curry Bickham of the other part

Executed by the said Hannah Maria Rickford Thomas Parker Rickford and Thomas Hawkins and attested as to each by one witness

Receipt indorsed signed and witnessed

18th April 1856

Indenture of Mortgage made between the said Thomas Hawkins of the one part and the said Hannah Maria Rickford and Thomas Parker Rickford of the other part

Reciting that the said Hannah Maria Rickford and Thomas Parker Rickford had agreed to lend to the said Thomas Hawkins the sum of £4,000 out of monies belonging to them on a joint account on having the repayment thereof with Interest accrued as thereinafter appearing

It is witnessed that in consideration of the sum of £4,000 to the said Thomas Hawkins paid by the said Hannah Maria Rickford and Thomas Parker Rickford (receipt acknowledged) the said Thomas Hawkins did covenant for payment on the 18th day of October then next to the said Hannah Maria Rickford and Thomas Parker Rickford or the survivor of them or the executors or administrators of such survivor their or his assigns of the sum of £4,000 with Interest at £5 per cent per annum without any deduction

And it is lastly witnessed that in consideration of the Premises He the said Thomas Hawkins did thereby assign unto the said Hannah Maria Rickford and Thomas Parker Rickford

All those Leasehold messuages or tenements and hereditaments in the 4th 5th 6th and 8th Schedules thereunto annexed particularly mentioned and described with their and every of their appurtenances And all the estate &c.

To hold the same unto the said Hannah Maria Rickford and Thomas Parker Rickford their executors administrators and assigns for all the residue then to come of the several terms of years created by the

[p. 9]

several Leases in the said Schedules mentioned or referred to at the rents and subject to the Covenants agreements and conditions in and by the said Leases respectively reserved and contained and on the Tenants' or Lessees' part to be paid observed and performed

Proviso on payment of the said Principal and Interest monies as aforesaid for reassignment of the said Premises unto the said Thomas Hawkins his executors administrators or assigns or as he or they should direct for the then residue of the said several terms for which the same were respectively holden

Covenant by said Thomas Hawkins for payment of the Interest half yearly

---

1 Marginal note: sic. 11 December 1835.

Proviso that the said sum of £4,000 was money belonging to the said Hannah Maria Rickford and Thomas Parker Rickford upon a joint account at Equity as well as at Law

>Covenants by the said Thomas Hawkins that the said Leases were valid subsisting Leases – that he had good right to assign – for quiet enjoyment after default   free from Incumbrances – for further assurance – and to keep said Premises insured from loss by fire

Usual Power of Sale after default
Proviso not to sue until default
Proviso exempting purchasers from necessity to see to application of Purchase monies – Receipt Clause – As to application of Purchase Monies &c.

>The sixth Schedule
>Same as in the last abstracted Indenture
>Executed by the said Thomas Hawkins Hannah Maria Rickford and Thomas Parker Rickford and attested by one witness as to each
>Receipt for consideration money signed by the said Thomas Hawkins and witnessed

5th August 1856
Memorandum (annexed to last abstracted Indenture) that of the sum of £4,000 lent to Mr Hawkins on the security of the (thereto) annexed Indenture the sum of £2,908.6.7 belonged to Mrs Rickford and Captain Rickford as Trustees of the Will of Thomas Rickford Esquire deceased and the sum of £1,091.13.5 belonged to Mrs Rickford as her own property

>Signed by the said Hannah Maria Rickford and Thomas Parker Rickford

(xv)   Supplemental Abstract of the Title of Thomas Hawkins Esquire to a Messuage Tenement or Public House called 'The Pigeons' situate in Friar Street in Reading in the County of Berks for the residue of a Term of 80 years from Michaelmas 1789 (1863). Original in the Greyfriars Church Archive.

The previous document showed that on 7 November 1846 Charles Curry Bickham sold his half share of the Castle Streeet Brewery to Thomas Hawkins. This document proves Bickham's ownership prior to that date, that he had purchased it from Jonathan Tanner on 22 April 1835. The Pigeons public house is one of the properties involved in these purchases.

Bickham took out a £6,000 mortgage with John Gardner to enable him to complete the purchase. After John Gardner's death in February 1836, Bickham's mortgage was with Mary Gardner and James Agg Gardner. Much of this document revolved around this loan, including a repayment by Bickham of £500, only for him to re-borrow the sum again later.

21st July 1835
Indenture of Mortgage made between Charles Curry Bickham of Reading in the County of Berks Common Brewer of the one part and John Gardner[1] of Cheltenham in the County of Gloucester Esquire of the other part

Reciting (inter alia) that Jonathan Tanner (therein named) became possessed of the messuage tenement or Public House mentioned or described in Number 2 of the 6th Schedule (to now abstracting Indenture) under or by virtue of a Lease granted or agreed to be granted by the Mayor and Corporation of the Borough of Reading for the term of 99 years from the month of May 1789 at the yearly rent of £5[2]

And reciting that by an Indenture dated on or about the 22nd day of April 1835 and expressed to be made between Alfred Compigne Gentleman of the first part William Stephens Banker Herbert Lewis Woollen Draper and George Chisman Cornfactor Assignees of the Estate and Effects of the said Jonathan Tanner a Bankrupt of the second part the said Jonathan Tanner of the third part the said Charles Curry Bickham of the fourth part and Joseph Whatley Gentleman of the fifth part It was thereby thirdly witnessed that for the consideration therein expressed the said Alfred Compigne William Stephens Herbert Lewis and George Chisman Did assign and the said Jonathan Tanner Did grant assign and confirm unto the said Charles Curry Bickham his executors administrators and assigns One full and equal undivided Moiety half part or share of and in All those Leasehold messuages or tenements Inns and Public Houses Lands and all and singular other the Leasehold Premises respectively described and comprised in the 4th 5th and 6th Schedules to the Indenture then in recital and which said messuages or tenements Inns and Public Houses Lands and other Leasehold Premises were the same as were mentioned

---

1 Variously Gardner or Gardener.
2 This public house was the Pigeons. Note that the lease was for 80 years from May 1789, not 99 years as here.

[p. 2]

or described in the 4th 5th and 6th Schedules written under or annexed to the Abstracting Indenture and of and in their Appurtenances To hold the same unto the said Charles Curry Bickham his Executors Administrators and Assigns thenceforth for all the residue of the several and respective Terms for years granted and agreed to be granted of the said Leasehold Premises respectively as thereinbefore mentioned and which was then to come and unexpired Subject to the payment of the several yearly and other rents and fines upon renewal and to the observance and performance of the covenants and agreements by and in the said several Leases and Agreements for Leases respectively reserved and contained and agreed to be reserved and contained and which were or ought to be thenceforth by and on the part and behalf of the several Lessees or Assignees of the said Leasehold Premises respectively paid observed performed and kept so far as concerned or relate to the said one moiety or half part of the same premises

And reciting that the said Charles Curry Bickham had requested the said John Gardner to advance him the sum of £6,000 which the said John Gardner had agreed to do on having the repayment thereof secured to him as thereinafter expressed

It was witnessed that in consideration of the sum of £6,000 to the said Charles Curry Bickham paid by the said John Gardner receipt acknowledged the said Charles Curry Bickham Did (inter alia) grant bargain sell and demise unto the said John Gardner his Executors Administrators and assigns

> All those Leasehold messuages or tenements Inns and Public Houses lands and all and singular other the Leasehold Premises mentioned or described in the 4th 5th and 6th Schedules written under or annexed to the now abstracting Indenture And of and in All other the Leasehold Premises (if any) a Moiety or other part or share of and in which was comprised in and assigned by the thereinbefore recited Indenture of Release of the 22nd day of April 1835 And of and in all and singular the rights members and appurtenances to the said Leasehold messuages lands and other Premises belonging or in anywise appertaining

[p. 3]

> To hold the said moiety hereditaments and all and singular other the Premises thereinbefore demised or expressed or intended so to be unto the said John Gardner his executors administrators and assigns thenceforth for all the residue then unexpired of the several and respective Terms of years granted and agreed to be granted as thereinbefore was recited or mentioned and for all other the Term Estate and Interest in the Premises respectively thereby demised or intended so to be of the said Charles Curry Bickham except the last day of each of the same terms for years term estate and interest respectively

Proviso that if the said Charles Curry Bickham his heirs executors administrators or assigns or any of them should well and truly pay or cause to be paid to the said John Gardner his executors administrators or assigns the sum of £6,000 with half a years interest for the same after the rate of £5 for £100 for a year on the 21st day of January next ensuing the date of the now Abstracting Indenture without any deduction &c. then the Demises and other Conveyances thereby made or intended so to be should cease determine and be void to all intents and purposes whatsoever

Covenants by the said Charles Curry Bickham for payment of Principal and Interest – that he had good right to demise – for quiet enjoyment after default – for further assurance for payment of rents and observance of covenants reserved and contained in said Leases – to obtain renewals thereof when necessary – or to pay expenses thereof – and to keep Premises insured from loss by Fire

Declaration that all persons in whom the said moiety of the said Leasehold Premises should vest should stand possessed thereof In trust for the said John Gardner his heirs executors administrators and assigns respectively subject to the right of redemption subsisting therein by virtue of now Abstracting Indenture

Declaration that after default the said John Gardner his heirs executors administrators and assigns respectively might grant Leases of said Leasehold Premises for any term or terms not exceeding 14 years at a yearly rent

Power of Sale in case of Default

> The sixth Schedule thereinbefore referred to
> Number 2 All that messuage tenement or Public House and Premises commonly called or known by the name or sign of 'The Pigeons' situate in the Parish of

[p. 4]

> Saint Lawrence in Reading aforesaid on the North side of the said Street there called Friar Street and formerly in the occupation of Robert Wilson and then or lately of George Williams
> Executed by the said Charles Curry Bickham and attested by two witnesses
> Receipt for £6,000 indorsed signed by the said Charles Curry Bickham and witnessed

20th November 1838

Acknowledgement (indorsed) of having received £500 in part of the principal sum of £6,000 secured by the above Abstracted Indenture

> Signed by Mary Gardner and James Agg Gardner executrix and executor of the said John Gardner and witnessed

15th February 1842

Indenture (indorsed on last Abstracted Indenture) made between the said Charles Curry Bickham of the one part and the said Mary Gardner Widow and James Agg Gardner Esquire both of Cheltenham in the County of Gloucester of the other part

> Reciting that the said John Gardner departed this life on the 28th day of February 1836 having previously made and published his last Will and

Testament in writing of which he appointed the said Mary Gardner and James Agg Gardner (at the date of the Will and therein called James Agg) the executrix and executor and on the 23rd day of November 1838 the sum of £500 was paid by the said Charles Curry Bickham to the said Mary Gardner and James Agg Gardner as such executrix and executor as aforesaid in part satisfaction of the Principal sum of £6,000 secured by the hereinbefore abstracted Indenture

And reciting that the sum of £5,500 the remainder of such Principal sum still remained due to the said Mary Gardner and James Agg Gardner as such executrix and executor as aforesaid

And reciting that the said Charles Curry Bickham having occasion for the sum of £500 had applied to the said Mary Gardner and James Agg Gardner to advance the same to him which they had agreed to do on having the repayment thereof with interest secured to them in the manner thereinafter expressed

[p. 5]

It was witnessed that in consideration of the sum of £500 to the said Charles Curry Bickham paid by the said Mary Gardner and James Agg Gardner – receipt acknowledged – He the said Charles Curry Bickham did thereby Covenant for payment of the said sum of £500 and Interest for the same after the rate of £5 per cent per annum on the 15th day of August next ensuing the date thereof – and that all the undivided Moiety or equal half part or share of the said Charles Curry Bickham by the hereinbefore abstracted Indenture demised or assured of and in (inter alia) the Leasehold Messuages Tenements and Premises mentioned or described in the 6th Schedule written under or annexed to the hereinbefore Abstracted Indenture and every part and parcel of the same and the Appurtenances should be charged and chargeable with and be a Security for the payment to the said Mary Gardner and James Agg Gardner their executors administrators or assigns as well of the sum of £500 then lent with Interest as aforesaid as of the said sum of £5,500 and the Interest thereof and that all and singular the trusts powers and provisions contained in the hereinbefore Abstracted Indenture for the levying raising paying and securing of the sum of £6,000 thereby secured and Interest should be construed and read as if the sum of £500 then lent had formed part of the principal sum by that Indenture secured and then due and should be applicable and exercisable to and for the levying raising paying and securing as well of the said sum of £500 and the Interest thereof as of the said sum of £5,500 and the Interest of the same

Proviso that inasmuch as the sum of £500 so as aforesaid advanced and paid by the said Mary Gardner and James Agg Gardner belonged to them jointly on a joint account if either of them the said Mary Gardner and James Agg Gardner should die during the continuance of that Security the receipts in writing of the survivor of them her or his executors administrators or assigns should be effectual discharges for the said sum of £500 and the Interest thereof

Executed by the said Charles Curry Bickham Mary Gardner and James Agg Gardner and attested as to each by one witness
Receipt for £500 subscribed signed by the said Charles Curry Bickham and witnessed

(xvi)   Further Supplemental Abstract of the Title of Thomas Hawkins Esquire to a Messuage Tenement or Public House called 'The Pigeons', situate in Friar Street in Reading in the County of Berks for the residue of a term of 80 years from Michaelmas 1789 (1863). Original in the Greyfriars Church Archive.

Thomas Rickford owned a half share of the Castle Street Brewery, including the premises of the Pigeons. He had been granted, along with his partner Charles Curry Bickham, the Lease of the Pigeons by the Corporation on 11 December 1835.[1] On 7 November 1846 Bickham had sold his half share to Thomas Hawkins, and so Rickford and Hawkins were thenceforward co-partners of Castle Street Brewery.

In 1852, Thomas Rickford died and by his will of 9 June his half share in the Brewery (including the Lease of the Pigeons) passed to Hannah Maria Rickford and Thomas Parker Rickford. On 17 April 1856, they sold the half share in Castle Street Brewery to Thomas Hawkins. Hawkins took out a £4,000 mortgage with the Rickfords as part of the payment.[2]

This document deals with the transference of the ownership of the mortgage for £4,000, with Thomas Parker Rickford being replaced by Charles William Calvert and John Wills, thereby explaining their role in the following document.

3rd August 1863
Indenture of Appointment made between Hannah Maria Rickford of Bradenham in the County of Bucks Widow of the first part Thomas Parker Rickford of Donhead Cottages Fremantle in the Town and County of Southampton Esquire of the second part Charles William Calvert of Ockley Court Dorking in the County of Surrey Esquire and John Wills of No. 3 Great Carters Lane Doctors Commons in the City of London Gentlemen of the third part and the said Hannah Maria Rickford Charles William Calvert and John Wills of the fourth part

Reciting that Thomas Rickford late of Reading in the County of Berks Common Brewer deceased by his last Will and Testament bearing date the 9th day of June 1852 after making sundry pecuniary and other bequests devised unto and to the use of his wife the said Hannah Maria Rickford his said son Thomas Parker Rickford and Edward Vines of Reading aforesaid Esquire their Heirs and Assigns the residue of his real Estate and bequeathed to them their Executors Administrators and Assigns the residue

---
1 See Document II (xiii).
2 See Document II (xiv).

of his Personal Estate Upon trust to sell the said residuary real Estate (including Leaseholds) and to call in sell and convert into money his said residuary Personal Estate and to stand possessed of and interested in the monies which should arise by the ways and means aforesaid Upon trust thereout to pay the said Testators Debts and funeral and testamentary expenses and a certain Legacy given by that his Will and to lay out and invest the surplus or residue of the said Trust Monies in the Public Stocks or Funds of Great Britain or on Government or real Securities at Interest with power to alter vary and transfer the same as therein mentioned and to stand possessed of all the said Trust monies Stocks funds and securities and the Interest Dividends and annual produce thereof Upon trust during the life of his said wife Hannah Maria Rickford to pay to her or her assigns the Interest Dividends and produce of the whole of the said Trust monies Stocks funds and securities for her own use and benefit and from and after the decease of the said Hannah Maria Rickford Upon trust to pay assign or transfer one equal half part or share thereof to his said Son Thomas Parker Rickford his Heirs Executors Administrators and Assigns to and for his and their own absolute use and benefit and to receive the Interest Dividends

[p. 2]
and annual produce of the remaining equal half part thereof and to pay the same from time to time as and when it should become receivable and not by way of anticipation into the proper hands of the said Testators Daughter Maria Golding King during her life and for her own sole and separate use free from marital control as a strictly personal and inalienable provision
And after the decease of his said Daughter then upon trust to pay the said Interest Dividends and produce to her Husband Isaac King and his assigns during his natural life and after the decease of the survivor of his said Daughter and her said Husband Upon trust for the Child or Children or other Issue of his the said Testators Daughter as therein mentioned
And the said Testator did thereby nominate constitute and appoint his said Wife and Son and the said Edward Vines Executrix and Executors of his said Will
And further declared that if the Trustees thereby appointed or to be appointed as thereinafter mentioned any or either of them should happen to die or be desirous of being discharged from or refuse decline or become incapable to act in the trust thereby in them respectively reposed before the said Trusts should be fully executed performed or discharged then when and so often as the same should happen it should and might be lawful to and for the surviving or continuing Trustees or Trustee or the Executors or Administrators of the last surviving Trustee by any Deed or Deeds Instrument or Instruments in writing to be sealed and delivered by them him or her in the presence of and attested by one or more credible witness or witnesses from time to time to appoint any other person or persons to be a Trustee or Trustees in the stead or place of the Trustee or Trustees so dying or desiring to be discharged or refusing declining or becoming incapable to act as aforesaid

And that when and so often as any new Trustee or Trustees should be so appointed all the Trust Estates monies and Premises which should then be vested in the Trustee or Trustees so dying or desiring to be discharged or refusing declining or becoming incapable to act as aforesaid either solely or jointly with any other Trustee or Trustees should be conveyed assigned and transferred in such sort and manner so as that the same should and might be legally and effectually vested in the surviving or continuing Trustee or Trustees and such new or other Trustee or Trustees or if there should be no surviving or continuing Trustee then in such new Trustee or Trustees only upon the same trusts as were thereinbefore declared of and concerning the same Trust Estates Monies and Premises respectively or such of them as should might be then subsisting or capable of taking effect And that every such new Trustee or Trustees should and might in all things act and assist in the management carrying on and execution of the trusts to which he or they should be so appointed as fully and effectually

[p. 3]

to all intents effects constructions and purposes whatsoever as if he or they had been originally in and by the then reciting Will nominated a Trustee or Trustees and as the Trustee or Trustees in or to whose place such new Trustee or Trustees should respectively come or succeed were or was enabled to do or could or might have done if then living and continuing to act in the Trusts thereby in him or them referred

And reciting that the said Thomas Rickford by a Codicil to his said Will bearing date the 15th day of August 1854 revoked the appointment in the said Will contained of the said Edward Vines as Trustee and Executor of the said Will.

And reciting that the said Thomas Rickford died on the 5th day of February 1855 without having revoked or altered his said Will except by adding the said Codicil thereto and that the said Will and Codicil were duly proved by the said Hannah Maria Rickford and Thomas Parker Rickford in the Prerogative Court of the Archbishop of Canterbury on the 9th day of March 1855.

And reciting that the residuary Estate of the said Thomas Rickford deceased then consisted of the sum of £2,908.6.7 invested with other monies of the said Hannah Maria Rickford amounting altogether to the sum of £4,000 on the security of an Indenture of Mortgage bearing date the 18th day of April 1856 and made between Thomas Hawkins of the one part and the said Hannah Maria Rickford and Thomas Parker Rickford of the other part.

And reciting that the said Thomas Parker Rickford was desirous of being discharged from the trusts of the thereinbefore recited Will of the said Thomas Rickford.

And reciting that the said Hannah Maria Rickford had requested the said Charles William Calvert and John Wills to become Trustees of the said Will in the place of the said Thomas Parker Rickford which they had agreed to do.

And reciting that it appeared by the Certificate of the Chief Clerk of His Honour, Vice Chancellor, Sir Richard Torin Kindersley the Judge to whose Court a certain cause of Wyndham v. Rickford was attached made in the said cause and bearing date the 31st day of July 1863 that the now abstracting Indenture had been approved and settled by the said Judge.

It is witnessed that in pursuance of the said Agreement and in execution of the power for that purpose given to her by the thereinbefore recited Will of the said Thomas Rickford and of all other powers enabling her in that behalf. She the said Hannah Maria Rickford did by the now Abstracting Indenture or Instrument in writing sealed and delivered by her in the presence of and attested by one credible witness appoint the said Charles

[p. 4]
William Calvert and John Wills to be Trustees of the said Will in the stead or place of the said Thomas Parker Rickford

And reciting that by an Indenture bearing even date with the now abstracting Indenture and made between the said Hannah Maria Rickford and Thomas Parker Rickford of the first part the said Charles William Calvert and John Wills of the second part and the said Hannah Maria Rickford Charles William Calvert and John Wills of the third part the said sum of £4,000 and the Interest thereof had been assigned by the said Hannah Maria Rickford and Thomas Parker Rickford unto the said Hannah Maria Rickford Charles William Calvert and John Wills their executors administrators and assigns And the Securities for the same had been vested in the said Hannah Maria Rickford Charles William Calvert and John Wills their heirs executors administrators and assigns respectively according to the nature and tenure thereof.

It is also witnessed that it is thereby agreed and declared between and by the said parties thereto that the said Hannah Maria Rickford Charles William Calvert and John Wills their executors administrators and assigns should stand and be possessed of and interested in the said sum of £4,000 and the Interest thereof so assigned to them as aforesaid as to the said Principal sum of £2,908.6.7 part thereof and the Interest for the same sum.

> Upon and for the trusts intents and purposes and with under and subject to the powers provisos and conditions in the thereinbefore recited Will of the said Thomas Rickford expressed and contained of and concerning his residuary Estate or such of the same Trusts intents and purposes as were then subsisting and capable of taking effect.

And as to the sum of £1,091.13.5 the residue of the said sum of £4,000 and the Interest thereof.

> In trust for the said Hannah Maria Rickford her Executors Administrators and Assigns absolutely.
>
> Executed by the said Thomas Parker Rickford Charles William Calvert and John Wills and attested by one witness.

Certificate (in margin of said abstracted Indenture) by Chief Clerk of Vice Chancellor Kindersley's approval – dated 31st July 1863.

3rd August 1863

Indenture of Transfer of Mortgage made between the said Hannah Maria Rickford and Thomas Parker Rickford of the first part the said Charles William Calvert and John Wills of the second part and the said Hannah Maria Rickford Charles William Calvert and John Wills of the third part.

Reciting the Indenture of Mortgage of the 18th day of April 1856

[p. 5]
    (abstracted in first Abstract).[1]

And reciting that the said principal sum of £4,000 still remained due and owing on the security of the same Indenture together with Interest thereon from the [blank] day of [blank] then last.

And reciting that the said sum of £4,000 had become vested in Equity in the said Hannah Maria Rickford Charles William Calvert and John Wills.

And reciting that the said Hannah Maria Rickford and Thomas Parker Rickford had accordingly agreed to assign the said Mortgage Debt of £4,000 and the Interest thereof unto the said Hannah Maria Rickford Charles William Calvert and John Wills and to assign (inter alia) the Leasehold Hereditaments comprised in the 6th Schedule thereto unto the said Hannah Maria Rickford Charles William Calvert and John Wills their executors administrators and assigns. Subject to the equity of redemption subsisting in the said several Premises.

And reciting that it appeared by the Certificate of the Chief Clerk of His Honour Vice Chancellor Sir Richard Torin Kindersley the Judge to whose Court a certain cause of Wyndham v. Rickford was attached made in the said cause and bearing date the 31st day of July 1863 that the now abstracting Indenture had been approved and settled by the said Judge.

It is witnessed that in pursuance of the said agreement and in consideration of the Premises They the said Hannah Maria Rickford and Thomas Parker Rickford Did and each of them Did thereby grant bargain sell and assign unto the said Hannah Maria Rickford Charles William Calvert and John Wills their Executors Administrators and Assigns.

> All that the said Principal sum of £4,000 secured by the thereinbefore recited Indenture of the 18th day of April 1856 together with all Interest then due and thenceforth to accrue due in respect thereof Together with all the benefit of the power of Sale and all other remedies for the recovery of the said Principal sum and the Interest thereof.

Together with full power and authority to demand sue for recover and receive and give valid receipts for the said sum of £4,000 and Interest in the Names or Name of the said Hannah Maria Rickford and Thomas Parker Rickford or the survivor of them or the executors or administrators of such survivor or their his or her being previously to the bringing or prosecuting of any action suit proceeding claim or demand in their or his or her Name or Names and at all times

---

1 See Document II (xiv), document pages 8 and 9.

indemnified and kept indemnified against all actions suits proceedings costs damages claims and demands which might be brought prosecuted

[p. 6]
sustained or incurred or which may become payable by reason of any action suit proceeding claim or demand which may be brought or prosecuted in the Names or Name of the said Hannah Maria Rickford and Thomas Parker Rickford or the survivor of them or the executors or administrators of such survivor by virtue of the power or authority thereinbefore given.

To have hold and receive the said Principal sum Interest and premises thereby assigned unto the said Hannah Maria Rickford Charles William Calvert and John Wills their Executors Administrators and Assigns absolutely.

And it is also witnessed that in further pursuance of the said agreement and in consideration of the Premises they the said Hannah Maria Rickford and Thomas Parker Rickford Did and each of them Did thereby bargain sell assign and transfer unto the said Hannah Maria Rickford Charles William Calvert and John Wills their executors administrators and assigns.

All the Leasehold Hereditaments in (inter alia) the 6th Schedule thereunto particularly mentioned and described with all and every of their appurtenances

And all the Estate &c.

To hold the same unto the said Hannah Maria Rickford Charles William Calvert and John Wills their executors administrators and assigns thenceforth for all the rest residue and remainder then to come and unexpired of the several terms of years in the several parts thereof respectively created.

Subject as all the said Premises respectively to the equity of Redemption then subsisting therein on payment of the said sum of £4,000 and Interest.

Covenant by the said Hannah Maria Rickford and Thomas Parker Rickford that they had done no act to incumber.

Proviso and Declaration by the said Hannah Maria Rickford Charles William Calvert and John Wills that the said sum of £4,000 belonged to them on a joint account and that in case any or either of them should die in the life time of the others or other of them the receipt or receipts in writing of the Survivors or Survivor of them should effectually discharge the Person or Persons paying the same sum and the Interest thereof from all responsibility as to the application thereof.

The Sixth Schedule to said abstracted Indenture.

All that Messuage Tenement or Public House commonly called or known by the name or sign of 'The Pigeons' situate lying and being in the parish of Saint Lawrence in Reading aforesaid on the North side of the said Street there called Friar Street [p. 7] formerly in the occupation of Robert Wilson late of George Williams then of Charles Hewitt and then or late of James Davis which said Messuage or Tenement and Premises were demised and leased to the said Thomas Rickford and Charles Curry Bickham by a certain indenture dated the 7th day of November 1835 and made between The Mayor Aldermen and Burgesses of the Borough of Reading of the one part and the said Thomas Rickford and Charles Curry Bickham of the other part.

Executed by the said Thomas Parker Rickford Charles William Calvert and John Wills and attested by one witness.

Certificate (in margin of said last abstracted Indenture) by Chief Clerk of Vice Chancellor's approval – Dated 31st July 1863.

(xvii) Assignment of the 'Pigeons' Public House in Friar Street to The Venerable Archdeacon Phelps (1863). Original indenture in the Greyfriars Church Archive.

This indenture signs over the remaining years on the Lease of the Pigeons public house from Thomas Hawkins to Rev William Whitmarsh Phelps. The building and land had already been purchased, by Mr Phelps on 23 April 1862.[1] By this date the Pigeons had been demolished, and Greyfriars Church had been restored and reconsecrated.

Dated 21 December 1863.

This Indenture made the twenty first day of December in the year of our Lord one thousand eight hundred and sixty three

Between Thomas Hawkins of Reading in the County of Berks Common Brewer of the first part Hannah Maria Rickford of Bradenham in the County of Buckingham Widow Charles William Calvert of Ockley Court Dorking in the County of Surrey Esquire and John Wills of Number 3 Great Carters Lane Doctors Commons in the City of London Gentleman of the second part and the Venerable and Very Reverend William Whitmarsh Phelps Archdeacon of Carlisle of Carlisle in the County of Cumberland of the third part

Whereas the said Thomas Hawkins is possessed of the Messuage tenement or Public House and premises hereinafter described and hereby assigned or intended so to be with the appurtenances for the residue of a Term of four score Years from the twenty ninth day of September one thousand seven hundred and eighty nine granted thereof by the Mayor Aldermen and Burgesses of the Borough of Reading aforesaid by an Indenture of Lease dated the eleventh day of December one thousand eight hundred and thirty five at the Yearly rent of Five Pounds and subject to the conditions and covenants therein mentioned subject nevertheless (with other hereditaments) to an Indenture of Mortgage

---

1 See Document II (xix).

dated the eighteenth day of April one thousand and eight hundred and fifty six for securing to the said Hannah Maria Rickford and Thomas Parker Rickford the sum of Four thousand Pounds and Interest as therein mentioned and which principal sum of Four thousand Pounds and Interest and the Securities for the same have now become vested in the said Hannah Maria Rickford Charles William Calvert and John Wills by means of an Indenture dated on or about the third day of August one thousand eight hundred and sixty three and made or expressed to be made between the said Hannah Maria Rickford and Thomas Parker Rickford Esquire of the first part the said Charles William Calvert and John Wills of the second part and the said Hannah Maria Rickford Charles William Calvert and John Wills of the third part

And whereas the said Thomas Hawkins has contracted with the said William Whitmarsh Phelps for the Sale to him of the said Messuage tenement Public House and premises hereinafter described and intended to be hereby assigned at the price or sum of Two hundred and ten Pounds And it has been agreed that the said sum of Two hundred and ten Pounds should be paid to the said Hannah Maria Rickford Charles William Calvert and John Wills in part discharge of the principal moneys and Interest secured to them by the hereinbefore recited Indenture of Mortgage they the said Hannah Maria Rickford Charles William Calvert and John Wills have consented to concur in these Presents in manner hereinafter mentioned

Now this Indenture witnesseth that in pursuance of the said agreement and in consideration of the sum of Two hundred and ten Pounds Sterling money in hand paid by the said William Whitmarsh Phelps at the request and by the direction of the said Thomas Hawkins (testified by his executing these Presents) to the said Hannah Maria Rickford Charles William Calvert and John Wills at or immediately before the execution hereof the receipt whereof they the said Hannah Maria Rickford Charles William Calvert and John Wills do and each of them doth hereby acknowledge and from the same do and each of them doth acquit release and discharge the said Thomas Hawkins his heirs executors and administrators and also the said William Whitmarsh Phelps his heirs executors administrators and assigns for ever by these Presents They the said Hannah Maria Rickford Charles William Calvert and John Wills at the request and by the direction of the said Thomas Hawkins testified as aforesaid Do and each of them Doth by these Presents bargain sell assign transfer set over and release And the said Thomas Hawkins Doth by these Presents bargain sell assign transfer set over and confirm unto the said William Whitmarsh Phelps his executors administrators and assigns

All that Messuage tenement or Public House and premises commonly called or known by the name or Sign of the 'Pigeons' situate lying and being in the Parish of Saint Lawrence in Reading aforesaid on the North side of the said Street now called Friar Street formerly in the occupation of Robert Wilson late of George Williams since of Charles Hewitt afterwards of James Davies which said Messuage or tenement and premises were demised and leased to Thomas Rickford and Charles Curry Bickham by a certain Indenture dated the eleventh day of December one thousand eight hundred and thirty five hereinbefore recited And all and singular houses outhouses edifices buildings ways waters water courses easements rights privileges and appurtenances whatsoever to the same Messuage and premises belonging or appertaining And all the estate right title interest term and terms of years yet to come and unexpired benefit property claim and demand whatsoever both at law and in equity of them the said Thomas Hawkins Hannah Maria Rickford Charles William Calvert and John Wills

To have and to hold the said Messuage tenement or Public House and all other the premises hereby assigned or intended so to be with their appurtenances unto the said William Whitmarsh Phelps his executors administrators and assigns from the day of the date of these Presents for all the residue now to come and unexpired of the said Term of Four Score Years created by the said Indenture of Lease subject to the Rent covenants and conditions therein contained on the part of the Lessees their executors administrators and assigns to be observed and performed But freed and discharged from all principal moneys and interest due and owing upon or intended to be secured by and from all claims and demands under the said Indenture of the eighteenth day of April one thousand eight hundred and fifty six and the third day of August one thousand eight hundred and sixty three

And each of them the said Hannah Maria Rickford Charles William Calvert and John Wills for herself and himself respectively and her and his heirs executors and administrators and as to and concerning only her and his respective acts deeds and defaults doth hereby covenant with the said William Whitmarsh Phelps his executors administrators and assigns that they the said Hannah Maria Rickford Charles William Calvert and John Wills respectively have not at any time heretofore made done executed permitted or knowingly suffered or been party or privy to any act deed matter or thing whatsoever by means whereof the said Messuage tenement or Public House hereditaments and premises intended to be hereby assigned or any part thereof are or is or may be charged or incumbered or in any manner prejudicially affected in title charge estate or otherwise howsoever

And the said Thomas Hawkins doth hereby for himself his heirs executors and administrators covenant with the said William Whitmarsh Phelps his executors administrators and assigns in manner following (that is to say) that for and notwithstanding any act deed matter or thing by them the said Thomas Hawkins Hannah Maria Rickford Charles William Calvert and John Wills or any of them made done or willingly suffered to the contrary they the said Thomas Hawkins Hannah Maria Rickford Charles William Calvert and John Wills now have in themselves or one of them hath in himself or herself good right full power and absolute authority to assign and assure the Messuage tenement or Public House and premises hereby assigned or intended so to be and every part and parcel of the same with the appurtenances in manner hereinbefore expressed concerning the same And also that it shall be lawful for the said William Whitmarsh Phelps his executors administrators and assigns peaceably and quietly to hold and enjoy the

[Second Sheet]
said hereditaments and premises hereby assigned as aforesaid and to receive and take the rents issues and profits thereof from the day of the date hereof for and during the remainder yet to come and unexpired of the aforesaid term of

Four Score Years without the lawful let suit trouble hindrance interruption or denial of or by the said Thomas Hawkins Hannah Maria Rickford Charles William Calvert and John Wills or any or either of them their or any or either of their executors or administrators or any other person or persons having or lawfully claiming or who shall or may hereafter have or lawfully claim any estate right title trust or interest in to or out of the same premises by from through or under or in trust for them any or either of them or any other person or persons whomsoever And that free and clear and freely and clearly and absolutely exonerated and discharged from all incumbrances whatsoever made done committed or suffered by them the said Thomas Hawkins Hannah Maria Rickford Charles William Calvert and John Wills or either of them or any other person or persons whomsoever now or hereafter rightfully claiming or possessing any estate right title or interest from through under or in trust for them or either of them

And further that he the said Thomas Hawkins and every other person having or lawfully claiming of any estate right title trust or interest in to or out of the said premises hereby assigned or any part thereof by from through under or in trust for the said Thomas Hawkins or any other person or persons whomsoever shall and will at any time or times hereafter during the said Term of Four Score Years upon the request and at the proper costs and charges of the said William Whitmarsh Phelps his executors administrators or assigns make do and execute or cause and procure to be made done and executed all and every such further or other lawful and reasonable act deed assignment and assurance in the Law whatsoever for the further better more perfectly and absolutely assigning assuring and confirming the said premises hereby assigned or intended so to be or any part thereof with the appurtenances unto the said William Whitmarsh Phelps his executors administrators and assigns for the remainder then to come and unexpired of the said Term of Four Score Years

And whereas inasmuch as the several deeds evidences and writings mentioned and comprised in the Schedule hereunder written relate as well to the said Messuage Tenement Public House and premises hereby assigned or intended so to be as to other hereditaments of greater value belonging to the said Thomas Hawkins and now comprised in the said Mortgage Securities it hath been agreed that the said Hannah Maria Rickford and Thomas Hawkins shall covenant for the production of the same in manner hereinafter contained

Now this Indenture further witnesseth that in consideration of the premises the said Hannah Maria Rickford for herself her executors and administrators so long as the Deeds evidences and writings specified in the Schedule to these Presents shall be in her custody or power as such Mortgagee or Transferee as aforesaid but not otherwise and also for the purpose of binding her assigns so far as it is competent for her so to do without creating any personal liability on her part for the acts or defaults of such assigns And the said Thomas Hawkins doth for himself his executors and administrators hereby covenant with the said William Whitmarsh Phelps his executors administrators and assigns in manner following that they the said Hannah Maria Rickford and Thomas Hawkins or one of them or his or her executors administrators or assigns shall and will from time to time and at all times hereafter (unless hindered or prevented by fire or other inevitable accident) upon the reasonable request and at the costs of the said William Whitmarsh Phelps his executors administrators or assigns produce and shew forth in England unto the said William Whitmarsh Phelps his executors administrators or assigns or his or their Counsel Attorney Agent or Solicitor or to or before any Court or Courts of Law or Equity or at or upon any Commission for the examination of Witnesses or otherwise as occasion shall require the several Indentures specified in the Schedule hereunder written in manifestation support or defence of the Title of the said William Whitmarsh Phelps his executors administrators or assigns to the said Messuage Tenement Public House and premises hereinbefore assigned or intended so to be or any part thereof And also shall and will at the like request and costs of the said William Whitmarsh Phelps his executors administrators or assigns make and deliver to the said William Whitmarsh Phelps his executors administrators or assigns true and attested Copies Extracts or Abstracts of and from the same Deeds evidences and writings or any of them and permit the same to be examined and compared with the Originals either by the said William Whitmarsh Phelps his executors administrators or assigns or by any other person or persons whom he or they should for that purpose appoint

In Witness whereof the said parties to these Presents have hereunto set their hands and seals the day and year first within written

The Schedule to which the above written Indenture refers

21st July 1835	Indenture between Charles Curry Bickham of the one part and John Gardener of the other part and Receipt indorsed thereon dated 23rd November 1838
15th February 1842	Indenture between the said Charles Curry Bickham of the one part and Mary Gardener Widow and James Agg Gardener of the other part
7th November 1846	Indenture between the said Charles Curry Bickham of the first part the said Mary Gardener and James Agg Gardener of the second part Edith Agg of the third part the said Thomas Hawkins of the fourth part and Grantham Robert Dodd of the fifth part
17th April 1854[1]	Indenture between the said Hannah Maria Rickford and Thomas Parker Rickford of the first part the said Thomas Hawkins of the second part and the said William Hobbs of the third part
18th April 1854	Indenture of Mortgage between the said Thomas Hawkins of the one part and the said Hannah Maria Rickford and Thomas Parker Rickford of the other part

---

1 Actually 1856. The next entry should also be 1856.

3rd April[1] 1863 Indenture of Transfer between the said Hannah Maria Rickford and Thomas Parker Rickford of the first part the said Charles William Calvert and John Wills of the second part and the said Hannah Maria Rickford Charles William Calvert and John Wills of the third part

[Signed and sealed] Thomas Hawkins
  Hannah Maria Rickford
    Charles William Calvert   John Wills

[On reverse]
Received the day and year first within written of and from the within named William Whitmarsh Phelps the sum of Two hundred and ten Pounds being the consideration Money within expressed to be paid by him to us.
£210.

[Signed] Hannah Maria Rickford C. W. Calvert   Jn Wills

Witness to the Signing by Hannah Maria Rickford
[Signed] Isaac King, Clerk, Magistrate for the County of Buckingham

Witness to the signing by Charles William Calvert and John Wills respectively
[Signed] Geo. Brocklesby

Signed Sealed and Delivered by the within named Hannah Maria Rickford in the presence of
[Signed] Isaac King, Clerk, Magistrate for the County of Buckingham

Signed Sealed and Delivered by the within named Charles William Calvert and John Wills respectively in the presence of
[Signed] Geo. Brocklesby, Clerk to Messrs Preston & Ley, Solicitors
16 Water Lane, Great Tower Street, London

Signed Sealed and Delivered by the within named Thomas Hawkins in the presence of
[Signed] Henry Collins, Solicitor Reading

---

1 Actually 3 August 1863.

(xviii) Correspondence: From J. J. Blandy, Town Clerk, on behalf of Reading Corporation, to John Neale, Purchaser's Solicitor, concerning the payment of £350 for the Pigeons public house (1861–2). Originals/copies in Greyfriars Church Archive.

This correspondence encompasses the disagreement between the Town Clerk of Reading and the Purchaser's Solicitor over the method of payment of the purchase money for the Pigeons public house. Mr Blandy, for the Council, wanted the money to be available for the works needed at the new Police Buildings at High Bridge House, but Mr Neale believed that the letter of the law meant that the money had to be deposited in the Bank of England, which meant that the Council could only use it for the purchase of land, and not this refurbishment.

Letter 1
To John Neale Esquire

Reading, 2nd December 1861

Dear Sir,
    Corporation to Phelps

On looking at this Draft Conveyance I see you have made the Secretary of State a party to it. This is quite unnecessary as the Corporation is advised and will only lead to delay and perhaps to difficulty as no application has been made to the Secretary of State for his sanction to the Sale. I trust therefore you will not desire to retain him as a party to the Deed. To satisfy you that you may safely dispense with him I send for your perusal a Case laid before Mr Rudall on the point and his opinion thereon, together with a Case laid before the Recorder and his opinion to which that of Mr Rudall refers.

You also recite payment of a portion of the purchase money into the Bank of England under the Act of 2 & 3 Vic. Cap. 40. This is at variance with the prayer of the Memorial and the Answer of the Lords of the Treasury. You will find by the Letter from their Secretary, which is set out at length in the Abstract, that they have consented to the whole £1250 being paid to the Borough Treasurer for the purpose of the Works at High Bridge House, and it is the intention of the Council so to apply it, but this cannot be done if the £350 is paid into the Bank, as it must then be laid out in the purchase of land under the Order of the Court of Chancery. I hope therefore that you will see no reason for not paying the whole £1250 to the Treasurer and altering the Draft Conveyance accordingly.

I was going to have perused the Draft and to have altered it in accordance with the above suggestions, but it occurred to me that you might prefer to have my views before you in this form and to alter the Draft for yourself.

Other matters have occupied my attention since the 16th ult. when I received the Draft, so that I could not give it earlier attention but if you can [cut page – probable text 'return it'] to me at once I can now dispose of it.

    I am, Dear Sir, Yours truly, J. J. Blandy Town Clerk

PS Shall I arrange with Messrs Alleston & Co for your securing the remainder of the Deeds in London?

Letter 2
To J. Neale Esquire

Friar Street, 7th December 1861

Dear Sir,

Corporation to Phelps

I have read Mr Whitaker's Opinion and with every respect for that Gentleman, must say that I think it quite unnecessary and incorrect that the £350 should be paid into the Bank of England, and if you insist upon doing this, I must return the draft Conveyance unapproved, and shall advise the Corporation to decline to complete the Contract.

The Local Act of 2 & 3 Vic. cap. 40 with an extract from the Schedule shewing that the 'Pigeons' property was embraced by it, was fully set out in the Memorial to the Lords of the Treasury, and the Act 23 Vic. cap. 16 was also referred to so that their Lordships had all necessary information before them at the time they gave their sanction to the appropriation of the £1250 to the works at the new Police Buildings, and as the Lords of the Treasury are the acknowledged Conservators of the property of Corporations, it cannot be supposed that they would have authorized such an application of the money if they had not been satisfied that they had the power to do so, and I do not think it is for the Corporation or the purchaser to say that the sanction so given is ultra vires.

To you it may appear a matter of indifference whether the purchase money is paid into the Bank of England or to the Borough Treasurer, but it is not so to the Corporation. If paid into the Bank it must be reinvested in land and cannot be applied to the erection of Police Buildings and the Corporation will be driven to the necessity of borrowing and charging the Town with £350 more as a Mortgage Debt probably at £2 per cent more Interest than they will be receiving for the money invested and they will be obliged to memorialize the Treasury for these further powers to borrow, the consent given being limited to £850 on the ground that with the £1250 it would be all that was wanted, and arrangements have been entered into by the Corporation upon that basis. In short, the mode in which you propose to deal with the purchase money will be attended with inconvenience in every form, without as it appears to me, any real necessity for it.

Have you considered this, or thought only of the trifling risk to which (under the worst circumstances that can arise) your Client may be exposed?

It is assumed (for there is no proof of its being a fact) that the 'Pigeons' property came to the Corporation under the Charter of Queen Elizabeth. That it is therefore liable conjointly with nearly all the other properties of the Corporation to the expense of repairing certain roads and Bridges and a payment of £10 a year to the Master of the Grammar School. That therefore the purchase money must be paid into the Bank of England because that mode of payment is prescribed by a Local Act which enables the Corporation to sell free from those particular liabilities. But the Lords of the Treasury have thought fit to sanction another mode of payment. Evidence of this will be given by two of their Lordships being made parties to and executing the Conveyance.

The receipt of the Treasurer will be endorsed, and the Corporation will covenant for quiet enjoyment free from incumbrances. Surely this is sufficient to protect the purchaser from all probable claims, and it is difficult to conceive in what way the validity of such a Conveyance can be impeached. At all events I cannot advise the Corporation to consent to the mode of payment you propose, and if you insist upon it, I fear it must end in their declining to execute a Conveyance.

I am, Dear Sir, Yours truly, J. J. Blandy Town Clerk

Letter 3
To John Neale Esquire
Friar Street, 12 December 1861

Dear Sir,
Corporation to Phelps

I do not see how we can refer the question to Counsel without incurring expense and delay which we all desire to avoid, and probably no opinion of Counsel would be altogether satisfactory. I have therefore written to the Lords of the Treasury on the subject and as soon as I hear from them I will communicate further with you.

I am, Dear Sir, Yours truly, J. J. Blandy Town Clerk

Letter 4
To John Neale Esquire
Friar Street, 31 December 1861

Dear Sir,
Corporation to Phelps

I have heard from the Lords of the Treasury who will be satisfied if the questions referred to in my letter to you of the 7th instant are settled between us in the manner proposed by yours of the 9th. I would therefore suggest that the papers should be laid before Mr W. Rudall (of whom I believe you have some knowledge) to advise between both parties at their joint expense.

If you concur in this suggestion please write me a line to that effect, and I will immediately lay the necessary Instructions before Mr Rudall.

I am, Dear Sir, Yours truly, J. J. Blandy Town Clerk

Letter 5
To John Neale Esquire
Friar Street, 8 January 1862

Dear Sir,
Corporation to Phelps

I send you the Draft Case as I propose to send it to Mr Rudall and if you will let me have it back approved in time for its being copied today I will have it laid before him tomorrow.

Yours truly, J. J. Blandy Town Clerk

Case for Mr W. Rudall to advise as within:

Herewith is sent the Copy of a Contract between the above parties for the sale and purchase of certain Properties in the Borough of Reading which are to form the site of a new Church requiring consecration.

Also, Copy of a Local Act (2 & 3 Vic. C 40) enabling the Corporation to sell certain of their Corporate Properties discharged from certain liabilities to which they were made subject by the Letters Patent of Queen Elizabeth in the Act recited.

A portion of the property agreed to be sold to Mr Phelps, viz the Pigeons Public House, is Scheduled to the Local Act and therefore has been assumed to have been derived by the Corporation from the Grant of Queen Elizabeth although the property cannot be identified with any thing specifically mentioned in the Letters Patent. The other Property agreed to be sold to Mr Phelps and which adjoins the Pigeons was granted to the Corporation by Henry 8th but the Pigeons cannot be distinctly identified as part of it.

It will be seen from the Local Act that the purchase moneys of any of the properties comprised in the Schedule thereto which may be sold are to be paid into the Bank of England to the account of the Accountant General Exparte the Corporation and to be by him invested in Exchange Bills until they can be reinvested in the purchase of Real Estate to become subject to the aforesaid liabilities.

The accompanying Memorial was presented to the Lords of the Treasury for their sanction to the sale to Mr Phelps and to the appropriation of the purchase money or so much thereof as their Lordships should see fit to certain Works in the Memorial particularly mentioned.

The following was their Lordships' Answer to the Memorial (set out Letter)

It will be seen from the above that the sanction given to the payment of the whole amount of Mr Phelps's purchase money to the Borough Treasurer – virtually supersedes the direction of the Local Act of 2 & 3 Vic. C 40 as to the payment of any part of the purchase money into the Bank of England.

This sanction of the Lords of the Treasury is based on the Act of 23 Vic C 16 which is sent herewith.

Mr Phelps's Solicitor objects to the whole £1250 being paid to the Borough Treasurer and proposes to pay so much thereof as represents the Pigeons Property (viz £350) into the Bank of England in accordance with the directions of the Local Act contending that the Act of 23rd Vic C16 deals only with the interests of the Corporation and not those of third parties and neither repeals or affects the Local Act 2nd & 3rd Vic C 40. The Corporation object to this and wish the whole purchase money paid to the Treasurer but Mr Phelps's Solicitor having declined the Town Clerk wrote the following letter to the Lords of the Treasury to which the accompanying reply has been received (Set out Letters)

As the Lords of the Treasury leave the question to be decided by the Legal Advisers of the parties they have agreed to refer it to the decision of Mr W. Rudall who is therefore requested to peruse the accompanying papers and to advise on behalf of both parties.

Whether it is proper that the whole purchase money of £1250 should be paid to the Treasurer of the Borough Fund or whether so much thereof as relates to the 'Pigeons' Property, which is one of the properties scheduled to the Local Act, must be paid into the Bank of England in order to its being conveyed free from the liabilities in such act referred to.

Letter 6
1862
Corporation to Phelps: Mr W. Rudall's Opinion

16.1.62 Made copy for Mr Phelps J. W. H. D.

Blandy, Town Clerk

Copy Opinion
I am of opinion that so much of the purchase money as is attributable to the 'Pigeons' property being one of the properties scheduled to the Local Act must be paid into the Bank of England, in the manner directed by the 2nd section of that Act.

The Act of the 23 of Vic. cap 16 and the other general acts relating to Municipal Corporations, do not affect the Local Act without express words of reference; and I think that the directions for the application of the purchase money contained in the first letter of the Lords of the Treasury and recalled by their second letter, were at least to the extent of the amount of purchase money above referred to, beyond all doubt ultra vires, See the recent case of Fitzgerald v Champnoys 2 Johnson & Hern 3/ And see the Judgment of Lord Turner in the Trustees of the Birkenhead Docks v Laird 4 De Geo M & G J 32 S. C. 18 Jur 883.

    [signed] William Rudall, Lincolns Inn, January 14. 1862

Letter 7
To J. Neale Esquire
                                            Friar Street, 15th January 1862
Dear Sir,
    Corporation to Phelps
    I have today received Mr Rudall's opinion of which I send you a copy – and as he concurs in the view taken by Mr Whittaker I shall tomorrow send the draft Conveyance to the Lords of the Treasury for approval.
    I am, Dear Sir, Yours truly, J. J. Blandy Town Clerk

Letter 8
1862
Corporation to Phelps

Letter of Town Clerk to The Right Honourable, The Lords Commissioners of Her Majesty's Treasury and Letter in reply.

Reading, 16th January 1862

My Lords,

<u>Corporation of Reading to Phelps</u>

With reference to a Letter I addressed to your Lordships on the 11th December last and one from your Lordships' Secretary to the Mayor of this Borough of the 24th of that month I now beg to inform your Lordships that the matter in question has been submitted for the opinion of Counsel and that the parties are advised that so much of the purchase money as relates to the 'Pigeons' property viz £350 must be paid into the Bank of England in the manner directed by the second Section of the Local Act of 2 & 3 Vic. cap. 40 and I am therefore directed on behalf of the Council of this Borough to request that your Lordships will be pleased to vary the approval expressed in the letter of your Lordships' Secretary of the 25th July last to the Mayor of Reading by directing that so much of the purchase money as relates to the Bridewell property only be applied towards the cost of the works at High Bridge House and that the sum of £1150 instead of £800 be raised by Mortgage in the manner previously directed by your Lordships.

I enclose the Draft Conveyance to Mr Phelps for the approval of your Lordships' Solicitor and have the honour to be

My Lords, Your Lordships' Most obedient humble servant

J. J. Blandy Town Clerk

The Right Honourable The Lords Commissioners of Her Majesty's Treasury

Letter 9
[Reply from The Lords Commissioners of Her Majesty's Treasury to J. J. Blandy, Town Clerk]

Treasury Chambers, 24th January 1862

Sir,

The Lords Commissioners of Her Majesty's Treasury have had before them the letter from the Town Clerk of Reading dated the 16th Instant, and its Inclosure (herewith returned) further relative to the sale of certain Corporate property sanctioned by this Board, and the investment of the proceeds, and I am directed by their Lordships to acquaint you that as the arrangements now proposed differs both in regard to the amount to be raised by Mortgage as to the application of the proceeds of the sale from that contained in the prayer of the Memorial forwarded to this Board in June last, My Lords cannot entertain the proposal until it has been submitted to them in a fresh Memorial after due notice has been given.

I am, Sir, Your obedient servant F. Peel

Letter 10
To John Neale Esquire

Friar Street, 25 January 1862

Dear Sir,
    Corporation to Phelps

I send you copy of the Letter I wrote on the 16th instant to the Lords of the Treasury and of the reply which has been this morning received. Greatly as I regret the delay and inconvenience which must now occur, nothing but the view you have felt it necessary to take of the Title and your proposal to depart from the course prescribed by the Lords of the Treasury as to payment of the Purchase money has got us into this dilemma.

    I am, Dear Sir, Yours truly, J. J. Blandy Town Clerk

Letter 11
To J. Neale Esquire

Friar Street, 28 January 1862

Dear Sir,
    Corporation to Phelps

You must not suppose that my letter was written under the influence of irritation or that it was intended to imply unkind censure upon you for the course you have taken. It was rather the expression of my regret at the results which have ensued from the adoption of that course; and I assure you my regret is as unfeigned on account of the interference the delay will occasion in the prosecution of Mr Phelps' good intentions, as it is on account of the inconvenience it will occasion to the Corporation.

If you will refer to the Abstract of Title you will see that the Memorial <u>was</u> properly drawn, and fully set out the Local Act of 2 & 3 Vic. Cap 40, and clearly shewed the application of its provisions to the 'Pigeons' property, and that you therefore had before you at the outset in the Abstract the letter of the Lords of the Treasury which is now considered ultra vires.

My regret therefore arises not so much upon the fact that this question has been raised, as that it was not raised at an earlier period when we were dealing with requisitions and observations on the title as in that case it might have been rectified while we were necessarily delayed by other questions; but instead of this the direction for the payment of the £1250 to the Borough Treasurer was never made the subject of objection or remark, and no intimation was given me of your intention to depart from the course laid down by the Lords of the Treasury until I discovered it in the recitals of the draft Conveyance. Now I am sure you will, upon reflection, see with me that so important a deviation from the directions under which alone the Corporation were authorized to convey the property ought to have been made a matter of substantial objection at the outset, and that however necessary it might afterwards be thought to make it so, it is a matter for regret that so much time must now be lost in consequence of our having to retrace our steps and to get a different authority from the Treasury Commissioners upon a new Memorial, to be stated (<u>not</u> according to Mr Rudall's opinion) but substantially as it was before, only giving clear and definite expression to what I now know to be your views. It could not be supposed that I should anticipate such an objection. On the contrary I was satisfied with the directions of the Lords of the Treasury myself, and had no suspicion that you would hesitate to act upon them; and it is really a pity that if you had any intention to do otherwise you did not specifically communicate that intention to me and not leave me to find it out by the form in which you prepared the Conveyance. However the mischief is done, and regret is useless. But pray, accept my assurance that the interest I feel in the matter is quite sufficient without solicitations to induce me to use every exertion I can consistently with a due regard to other things to bring this business to the earliest possible termination.

    I am, Dear Sir, Yours very truly, J. J. Blandy Town Clerk

Letter 12
To J Neale Esquire

Friar Street, 21 March 1862

Dear Sir,

    Corporation to Phelps

I have this morning received the draft Conveyance approved by the Lords of the Treasury and have therefore the pleasure of returning your Draft and the Draft Deed of Covenant approved on behalf of the Corporation.

You may now proceed with all the expedition you please but the first thing you should do is to pay the £350 into the Bank of England, because until that has been done and the Office copy Receipt and Certificate sent to me the Conveyance cannot be executed. You should therefore at once remit the £350 to your agents with instructions to pay it into the Bank in accordance with the requirements of the Local Act of 2 & 3 Vic. Cap. 40 and to apply for office copies of the Receipt and Certificate. In the meantime you can have the two Deeds engrossed and sent to me for examination, and as soon afterwards as you can let me have the office copies Receipt and Certificate I will get the Conveyance executed.

To save you trouble I send you a copy of the Act of 2 & 3 Vic. C. 40 and shall be happy to give you any further information or assistance you may require.

    I am, Dear Sir, Yours very truly, J. J. Blandy Town Clerk

(xix)   Conveyance of the Site of the late Greyfriars Church and other hereditaments situate in Friar Street Reading in the County of Berks (23 April 1862). Original indenture in the Greyfriars Church Archive

This is the actual indenture of conveyance of the Greyfriars site from the Borough Council to Rev William Whitmarsh Phelps, marking the end of the time that Greyfriars Church was a Bridewell, and the start of its restoration to ecclesiastical use.

The Mayor, Alderman and Burgesses of the Borough of Reading to the Reverend William Whitmarsh Phelps

[First Sheet]
This Indenture made the twenty third day of April in the Year of our Lord one thousand eight hundred and sixty two Between the Mayor Aldermen and Burgesses of the Borough of Reading in the County of Berks (by the Council of the same Borough) of the first part Charles Stephens of Earley Court in the County of Berks Esquire the Treasurer of the Borough Fund of the same Borough of the second part Sir William Dunbar Baronet and Lieutenant Colonel Luke White two of the Lords Commissioners of Her Majesty's Treasury of the third part and the Reverend William Whitmarsh Phelps of Reading aforesaid Clerk of the fourth part

Whereas by an Act of Parliament passed in the Session holden in the second and third years of the Reign of Her present Majesty intituled 'An act to enable the Mayor Aldermen and Burgesses of the Borough of Reading in the County of Berks to sell certain Real Estate discharged from certain liabilities and to invest the purchase monies arising from such Sales in the purchase of other real Estate to be charged with such liabilities' After amongst other things reciting certain Letters Patent of Her late Majesty Queen Elizabeth under the Great Seal of England dated in the second year of Her Reign It was amongst other things enacted that from and after the passing of that Act it should and might be lawful for the Council for the time being of the Borough of Reading aforesaid (with the approbation of the Lords Commissioners of Her Majesty's Treasury or any three of them) at such time or times as the said Council should deem expedient absolutely to sell alienate dispose of and convey all and every or any of the Messuages lands Tenements hereditaments and premises comprised in the Schedule to that Act (and from which Schedule the Schedule to these Presents is an Extract) subject and without prejudice nevertheless to the subsisting Leases thereof for the time being and to make every such Sale alienation disposition and conveyance of the said Messuages lands Tenements hereditaments and premises freed and absolutely and for ever exonerated and discharged of and from an Annual sum of Ten Pounds payable to the Schoolmaster of the Free School within the said Borough as his Stipend and salary and of and from all liability thereto or to the payment thereof and from all remedies claims and demands in respect thereof and also freed and absolutely and forever exonerated and discharged of and from all repairs of the Bridges ways roads streets and places therein mentioned or any other Bridges ways roads streets and places whatsoever to the repairs whereof the said Mayor Aldermen and Burgesses or the Lessees tenants or occupiers of any of their lands or hereditaments were (previously to and at the time of the passing of the said Act or would have been in case that Act had not been passed) subject or liable and from all costs charges and expenses of repairing sustaining rebuilding and making all and every or any such Bridges ways roads streets and places respectively and all liability thereto or to contribution towards the same and from all remedies claims and demands whatsoever by the Queen's Most Excellent Majesty her heirs and Successors and all and every other Bodies and Body Politic or Corporate and person or persons whomsoever in respect or by reason of any such liability as aforesaid And of and from all burdens duties charges and liabilities whatsoever to which such Messuages lands tenements and hereditaments or the rents and profits thereof or any part thereof were subject or liable at the time of passing the said Act under or by virtue or means of the therein recited Letters Patent either expressly or in construction of Law (save and except only the Annual rent of Twenty two Pounds reserved to the Crown by the said Letters Patent) until such time as the same Annual rent should have been purchased or acquired by the said Mayor Aldermen and Burgesses under the power for that purpose thereinafter contained And the Council for the time being of the said Borough should and was thereby authorized to make such sales alienations and dispositions as aforesaid either by Public Auction or by Private Contract or partly in each mode and in such manner and on such terms and conditions as should have been approved of by the said Lords Commissioners of Her Majesty's Treasury or any three of them And it was further enacted that the purchaser or purchasers of all or any of the said Messuages lands tenements and hereditaments which should be sold under the powers and authorities in the said Act contained should pay his her or their purchase money or monies into the Bank of England in the name and with the privity of the Accountant General of the Court of Chancery to be placed to his Account there Exparte the Mayor Aldermen and Burgesses of the Borough of Reading pursuant to the method prescribed by the Act of the Twelfth Year of the Reign of His late Majesty King George the first Chapter thirty two and the General Orders of the said Court and without fee or reward according to the Act of the Twelfth Year of the Reign of His late Majesty King George the second Chapter twenty four and the Receipt or Receipts of the Cashier or Cashiers of the Bank of England and the Certificate or Certificates of the said Accountant General of the payment into the Bank of England by such purchaser or purchasers of his her or their purchase money or monies or any part thereof as aforesaid annexed to the same and filed in the Register Office of the said Court of Chancery or any Office Copy or Copies of any such Certificate and Receipt should from time to time be and be deemed and taken to be a good and sufficient discharge and good and sufficient discharges to such purchaser or purchasers and his her and their heirs executors administrators and assigns for so much or such part or parts of the purchase money or monies for which such Certificate or Certificates and receipt or receipts respectively should be so given as aforesaid and after filing such Certificate of Certificates and receipt or receipts such purchaser or purchasers and his her or their heirs executors administrators and assigns should be absolutely acquitted and discharged of and from the same monies and should not be answerable or accountable for any loss misapplication or nonapplication thereof And it was also enacted that the like notice of the intention of the Council of the said Borough of Reading to make application to the Lords Commissioners of Her Majesty's Treasury for or in relation to any act matter or thing whatsoever to the doing making executing effecting or authorizing of which the approbation of the said Lords Commissioners or any three of them as by the said Act made necessary and the like means and opportunities for the inspection of a Copy of the Memorial intended to be sent to the said Lords Commissioners should be given and afforded as in the therein recited Act of the sixth year of the reign of His late Majesty King William the fourth (being an Act to provide for the regulation of Municipal Corporations in England and Wales) was provided or required with respect to the obtaining such approbation of the said Lords Commissioners to any Sale alienation demise or lease purposed to be made under the authority of the said last mentioned Act and to the making of which such approbation was by the same Act made necessary

[Second Sheet]
And it was further enacted that all and every persons and person who would become the purchaser or purchasers of all or any part of the Messuages or Tenements lands hereditaments and other the premises by the said Act authorized to be sold and disposed of and the respective heirs and assigns of such purchaser or purchasers should and might from and after the payment of his her or their purchase money into the Bank of England as thereinbefore provided have hold occupy possess and enjoy the said Messuages or tenements lands hereditaments and premises and the rents issues and profits thereof freed exonerated and discharged of and from the said yearly sum of Ten Pounds payable to the Schoolmaster for the time being of the said Free School as his stipend and salary and from all liability thereto and all claims and demands in respect thereof and for the repairs and rebuilding of the said Bridges ways roads streets and places and from all costs and expences and all liability thereto and all remedies claims and demands whatsoever by the Queen's Most Excellent Majesty her heirs and successors and all other Body or Bodies Politic or Corporate or person or persons whomsoever in respect thereof and likewise of and from all and every other the burdens duties charges and liabilities exonerated and discharged from which the Messuages lands tenements and hereditaments thereinbefore mentioned or referred to was by that Act authorized to be sold alienated or demised as aforesaid

And Whereas under the authority of the said recited Act and with the approbation of the Lords Commissioners of Her Majesty's Treasury the said Mayor Aldermen and Burgesses purchased the said Annual rent of Twenty two Pounds in the same Act mentioned and by an Indenture dated on or about the seventeenth day of April one thousand eight hundred and forty five and made or expressed to be made between Thomas Bros the Younger Esquire of the first part Arthur Lennox Esquire commonly called Lord Arthur Lennox and Alexander Pringle and Henry Baring Esquires three of the Lords Commissioners of Her Majesty's Treasury of the second part and the said Mayor Aldermen and Burgesses of the third part All that the said Annual rent of Twenty two Pounds reserved and made payable in and by the said Letters Patent of Her said late Majesty Queen Elizabeth howsoever the same might be or might thereafter have been called known distinguished or described and all arrears and future payments thereof and all powers remedies and authorities whatsoever vested in or appertaining to the said Thomas Bros the Younger for recovering and compelling payment of the said Annual Rent were granted bargained sold aliened and confirmed remised released and discharged Unto and to the Use and behoof of the said Mayor Aldermen and Burgesses of the Borough of Reading their successors and assigns absolutely for ever and to the intent and so that as provided and enacted by the said recited Act of the second and third Years of the Reign of Her present Majesty the same Annual rent might thenceforth sink into and be absolutely extinguished in the Lands Tenements and hereditaments tolls profits and other the premises out of which the same was or might be issuing and payable or which were or which but for such extinguishment would have been charged with or liable to the payment thereof and so as that the same Rent should not nor should any part thereof be thenceforth payable or recoverable

And Whereas the said Mayor Aldermen and Burgesses are seized of the Messuage land Tenements and hereditaments hereinafter firstly mentioned or described and hereby granted or intended so to be and their appurtenances and the inheritance in fee simple of the same free from all Incumbrances

And Whereas the said Mayor Aldermen and Burgesses by the Council of the said Borough deeming it expedient to sell and alienate the Messuage buildings land Tenements and hereditaments hereinafter mentioned or described and hereby granted or intended so to be accordingly under the authority of the Act of Parliament passed in the Fifth and sixth Years of the Reign of his late Majesty King William the fourth intituled An act to provide for the regulation of Municipal Corporations in England and Wales subject to the approbation of the Lords Commissioners of Her Majesty's Treasury agreed with the said William Whitmarsh Phelps for the absolute sale to him of the said Buildings land Tenements and hereditaments hereinafter firstly mentioned or described and hereby granted or intended so to be and their appurtenances and the inheritance in fee simple of the same free from all Incumbrances for the sum of Nine hundred Pounds Sterling And under the authority of the hereinbefore recited Act of Parliament of the second and third Years of the Reign of Her present Majesty the said Mayor Aldermen and Burgesses by the Council of the said Borough subject to the approval of the Lords Commissioners of Her Majesty's Treasury agreed with the said William Whitmarsh Phelps for the absolute sale to him of the Messuage and hereditaments hereinafter secondly mentioned or described and hereby granted or intended so to be and their appurtenances and the inheritance in fee simple of the same free from all Incumbrances except the Lease hereinafter mentioned for the sum of Three hundred and fifty Pounds Sterling

And Whereas pursuant to the provisions of the said Acts of Parliament the said Council by Memorial dated the eleventh day of February one thousand eight hundred and sixty two represented the circumstances of the case to the Lords Commissioners of Her Majesty's Treasury and applied to the said Lords Commissioners to approve of such Sales to the said William Whitmarsh Phelps as aforesaid And Notice of the intention of the said Council to make such application as aforesaid was fixed to the Outer door of the Town Hall within the said Borough one Calendar Month before the making of such application and a Copy of the said Memorial intended to be sent to the said Lords Commissioners and so sent as aforesaid was kept in the Town Clerks Office during such Calendar Month and was freely open to the inspection of every Burgess at all reasonable hours during the same Month

And Whereas by an Act passed in the Session of Parliament held in the Twelfth and thirteenth Years of the Reign of Her present Majesty intituled An Act to reduce the number of signatures required to Instruments issued by the Lords of the Treasury it is enacted that where any Warrant appointment authority approval instrument or act whatsoever is by any Act of Parliament or otherwise required to be issued made signified or done by or under the hands of the Commissioners of Her Majesty's Treasury or by or under the hands of any three or more of them every such Warrant appointment authority approval instrument or act may be issued made signified or done by or under the hands of any two or more of the said Commissioners and when so issued made signified or done as aforesaid should be binding and have the same effect to all intents and purposes as

[Third Sheet]
If issued made signified or done by or under the hands of the said Commissioners or by or under the hands of any three or more of them as the case might require
And Whereas the said Lords Commissioners of Her Majesty's Treasury have signified their approval of the said Sale to the said William Whitmarsh Phelps as is testified by two of the said Lords Commissioners being parties to and executing these Presents
And Whereas pursuant to the hereinbefore firstly recited Act of Parliament the said William Whitmarsh Phelps did on the twenty seventh day of March one thousand eight hundred and sixty two pay the said sum of Three hundred and fifty Pounds (the purchase Money for the Messuage and hereditaments hereinafter secondly mentioned or described and hereby granted or intended so to be) into the Bank of England in the name and with the privity of the Accountant General of the Court of Chancery to his account there 'Exparte the Mayor Aldermen and Burgesses of the Borough of Reading' as appears by the Receipt of W Hoddle one of the Cashiers of the said Bank and the Certificate of the said Accountant General annexed to the same and filed in the Register Office of the said Court of Chancery and Copies of which receipt and Certificate are indorsed on the back of these Presents
Now this Indenture witnesseth that in pursuance and performance of the said agreement and in consideration of the sum of Nine hundred Pounds Sterling to the said Charles Stephens as such Treasurer aforesaid now truly paid by the said William Whitmarsh Phelps being in full for the absolute purchase of the Buildings land Tenements and hereditaments hereinafter firstly mentioned or described and hereby granted or intended so to be and their appurtenances free from all Incumbrances the receipt of which said sum of Nine hundred Pounds the said Charles Stephens doth hereby acknowledge and from the same the said Charles Stephens and also the said Mayor Aldermen and Burgesses do hereby respectively for ever release and discharge the said William Whitmarsh Phelps his heirs executors administrators and assigns And also, in consideration of the said sum of Three hundred and fifty Pounds so by the said William Whitmarsh Phelps paid into the Bank of England in the name and with the privity of the Accountant General of the Court of Chancery to his account there 'Exparte the Mayor Aldermen and Burgesses of the Borough of Reading' as hereinbefore recited and being in full for the absolute purchase of the Messuage and hereditaments hereinafter secondly mentioned or described and hereby granted or intended so to be free from all Incumbrances except the Lease hereinafter

mentioned And by virtue and in exercise of the several powers or authorities by the hereinbefore recited Acts of Parliament given to or vested in the said Mayor Aldermen and Burgesses and every or any other power or authority in any wise enabling them in such behalf They the said Mayor Aldermen and Burgesses by the Council of the said Borough with the approbation of the said Lords Commissioners of Her Majesty's Treasury testified by the said two Lords Commissioners parties hereto executing these Presents Do by these Presents sell alienate dispose of grant convey and confirm unto the said William Whitmarsh Phelps his heirs and assigns for ever

Firstly All that piece of Land situate on the North side of Friar Street in the Parish of Saint Lawrence in Reading in the County of Berks with the Ruins of the Church of the Grey Friars and all other Buildings (except as hereinafter mentioned) standing and being thereon some of which were lately used for the purposes of a Bridewell or House of Correction and for a Residence and Offices for the Keeper of the same (Except such portions of the said Buildings as have been recently erected for the better accommodation and detention of Prisoners confined in the said Bridewell which the said Mayor Aldermen and Burgesses are to be at liberty at any time within two years from the Twenty second day of May one thousand eight hundred and sixty one to take down remove and carry away without doing any damage or making any compensation to the said William Whitmarsh Phelps for the same) And the Ground Plot of which said piece of Land hereby granted or intended so to be is shown in the Plan drawn on the back of the third Skin of these Presents by being coloured Red and the boundaries and dimensions whereof are thereon also shown and their respective rights members and appurtenances[1]

And secondly All that Messuage now used as a Public House called the 'Pigeons' situate on the North side of Friar Street aforesaid and adjoining the piece of Land hereinbefore firstly mentioned or described and being the Messuage mentioned or comprised in the Schedule to these Presents and which said Messuage called the 'Pigeons' was by an Indenture of Lease dated the eleventh day of December one thousand eight hundred and thirty five demised by the said Mayor Aldermen and Burgesses to Thomas Rickford and Charles Curry Bickham for the Term of Eighty Years from the Twenty ninth day of September one thousand seven hundred and eighty nine at the Yearly Rent of Five Pounds and the Ground Plot thereof is shown in the said Map or Plan by being coloured Blue and the boundaries and dimensions whereof are therein also shown and the respective rights members and appurtenances And all Outhouses edifices buildings cellars sollars areas Courts Courtyards pumps cisterns sewers gutters drains wydraughts[2] ways paths passages lights waters watercourses liberties privileges easements profits commodities advantages and emoluments whatsoever to the said land hereditaments and premises hereby granted or intended so to be or any of them respectively belonging or in anywise appertaining or reputed known held occupied or enjoyed as part parcel or member thereof or any part thereof And the reversion and reversions remainder and remainders yearly and other rents issues and profits of the said

---

1 See Figure 5.
2 Wydraught, or withdraught, is an obsolete term for a privy or sewer.

Messuage land tenements hereditaments and premises hereby granted or intended so to be And all the estate right Title property benefit claim and demand whatsoever or howsoever of the said Mayor Aldermen and Burgesses of in to out of or upon the same hereditaments and premises

To have and to hold the said Messuage buildings land Tenements hereditaments and premises hereby granted or intended so to be Unto and to the Use of the said William Whitmarsh Phelps his heirs

[Fourth Sheet]
And assigns for ever Subject to the said Lease dated the eleventh day of December one thousand eight hundred and thirty five but absolutely and for ever exonerated and discharged from all Stipends rents payments repairs costs charges expenses remedies claims and demands burdens duties and liabilities discharged wherefrom the said premises are authorized to be sold and conveyed by virtue of the said Acts of Parliament or either of them and from all other Incumbrances whatsoever

And the said Mayor Aldermen and Burgesses for themselves and their Successors do hereby covenant with the said William Whitmarsh Phelps his heirs and assigns in manner following that is to say that notwithstanding any act deed matter or thing by them the said Mayor Alderman and Burgesses made done permitted or suffered to the contrary (except as hereinafter excepted) they the said Mayor Aldermen and Burgesses by the said Council now have good right and absolute authority to sell alienate grant convey and confirm the said Messuage buildings land Tenements hereditaments and premises hereby granted and conveyed or intended so to be Unto and to the Use of the said William Whitmarsh Phelps his heirs and assigns for ever in manner aforesaid according to the true intent and meaning of these Presents

And that it shall be lawful for the said William Whitmarsh Phelps his heirs and assigns from time to time and at all times hereafter peaceably and quietly to hold possess and enjoy the said Messuage buildings land tenements hereditaments and premises hereby granted or intended so to be and receive and take the rents and profits thereof without any lawful let suit trouble eviction claim or demand whatsoever of or by the said Mayor Aldermen and Burgesses or their Successors or any person or persons lawfully claiming or to claim by from through under or in trust for them other than and in respect of the exception aforesaid

And that free and clear and freely clearly and absolutely acquitted exonerated released and for ever discharged or otherwise by the said Mayor Aldermen and Burgesses and their Successors well and sufficiently saved defended kept harmless and indemnified of from and against all estates titles troubles charges debts and incumbrances whatsoever either already or to be hereafter had made executed occasioned or suffered by the said Mayor Aldermen and Burgesses their predecessors or successors or by any other person or persons lawfully claiming or to claim by from or under or in trust for them the hereinbefore mentioned Indenture of Lease dated the eleventh day of December one thousand eight hundred and thirty five only excepted

And further that the said Mayor Aldermen and Burgesses and their Successors and all and every person or persons having or claiming or who shall or may have or claim any estate right title or interest at law or in Equity in to or out of the said Messuage buildings land tenements hereditaments and premises hereby granted or intended so to be or any of them or any part thereof by from under or in trust for the said Mayor Aldermen and Burgesses or their Successors shall and will from time to time and at all times hereafter upon every reasonable request and at the costs and charges of the said William Whitmarsh Phelps his heirs or assigns do execute make and perfect or cause to be done executed made and perfected all such further and other lawful and reasonable acts deeds things and assurances in the Law whatsoever for the further better more perfectly and absolutely granting conveying and assuring the said Messuage buildings land tenements hereditaments and premises hereby granted or intended so to be Unto and to the Use of the said William Whitmarsh Phelps his heirs or assigns or his or their Counsel in the Law shall be devised advised and required

And the said William Whitmarsh Phelps doth hereby for himself his heirs executors and administrators Covenant with the said Mayor Aldermen and Burgesses their Successors and assigns that the remains of the late Church of the Grey Friars now standing on the said piece of Land hereinbefore firstly mentioned or described and hereby granted or intended so to be shall within the space of Ten years from the date of these Presents be restored and adapted to the purposes of Religious Worship according to the Rites and Doctrines of the United Church of England and Ireland

Provided nevertheless that nothing in these Presents contained shall be construed to restrain the said William Whitmarsh Phelps his heirs or assigns from erecting Houses Schools or any other Buildings upon any portions of the said Land hereby granted or intended so to be which shall not be required for a Church as aforesaid nor from selling and disposing of such portions of the same Land at his and their freewill and pleasure

In Witness whereof the said Mayor Aldermen and Burgesses have affixed their Common Seal and the said Charles Stephens and the said two Lords Commissioners of Her Majesty's Treasury and the said William Whitmarsh Phelps have respectively set their hands and seals the day and year first hereinbefore written.

The Schedule referred to in the above written Indenture.

Situation of Property	Friar Street North
Lessee or Assignee	Messieurs Rickford and Bickham
Present or last Known Occupier	George Williams
Description of Property	Messuage with the appurtenances called the 'Three[1] Pigeons'
Yearly Rent	Five Pounds
How holden by the Tenant or Assignee	By Lease for Eighty Years from Michaelmas 1789.

---

1 The word Three is added by a caret.

[*Below this table there are 5 red wax seals, each on a green cloth background, with a signature:*

James Boorne (Chairman) – seal of the Borough of Reading
Charles Stephens – Treasurer of the Borough Fund of the Borough of Reading
William Dunbar – Lords Commissioner of Her Majesty's Treasury
Luke White – Lords Commissioner of Her Majesty's Treasury
William Whitmarsh Phelps – Purchaser]

[Reverse of the First Sheet]
29th March 1862
I do hereby certify that pursuant to an Act of Parliament passed in the 2nd and 3rd years of the Reign of Her Majesty Queen Victoria entitled an Act to enable the Mayor &c. of Reading &c. The Reverend William Whitmarsh Phelps the Purchaser has paid into the Bank of England the sum of three hundred and fifty pounds which is placed to my account as Accountant General and to the credit of Exparte the Mayor Aldermen and Burgesses of the Borough of Reading in the Books kept at the Bank and in my office as appears by the receipt of Mr W. Hoddle one of the Cashiers of the Bank dated the 27th March 1862 hereto annexed
   W. Russell A.G.

             London the 27th March 1862
Received pursuant to an Act of Parliament passed in the 2nd and 3rd year of the Reign of Her Majesty Queen Victoria entitled an Act to enable the Mayor of Reading &c. of the Revd William Whitmarsh Phelps the Purchaser the sum of three hundred and fifty pounds which money is placed to the account of William Russell Esquire as Accountant General of the Court of Chancery and to the credit of Exparte the Mayor Alderman and Burgesses of the Borough of Reading in the Books kept at the Bank for the Suitors of the said Court of Chancery.
   For the governor and Company of the Bank of England. W. Hoddle
£350
Ent[ere]d
[Signed] W. J. Whaley
Received the day and year first within written of and from the within named William Whitmarsh Phelps the sum of Nine hundred Pounds being the consideration money within expressed to be paid, by him to me.
[Signed] Charles Stephens Treasurer of the Borough Fund of the Borough of Reading.
Witness [Signed] Samuel Preston
Signed sealed and delivered by the within named Charles Stephens in the presence of [Signed] Samuel Preston Clerk to Mr Blandy Town Clerk Reading.

The Common Seal of the within named Mayor Aldermen and Burgesses was affixed hereto in the presence of [Signed] J. J. Blandy Town Clerk

Signed Sealed and Delivered by the within named Lords Commissioners of Her Majesty's Treasury in the presence of Thomas Halligan, Office Keeper Treasury

Signed sealed and delivered by the within named William Whitmarsh Phelps in the presence of [Signed] John Neale Solicitor Reading,
[Signed – illegible] his clerk

(xx) Covenant for the Production of Title Deeds – The Mayor Aldermen and Burgesses of the Borough of Reading to The Reverend W. W. Phelps (23 April 1862). Original in the Greyfriars Church Archive.

This Indenture made the twenty third day of April in the Year of our Lord one thousand eight hundred and sixty two Between the Mayor Aldermen and Burgesses of the Borough of Reading in the County of Berks of the one part and The Reverend William Whitmarsh Phelps of Reading aforesaid Clerk of the other part
Whereas by Indenture bearing even date with and executed immediately before the execution of these Presents and made or expressed to be made between the said Mayor Aldermen and Burgesses (by the Council of the said Borough) of the first part Charles Stephens of Earley Court in the County of Berks Esquire the Treasurer of the Borough Fund of the same Borough of the second part Sir William Dunbar Baronet and Lieutenant Colonel Luke White two of the Lords Commissioners of Her Majesty's Treasury of the third part and the said William Whitmarsh Phelps of the fourth part Firstly All that piece of Land situate on the North side of Friar Street in the Parish of Saint Lawrence in Reading in the County of Berks with the Ruins of the Church of the Grey Friars and all other Buildings (except thereinafter mentioned) standing and being thereon some of which were used for the purpose of a Bridewell or House of Correction and for a Residence and Offices for the Keeper of the same (except such portions of the said Buildings as had been recently erected for the better accommodation and detention of Prisoners confined in the said Bridewell as therein mentioned) And Secondly All that Messuage then used as a Public House called the 'Pigeons' situate on the North side of Friar Street aforesaid and adjoining the piece of Land therein and hereinbefore firstly mentioned or described have been granted and conveyed Unto and to the Use of the said William Whitmarsh Phelps his heirs and assigns for ever
And Whereas the Deeds evidences and writings mentioned in the Schedule hereto relate not only to the said Messuage buildings land tenements and hereditaments comprised in and granted by the hereinbefore recited Indenture but also to other hereditaments of the said Mayor Aldermen and Burgesses of greater value And it hath therefore been agreed that the said Mayor Aldermen and Burgesses shall retain the possession of the same Deeds evidences and writings and should enter into such Covenant in respect of the same as in hereinafter contained

Now this Indenture Witnesseth that in pursuance of the said agreement and in consideration of the premises They the said Mayor Aldermen and Burgesses do for themselves and their Successors Covenant with the said William Whitmarsh Phelps his heirs and assigns that the said Mayor Aldermen and Burgesses their Successors or assigns shall and will unless hindered or prevented by fire or some other inevitable accident from time to time and at all times hereafter upon every reasonable request and at the costs and charges of the said William Whitmarsh Phelps his heirs or assigns produce and show forth or cause to be produced and shown forth unto the said William Whitmarsh Phelps his heirs or assigns or to the Counsel Attornies Agents or Solicitors of him them or any of them or at any Trial or hearing in any Court of Law or Equity or at any Commission examination or otherwise as occasion shall require all and every or any of the Deeds evidences and writings specified in the Schedule hereto for the better manifesting maintaining defending and proving the estate interest title or property of the said William Whitmarsh Phelps his heirs or assigns or any of them in and to the said Messuage buildings land and hereditaments so granted by the said Indenture bearing even date herewith or any part or parcel thereof And also shall and will from time to time and at all times hereafter at the request costs and charges of the said William Whitmarsh Phelps his heirs and assigns deliver or cause to be delivered unto the said William Whitmarsh Phelps his heirs or assigns such true and attested Copies or true Copies unattested or Abstracts of or Extracts from the said Deeds evidences and writings or any of them as he or they may require And shall and will in the meantime keep the same Deeds evidences and writings safe undefaced unobliterated and uncancelled

In Witness whereof the said Mayor Aldermen and Burgesses have hereunto affixed their Common Seal the day and year first above written

The Schedule referred to in the above written Indenture

23rd Sept 2nd Elizabeth	Letters Patent of Queen Elizabeth to the Mayor and Burgesses of Reading.
1st July 1835	Indenture between Thomas Bros Esquire of the first part John Alliston of the second part Thomas Bros the younger Esquire of the third part.
17th April 1845	Indenture between the said Thomas Bros the younger of the first part Arthur Lennox Esquire commonly called Lord Arthur Lennox and Alexander Pringle and Henry Baring Esquires three of the Lords Commissioners of Her Majesty's Treasury of the second part and the said Mayor Aldermen and Burgesses of the third part.
17th April 1845	Indenture between the said Thomas Bros the elder and John Alliston of the one part and the said Mayor Aldermen and Burgesses of the other

	part being a Covenant for the production of Title Deeds.
31st March 1854	Attested Copy of Deed Poll under the Seal of the said Mayor Aldermen and Burgesses and under the hand of Richard Fellowes Esquire being a Mortgage to the said Richard Fellowes.
11th February 1862	Memorial of the Council of the Borough of Reading to the Lords Commissioners of Her Majesty's Treasury relative to the sale of the said hereditaments. Notice of Town Clerk to make application to the said Lords Commissioners for approbation of Sale of the said hereditaments to the said William Whitmarsh Phelps.

[This is followed by the seal of the Borough of Reading with the signature of James Boorne (Chairman)]

[Reverse of First Sheet]
The Common Seal of the within named Mayor Aldermen and Burgesses was affixed hereto in the presence of J. J. Blandy [signature] Town Clerk

(xxi)   Abstract of the Title of Mr John Weedon to a Freehold Estate on the North side of Friar Street in the parish of St Lawrence Reading (1849). Royal Berkshire Archives R/D49/1/1

This document contains a wealth of detail about past ownership of the area known as the Grey Friars Estate from the early eighteenth century to the mid-nineteenth, including the intriguing mention of a bowling alley!

4th & 5th February 1806
Indentures of Lease and Release made between Joseph Hill of Savile Row in the parish of Saint James Westminster in the County of Middlesex Esquire of the first part, Thomas Hill Mortimer of Savile Row aforesaid Gentleman of the second part, Lancelot Austwick of Reading in the County of Berks Esquire of the third part and George Booth Tyndale of Lincolns Inn Fields in the County of Middlesex Gentleman of the fourth part.

Reciting that by Indentures of Lease and Release bearing date respectively the 15th and 16th days of November then last the Release made between Joseph Heycock of Saddington in the County of Leicester Gentleman of the first part the said George Booth Tyndale of the second part Henry Le Grice of Lincolns Inn Fields aforesaid Gentleman of the third part the said Joseph Hill of the fourth part and the said Thomas Hill Mortimer of the fifth part and by virtue of a common Recovery suffered as of the then last Michaelmas Term pursuant to an Agreement in the said Indenture of Release contained wherein the said George Booth Tyndale was tenant the said Henry Le Grice was demandant and the said Joseph Heycock was Vouchee and by virtue of an Indenture (indorsed on the said Indenture of Release of the 16th day of November then last) bearing date the 18th day of January then last past and made between the said Joseph Heycock and Mary his Wife of the one part and the said Joseph Hill and Thomas Hill Mortimer of the other part declaring the uses of a fine levied by the said Joseph Heycock and Mary his Wife as of Michaelmas Term then last The Messuages tenements lands and hereditaments in the now abstracting Indenture particularly described and intended to be thereby appointed and released were limited and assured and did then stand limited To such uses upon such trusts and to and for such intents and purposes and with under and subject to such powers provisos and declarations as the said Joseph Hill by any deed or deeds writing or writings with or without power of revocation to be sealed and delivered by him in the presence of and to be attested by two or more credible witnesses should from time to time direct limit or appoint and in default of and until such direction limitation or appointment To the use of the said Joseph Hill and his assigns during his life with remainder To the use of the said Thomas Hill Mortimer and his heirs during the life of the said Joseph Hill In trust for the said Joseph Hill and his assigns with remainder To the use of the said Joseph Hill his heirs and assigns for ever

And that the said Lancelot Austwick had contracted and agreed with the said Joseph Hill for the purchase of the Inheritance in fee simple in possession of the said Messuages tenements lands and hereditaments for the sum of Three thousand Pounds

It is by the Release witnessed that in consideration of the sum of Three thousand pounds by the said Lancelot Austwick to the said Joseph Hill paid The said Joseph Hill by force and virtue and in exercise and execution of the power and authority to him given and reserved in and by the said therein recited Indenture of Release (at the request of the said Lancelot Austwick by the now abstracting Deed or writing sealed and delivered by the said Joseph Hill in the presence of the two credible persons whose names were thereupon endorsed as witnesses to the execution of the now abstracting Indenture by the said Joseph Hill) did direct limit and appoint and likewise grant bargain sell alien release and confirm And the said Thomas Hill Mortimer according to his estate and interest in the premises at the request and by the direction of the said Joseph Hill and at the nomination of the said Lancelot Austwick did bargain sell alien and release unto the said George Booth Tyndale and his heirs (in his actual possession &c.)

>All that messuage or tenement with the garden and Strip of Ground and appurtenances thereunto belonging then in the tenure or occupation of Theodosia Hill and Frances Hill Spinsters

>And also all those several messuages or tenements lands and hereditaments then in the occupation of the several persons

thereinafter named as undertenants of the said Theodosia Hill and Frances Hill (that is to say)

All that messuage or tenement with the Garden and appurtenances thereunto belonging then in the tenure or occupation of [Blank] Vincent widow

And all that messuage or tenement with the strip of garden ground and appurtenances thereunto belonging then in the tenure or occupation of John Ball

And all that messuage or tenement with the strip of garden ground and appurtenances thereunto belonging then in the tenure or occupation of [Blank] Beazley Widow

And all that messuage or tenement with the stables outhouses and appurtenances thereunto belonging then in the tenure or occupation of Thomas Smith

And all that messuage or tenement with the stables outhouses and appurtenances thereunto belonging then in the tenure or occupation of James Clark

And all that messuage or tenement with the stables outhouses and appurtenances thereunto belonging then in the tenure or occupation of William Shailor

And all that messuage or tenement with the stables outhouses and appurtenances thereunto belonging then in the tenure or occupation of John Slaughter

And all that messuage or tenement with the Granary and appurtenances thereunto belonging then in the tenure or occupation of William Wentworth

And also that messuage or tenement with the workshop and appurtenances thereunto belonging then in the tenure or occupation of William Thane

And all that piece or parcel of meadow land containing by estimation one acre and eight perches more or less then in the tenure or occupation of the Reverend William Marsh

And all that piece or parcel of meadow land containing by estimation two roods and thirty-four perches more or less then in the tenure or occupation of the said William Marsh

And all that piece or parcel of meadow land containing by estimation one acre one rood and thirteen perches more or less then in the tenure or occupation of Holland Thomas Higgs and Charles Poulton

And all that piece or parcel of meadow land containing by estimation three roods and seventeen perches more or less then in the tenure or occupation of the said Holland Thomas Higgs and Charles Poulton

And all that piece or parcel of meadow land containing by estimation one acre and six perches more or less And all that piece or parcel of meadow land containing by estimation three roods and eight perches more or less both which two last mentioned pieces or parcels of Land were then in the tenure or occupation of the said Charles Poulton

And all that piece or parcel of meadow land commonly called or known by the name of The Grove containing by estimation thirty perches more or less then in the tenure or occupation of the said Holland Thomas Higgs

And all those gardens containing by estimation two acres two roods and thirty-two perches more or less then in the tenure or occupation of John Patey

And all those gardens containing by estimation twenty perches more or less then in the tenure or occupation of John Shailor

And all that yard with the pigsties and appurtenances thereunto belonging containing by estimation eighteen perches more or less then in the tenure or occupation of the said John Shailor

And also that small garden with the stables thereunto adjoining and appurtenances thereunto belonging containing by estimation fourteen perches more or less then in the tenure or occupation of said Holland Thomas Higgs

All which said messuages or tenements gardens stables outhouses lands hereditaments and premises were situate lying and being in the parish of Saint Lawrence in Reading aforesaid and were bounded by the Road leading to Caversham on the West by Vastern or Fostern Meadow called or known by the name of Home Fast on the East by a brook called Pottmans on the north and by Fryers Street on the South All which said lands and hereditaments were formerly purchased by Joseph Heycock deceased of and from John Dalby Esquire Alice Dalby Spinster and Elizabeth Dalby Spinster and were conveyed to the said Joseph Heycock deceased and his heirs by Indentures of Lease and Release bearing the date respectively the 2nd and 3rd days of August 1722 and in which Indentures the messuages or tenements lands and hereditaments thereby conveyed were particularized by the following description viz

All that garden plot or parcel of ground containing by estimation three quarters of an acre were it more or less bounded with the Highway leading from Reading towards Caversham on the West part and certain Lands in Reading aforesaid usually called the Fryers on the East part situate lying and being in the Parish of Saint Lawrence in Reading aforesaid and within the Manor of Battel in the County of Berks together with all the messuages or tenements structures edifices and buildings thereon set up and erected All which premises theretofore were in the several tenures or occupations of Benjamin Burrows and the Widow Alexander and afterwards of the said Edward Dalby his undertenants or assigns and were purchased by John Dalby deceased to him and to his heirs for ever of and from his brother the said Edward Dalby and the same were then in the occupation of Samuel Dean or his undertenant or undertenants and Giles Newberry

And also all that little messuage or tenement with the appurtenances thereof

And also the piece of ground on which there lately stood a hovell at East end of the said messuage extending itself the breadth of the said East end of the said messuage unto the Wall or Bank of the Fryers Garden there

And also all the ground thereunto belonging or therewith used or enjoyed or appurtenant thereunto which last mentioned premises then late were in the occupation of Elizabeth Downing Widow and then of [Blank] Read Widow and were situate lying and being at the West end of Fryer Street in the said parish of Saint Lawrence in Reading aforesaid turning down to Pottman Brook bounded on the Road or Highway on the south part thereof the said garden called the Fryers Garden on the East part thereof the gateway through the brick wall leading unto the messuage or tenement part of the above granted premises theretofore in the occupation of Thomas Abery and then of the before named Giles Newberry on the West part and with a stable and outhouse part of the above granted premises theretofore in the occupation of the said Thomas Abery and then of the said Samuel Deane on the North part and were then lately purchased by the said John Dalby to him and his heirs and assigns for ever of and from the said Elizabeth Downing and her son William Downing

And also all that tenement and the Lands called or known by the name of the Fryers Ground situate in Reading aforesaid on the North side of Fryers Street there together with the orchard or the ground then lately called the Orchard thereunto belonging containing by estimation six acres were it more or less bounding on the Highway leading from Reading aforesaid towards Caversham on the West a garden formerly a Bowling Alley on the East upon the Fosterns on the North and upon the Town of Reading upon the South which said last mentioned premises then lately were purchased by the said John Dalby deceased to him and his heirs and assigns for ever of and from Richard Neville Esquire Thomas Hobby Esquire Dorothy Vachell Widow Thomas Vachell Esquire and others and then or then late were in the occupation of Thomas Alexander of Reading aforesaid Butcher And all other the messuages lands and hereditaments (if any) situate lying and being in or near the Parish of Saint Lawrence in Reading aforesaid and comprised in the said Indenture of the 16th November then last and the Recovery and Fine so suffered and levied as aforesaid.

Together with all houses &c.
And the reversion &c.
And all the Estate &c.

To hold the same with their appurtenances (free from the payment of the Land Tax which had been redeemed) unto the said George Booth Tyndale and his heirs

To the use and behoof of the said George Booth Tyndale his heirs and assigns for ever. But nevertheless In trust for the said Lancelot Austwick his heirs and assigns for ever and to be conveyed and disposed of as he or they should from time to time direct or appoint.

Covenant by the said Joseph Hill that neither he nor the said Thomas Hill Mortimer had done any act to incumber

> Executed by the said Joseph Hill and Thomas Hill Mortimer and attested by two witnesses and receipt for three thousand pounds consideration money endorsed signed by the said Joseph Hill and witnessed

The Bargain and Sale for a year is from the said Joseph Hill and Thomas Hill Mortimer to the said George Booth Tyndale in consideration of five shillings executed by the said Joseph Hill and Thomas Hill Mortimer attested

18 April 1826

Will of the said Lancelot Austwick whereby he gave to his Daughter Ann Austwick all the household goods furniture plate and certain other effects which should be in and about his house at Reading aforesaid at the time of his decease and after disposing of other Goods and Bank Stock he gave and devised

> All his freehold messuage lands and estate at Reading aforesaid with their appurtenances

Unto and to the use of William Stephens the younger of Reading aforesaid Esquire John Knight of Farnham in the County of Surrey Brewer and John Tyrrell of Lincolns Inn Esquire Barrister at Law their heirs and assigns for ever nevertheless upon the trusts thereinafter declared of or concerning the same viz

> Upon trust that his said Trustees and the Survivors and Survivor of them and the heirs and assigns of such Survivor should at such time or times as they or he should think proper but with the consent of his Son Harwood Austwick and Mary Ann his wife during their joint lives and after the decease of one of them with the consent of the Survivor of them during his or her life and after the decease of such Survivor at the discretion of the said Trustees or Trustee sell and dispose of all or any part of his said messuage lands and estate thereinbefore devised at such price or prices as to his said Trustees or Trustee should seem meet and execute all necessary Conveyances and give receipts for the purchase monies thereof which should effectually discharge the person or persons to whom the same responsibility should be given from being answerable for any loss or misapplication of the money in such receipts respectively expressed to be received.

> With a Power at any time before the Sale to grant Leases for any number of years not exceeding twenty-one years which has not been exercised

And the said Testator declared that the receipts of his Trustees or Trustee should actually discharge the person or persons to whom the same should be given from being answerable for the application monies therein respectively expressed to be received

And the said Testator appointed his said Son Harwood Austwick and the said William Stephens John Knight and John Tyrrell executors of his said Will

Executed by the said Testator in the presence of three subscribing witnesses

Proved (together with two Codicils thereto not affecting real Estate) in the Prerogative Court of Canterbury 16 April 1829 by the said Harwood Austwick and William Stephens Esquire two of the executors

30th November 1846

Indenture of Statutory Release made between William Stephens of Prospect Hill in the parish of Tilehurst in the County of Berks Esquire and John Knight of Farnham in the County of Surrey Esquire of the first part Harwood Austwick of Gloucester Terrace Hyde Park in the County of Middlesex Esquire of the second part George Booth Tyndale of Hayling Island in the County of Southampton Esquire of the third part and John Mitchell Furnell of Reading in the said County of Berks Gentleman of the fourth part

> Reciting the before abstracted indentures of Lease and Release of the 4th and 5th February 1806
>
> And that in or about the year 1808 the said Lancelot Austwick pulled down five of the said messuages which abutted on Friar Street aforesaid and on the site thereof or of some part thereof erected a Capital Messuage or Dwellinghouse for his own residence and also removed or altered the internal division fences of the said pieces of Land and Gardens
>
> And reciting the said abstracted Will of the said Lancelot Austwick and his death in the month of February in the year 1829 without having revoked or altered his said recited Will (Except by two Codicils thereto not affecting real Estate) and the same was duly proved by two of the executors thereof in the Prerogative Court of Canterbury on the 16th day of April in the same year
>
> And reciting that the said Harwood Austwick was the only Son and Heir at Law of the said Testator
>
> And reciting that the said John Tyrrell departed this life in the month of August 1840 leaving the said William Stephens and John Knight him surviving
>
> And reciting that the said Mary Ann Austwick departed this life in the month of November 1835
>
> And reciting that the said William Stephens and John Knight as such surviving Trustees with the consent of the said Harwood Austwick had contracted with the said John Mitchell Furnell for the absolute sale to him of the said Capital messuage or Dwellinghouse five messuages or tenements lands hereditaments and premises in fee simple in possession free from tithe and tithe rent charge and also from the Land tax which had been redeemed and from all incumbrances for the sum of Five thousand Pounds

It is witnessed that in consideration of the sum of Five thousand Pounds to the said William Stephens and John Knight paid by the said John Mitchell Furnell The said William Stephens and John Knight (with the consent of the said Harwood Austwick testified &c.) did and each of them did thereby grant bargain sell release and convey And the said Harwood Austwick did thereby grant release and convey and ratify and confirm And the said George Booth Tyndale (at the request and by the direction of the said William Stephens and John Knight testified &c. and of the said Harwood Austwick testified &c.) did thereby grant release and convey unto the said John Mitchell Furnell and his heirs

> All that capital messuage or Dwellinghouse and all those five messuages or tenements lands hereditaments and premises therein before particularly described or referred to and which (or the sites thereof) were comprised in and conveyed to the said Testator by the therein recited Indentures of Lease and appointment and Release or intended so to be and were also comprised in the said therein recited Devise and which were then better known by the following description viz
>
> All that Capital Messuage or Dwellinghouse abutting on Friar Street aforesaid so erected by the said Lancelot Austwick with the stable Coach Houses outbuildings yards gardens lawns and pleasure grounds thereunto belonging
>
> And all that piece or parcel of pasture Land with the Land covered with water therein lying behind the said Capital Messuage and Hereditaments formerly and for many years before his decease in the occupation of the said Testator and lately of Mrs Isabella Harwood Widow as the Tenant thereof
>
> And also all those five messuages or Tenements with the yards gardens and appurtenances thereto belonging abutting on the Caversham Road aforesaid in the respective occupations of Sarah Eyre Widow Francis Hughes Mary Webb Spinster George Strong and Susan Cresswell Widow as the tenants thereof
>
> All which hereditaments and premises thereby released (including the site of the said Buildings) containing together by admeasurement 10 acres 39 perches and were situate in the parish of Saint Lawrence in Reading aforesaid and were bounded by the Road leading to Caversham on the West partly by Vastern or Fostern Meadow (formerly called by the name of Home Fast) and partly by land and Hereditaments belonging to William Trimmer and others respectively on the East by a Brook called Pottmans on the North and partly by Friar Street and partly by buildings belonging to the Corporation of Reading on the South and the same were delineated in the Map or plan drawn in the margin of the now abstracting Indenture
>
> Together with all outhouses &c
>
> And the reversion &c.
>
> And all the Estate &c.
>
> And all Deeds &c.

To hold the said Capital messuage or Dwellinghouse five messuages or tenements piece or parcel of Land Outbuildings yards Gardens lawns pleasure Grounds and all other the Hereditaments and premises thereinbefore described and thereby released and conveyed or intended so to be with their rights members and appurtenances free from tithe and tithe rent charge and also from the Land tax which had been redeemed and from all incumbrances unto the said John Mitchell Furnell his heirs and assigns for ever

To the use of the said John Mitchell Furnell his heirs and assigns for ever

Separate Covenants by the said William Stephens and John Knight that they had not done any act to incumber

Covenant by the said George Booth Tyndale that he had not done any act to incumber

Covenants by the said Harwood Austwick (limited to his own Acts and those of the said Testator) that the parties thereto of the first second and third parts some or one of them were rightfully seized of the said hereditaments for a good estate of Inheritance in fee simple – had power to convey for quiet enjoyment subject to the existing tenancies of the said five messuages – free from incumbrances

and for further assurances

Executed by the said William Stephens John Knight Harwood Austwick and George Booth Tyndale duly attested and receipt for Five thousand Pounds the consideration money indorsed signed by the said William Stephens and John Knight and witnessed

1st December 1846

By Indenture of Statutory Release (endorsed on last abstracted Indenture) made between the said John Mitchell Furnell of the first part John Weedon of Reading aforesaid Gentleman of the second part and Edward Micklem of Reading aforesaid Esquire of the third part

Reciting that the messuages or tenements lands and hereditaments comprised in and conveyed by the therein within written Indenture were purchased by the said John Mitchell Furnell at the request and on the part and behalf of the said John Weedon and the sum of Five thousand Pounds therein within mentioned to be paid by the said John Mitchell Furnell as the consideration of and for the purchase of the said messuages lands and hereditaments was the proper money of the said John Weedon and the name of the said John Mitchell Furnell was made use of in the therein written Indenture In trust for the said John Weedon his heirs and assigns upon and for no other trust intent or purpose whatsoever as the said John Mitchell Furnell and John Weedon did thereby respectively admit and acknowledge

It is witnessed that in consideration of the premises the said John Mitchell Furnell at the request and by the direction of the said John Weedon testified &c. did thereby grant bargain sell release and convey unto the said John Weedon and his Heirs

All and singular the messuages or Tenements lands and hereditaments comprised in and conveyed by the therein within written Indenture or intended so to be with their rights members and appurtenances

And all the Estate &c.

To hold the said messuage or Tenements lands and hereditaments thereby released and conveyed or intended so to be with their rights members and appurtenances unto the said John Weedon and his Heirs

To the uses thereinafter expressed and declared viz

To the use of such person or persons for such estate or estates interest or interests and in such parts shares and proportions as the said John Weedon should at any time or times and from time to time thereafter by any Deed or Deeds in writing duly executed and attested direct limit or appoint

And in default of and until any such direction limon or appointment and in the mean time subject thereto

To the use of the said John Weedon and his assigns for the term of his natural life

And from and immediately after the determination of that Estate in the life time of the said John Weedon

To the use of the said Edward Micklem his executors and administrators during the natural life of the said John Weedon

In trust nevertheless for the said John Weedon and his assigns

And from and immediately after the decease of the said John Weedon

To the use of the said John Weedon his heirs and assigns for ever

Declaration by the said John Weedon that no woman becoming his widow should be entitled to Dower out of the said Hereditaments and premises

Covenant by the said John Mitchell Furnell that he had done no Act to incumber

Executed by the said John Mitchell Furnell and John Weedon and duly attested

(xxii) Abstract of the Title of Mr Francis Morgan Slocombe to a Freehold piece of Land part of the Greyfriars Estate in the parish of St Lawrence Reading (1862). Original in the Greyfriars Church Archive.

The first 12 pages are an almost exact copy of the previous document, 'Abstract of the Title of Mr John Weedon to a Freehold Estate on the North side of Friar Street in the Parish of Saint Lawrence Reading', and so are omitted here.

[p. 13]
27th December 1847
By Indenture of Statutory Release Between the said John Weedon of the 1st part Francis Morgan Slocombe of Reading Gentleman of the 2nd part and Edward Mullins of Great James Street Bedford Row Gentleman of the 3rd part

Reciting the hereinbefore abstracted Indenture of the 30th of November 1846

Also reciting the lastly abstracted Indenture

And reciting that said Francis Morgan Slocombe had contracted with said John Weedon for the absolute purchase of said capital messuage or

Dwellinghouse with the yard Garden and land thereunto adjoining thereinafter particularly described free from incumbrances at the price of £1930

It is witnessed that in consideration of £1930 by said Francis Morgan Slocombe paid to said John Weedon the receipt whereof is acknowledged He said John Weedon in execution of the powers reserved to him by the lastly thereinbefore recited Indenture did irrevocably direct limit and appoint that from thenceforth the said Capital Messuage or Dwellinghouse Yard Garden Land and Hereditaments thereinafter particularly described and released should go remain and be To the uses upon the Trusts and for the ends intents and purposes thereinafter expressed concerning the same

[p. 14]

And it is further witnessed that for the considerations aforesaid said John Weedon Did by those presents made in pursuance of and Act &c. Grant bargain sell alien release and convey ratify and confirm unto said Francis Morgan Slocombe and to his Heirs Appointees and Assigns

All that Capital Messuage or Dwellinghouse abutting on Friar Street in the parish of Saint Lawrence Reading in the County of Berks some years since erected by Lancelot Austwick Esquire with the yard Garden and Land thereunto adjoining and lying behind the same which said Hereditaments and premises contain by admeasurement on the South or Front side thereof next Friar Street 104 feet 4 inches and in depth on the East side thereof 193 feet 2 inches in the rear on the north side thereof 352 feet 6 inches and on the West and South West sides thereof together 308 feet were the same several dimensions a little more or less and were bounded on the north by other land of said John Weedon on the East by a road leading out of Friar Street called Grey Friars Road on the South partly by Friar Street and partly by building belonging to the Corporation of Reading and on the West and South West partly by other land and buildings belonging to said John Weedon and partly by said buildings belonging to the Corporation of Reading all which Hereditaments were more particularly delineated and shewn forth in the plan thereof drawn in the margin of now reciting Indenture and coloured red yellow and green with a right of way for said Francis Morgan Slocombe his appointees Heirs and assigns and his and their Tenants Tradesmen Agents and workmen at all times to said Hereditaments unto and over said Grey Friars Road

Together with the boundary wall to said hereditaments built thereon by said Francis Morgan Slocombe

And all Houses &c.

And the Reversions &c.

[p. 15]

And all the Estate &c.

To hold free from Tithe and Tithe Rent Charge and also from Land tax which had been redeemed and from all incumbrances unto said Francis Morgan Slocombe and his heirs

> To such uses upon such Trusts and for such ends intents and purposes and with under and subject to such powers provisos Declarations and agreements and in such manner and form as said Francis Morgan Slocombe should from time to time by any Deed or Deeds in writing to be by him sealed and delivered in the presence of and attested by one or more witness or witnesses direct limit or appoint
>
> To the use of said Francis Morgan Slocombe and his assigns during the term of his natural life without impeachment of waste
>
> To the use of said Edward Mullins his executors and administrators during the life of and in trust for said Francis Morgan Slocombe and his assigns
>
> To the use of said Francis Morgan Slocombe his heirs and assigns for ever
>
> Declaration by said Francis Morgan Slocombe against Dower

Covenants by said John Weedon for himself his heirs executors and administrators that said Power of Appointment was a valid and subsisting Power – that he had good right to appoint – For quiet enjoyment – Free from incumbrances And for further assurance – And that no buildings should be erected or Cesspool constructed within 35 feet of the north wall for 150 feet from East to West

Further Covenant by said John Weedon for the production and giving copies of Deeds mentioned in Schedule

Covenant by said Francis Morgan Slocombe to put up wall to complete separation of Properties and to allow the removal of certain erections within six months from date of Deed.

The Schedule referred to –

4th & 5th February 1806
Indentures of Lease and Release the Release between Joseph Hill of 1st part Thomas Hill Mortimer of 2nd part Lancelot Austwick of 3rd part and George Booth Tyndale of 4th part

30th November 1846
Indenture between William Stephens and John Knight of 1st part

[p. 16]
Harwood Austwick of 2nd part George Booth Tyndale of 3rd part and John Mitchell Furnell of 4th part

1st December 1846
Indenture between John Mitchell Furnell of 1st part John Weedon of 2nd part and Edward Micklem of 3rd part

> Executed by said John Weedon and Francis Morgan Slocombe and attested and receipt for £1930 consideration money endorsed signed and witnessed

28th December 1847

By Indenture of Mortgage between said Francis Morgan Slocombe of the one part and John Weedon of the other part

> Reciting lastly abstracted Indenture
>
> And reciting that said Francis Morgan Slocombe had requested said John Weedon to lend him £1000 on Mortgage of hereditaments comprised in recited Indenture which he had agreed to do

It is witnessed that in consideration of £1000 to said Francis Morgan Slocombe paid by said John Weedon the receipt whereof is acknowledged He said Francis Morgan Slocombe Did direct limit and appoint that said Capital Messuage or Dwellinghouse land and Hereditaments comprised in said thereinbefore recited Indenture should henceforth go remain and be &c. that said recited Indenture should inure

> > To the use of said John Weedon his heirs and assigns subject to the proviso for redemption thereinafter contained

Proviso for Redemption and Reconveyance of said Hereditaments on payment by said Francis Morgan Slocombe his heirs or assigns unto said John Weedon his executors administrators and assigns of said sum of £1000 with interest thereon at 5 per Cent per Annum at the times and in manner thereinafter mentioned

Power of Sale in default of payment with the usual indemnity to Purchase and to Mortgage

Covenants by said Francis Morgan Slocombe for himself his heirs executors and administrators with said John Weedon his heirs executors administrators and assigns to keep premises in repair – For payment of principal and interest – that he had good right to appoint – For quiet enjoyment after default – Free from incumbrances – For further Assurance – And for insuring House and buildings

Proviso for continuance of Mortgage for three years

[p. 17]

> > Executed by both parties and attested and receipt for consideration money indorsed signed and witnessed

23rd February 1850

Indenture of Transfer between said John Weedon of the one part and William Blandy of Reading aforesaid Banker and Thomas Skeete Workman of Reading aforesaid Surgeon of the other part

> Reciting lastly abstracted Indenture
>
> Also reciting that said William Blandy and Thomas Skeete Workman had proposed to pay to said John Weedon said sum of £1000 upon having a transfer to them of same and all interest thereafter to grow due and also upon having the hereditaments comprised in said recited Indenture conveyed to them subject to the right of redemption then subsisting

It is witnessed that in consideration of £1000 to said John Weedon paid by said William Blandy and Thomas Skeete Workman the receipt whereof is acknowledged He said John Weedon Did bargain sell assign transfer and set over unto said William Blandy and Thomas Skeete Workman their executors administrators and assigns

>All that said sum of £1000 secured by said recited Indenture and charged upon said Capital Messuage or Dwellinghouse land and Hereditaments and all interest to grow due for same with the full benefit of said Indenture and Mortgage
>And all the Estate &c.

To hold receive and take said sum of £1000 and all interest thereafter to grow due unto said William Blandy and Thomas Skeete Workman their heirs executors administrators and assigns as and for their own proper monies

Power of Attorney from said John Weedon to said William Blandy and Thomas Skeete Workman to apply for and compel payment of said principal sum of £1000 and interest

And it was further witnessed that for considerations aforesaid said John Weedon by now abstracting Indenture made in pursuance of an Act &c. Did Bargain sell alien and release unto said William Blandy and Thomas Skeete Workman their heirs and assigns

>Said Capital Messuage land and Hereditaments
>And the Reversions &c.
>And all the Estate &c.

[p. 18]
>To hold unto and to the use of said William Blandy and Thomas Skeete Workman their heirs and assigns for ever subject to the Proviso for Redemption contained in said recited Indenture of Mortgage

Covenant by said John Weedon that he had done no act to incumber

Covenant by said William Blandy and Thomas Skeete Workman for indemnification of said John Weedon

>Executed by said John Weedon and attested and receipt for £1000 consideration money indorsed signed and witnessed

6th January 1852
Memorandum indorsed on last Abstracted Indenture under the hand of said William Blandy acknowledging receipt of principal sum of £1000 and Interest and undertaking to reconvey the therein within mentioned Messuage land and Hereditaments

16th November 1853
Indenture of Reconveyance between said William Blandy of the 1st part said Francis Morgan Slocombe of the 2nd part and said Edward Mullins of the 3rd part

>Reciting said Abstracted Indenture of Mortgage of 28th of December 1847
>Also reciting said Abstracted Indenture of the 23rd of February 1850
>And reciting the death of said Thomas Skeete Workman on the 19th of February 1851
>And reciting that on the 6th day of January 1852 said Francis Morgan Slocombe paid to said William Blandy said principal sum of £1000 with

all interest due thereon as he did thereby acknowledge but no Reconveyance of Capital Messuage Dwellinghouse land and Hereditaments was then made

It is witnessed that in consideration of said sum of £1000 sterling by said Francis Morgan Slocombe paid to said William Blandy in full satisfaction and discharge of all principal money and interest due and owing under said Indenture of Mortgage the payment and receipt whereof is acknowledged He said William Blandy Did grant Release and convey and also remise and quit claim unto said Francis Morgan Slocombe his heirs and assigns

> Said Capital messuage land and Hereditaments
> And the reversions &c.
> And all the Estate &c.

[p. 19]

> To hold (freed and absolutely remunerated and discharged from said principal sum of £1000 and all interest payable in respect thereof) unto said Francis Morgan Slocombe and his Heirs
>> To such uses upon such Trusts and for such ends intents and purposes and with under and subject to such powers provisos declarations and agreements and in such manner and form as said Francis Morgan Slocombe should from time to time by any Deed or Deeds in writing to be by him sealed and delivered in the presence of and attested by one or more Witness or Witnesses direct limit or appoint and in default of and subject to such direction limitation or appointment
>> To the use of said Francis Morgan Slocombe and his assigns during the term of his natural life without impeachment of waste
>> To the use of said Edward Mullins his executors and administrators during the life of and in Trust for said Francis Morgan Slocombe and his assigns
>> To the use of said Francis Morgan Slocombe his heirs and assigns for ever

Declaration by said Francis Morgan Slocombe against Dower
Covenant by said William Blandy that he had not incumbered
> Executed and attested

Same date

Statutory Declaration by said William Blandy as follows 'I William Blandy of Reading in the County of Berks Banker do solemnly and sincerely declare that I am the person named in a certain Indenture bearing date the 23rd of February 1850 expressed to be made between John Weedon of Reading aforesaid Esquire of the one part and William Blandy of Reading aforesaid Banker and Thomas Skeete Workman of Reading aforesaid Surgeon of the other part being an Indenture whereby the said John Weedon in consideration of the sum of £1000 to him paid by myself and the said Thomas Skeete Workman transferred to myself and the said Thomas Skeete Workman a certain Mortgage debt of £1000 charged on certain Hereditaments in Friar Street Reading aforesaid by Indenture of Mortgage dated the 28th of December 1847 and made between

Francis Morgan Slocombe of Reading aforesaid Gentleman of the one part and the said John Weedon

[p. 20]
of the other part
And I further solemnly and sincerely declare that the sum of £1000 so paid to the said John Weedon as aforesaid by myself and the said Thomas Skeete Workman was advanced by us out of money belonging to myself and the said Thomas Skeete Workman jointly on a joint account and that the same sum and the interest thereof by reason of the death of the said Thomas Skeete Workman which took place on or about the 19th of February 1851 became payable to myself alone as the survivor in exclusion of the Executors and administrators of the said Thomas Skeete Workman' And I make &c.

As to the Western Extremity
of the Piece of Land

17th July 1852
Indenture between Sarah Weedon of Reading Widow of the 1st part said Francis Morgan Slocombe of the 2nd part and said Edward Mullins of the 3rd part

> Reciting hereinbefore abstracted Indentures of the 30th of November and 1st of December 1846
> And reciting the Will and Codicil of said John Weedon by which he devised his real Estate to Sarah Weedon Edward Micklem and Thomas Champion in Trust with full powers to sell same
> And reciting the death of said John Weedon on the 19th of March 1850 and the proof of his Will and Codicil by the said Sarah Weedon alone on the 6th of May 1850 in the Prerogative Court of Canterbury
> And reciting that by Deed Poll under the hands of and seals of said Edward Micklem and Thomas Champion dated the 6th of July 1850 they renounced and disclaimed all Estate Title Trusts and powers under the Will and Codicil of said John Weedon
> And reciting that said Francis Morgan Slocombe had contracted with said Sarah Weedon for the purchase of the Piece of Land thereinafter described for the sum of £23

It is witnessed that in consideration of £23 to said Sarah Weedon paid by said Francis Morgan Slocombe the receipt whereof was acknowledged She said Sarah Weedon as Devisee in Trust under said Will and Codicil or one of them Did grant Release and convey unto said Francis Morgan Slocombe and his heirs

> All that piece or parcel of Land being part and portion of the Grey Friars Estate situate on the South West side of Property also forming part

[p. 21]
> of the said Estate sold and conveyed by John Weedon deceased to said Francis Morgan Slocombe and being in the parish of Saint Lawrence in the Borough of Reading in the County of Berks and

containing in length on the North East side thereof 168 feet 6 inches and on the South West side thereof 165 feet and in breadth on the South side thereof 8 feet and on the North or North West side thereof 3 feet 10 inches were the same several dimensions a little more or less (bounded on the North East side thereof by land belonging to said Francis Morgan Slocombe on the South West and South sides thereof by land belonging to said Sarah Weedon and on the north or north west side thereof by land and premises belonging to George Simmonds Strong which piece of land was partly delineated in the plan drawn at the back of now abstracting deed and coloured Green Together with the boundary Wall to said piece or parcel of Land erected and built thereon by said Francis Morgan Slocombe

And all the Estate &c.

To hold unto said Francis Morgan Slocombe and his heirs To such uses Upon such Trusts and for such intents and purposes as

said Francis Morgan Slocombe should appoint and in default of and subject to such appointment To the use of said Francis Morgan Slocombe and his assigns for life

To the use of said Edward Mullins his executors and administrators during the life of and In trust for said Francis Morgan Slocombe and his assigns

To the use of said Francis Morgan Slocombe his heirs and assigns for ever

Declaration against Dower

Covenant by said Sarah Weedon that she had not incumbered

And to produce and give copies of Indentures in Schedule

[p. 22]

The Schedule contains

The Abstracted Indentures of the 4th and 5th February 1806 the 30th November 1846 1st December 1846 and The thereinbefore recited Deed Poll of 6th July 1850

Executed and attested and receipt for consideration money indorsed signed and witnessed

(xxiii) Conveyance of pieces of land part of the Greyfriars Estate in the parish of St Lawrence Reading (1862). Original in the Greyfriars Church Archive

This indenture is the record of the conveyance of the strip of land immediately to the north of the church, that included the area of the north transept and an access strip along the north of the site to enable a vestry to be built against the north transept.[1]

---

1 See Figure 7.

19 June 1862
Mr F. M. Slocombe to Reverend W. W. Phelps

[First Sheet]
This Indenture made the nineteenth day of June in the year of our Lord one thousand eight hundred and sixty two Between Francis Morgan Slocombe of Reading in the County of Berks Gentleman of the first part The Reverend William Whitmarsh Phelps of Reading aforesaid Clerk of the second part and John Neale of the same place Gentleman of the third part

Whereas by an Indenture bearing date on or about the sixteenth day of November one thousand eight hundred and fifty three and made or expressed to be made between William Blandy Banker of the first part the said Francis Morgan Slocombe of the second part and Edward Mullins Gentleman of the third part For the considerations therein mentioned the piece of land hereinafter firstly described and hereby appointed and conveyed was (with other hereditaments) conveyed unto the said Francis Morgan Slocombe and his heirs to such uses upon such trusts and for such ends intents and purposes and with under and subject to such powers provisos declarations and agreements and in such manner and form as the said Francis Morgan Slocombe should from time to time by any Deed or Deeds in writing to be by him sealed and delivered in the presence of and attested by one or more witness or witnesses direct limit or appoint And in default of and subject to such direction limitation or appointment To the use of the said Francis Morgan Slocombe and his assigns during the term of his natural life remainder To the use of the said Edward Mullins his executors and administrators during the life of and in trust for the said Francis Morgan Slocombe and his assigns with remainder To the use of the said Francis Morgan Slocombe his heirs and assigns for ever

And whereas by an Indenture bearing date on or about the seventeenth day of July one thousand eight hundred and fifty two and made or expressed to be made between Sarah Weedon widow of the first part the said Francis Morgan Slocombe of the second part and the said Edward Mullins of the third part For the considerations therein mentioned the piece or parcel of land hereinafter secondly described and hereby appointed and conveyed was (with other hereditaments) conveyed unto the said Francis Morgan Slocombe and his heirs To such uses upon such trusts and for such intents and purposes as the said Francis Morgan Slocombe should appoint And in default of and subject to such appointment To the use of the said Francis Morgan Slocombe and his assigns for life remainder To the use of the said Edward Mullins his executors and administrators during the life of and in trust for the said Francis Morgan Slocombe and his assigns with remainder To the use of the said Francis Morgan Slocombe his heirs and assigns for ever

And whereas the said Francis Morgan Slocombe hath contracted with the said William Whitmarsh Phelps for the absolute Sale to him of the pieces or parcels of Land hereinafter described and hereby appointed and conveyed or intended so to be and the fee simple and inheritance thereof in possession free from incumbrances at or for the price or sum of three hundred pounds

Now this Indenture Witnesseth that in pursuance of the said Contract and in consideration of the sum of Three hundred pounds of Sterling money in hand well and truly paid by the said William Whitmarsh Phelps to the said Francis Morgan Slocombe on the execution hereof the receipt of which said sum of three hundred pounds and that the same is in full for the absolute purchase of the said piece of land hereinafter described and hereby appointed and conveyed or intended so to be the said Francis Morgan Slocombe Doth hereby acknowledge and therefrom Doth by these presents release exonerate and for ever discharge the said William Whitmarsh Phelps his heirs executors administrators and assigns and every of them for ever by these presents He the said Francis Morgan Slocombe in pursuance and by virtue and in exercise of the powers and authorities given or reserved to him by the hereinbefore in part recited Indenture of the sixteenth day of November one thousand eight hundred and fifty three and the seventeenth day of July one thousand eight hundred and fifty two Doth by this present Deed or Instrument in writing by him sealed and delivered in the presence of and attested by one or more witness or witnesses direct limit and appoint That the pieces or parcels of land hereinafter particularly described and hereby conveyed with their appurtenances shall from henceforth be to the uses upon the trusts and for the ends intents and purposes hereinafter limited expressed and declared

And this Indenture also Witnesseth that in further pursuance of the said Contract and for the considerations aforesaid the said Francis Morgan Slocombe Doth by these presents grant release convey and confirm unto the said William Whitmarsh Phelps and his heirs

Firstly All that piece or parcel of land (being part of the hereditaments comprised in and conveyed to the said Francis Morgan Slocombe by the hereinbefore recited Indenture of the sixteenth day of November one thousand eight hundred and fifty three) situate on the North side of the Building in Friar Street Reading aforesaid lately used as a Bridewell but now called the Grey Friars Church as the same with its several dimensions and boundaries is shown by the Plan drawn on the back of these presents and distinguished by the Colour red

Secondly All that piece or parcel of land (being part of the hereditaments comprised in and conveyed to the said Francis Morgan Slocombe by the hereinbefore recited Indenture dated the seventeenth day of July one thousand eight hundred and fifty two) also situate on the North side of land at the West end of the Building in Friar Street Reading aforesaid lately used as a Bridewell but now called the Grey Friars Church as the same with its several dimensions and boundaries is shewn by the plan drawn on the back of these presents and distinguished by the Colour Blue Together with all ways passages waters watercourses sewers gutters bounds fences walls easements privileges profits commodities advantages and appurtenances whatsoever to the said pieces or parcels of land belonging or appertaining or reputed to belong or appertain And the reversion and reversions remainder and remainders rents issues and profits thereof And all the estate right title interest use trust possession inheritance property claim and demand whatsoever both at Law and in equity of him the said Francis Morgan Slocombe of in to out of or upon the same pieces or parcels of land or any part thereof

To have and To hold the said pieces or parcels of land and all and singular other the hereditaments and premises hereby appointed and conveyed or intended so to be with their appurtenances unto the said William Whitmarsh Phelps and his heirs To the uses upon the trusts and for the ends intents and purposes hereinafter declared that is to say To such uses upon such trusts and for such ends intents and purposes as the said William Whitmarsh Phelps shall from time to time or at any time by deed or deeds appoint and in default of and until such appointment and subject thereto To the use of the said William Whitmarsh Phelps and his assigns during the term of his natural life without impeachment of waste And after the determination of that estate by any means in his life time To the use of the said John Neale his executors and administrators during the life of and in trust for the said William Whitmarsh Phelps and his assigns And after the determination of the said hereinbefore lastly limited estate To the use of the said William Whitmarsh Phelps his heirs and assigns for ever

And it is hereby declared that no Widow of the said William Whitmarsh Phelps shall be entitled to dower out of the said pieces or parcels of land or any part thereof

And the said Francis Morgan Slocombe doth hereby for himself his heirs executors and administrators Covenant and declare with and to the said William Whitmarsh Phelps his heirs and assigns in manner following that is to say that notwithstanding any act deed matter or thing made done permitted or suffered by the said Francis Morgan Slocombe to the contrary the hereinbefore recited powers of appointment are at the time of the execution of these presents valid and subsisting powers And also that notwithstanding any such act deed matter or thing as aforesaid the said Francis Morgan Slocombe now hath in himself good right full power and lawful and absolute authority to appoint release and convey the said pieces or parcels of lands and hereditaments with their appurtenances To the uses and in manner aforesaid And also that the said pieces or parcels of land hereby appointed and conveyed shall and may from

[Second Sheet]
Henceforth and at all times hereafter be to the uses hereinbefore declared concerning the same and be peaceably and quietly held and enjoyed accordingly without let suit eviction ejection interruption disturbance or denial of or by the said Francis Morgan Slocombe or any other person or persons whomsoever rightfully claiming under or in trust for him

And that freely clearly and absolutely indemnified by the said Francis Morgan Slocombe his heirs executors or administrators of from and against all former estates rights titles liens charges and incumbrances whatsoever made created or suffered by the said Francis Morgan Slocombe or any person or persons whomsoever rightfully claiming under or in trust for him

And moreover that the said Francis Morgan Slocombe and all persons rightfully claiming any estate or interest legal or equitable in the said hereditaments and premises under or in trust for him will from time to time and at all times hereafter at the request and costs of the said William Whitmarsh Phelps his appointees heirs or assigns enter into execute and perfect all such further and other lawful and reasonable acts deeds appointments conveyances and assurances whatsoever for the further better or more satisfactorily appointing assuring and confirming the said pieces or parcels of Land and hereditaments To the uses aforesaid according to the true intent and meaning of these presents as the said William Whitmarsh Phelps his appointees heirs or assigns or his or their Counsel in the Law shall require and as shall be tendered to be done and executed

And the said William Whitmarsh Phelps doth hereby for himself his heirs executors administrators and assigns covenant with the said Francis Morgan Slocombe his heirs executors administrators and assigns that he the said William Whitmarsh Phelps his heirs or assigns will forthwith erect or cause to be erected a good brick or flint wall fair on both sides of the height of six feet at the least to separate that portion of the said pieces or parcels of Land hereby appointed and conveyed and marked A to B on the said plan drawn on the back of these presents from the adjoining Land of the said Francis Morgan Slocombe on the North side And also that the Glass to be used in the Windows shewn on the said plan shall be Church or nontransparent Glass And also shall allow the present Wall which bounds the front yard of the said Francis Morgan Slocombe on the West to remain to a height corresponding with the Wall of the said Francis Morgan Slocombe next Friar Street or otherwise shall erect or cause to be erected a new Wall on the said Western boundary of the said height and hereafter maintain the same Wall

And whereas on the treaty for the said Sale it was agreed that the Title Deeds and evidences of Title mentioned in the Schedule hereunder written which relate to other hereditaments of greater value belonging to the said Francis Morgan Slocombe should remain in the custody of the said Francis Morgan Slocombe on his entering into the Covenant for production and furnishing copies thereof hereinafter contained

Now this Indenture lastly witnesseth that in pursuance of the said agreement and in consideration of the premises He the said Francis Morgan Slocombe doth hereby for himself his heirs executors administrators and assigns Covenant with the said William Whitmarsh Phelps his appointees heirs and assigns that he the said Francis Morgan Slocombe his heirs or assigns shall and will (unless prevented by fire or other inevitable accident) at all times hereafter upon every reasonable request and at the costs of the said William Whitmarsh Phelps his appointees heirs or assigns produce or cause to be produced to him or them or his or their Counsel Attornies Solicitors or Agents or at any Trial or hearing in any Court or otherwise as occasion shall require in England all and every the Deeds and evidences specified in the Schedule hereunder written for the proof manifestation or support of the Title of the said William Whitmarsh Phelps his appointees heirs and assigns to the said pieces or parcels of Land and hereditaments hereinbefore described and hereby appointed and conveyed or intended so to be and every part thereof

And also (unless prevented as aforesaid) at such request and costs as aforesaid make and deliver to the said William Whitmarsh Phelps his heirs and assigns true and attested copies abstracts or extracts of or from the said deeds and evidences or any of them and permit the same to be examined with the originals by the said William Whitmarsh Phelps his appointees heirs or assigns or any person appointed by him

And lastly shall and will in the meantime keep and preserve the same Deeds and Evidences undefaced unobliterated and uncancelled (accidents by fire or other inevitable cause excepted)

In witness whereof the said parties to these presents have hereunto set their hands and seals the day and year first within written

The Schedule referred to.

4th and 5th February 1806	Attested Copies of Indentures of Lease and Release the latter made between Joseph Hill Esquire of the first part Thomas Hill Mortimer Gentleman of the second part Lancelot Austwick Esquire of the third part and George Booth Tyndale Gentleman of the fourth part
30th November 1846	Attested Copy of Indenture between William Stephens Esquire and John Knight Esquire of the first part Harwood Austwick Esquire of the second part the said George Booth Tyndale Esquire of the third part and John Mitchell Furnell Gentleman of the fourth part
1st December 1846	Attested Copy of Indenture between the said John Mitchell Furnell of the first part John Weedon Gentleman of the second part and Edward Micklem Esquire of the third part
27th December 1847	Indenture between the said John Weedon of the first part the said Francis Morgan Slocombe of the second part and Edward Mullins Gentleman of the third part
28th December 1847	Indenture of Mortgage between the said Francis Morgan Slocombe of the one part and the said John Weedon of the other part
23rd February 1850	Indenture of Transfer of Mortgage between said John Weedon of the one part and William Blandy Banker and Thomas Skeete Workman Surgeon of the other part
6th January 1852	Memorandum (endorsed on last Indenture) under the hand of the said William Blandy
16th November 1853	Indenture between the said William Blandy of the first part the said Francis Morgan Slocombe of the second part and said Edward Mullins of the third part
Same Date	Statutory Declaration of said William Blandy
17th July 1852	Indenture between the said Sarah Weedon of the first part the said Francis Morgan Slocombe of the second part and said Edward Mullins of the third part

[Signatures and seals of]   F. M. Slocombe   W. W. Phelps

[Reverse of First Sheet]
Received the day and year first within written of and from the within named William Whitmarsh Phelps the sum of Three hundred pounds being the consideration money within expressed to be paid by him to me.
[Signed] F. M. Slocombe
Witness:
[Signed] Henry Creed
£300
Signed Sealed and Delivered by the within named Francis Morgan Slocombe in the presence of
    [Signed] Henry Creed
    Clerk to Mr Slocombe, Solicitor, Reading
Signed Sealed and Delivered by the within named William Whitmarsh Phelps in the presence of
    [Illegible signature] Clerk to Mr J. Neale, Solicitor Reading

(xxiv) Draft deed of Agreement between the bishop patron and incumbent as to the patronage of a church intended to be built on the north side of Friar Street in the Parish of St Lawrence Reading in the County of Berks (1862). Original in the Greyfriars Church Archive.

This Indenture made the 8th day of August A.D. 1862 Between The Right Reverend Father in God Samuel by Divine permission Lord Bishop of Oxford of the first part The Reverend John Ball the Vicar of the Vicarage and Parish Church of St. Lawrence Reading in the County of Berks of the second part and the said John Ball the Reverend William Whitmarsh Phelps Incumbent of the Church of the Holy Trinity in Reading aforesaid John Neale of Reading aforesaid Gentleman John Simonds of Reading aforesaid Banker and the Reverend Peter French Incumbent of the Parish Church of the Holy Trinity Burton upon Trent in the County of Stafford of the third part Whereas by an Act of Parliament made and passed in the Session held in the 8th and 9th Years of the Reign of Her Majesty Queen Victoria intituled 'An Act for further amendment of the Church Building Acts' It is Enacted that if before or during the building of any new Church or previous to its Consecration the Bishop of the Diocese and the Patron and Incumbent of the Parish in which such new Church has been or is intended to be

[p. 2]
built shall enter into an agreement in writing that the right of nomination to such new Church shall on its Consecration belong to and be exercised by any Body Corporate aggregate or sole or by any person or persons such agreement shall be binding on such respective parties their Successors heirs and assigns

and they shall be compelled to fulfil the same And Whereas by another Act of Parliament made and passed in the session held in the 11th and 12th Years of the same Reign intituled 'An Act to amend the Law relative to the assignment of Ecclesiastical Districts' After Reciting the Enactment hereinbefore recited and also reciting that doubts had been entertained whether such provision extended beyond a power on the part of such Bishop Patron and Incumbent to enter into such agreement for more than one turn or right of presentation And that it was expedient that such doubts should be removed It was Enacted and declared that any Agreement already made or thereafter to be made between such Bishop Patron and Incumbent under the provisions of the hereinbefore recited Act purporting to be an agreement made between such parties with respect to any new Church before or during its building or previous to its Consecration

[p. 3]
that the right of presentation thereto should on its Consecration be vested either in perpetuity or otherwise in any body corporate aggregate or sole or any person or persons their heirs or assigns should be valid and effectual for the purpose of vesting such patronage according to such Agreement And Whereas for the use and accommodation of certain of the Inhabitants of the said Parish of Saint Lawrence, Reading, and to promote the service of Almighty God according to the Liturgy and Rites of the United Church of England and Ireland it is intended to erect a new Church (to be Consecrated by the name and style of 'Grey Friars' Church') upon a parcel or parcels of Land situate on the North side of Friar Street in the Parish of Saint Lawrence aforesaid and which parcel or parcels of Land have lately been purchased by the said W. W. Phelps and have since been conveyed by him to the Ecclesiastical Commissioners for England under the provisions of the Acts of Parliament commonly called and known as The Church Building Acts as and for a site for the said new Church to be called Grey Friars Church with surrounding Yard and Enclosures

[p. 4]
and to be devoted when Consecrated to Ecclesiastical purposes for ever And Whereas the sum of Money necessary for the erection of the said intended new Church has lately been subscribed of which sum the said William Whitmarsh Phelps John Neale John Simonds and Peter French have out of their own moneys contributed the sum of £2,000 And Whereas it is in contemplation to procure or obtain the assignment to the said Church (when erected and consecrated) of an Ecclesiastical District Now this Indenture Witnesseth that by virtue and in exercise of the power or provision in that behalf contained in the said Acts of Parliament of the 8th and 9th and the 11th and 12th Years of the Reign of Her said Majesty or either of them and of every other power and provision in anywise enabling them in this behalf the said Samuel Lord Bishop of Oxford as the Bishop of the Diocese within which the said Parish and Parish Church of St Lawrence Reading is situate and also as the Patron of such last mentioned Parish and the said John Ball as the Incumbent of the same Parish and Parish Church for themselves and their respective successors heirs and assigns hereby Covenant

[p. 5]
and agree with the said John Ball William Whitmarsh Phelps John Neale John Simonds and Peter French their heirs and assigns that the patronage of or right of nomination to the said new Church to be built in the said Parish of Saint Lawrence Reading as aforesaid shall from and after the Consecration of such Church belong to and be vested in the said John Ball William Whitmarsh Phelps John Neale John Simonds and Peter French their heirs and assigns for ever but upon the trusts and for the purposes and with and subject to the power and provisoes hereinafter declared and contained concerning the same And it is hereby accordingly agreed and declared between and by the parties to these presents that the said Patronage of or right of nomination to the said new Church shall for ever hereafter be held by the said John Ball William Whitmarsh Phelps John Neale John Simonds and Peter French their heirs and assigns Upon Trust that they the said John Ball William Whitmarsh Phelps John Neale John Simonds and Peter French and the survivors and survivor of them and the heirs of such survivor and their or his assigns or other the Trustee or Trustees for the time being of these presents do and shall immediately upon the Consecration

[p. 6]
of the said new Church and thereafter from time to time for ever when and as often as the said new Church shall become vacant by the death resignation deprivation or Cession of the Incumbent or Minister thereof or otherwise nominate or appoint to the same Church or Incumbency such fit and pious person of godly life and conversation being in Holy Orders capable of accepting and holding the same as the said Trustees or Trustee for the time being of these presents or the major part in number of them or if there shall happen to be but one Trustee for the time being then as such Trustee shall determine upon And do and shall perform and execute all such other acts deeds matters and things as shall or may be requisite for enabling the person so from time to time nominated or appointed as aforesaid to become and continue the Minister of such Church and to hold and enjoy such Incumbency and all emoluments rights privileges and appurtenances thereunto or to such office of Minister belonging And it is hereby expressly declared that any one of the Trustees or the sole Trustee for the time being of these Presents if duly qualified in other respects may at any time be nominated or appointed

[p. 7]
under the trust hereinbefore declared notwithstanding his being one of the persons or the only person by whom such nomination or appointment shall be made And it is hereby agreed and declared between and by the said parties to these Presents that when and so often as any of the Trustees for the time being of these Presents whether hereby constituted or to be appointed as hereinafter mentioned or otherwise shall die or shall leave the United Kingdom and reside abroad or shall be desirous of being discharged from or refuse or decline or become incapable to act in the Trusts hereinbefore declared then and in such case and so often as the same shall happen it shall be lawful for the persons

who shall for the time being be Trustees of these Presents and shall be within the United Kingdom and willing and capable to exercise the present power (including as one of such Trustees the person (if any) who shall be about to retire) or the major part in number of such persons or if there shall be but one such person then for such one person and they and he are and is hereby directed with all convenient speed by any deed or deeds Instrument or Instruments in writing

[p. 8]
to be sealed and delivered by them or him in the presence of and to be attested by two or more credible Witnesses from time to time to nominate substitute or appoint any other male person or persons of full age and of godly life and conversation and a member of the said United Church of England and Ireland to be a Trustee in the place of such Trustee so dying or leaving this Kingdom or desiring to be discharged or refusing declining or becoming incapable to act or ceasing to be a Trustee as aforesaid And that when and so often as any new Trustee or Trustees shall be nominated substituted and appointed as aforesaid the said Patronage or right of nomination hereinbefore vested in the said persons parties hereto of the 3rd part or intended so to be shall with all convenient speed be conveyed and assured in such manner as that the same shall and may be legally and effectually vested in the persons or person who after such appointment shall be the Trustees or Trustee of these Presents to be held upon the same Trusts as in hereinbefore declared of and concerning the same so far as the same shall be then subsisting or capable of taking effect And it

[p. 9]
is hereby agreed and declared that the Trustee or Trustees so to be nominated substituted or appointed as aforesaid shall and may in all things act and assist in the management carrying on and execution of the Trusts to which he or they shall be so appointed in conjunction with the other then surviving or continuing Trustees or Trustee if there shall be any such surviving or continuing Trustee or Trustees and if not then by himself or themselves as fully and effectually and shall and may have and exercise or join in exercising the same powers or authorities and discretions to all intents and purposes whatsoever as if he or they had been originally in and by these Presents nominated a Trustee or Trustees and as well before as after the said Patronage or right of nomination shall have been so conveyed and assured as aforesaid In Witness &c.

Approved for the Bishop of Oxford. [Signed] John M Davenport, Oxford 6 May 1862

Approved [Signed] John Ball B.D. Vicar of St Lawrence Reading

[p. 10]
[Schematic diagram of how the document will be signed]

S (Bishop's seal) Oxon

John Ball B.D. as Vicar of St Lawrence, Reading (Seal)
John (Seal) Ball
W.W. (Seal) Phelps
John Neale (Seal)
John (Seal) Simonds
Peter French (Seal)

Signed sealed and delivered by the within named Samuel Lord Bishop of Oxford in the presence of
[Signed] John M Davenport, Oxford, Secretary to his Lordship

Signed sealed and delivered by the within named John Simonds in the presence of
[Signed] S. Fullbrook, King Street, Reading Gentleman

Signed sealed and delivered by the within named Reverend W. W. Phelps and John Neale in the presence of
[Signed] J. W. H. Davis Clerk to Mr Neale, Solicitor, Reading

Signed sealed and delivered by the within named Peter French in the presence of
[Signed] J. H. Law

Signed sealed and delivered by the within named John Ball in the presence of both as Vicar of St Lawrence and as Trustee
[Signed] J. H. Law Clerk to Mr J. Neale, Solicitor, Reading

(xxv)   Correspondence respecting the conveyancing of the Greyfriars property from the Rev W. W. Phelps to the Ecclesiastical Commissioners (1862–3). Originals in the Greyfriars Church Archive.

Letter 1
All Communications for this Board to be addressed to – The Secretary, Ecclesiastical Commission, 11, Whitehall Place, London SW
To John Neale, Esquire, Reading.
                                                            11, Whitehall Place, SW
                                                            14th May 1862
Sir,
                    File No. 26664
                 Proposed New Church
                in Reading St. Lawrence
    I have on behalf of the Ecclesiastical Commissioners for England to acknowledge the receipt of your letter of the 8th instant relative to the conveyance to this Board of a site for a new Church in the Parish of St Lawrence Reading and in reply I beg to transmit the circular letter and form of Undertaking which are used in cases of this kind. Upon the return of the

Undertaking duly executed, the matter will be referred to the Commissioners' Solicitors who will communicate with you as to the title of the property. Their investigation into title however is carried only so far as may be necessary to ensure the safety of the Board in accepting the conveyance.

I am, Sir, Your very obedient Servant, [Signed] James J. Chalk

Letter 2
To John Neale, Esquire, Reading

11, Whitehall Place, SW
14th May 1862

Sir,

File No. 26664
Proposed New Church in Reading St. Lawrence
Conveyance of Site

In answer to your application of the 8th instant I have the honour to acquaint you that the Ecclesiastical Commissioners for England are willing to accept a conveyance of the land therein alluded to as a site for a proposed new church in the Parish of St Lawrence, Reading, on condition that a satisfactory title to the lands in question be shown, and that the costs to be incurred by the Board in respect of the contemplated Conveyance be defrayed by the promoters of the measure.

Should you determine to proceed in the matter you will be pleased to furnish me with a written Description of the land, and with a map or plan thereof drawn to a scale of not less than one chain to an inch. You will also be so good as to return the accompanying form of undertaking duly filled up signed and attested.

I am, Sir, Your very obedient Servant, [Signed] James J. Chalk

[Form of Undertaking]

Ecclesiastical Commissioners for England
File No. 26664
Proposed New Church in Reading St. Lawrence
Conveyance of Site

The Ecclesiastical Commissioners for England having consented to accept a Conveyance of certain Land as a site for a proposed new Church in the Parish of Saint Lawrence Reading on condition that a satisfactory Title to the Land in question is shown, and that the Costs to be incurred by the Board in respect of the contemplated Conveyance be defrayed by the promoters of the measure. I the undersigned hereby undertake to pay all Costs and charges which the said Commissioners may incur in respect of such Conveyance.

Dated this [blank] day of [blank] 1862,
    Name,   Address
Witness
    Name,   Address

Letter 3
To John Neale, Esquire, 13 Friar Street, Reading

11, Whitehall Place, SW
23rd May 1862

Sir,

File No. 26664
Proposed New Church
in Reading St. Lawrence
Conveyance of Site

I have the honour to acknowledge the receipt of your communication of the 21st instant and to acquaint you that Messrs. White, Borrett, and White, of No. 6, Whitehall Place, have been instructed to take the necessary steps on behalf of the Ecclesiastical Commissioners for England for completing the proposed Conveyance in this case.

I am, Sir, Your very obedient Servant, [Signed] James J. Chalk

Letter 4
To John Neale Esquire, Solicitor Reading

London, 6 Whitehall Place SW
24 May 1862

Dear Sir:

Reading St Lawrence: Church site

We have today received instructions from the Ecclesiastical Commissioners herein. We presume that the three conveyances to Mr Phelps all contain recital of previous title, and that you acted for him in each purchase. If this is so we shall be satisfied with an abstract of each of these purchase deeds, and your certificate that such abstract is correct, the prior title satisfactory and that there are no incumbrances. As far as we can judge without seeing the abstracts, this will be sufficient for our purposes.

Yours faithfully, White Borrett & White

Letter 5
To John Neale Esquire, Solicitor Reading

London, 6 Whitehall Place SW
19 June 1862

Dear Sir:

Reading St Lawrence: Church site
Would you oblige us with a reply to our letter of the 24th May?
Yours faithfully, White Borrett & White

Letter 6
To John Neale Esquire, Solicitor Reading

London, 6 Whitehall Place SW
22 July 1862

Dear Sir:
Reading: Church site

We send by Book Post this engrossment and abstract. Would you be good enough to return the abstract certified, when you send us the deed enacted.

  Yours faithfully, White Borrett & White

Letter 7
To John Neale Esquire, Reading

           London, 6 Whitehall Place SW
           12th August 1862

Dear Sir:
  Reading St Lawrence
  We have duly received this Deed which we have reported for seal at the Commissioners' last Meeting next Thursday. We have also received Abstract certified and our Draft.

  Yours faithfully, White Borrett & White

Letter 8
To John Neale Esquire, Reading

           London, 6 Whitehall Place SW
           29th August 1862

Dear Sir:
  Reading St Lawrence
  We send you an account of our Charges relating to this matter on payment of which the Deed will be forwarded to the Diocesan Registry £9.12.10

  Yours faithfully, White Borrett & White

      The Ecclesiastical Commissioners for England
           To
       Messrs White Borrett & White
        File No. 24664[1]
        Reading St Lawrence
         Church Site

	£	s	d
1862 May 24th			
On receipt of instructions from Secretary perusing Commissioners File of papers taking notes of same for future reference		13	4
Letter to Mr Neale that Instructions received and as to evidence of Title we required		5	0
June 19th			
Letter to Mr Neale for reply		5	0

---

1 Actually No. 26664.

June 25th
On receipt of Letter from Mr Neale with 3 Abstracts of Title perusing

Abstract No 1 6 sheets		13	4
The like No 2 12 sheets	1	6	8
The like No 3 5 sheets		13	4

July 4th

Preparing Certificate of Title and Copy	7	6
Instructions for Draft Conveyance	6	8
Drawing same	15	0
Copy	5	0
Tracing to annexe	5	0
Letter to Mr Neale with Draft Conveyance for approval and returning Abstract to be certified and Book Post	5	0

July 18th
On receipt of Letter from Mr Neale returning Draft Conveyance approved, Engrossing Deed

	10	0
Parchment	5	0
Plan	10	6

July 22nd

Letter to Mr Neale with Engrossment for execution and Draft and Book Post	5	0

August 1st

Attending Mr Neale's Clerk on his calling when he explained that it had become necessary to alter site and arranging to alter deed and plan so as to avoid the necessity of having the same reingrossed as the Bishop was about to consecrate the Church before leaving England	6	8
Altering plan and Engrossment accordingly and subsequently attending Mr Neale's Clerk and handing him same	6	8

August 12th

On receipt of Letter from Mr Neale with Deed executed and Draft Letter in reply acknowledging receipt	3	6
Drawing Report to Commissioners with Deed for seal and Copy	7	6
Attending for Deed when sealed and Examining attestations and completing Draft	6	8
Letter to Mr Neale that Deed was sealed and as to deposit of same in Diocesan Registry	3	6

On receipt of Costs Drawing final Report to Commissioners and with Duplicate Bill of Charges to accompany Copy	7	6
Letters Messengers &c.	4	6
£9	12	10

Letter 9
To John Neale Esquire, Reading
[Black bordered]

London, 6 Whitehall Place SW
9th September 1863

Dear Sir:
    Reading St Lawrence Church Site
       We shall be obliged by your sending us a Cheque for our Charges in this matter. We sent you the account <u>29th August 1862.</u>
       Yours faithfully, White Borrett & White

Letter 10
To John Neale Esquire, Reading
[Black bordered]

London, 6 Whitehall Place SW
11th September 1863

Dear Sir:
    Reading St Lawrence Church
       We are obliged by your Cheque for £9.12.10 our Charges in this matter and enclose a stamped receipt.
       Yours faithfully, White Borrett & White

[Receipt]
Reading St Lawrence
Received, this 11th day of September 1863 of J. Neale Esquire the sum of nine pounds twelve shillings and ten pence the amount of our Costs herein.
£9.12.10 White Borrett & White

(xxvi) Draft Conveyance of a Church Site in Reading St Lawrence Parish Church County of Berks Diocese Oxford. The Revd W. W. Phelps to the Ecclesiastical Commissioners for England (1862). Original in the Greyfriars Church Archive.

White Borrett & White, 6 Whitehall Place
J. Neale, Reading

Under the Authority and for the purposes of an Act of Parliament passed in the 58th Year of the Reign of King George the 3rd[1] intituled 'An Act for building and promoting the building of additional Churches in populous Parishes' and of another Act passed in the 59th Year of the same Reign[2] intituled 'An Act to amend and render more effectual an Act passed in the last Session of Parliament for building and promoting the Building of additional Churches in populous Parishes' and of another Act passed in the 3rd Year of the reign of King George the 4th[3] intituled 'An Act to amend and render more effectual two Acts passed in the 58th and 59th Years of His late Majesty for building and promoting the building of additional Churches in populous Parishes' and of another Act passed in the Session of Parliament holden in the 1st and 2nd Years of the Reign of Her present Majesty Queen Victoria[4] intituled 'An Act to amend and render more effectual the Church Building Acts' and of another Act passed in the Session holden in the 8th & 9th Years of the same reign[5] intituled 'An Act for the further amendment of the Church Building acts' and of the other Acts commonly called the 'Church Building

[p. 2]
Acts' and particularly of an Act passed in the Session holden in the 19th and 20th Years of the same Reign[6] intituled 'An Act for transferring the powers of the Church Building Commissioners to the Ecclesiastical Commissioners for England'
I the Reverend William Whitmarsh Phelps of Reading in the County of Berks Clerk being seized for an Estate of inheritance in fee simple in possession free from Incumbrances of the Plot of Land hereinafter described and intended to be hereby conveyed Do by these Presents freely and voluntarily and without any valuable consideration give grant and convey unto the said Ecclesiastical Commissioners for England All that Plot of Land containing Thirty perches situate in the Parish of St Lawrence Reading in the County of Berks bounded on the North and part of the East by Land belonging to Francis Morgan Slocombe Esquire on part of the South by Friar Street on the remainder of the South and East by the Pigeons Public House and on the West by other Land of me the said William Whitmarsh Phelps as the same is more particularly

---

1 58th Geo 3rd C45.
2 59th Geo 3rd C134.
3 3rd Geo 4th C72.
4 1st & 2nd Vic C107.
5 8th & 9th Vic C70.
6 19th & 20th Vic C55.

delineated on the Plan thereof drawn in the Margin of these Presents[1] and thereon coloured Pink together with all ways fences watercourses lights easements and appurtenances to the

[p. 3]
said plot of Land belonging or enjoyed therewith
And all the estate right Title and interest of me the said William Whitmarsh Phelps therein or thereto To hold (free from Land Tax and Tithe Rent charge) to the said Ecclesiastical Commissioners for England and their Successors for the purposes of the said Acts as and for a site for an intended new Church to be called Grey Friars Church with surrounding Yard and enclosure thereto and to be devoted when consecrated to Ecclesiastical purposes for ever by virtue and according to the true intent and meaning of the said several recited Acts
In witness whereof I the said William Whitmarsh Phelps have hereunto set my hand and seal and we the said Ecclesiastical Commissioners for England have hereunto affixed our Common Seal this first day of August 1862

Signed sealed and delivered by the within named William Whitmarsh Phelps in the presence of John Neale Solicitor Reading

---

1 For the Plan, see Figure 8.

III. Restoration of the Church

(i) Greyfriars Church, Reading. Circulars and Appeals Relative to the Restoration, together with a List of Subscribers, Balance Sheet &c. (1861–6) Booklet in the Greyfriars Church Archive.

First Circular:
Royal Berkshire Archives D/EPB/C95/1a

Dated 4 June 1861
RESTORATION OF THE GREYFRIARS CHURCH.

To the INHABITANTS of the BOROUGH of READING.
FELLOW TOWNSMEN,
Having from the earliest period of my residence among you, now twenty years ago, heard and joined in a regret that the noble fragment of antiquity above designated – I believe the only strictly ecclesiastical one we possess, – should not be restored to the sacred purpose for which it was designed, and once more exhibit the combination of holy use and graceful ornament, of which, in the midst of its venerable decay, it is so suggestive, I have at length been led to form the resolution of making an effort towards effecting that object.

My reasons for occupying so prominent a position, are not because I had means at my own disposal that could justify my indulging the ambition of being a benefactor to the town, nor that I had been entrusted by others with funds for carrying out that object. Undoubtedly, as I most gratefully acknowledge, my proposal was subsequently strengthened by the offer of various subscriptions. But I had, previously to this, after much consideration, and notwithstanding the magnitude of the undertaking, addressed myself unhesitatingly and fearlessly to the Restoration of the edifice that has so long been used as the Borough Bridewell.

First, because I see in the large and increasing population of the town, and particularly of that part of it in which the building in question is situated, an urgent demand for a greater supply of accommodation for religious worship, and feel it my duty, as a clergyman, to embrace an opportunity of affording every inhabitant desiring to avail himself of it, the privilege of attending Divine Worship, and being instructed in the truths of the Gospel of Christ, within the walls of a sanctuary in connection with the Church of England.

Also, because I believe that ample means for effecting this, along with other good and useful works of the day, are at the disposal of those who may reasonably be expected to take an interest in it.

And I have undertaken it *now* because a portion of land adjoining the ruins on the west side, and indispensable for the satisfactory accomplishment of the work, was about to pass into other hands; and also because I discover in the public improvements already carried out, and further contemplated in the heart of the town, in the Forbury and in other suburbs, a taste and spirit that do credit to the public feeling, and to those who have directed it, and this 'tide in the affairs of men', I think, should be taken at the full and not neglected.

Had any other and more suitable person stepped forward to this undertaking, I should have been glad. But as such is not the case, I offer my services to the work, which by God's blessing I shall not despair of seeing accomplished.

It is calculated that for the completion of the work on the scale it deserves, the sum of not less than £5,000 should be expended on the Building, and that £3,000 would be required for the endowment, and £2,000 for the site. In explanation of the last named item it may be observed, that the sum of £696 has been paid to the Executors of the late Mr. Weedon, for the piece of land adjoining the Ruins on the west side, and forming a frontage at the corner of the Caversham Road; and that the sum at which the Corporation have agreed to sell the Site of the Greyfriars Church, with the beautiful and extensive Ruins, and other Buildings, standing thereon, is £1250.

It is much to be wished that the sittings of the Restored Church should be in great part free. To what extent this can be done, compatibly with due regard to the support of the Minister, must depend on the liberality with which this proposal is met by the public. It will be obvious that the same liberality and public spirit must be the gauge of the architectural elegance, which it were to be desired should attract and gratify the eye, in an edifice of so much interest, and that will occupy so striking a position in the town.

The patronage will be vested in perpetuity in five Trustees, who will have power to fill up vacancies in their own number as they occur. The first Trustees will be:–

    REV. J. BALL, [1]
    REV. W. W. PHELPS,
    JOHN NEALE, ESQ., [2]
    JOHN SIMONDS, ESQ.,
    REV. PETER FRENCH.

Contributions will be received by the Rev. W. W. Phelps, and at the Banks. The amount already subscribed is—

	£	s.	d.
By four of the Trustees	2000	0	0
By thirty-five other friends to the object, whose names will appear in a future list of Subscribers	1514	18	0

Respectfully, therefore, and earnestly inviting your attention to the object, and your cordial and effectual co-operation and support to the work, which it will be remembered cannot be accomplished without effort and sacrifice, and a scale of contributions altogether different from that of benevolent objects that periodically recur,

    I have the honour to subscribe myself, Fellow Townsmen, Your faithful
    humble servant, W.W. PHELPS.
Reading, June 4th, 1861.

---

1 On the decease of the Rev John Ball in 1865 the vacancy was filled by the appointment of the Rev Edmund Hollond.
2 J. M. Strahern, Esquire, was appointed to fill the vacancy caused by Mr Neale's death in 1865.

Second Circular:
Royal Berkshire Archives D/EPB/C95/3a

Dated 24 April 1862

To the Editor of the Berkshire Chronicle. SIR,

I am happy to inform you, and the public through your columns that, after some delay occasioned by the necessity of obtaining the consent of the Lords of the Treasury, the seal of the Corporation was affixed on Wednesday last to a deed, whereby the fee simple of the site and buildings of the Greyfriars Church, recently occupied as the Bridewell, were conveyed to myself. I have undertaken, on my own responsibility, and within a specified period, to restore that remarkable relic of ecclesiastical antiquity, so as to be available for the services of the Church of England. But the confidence with which I incurred the risk and responsibility, and threw myself on the liberality of my fellow townsmen and countrymen, when the subject was first mooted in June last, has suffered no abatement whatsoever.

To replace unsightly buildings in a prominent part of the town by an edifice appropriate to its sacred object – to obliterate the reproach of a long-standing desecration – to cherish and hand down the venerable memories of the town by the restoration of so ancient and beautiful a structure, and, more than these, to provide amidst a large and increasing population, at a considerable distance from either of our churches, an opportunity of attending Divine Worship, and being instructed in the Truth as it is in Christ Jesus in the national church; these are objects of an interest and importance which, I persuade myself, will awaken the sympathy and enlist the liberality which have happily characterised so many of our recent improvements; and I either deceive myself, or it will eventually be found, that the instances of generous contribution referred to have furthered rather than retarded the restoration of the Greyfriars Church.

Encouraged by the support already given and promised, I shall not hesitate to commence the work immediately.

To allow a sufficient margin for endowment, it was stated in my first letter that £10,000 would be required, an amount that alarmed many of my friends. The sum subscribed, however, through private efforts, has already reached half of that amount. A list of the subscribers will be published next week. If the friends to this object who have not already given it their support, will respond with equal promptitude to this appeal, by payments made into the banks of Messrs. Stephens, Blandy and Co, and Messrs. Simonds, or by informing me of the contributions they intend to make, I shall hope through God's blessing, at a very early day to find that none of them regret the investment they have made.

I remain, Sir, yours very truly, W. W. PHELPS.
Trinity Parsonage, April 24th, 1862.

Third Circular:
Royal Berkshire Archives D/EPB/C95/6a

Dated 26 November 1862

THE GREYFRIARS' CHURCH, READING.
This noble fragment of ecclesiastical antiquity is in course of restoration to the sacred purpose for which it was designed, and about again to exhibit the combination of holy use and graceful ornament, of which, even during its desecration, it was so suggestive.

The large and increasing population of the town of Reading, and particularly of that part of it in which the building is situated, showed an urgent demand for increased Church accommodation, and induced the endeavour to embrace an opportunity of affording to every inhabitant of the locality desiring to avail himself of it, the privilege of attending Divine worship, and of being instructed in the truths of the Gospel of Christ, within the walls of a sanctuary in connection with the Church of England.

Accordingly, the site of the Greyfriars' Church, with its beautiful and extensive ruins (so long used as the Borough Bridewell), and the public-house adjoining, have been purchased of the Corporation for £1,250, and the leasehold interest in the public-house of the lessee for £210. A piece of land contiguous to the ruins on the west side, has also been purchased fer £696, and a further portion on the north side for £300. These several items make the total cost of the site and ruins amount to £2,456.

It is estimated that, for the completion of the undertaking on the scale its importance demands, not less than £5,000 should be expended on the building, and £3,000 raised for the endowment, in order (compatibly with a due regard to the support of the Incumbent Minister) to warrant the appropriation of a large portion of the sittings to the free use of the poor.

It is arranged that the patronage shall be vested in perpetuity in five Trustees, with power to fill up vacancies in their own number as they occur, the first Trustees being—

    The Reverend   JOHN BALL,
    The Reverend PETER FRENCH,
    JOHN NEALE, Esquire,
    The Reverend WILLIAM W. PHELPS,
    JOHN SIMONDS, Esquire.

The Lord Bishop of Oxford, as Diocesan, and also as Patron of the Living of St. Lawrence (in which parish the Church is situated), and the Reverend John Ball, as Vicar of that parish, have executed an instrument consenting to that arrangement.

The promoters of this undertaking desire to make grateful reference to the response of the public to their first appeal, as indicated by the annexed List of Subscriptions,[1] amounting to £6061 3s. 1d.; and they have, moreover, the gratification to state, that *on condition of private contributions to the*

---

[1] Not included here, as the full subscription list is given below.

Endowment Fund being received to the amount of £2,000, they are promised a sum of £1,000 for that object. In the event of the realization of which sum, and of the amount further required for the completion of the building, they confidently hope that the Church may be opened for Divine worship in as complete a form as the site at their disposal at present admits of, in the course of the next autumn.

Respectfully and earnestly, therefore, would they invite attention to this most interesting object, and solicit effective cooperation in a work, which it will be obvious cannot be fully accomplished, to the glory of God, and the good of immortal souls, without greater effort and sacrifice than are demanded by benevolent objects which periodically recur.

And they venture further to call attention to the fact, that the restoration of this beautiful edifice, has been for many years in abeyance, and the project now before the public was only adopted for execution, when the land adjoining the Ruins on the west side, forming a considerable frontage at the corner of the Caversham-road, and indispensable to the satisfactory accomplishment of the work, was about to pass into other hands; in which event, the restoration which now promises to become so striking an adornment as well as valuable acquisition to the town of Reading, and an object of even national interest, would for an indefinite period, if not altogether, have been lost.

Trinity Parsonage, Reading
26th November 1862.

Subscriptions received at the Reading Banks, and the London Banks connected with the same, and also by the Rev. W. W. Phelps, Oxford-road, Reading.

Fourth Circular:

Circular issued on or about 20 January 1863

THE GREYFRIARS' CHURCH, READING.
The restoration of this Church having progressed so rapidly and satisfactorily as to afford evidence of what were the wishes and intentions with which it was undertaken, the Reverend W. W. Phelps trusts that no further assurance is needed from him, that it is his earnest desire to see the work brought to such a completion, as will render the restored building not only available for the sacred purpose of religious worship, but also an object of general interest, as an ornament to the town and county.

In order that this might be effected, no efforts have been spared to trace out and revive all the material features of the original structure; and it is hoped that the progress which has been made (and which several discoveries in the process of the work have happily favoured) proves that those efforts have not been in vain.

In a work of such magnitude, which it was foreseen and stated from the first would require an outlay of £10,000, it was necessary to secure at the onset a sufficient number of *large* contributions to give a reasonable assurance of ultimate success. This has happily been afforded; and the sum of £6,000 and upwards raised; but as the large amount of about £4,000 has yet to be raised, for which he must look to more promiscuous offerings, he trusts that he may now suitably appeal to his fellow townsmen in particular, and generally to all who feel an interest in a work of this sort, to come forward and assist in its performance. He desires such public support, not merely for the sake of the sum which even small contributions will realize, but also and still more for the expression it would give of sympathy and goodwill to the undertaking.

Different reasons will suggest themselves to different minds why a helping and liberal hand should be stretched forth for this object; and among the most powerful of such reasons, will be the great need that must shortly be felt of increased accommodation for the public worship of God, in the thickly populated and rapidly extending neighbourhood in which the Greyfriars Church is situated, and which the Vicars of the parishes of St. Lawrence and St. Mary have consented to assign as a district to it.

Were it possible for him to do so, Mr. Phelps would gladly solicit the support of every resident in the town by a personal application, but as this is manifestly impracticable, he ventures to request that all into whose hands this address may come, will both contribute what they can themselves, and endeavour as far as possible to interest others to do the same.

Contributions may be paid at either of the Reading Banks, or by Post Office Orders, and Postage Stamps to the Rev. W. W. Phelps, Trinity Parsonage, Reading.

Collecting Boxes and Cards will also be gladly supplied to any Friends who may be willing to solicit and receive Subscriptions.

Fifth Circular:
Royal Berkshire Archives D/EPB/C95/7a

Dated 1 May 1863

The GREYFRIARS' CHURCH, READING.
The Restoration of this beautiful edifice had been for many years wished by the lovers of ecclesiastical antiquity, but continued in abeyance, and has at length been adopted for execution, just at a conjuncture when land adjoining the Ruins, and essential to the satisfactory accomplishment of the work, was about to pass into other hands, under circumstances which must have retarded it for a very protracted period, if indeed it had not precluded it altogether.

The work has now proceeded towards its completion, as regards outward form, in a manner that has called forth universal admiration, and more than realized all that had been anticipated from its grand and simple beauty and admirable proportions. It is estimated that further contributions will be required to the extent of about £500, to be laid out on the building, besides £3,000 to form an endowment fund. The liberal and most encouraging support which has been given, to the extent (as the appended list of Subscribers will show)[1] of £6,518 19s. 1d. forbids the originators to doubt that the further sum will be

---

[1] Not included here, as the full subscription list is given below.

raised, more especially when it is known, that towards the endowment, a promise of £1,000, three per cent. stock has been made, contingently upon £2,000 being contributed from private sources.

But, however confident of ultimate success, they beg to remind such as are favourable to the design, that they have arrived at a point in their formidable undertaking when Subscriptions are wont to flag, owing to a variety of fresh projects submitted to public notice, and at which therefore their hands might be most beneficially sustained by a renewed effort of their friends, and this desirable work most effectively expedited, and brought to completion at an early day; a work, be it remembered, no less strikingly beneficial than ornamental, whereby provision will have been made for proclaiming the glad tidings of the Gospel of Christ, within the walls of a sanctuary in connection with the United Church of England and Ireland, to a large and increasing population, principally poor, and greatly in need of an additional supply of the public means of Grace.

The Patronage is vested in the following Trustees, with power to fill up vacancies in their own number.

    The Rev. JOHN BALL,
    The Rev. PETER FRENCH,
    JOHN NEALE, Esq.,
    The Ven. W. W. PHELPS, Archdeacon and Canon of Carlisle,
    JOHN SIMONDS, Esq.

Donations received by Messrs Simonds and Co., Messrs. Stephens, Blandy and Co., and the London and County Bank, Reading; also by Messrs Williams, Deacon and Co., Messrs Willis, Percival, and Co., and the London and County Bank, Lombard-street, London; and by the Ven. Archdeacon Phelps, Reading.

Trinity Parsonage, Reading.
May 1st, 1863

Sixth Circular:

Dated 30 June 1864

GREYFRIARS' CHURCH.
To the Inhabitants of the Town of Reading.

In the month of June, 1861, I submitted to you the project of restoring the Ruins of the Greyfriars Church in this town, from the desecration which had for a long period consigned them to the condition of a Borough Bridewell.

I then stated that £10,000 would be required to effect this object: viz., £7,000 for the building, and £3,000 for endowment; but large as this sum was, I did not hesitate to appeal to, and rely upon, the liberality that had been evinced in the many and important improvements that had, of late years, been effected in the Town.

This confidence has not been disappointed, and at the end of three years I have the great satisfaction of announcing that the whole sum asked for (£10,000) has been raised; that the building has been restored in a manner which, I believe, has given general satisfaction; that it was consecrated on the 2nd December last, and has, since that time, afforded Church accommodation to a large congregation, in a locality where it had long been greatly needed.

Whilst, however, the work of restoration was in hand, several interesting discoveries were made indicating the original form of the building; and it was found impossible to resist the solemn and touching appeal of exhumed antiquity, which pleaded for the restoration of so much combined beauty and simplicity. This involved an outlay, not originally contemplated, to the extent of £1,840 14s. 8d.

That sum will, I believe, upon examination, be thought well accounted for by the addition of the north transept, including the purchase of additional site, the demolition and reconstruction of the eastern end of the building, and of three Arches, including the beautiful Chancel Arch, as also by other substantial improvements, suited to the now ascertained proportions and importance of the edifice.

For this addition to the expense, the originator of the restoration of course holds himself responsible, and can, in no case, complain of want of liberality on the part of those friends to the undertaking, who have come forward so munificently to its support.

Should they, however, or should any others who have not yet contributed, approve of the enlargement of the original design that has been adopted, and be disposed to share the expense with him, he begs to say that their contributions towards the entire work will be thankfully received and recorded.

W. W. PHELPS.

Reading, June 30th, 1864.

Contributions may be paid at either of the Reading Banks, or by Post Office Order to the Ven. W. W. Phelps, the Abbey, Carlisle.

Seventh Circular:

Dated 21 December 1866

To the Editor of the Reading Mercury.

Sir,

I have the satisfaction to inform those of your readers who have borne part in the restoration of Greyfriars Church, that the subscription list is now closed.

It will be in their recollection that the cash account was audited two years ago, (Dec. 21st, 1864), by Messrs R. C. Dryland and S. Fullbrook, who reported that the whole amount of expenditure had at that time been paid; and that the account stood:

	£	s.	d.
In debt to myself	1233	9	3
Since that period the following payments have been added to the amount:			
Legal Expenses	16	7	4

	£	s.	d.
Mr W. Brown, Surveyor	5	5	0
Registrar's fees – Consecration	12	4	0
Ditto License to Marry, &c.	2	2	0
Making the total deficiency	1269	7	7

The liberality of those friends to the undertaking has by the following contributions made up that balance, and closed the account:
[There followed a list of final contributions which added to the same total.]

It only remains that to the ascription of praise to Him, by whose blessing I am thus enabled – within five years and a half from the commencement of the undertaking, and three years from the consecration of the church, – to record the fact that the subscriptions have overtaken the outlay, I add my grateful thanks to every individual who has contributed to the work: whilst an especial acknowledgement is due to those latest as well as earliest contributors who have testified in deed as well as in word, their unwillingness that I should myself bear a larger portion of the expense than I voluntarily incurred at the outset.

A few statements will be subjoined, which it is thought may not be without interest to those who have watched the restoration with favour from its commencement.

I am, sir, Your obedient servant,
W. W. Phelps
St Lawrence Vicarage, Appleby
P.S.
1. The whole expense of the work has been as follows:

	£	s.	d.
Ruins & site purchased of Corporation of Reading	1250	0	0
Corporation for lowering the road	50	0	0
Land of Mrs Weedon	696	0	0
Land of Mr F. M. Slocombe	300	0	0
Lease of 'Pigeons' public house	220	0	0
Surveyor valuing 'Pigeons' public house	5	5	0
Builder	3250	0	0
Carpenter	2073	3	0
Glazier, &c.	191	6	3
Ironmonger	22	10	2
Upholsterer	23	6	5
Printing	40	9	11
Gas fitting	186	18	3
Warming Apparatus	72	10	0
Gas and Water laid on	16	15	2
Law expenses	153	12	2
Architect	296	13	0
Sums under £5	24	14	3
Mr Davenport's fees, consecration	12	4	0
Mr Davenport's fees, license to marry and baptise	2	2	0
	£8887	9	7

2. Analysis of the Subscription List.

		£	s.	d.
28	Contributions of £100 and upwards	6443	0	4
12	Contributions of £50 and under £100	630	0	0
29	Contributions of £20 and under £50	664	0	0
33	Contributions of £10 and under £20	360	7	0
288	Contributions of under £10	790	2	3
		£8887	9	7

3. It is to be borne in mind that the Restoration of Greyfriars Church, Reading, was assisted by no grant whatsoever from the Public Church Building Societies. Assistance was declined by the Oxford Diocesan Church Building Society, on the ground that application should have been made, and plans submitted, before the work had begun. This unfortunately was impossible, as the plan could only develop itself in the course of experiments made on ancient walls, the strength of which had to be tested, and on foundations that they had discovered in the process of the work.

TOTAL OF CONTRIBUTIONS				£	s.	d.
The Building Fund				8887	9	7
ENDOWMENT FUND	£	s.	d.			
Given in two sums	2750	0	0			
A Lady	100	0	0			
Bartlett, W. R., Esq.	5	5	0			
King, Mrs	5	0	0			
				2860	5	0
				£11,747	14	7

Combined List of Subscribers to the Greyfriars Church Building Fund

	£	s.	d.
Abraham, Miss	50	0	0
Adams, Mrs	1	0	0
Aitcheson, D., Esq.	1	0	0
Alexander, Mrs	1	0	0
Alfrey, R., Esq.	5	0	0
Allsop, Mr	1	1	0
A., M.	1	0	0
Andrews, Rev. C.	2	2	0
Austwick, H., Esq.	20	0	0
Aylmer, Col.	0	16	0
Bailey, John, Esq.	1	1	0
Ball, Rev. John	20	0	0
Ball, G., Esq.	20	0	0
Ball, Miss	5	5	0
Ball, Mrs G. (collection)	9	9	0

Ball, Mr James	5	0	0
Banbury, W., Esq.	10	10	0
Bartle, Miss	1	1	0
Barcham, Mr	3	3	0
Baster, Mrs	150	0	0
Bato, Mr		10	0
Bazett, Col.	50	0	0
Bazett, R. Y., Esq.	5	0	0
Beddome, R. B., Esq.	1	1	0
Bedford, Mr J.	2	2	0
Bell, Rev. C. D. *Ambleside*	5	0	0
Bennett, Jos. H., Esq. *Tutbury Castle*	5	0	0
Benyon, R., Esq., M.P.	100	0	0
Bevan, R. C. L., Esq.	100	0	0
Binfield, Miss (Sale of Hymn)	8	13	0
Binney, Miss	100	0	0
Blackwell, Mr	2	0	0
Blakiston, Sir Matthew	1	0	0
Blandy, J. J., Esq.	10	10	0
Blatch, Rev. James	25	0	0
Blyth, James, Esq.	20	0	0
Boorne, Mr J.	5	5	0
Bouverie, Hon. P. P., M. P.	20	0	0
Boxes, Sundry	5	2	11
Bracher, Mr R.	10	10	0
Bradley, Mr R., jun.	1	1	0
Briscoe, the Misses	10	0	0
Brooke, S. B., Esq.	15	5	0
Brown, Mr J. D.	2	0	0
Brown, the Misses	2	0	0
Bulley, Rev. Dr., the President of Magdalen College *Oxford*	10	0	0
Bunny, Major	1	12	0
Burfoot, Mrs H.	100	0	0
Butler, Mr C. J.	5	5	0
Carlisle, Hon. & Rt. Rev. Samuel Waldegrave, Bishop of	20	0	0
Carter, Mr W.	5	0	0
Carus, Rev. Canon	2	2	0
Champ, Mrs		10	0
Cherry, Rev. H. C.	2	0	0
Chessall, Miss		10	0
Chilcote, Mrs	1	0	0
Christopher, Rev. A. M.	2	0	0
Clark, Rev. H.	2	0	0
Clark, Rev. W.	2	0	0
Clerical Friend		10	0
Clutton, Mrs	1	0	0

Coles, the Misses	1	1	0
Coles, Miss (collection)	1	4	6
Connop, Rev. John	10	10	0
Consecration, collected Dec. 2nd, 1863	129	9	1
Cookesly, Rev. Dr. and Mrs	1	0	0
Cooper, Messrs L. and W.	5	5	0
Copland, the Misses *Sudbury Lodge, Harrow*	5	0	0
Coulthard, Rev. R.	5	0	0
Country Parson	25	0	0
Cowan, C., Esq., M. D.	10	0	0
Cowlard, Mrs	5	0	0
Cowper, Mr R.	2	0	0
Cowslade, Messrs (charges remitted)	15	12	0
Croasdaile, Mrs, sen. *Ireland*	1	1	0
Crocket, Jos., Esq.	25	0	0
Currie, Miss	1	0	0
Cusack, Rev. E.	2	0	0
Cust, Rev. A. Purey	5	0	0
Darter, Mr W. S.	10	0	0
Davies, Mr	1	0	0
Deane, R., Esq.		10	0
Dewe, the Misses	100	0	0
Dilwyn, Mrs	1	0	0
Dixon, Mr and Mrs	1	0	0
Dod, Miss (collection)	1	3	7
Dorset, the Misses	50	0	0
Downshire, Marquis of	100	0	0
Drake, W. R., Esq.	5	5	0
Dryland, R. C., Esq.	100	0	0
Dunlop, Mr	10	0	0
Durell, Rev. T. V.	6	6	0
Easton, C., Esq.	2	0	0
Eliot, W., Esq.	2	0	0
Elliott, Rev. E. B., *Brighton*	2	?	0
Elliott, Mrs	5	0	0
Estcourt, Rt. Hon. T. S.	1	0	0
Eyre, Rev F. J.	2	2	0
Farrow, Mr E. L.	2	2	0
Fenton, Miss	1	0	0
Ferguson, Mr W. H.	2	2	0
Filleul, Rev. P., *Jersey*	5	0	0
Fisher, Mrs, *Basildon*	15	0	0
Fisher, R., Esq., sen.	1	1	0
Fisher, R., Esq., Jun.	1	0	0
Fisher, W. Esq.	5	5	0
Fisher, Miss Jane	5	0	0

Fisher, Miss C. S.	1	1	0
Flanagan, Mr	1	1	0
Fletcher, Mrs Admiral	1	0	0
Fletcher, Miss	1	1	0
France, Rev. Thomas	5	0	0
French, Rev. Peter	921	3	8
Ditto, interest on note	1	3	8
Friend		10	0
Friend		10	0
Friend, by J. Lee, Esq.	2	10	0
Friend, by Mrs G. Valpy	5	0	0
Friends, two	1	10	0
Friends, two	210	0	0
Frowd, Rev. Dr., *Bath*	50	0	0
Frowd, Rev. Edward	5	0	0
Frowd, Miss, *Bath*	253	13	5
Frowd, Miss Ann, *Bath*	20	0	0
Frowd, Miss Susan	70	0	0
Frowd, Miss Sarah Thaine	170	0	0
Ditto, sale of lines	15	2	0
Fuller, Joseph, Esq.	5	5	0
Fullbrook, Mr S.	2	2	0
Gay, George, Esq.	20	0	0
George, Mrs		10	6
Gilliat, Mrs, *Fernhill*	2	0	0
Gilliat, A., Esq.	5	0	0
Gilliat, J. S., Esq.	5	0	0
Gleed, Rev. G.	5	0	0
Goddard, Mrs G. A.	1	0	0
Goldsmid, Sir F., M. P.	100	0	0
Goodhart, Rev. C. J.	1	0	0
Gordon, Sir H. Percy, Bart	1	0	0
Gosling, Mr J.	2	0	0
Graham, Thos., Esq.	21	0	0
Gregg, Rev. J. R.	1	0	0
Green, Miss	5	0	0
H., Miss	2	1	0
Halcomb, Miss	2	2	0
Harford, S., Esq., *Blaise Castle*	5	0	0
Harrington, Mrs	1	0	0
Harris, Thos., Esq.	60	0	0
Harris, Mrs T.	5	0	0
Harrison, Miss		10	0
Haslam, Mr James	10	0	0
Hatchard, Rev. T. D.	1	1	0
Hawkes, Mr H.	3	3	0
Hawkins, T., Esq.	20	0	0
Hawkins, Mrs, sen.	1	0	0

Hawkins, Mrs B.	6	0	0
Hawkins, Miss	1	0	0
Hawkins, Miss (collection)		13	0
Hayes, Rev. Sir J., Bart.	5	0	0
Hayward, Johnson, Esq.	5	0	0
Heelas, Messrs	20	0	0
Herringham, Mrs	12	0	0
Hewett, Robert, Esq.	10	0	0
Hewitt, Rev. A.	10	0	0
Hewitt, F., Esq.	2	2	0
Hewitt, Thos., Esq.	5	0	0
Hewitt, A. T., Esq.	2	2	0
Higgs, Mrs	20	0	0
H., J.	20	0	0
Hepinstal, Miss	1	0	0
Hind, Miss, *Ardley*	5	0	0
Hodges, Mr W.	2	2	0
Holding, Rev. John	50	0	0
Holding, Miss	1	0	0
Holding, the Misses, *Kingsclere*	5	0	0
Hollond, Rev. Edmund	150	0	0
Hopkins, Rev. W. T.	2	2	0
Hounslow, Mr J. W.	10	10	0
Howard, Rev. J. F.	2	2	0
Howell, Mrs		10	0
Howes, Mr R.	5	5	0
Howman, Rev. G. E.	5	0	0
Hughes, H., Esq.	5	0	0
Hughes Hughes, W., Esq.	2	2	0
Hughes Hughes, W., Esq., jun.	2	2	0
Huish, Mr		10	0
Hunter, Sir Paul	5	0	0
James, Rev. John	1	0	0
Jennings, R., Esq.	1	1	0
Johnson, Mr Joseph	2	2	0
Johnstone, Captain, R. N.		16	0
Keating, Hon, Mr Justice	5	0	0
Keeley, Mr W.	5	0	0
Keeley, Mrs (Box)		16	2
Kemble, Mrs H.	25	0	0
Kennard, Rev. R. R.	1	1	0
Key, Dowager Lady	1	1	0
King, Mrs	5	0	0
Lake, G. H., Esq.	1	0	0
Lanfear, Miss	1	1	0
Langley, Rev. John	10	0	0
Laurie, Mr G.	1	0	0
Lee, John, Esq.	5	0	0

Levett, Mrs	5	0	0
Lind, Mrs	1	0	0
Lodge, James, Esq.	10	0	0
London and County Bank (Reading)	25	0	0
Lovejoy, Mr G.	5	0	0
Lumbert, Miss	1	0	0
Lush, Miss (collected)	1	6	0
M.	1	0	0
Maberley, Miss	25	0	0
McMurdo, Miss	2	0	0
McMurdo, E. L. Esq.	5	0	0
Maitland, W. Fuller, Esq.	5	0	0
Maitland, Mrs Fuller	5	0	0
Major, Rev. Dr.	1	1	0
Marsh, Rev. William D. D.	5	0	0
Martin, Sir H., Bart.	1	1	0
Masters, Captain		10	0
Mathers, Miss, *Highbury Grange*	3	0	0
Mathews, John, Esq., *Chieveley*	10	0	0
Mathews, J., Esq.	1	0	0
Mathews, Miss	5	0	0
Matthews, Miss	3	0	0
Mattingley, the Misses	1	1	0
May, Walter, Esq. and Mrs May	40	0	0
Mayers, Miss	1	1	0
Midwinter, Mr W.	5	5	0
Mitchell, Miss	2	0	0
Monck, Mrs, *Caversham*	2	0	0
Monck, Miss, Velvet Communion Cloth			
Montressor, Major	5	0	0
Moore, Rev. E.	5	0	0
Morrell, Rev. R. P.	1	0	0
Morris, Mrs J. T.	5	5	0
Moses, W., Esq., M. D.	5	0	0
Mortimer, Rev. Dr.	1	0	0
Mount, W., Esq.	20	0	0
Mundy, Mrs	1	1	0
Murray, Miss Scott	3	0	0
Myddleton, Miss	1	0	0
Neale, John, Esq.	500	0	0
Neale, John, Esq., Law Expenses	153	12	2
Neale, John, Esq., Communion Plate			
Neale, Miss M.	100	0	0
Neale, Miss M. (Box)	1	19	5
Neale, Miss M., Servants of	6	5	3
Neville, Hon. Mirabel J.	1	0	0
Nicholas, J. L., Esq.	1	1	0

Nicholls, Miss	1	0	0
Nind, Rev. P. H.	2	2	0
Nixon, the Misses,		10	0
Palmer, R., Esq., *Holme Park*	50	0	0
Palmer, Mr G.	21	0	0
Papillon, Major	6	0	0
Parish Clerk	1	1	0
Parratt, J. E. T., Esq.	2	0	0
Payne, Rev. W.	10	0	0
Pears, Rev. Dr., *Repton*	5	0	0
Pechell, Mrs	4	0	0
Pecover, Mr	1	0	0
Pell, Miss	3	3	0
Perfect, Robert, Esq.	1	1	0
Perrot, Mr	1	1	0
Phelps, Ven. Archdeacon	500	0	0
Phelps, Mrs	100	0	0
Phelps, Rev. W. W., *Punjab*	10	0	0
Phelps, Rev. H. H.	2	0	0
Phelps, Rev. John	2	0	0
Phelps, Miss Ann	3	0	0
Phillips, Mr G.	1	0	0
Pidgeon, Messrs C. and J.	3	3	0
Ditto (Box)	2	0	0
Pike, Mr J.		10	0
Piercy, Rev. Peter	1	1	0
Plumptre, J. P., Esq.	5	0	0
Postage Stamps		10	0
Postman and Friends (collected)	3	3	0
Powys, Hon. and Rev. A. L. P. P.	3	3	0
Pratt, Miss	1	0	0
Preston, Mr S.	2	2	0
Ditto (collection)	1	9	0
Pring, Mr	1	0	0
Purvis, Captain	5	0	0
Puttrell, Miss	10	0	0
P. W.	15	0	0
Quentery, Miss	5	0	0
Radnor, Rt. Hon. Earl of	100	0	0
Raimondi, Miss	5	5	0
Ditto, Friends by	3	0	0
Raine, Miss C.	2	0	0
Rawlence, Mrs	1	0	0
Rector, A	1	1	0
Reed, Mr A.	5	0	0
Ditto (collection)	2	13	1
Ditto (Box)	2	15	11
Roberts, Mrs	2	2	0

Robinson, Rev. J. E., *Chieveley*	1	1	0
Robinson, Rev. Dr.	5	5	0
Row, William, Esq.	5	0	0
Ruddock, Messrs	2	2	0
St. Maur, Lady Henrietta	50	0	0
Salmon, Mr F.	1	0	0
Salmon, Mr W.	1	1	0
Saul, Mrs	1	0	0
Savory. Mr J.	1	1	0
Sawyer, C., Esq.	5	0	0
Sellar, Mr A.	1	1	0
Sellwood, R., Esq.	2	2	0
Selwyn, Rev. E.	5	0	0
Selwyn, Rev. E. J.	5	0	0
Shackel, W., Esq.	1	1	0
Sheepshanks, Miss	10	0	0
Sheppard, Mrs H	2	0	0
Sheppard, Mr. A., Reading Desk			
Sherwood, R., Esq.	10	0	0
Sherwood, Mrs R.	10	0	0
Sherwood, Mr W.		10	6
Shuter, Mrs T. A.	15	0	0
Simonds, John, Esq.	600	0	0
Simonds, Mrs Charles	320	0	0
Simonds, Miss	3	0	0
Ditto, Friend by	1	0	0
Slocombe, W. Esq.	5	5	0
Smith, Mrs Bailey	1	0	0
Smith, C. W., Esq.	4	4	0
Smith, Jason, Esq.	50	0	0
Smith, J. S., Esq.	2	2	0
Smith, R. P., Esq., M. D.	20	0	0
Smith. Mr S.	1	1	0
Snowdon, T. F., Esq.	10	0	0
Spokes, Mr P.	5	0	0
Sprague. T., Esq.	5	0	0
Sprague, T. B., Esq.	5	0	0
Stephens & Blandy, Messrs	50	0	0
Stephens, Mrs, *Caversham*	5	0	0
Stevens, Mr W., *Yateley*	1	1	0
Stevens, Miss	1	1	0
Stewart, Mr Duncan		10	0
Stirling, Rev. C.	8	8	0
Stone, Mrs	5	0	0
Stokes, Mr S.	1	1	0
Strachan, Miss		10	0
Strange, W. J. Esq.	5	5	0
Stuart, Clarence E., Esq.	400	0	0

Styles, Mr T. V.		10	0
Sutton, Mr M.	100	0	0
Sutton, Mr A.	100	0	0
Sutton, Messrs, Laying out and planting the Ground			
Szlarska, Madame		16	0
Tanner, Miss	6	0	0
Tanner, Miss M. (collection)	1	0	0
Taylor, J., Esq., *Culverlands*	5	0	0
Taylor, Mr J. O.	10	0	0
Teachers of Trinity Church Boys' School	1	15	0
Terry, W., Esq.	2	2	0
Terry, Miss	1	0	0
'The Love of Christ constraineth'	5	0	0
Thompson, Rev Sir H., Bart.	1	0	0
Thoyts, M. G., Esq.	20	0	0
Thwaites, A., Esq.	10	0	0
Tite, W., Esq., M. P.	5	0	0
Trench, Rev. F.	5	0	0
Trendell, J., Esq., *Abingdon*	2	2	0
Tristram, T. H., Esq., D. C. L.	2	2	0
Tubb, Mrs	1	1	0
Tucker, Rev. John	5	0	0
Tull, Mrs, *Peasemore*	5	0	0
Tull, H., Esq.	20	0	0
Twysden, Rev. T.	1	0	0
Tyndale, Rev. T.	1	1	0
Uhthoff, G., Esq.	1	1	0
Under Ten Shillings	5	18	0
Urmston, Mrs H. Brabazon, *Punjab*	2	2	0
Usborne, Miss E.	1	0	0
Valpy, Capt., R. N., and Mrs	100	0	0
Valpy, Rev. Gabriel	10	0	0
Valpy, Mrs G., Small Sums by	1	10	0
Valpy, Rev. Julius		10	0
Vanheythuson, Major	2	0	0
Vines, Charles, Esq.	2	2	0
Waller, Mr R. W.	2	2	0
Walter, John, Esq., M. P.	100	0	0
Wardell, Miss	1	0	0
Wasey, Miss, *Prior Court*	120	0	0
Webb, R. T., Esq.	5	0	0
Webb, Mrs R.	42	0	0
Weedon, Mrs	20	0	0
Wheeler, Miss, *High Wycombe*	5	0	0
Wheeler, Messrs, Font			
Wigfield, Mrs	5	0	0

Wilder, F., Esq.	5	0	0
Wilder, Rev. John	20	0	0
Willson, Mr C. F.	1	1	0
Willson, Mrs	1	1	0
Wilson, Alfred, Esq.	2	2	0
Wilson, C. Lea, Esq.	1	1	0
Wilson, Rev. Canon	3	3	0
Wilson, Col. Samuel	1	0	0
Wilson, Ford, Esq.	1	1	0
Wilson, the Misses	500	0	0
Wood, Mrs	1	1	0
Woodhouse, R. T., Esq., M. D.	4	4	0
Woodley, Mr T.	5	0	0
Woodman, Mr W. H.	50	0	0
Woodman, Miss (collected for Pulpit)			
Wootton, Mr W.	3	6	3
Workman, John, Esq.	25	0	0
Workman, Mrs J. (collection)	1	1	5
Ditto (Box)		14	8
Workman, Mrs W. R.	5	0	0
Worthington, Miss	5	5	0
Young Men's Association, Service Books			
Young, Miss, *Hare Hatch Lodge* (collected)	1	2	6
	8887	9	7

(ii) Correspondence by the Rev W.W. Phelps to the Earl of Radnor re the restoration of Greyfriars Church, Reading (1861–3). Royal Berkshire Archives D/EPB/C95/1–6, 6A, 7–8.

Royal Berkshire Archives D/EPB/C95/1
To: The Right Honourable The Earl of Radnor

Reading June 10, 1861

My Lord,

I trust your Lordship will not consider that, in addressing you again about the Grey Friars' Church, I am insensible to the kindness that dictated your Lordship's reply to a former letter on the same subject. The suggestions it contained deserved my serious consideration and I hope I have duly weighed them. But notwithstanding the uncertainty of all human efforts to secure permanency I have felt it my duty to proceed (as it will be seen by the enclosed reprint of a letter inserted in the Reading paper last week)[1] in the attempt to restore that venerable building for Church purposes, and to secure the patronage, as far as possible, in safe hands. Since I last addressed your

---

[1] D/EPB/C95/1a is a copy of Rev W. W. Phelps's first printed letter circular dated 4 June 1861, which appeared in the Reading newspapers on 8 June 1861. See Document III (i).

Lordship on the subject, our indefatigable Diocesan has become, by exchange, the patron of St. Lawrence, and thereby secured to himself the patronage of all three of our parish Churches. Your Lordship will hardly wonder if I, and those who think with me, are desirous of emulating his Lordship's energy, by endeavouring to do what may be permitted us, in our little day and generation, for what we believe to be the Faith of the Gospel.

I need not say how greatly your Lordship's support would encourage us in our arduous undertaking.

I have the honour to be, my Lord, your Lordship's faithful, humble servant,

W. W. Phelps

Royal Berkshire Archives D/EPB/C95/2
To: The Right Honourable The Earl of Radnor
                    Trinity Parsonage, Reading June 12. 1861
My Lord,

I beg to acknowledge, with my best thanks, your Lordship's letter of yesterday, (the 11th), and to express my regret that, at your Lordship's advanced age, my application may have occasioned trouble or inconvenience, which I would much rather have prevented.

In explanation of a former correspondence, to which I referred, I enclose a letter received from your Lordship in December last, the favor I had then requested, and with which your Lordship kindly expressed a regret that you could not comply, was That your Lordship would become one of the Trustees of our proposed Church. Your Lordship is startled at the magnitude of the undertaking and at this I cannot be surprised. Upon closer inspection, however, I hope it will appear to your Lordship, that though great it is not impracticable; nor by any means involved in the uncertainty which characterizes building projects in general.

I have stated, in my printed address, the amount that would be required to compleat the work <u>on the scale it deserves</u>. In reckoning that £5000 would be wanted for <u>the building</u>, on that scale a good margin has been given for contingencies.

But <u>half</u> that sum would suffice, to put the standing ruins in a condition suitable for Church worship – <u>in a plain and uncostly way</u>.

Again, I have reckoned £3000 for Endowments, but, if necessary, half that sum, or even <u>£1000</u>, would suffice.

For the site (or rather two contiguous sites) with the buildings thereon, the sum has been fixed, £1946: on this of course there can be no reduction.

Thus, though we propose going for so large a sum as £10,000, we believe the work <u>can</u> be achieved for under 6000. And of this we have £3,500 subscribed among <u>a few</u> friends of the object. A great local Interest has been expressed in it, from which it is fair to expect some fruit: which nothing, that I know of, will ripen more than a Subscription from your Lordship. I am, my Lord, with great respect and many apologies for this <u>long</u> letter,

Your Lordship's obedient, humble servant.

W. W. Phelps

Royal Berkshire Archives D/EPB/C95/3
To: The Right Honourable The Earl of Radnor

Reading May 15, 1862

My Lord,

May I venture to hope your Lordship will not consider me obtrusive if I once more – under somewhat altered circumstances – call your attention to the Restoration of the Greyfriars' Church at Reading.

Since I last applied to your Lordship on the subject the encouragement given to the project has been considerable and the work of restoration has been commenced. The Bishop of Oxford has also given his approval to a form of agreement which secures the patronage to the Trust in perpetuity.

I take the liberty of enclosing a copy of a letter I lately inserted in our local papers, together with the first published list of Subscribers.[1]

Should your Lordship see fit to permit me to add your name to the latter, it could not fail, from its well appreciated weight in the County, to assist me very materially in accomplishing the onerous task I have taken in hand.

I have the honour to remain, my Lord,
Your Lordship's obedient humble servant.
W. W. Phelps

---

1 D/EPB/C95/3a is a letter to editor of *Berkshire Chronicle* of 24 April 1862 and is transcribed in Document III (i).

16. Interior view of the West End of Greyfriars Church before restoration.

Royal Berkshire Archives D/EPB/C95/4
To: The Right Honourable The Earl of Radnor

Reading, May 21, 1862

My Lord,
Your Lordship is so good as to say at the close of your letter of the 17th Inst., that you feared I should consider it very unsatisfactory and disappointing. I cannot however admit that it was so. To have been honoured with a Subscription from your Lordship would, of course, have been what I most wished, but next to that I can truly say that I desire nothing more than an opportunity of replying to queries such as those your Lordship has put me. I shall do so with pleasure now, notwithstanding your Lordship's express Statement that you do not promise me any aid.

My own Incumbency, the Perpetual Curacy of Trinity Church, being in the Parish of St. Mary, is altogether distinct from the locality of the Greyfriars Church. It was built in 1827 by the late Reverend George Hulme, of Shinefield, who was its first Incumbent; and at whose request, made on his death-bed, I was appointed his Successor by the Trustees to his will, who are the present Patrons: but on the expiration of 60 years from the foundation of the Church, the patronage passes to the Vicar of the Parish. In the adjoining parish of St. Lawrence stand the beautiful ruins of an old Church of the Greyfriars built probably in the 13th century, well-admitting of restoration and adaptation to the services of our Church. About a year ago I conceived the project of undertaking such restoration. The motives by which I was influenced were, principally, my desire that, whilst such an object could be effected, during the incumbency of my friend Rev. J. Ball, on whose consent as Vicar I could calculate, it might be converted into a district Church for his parish, the patronage of which should be vested in perpetuity in Trustees holding the religious views called Evangelical, which I myself hold. I also knew that it was admirably situated in the midst of a large and increasing population at a considerable distance from any Church. The restoration itself, I also thought, would create considerable interest.

I am well aware that there must be uncertainty attaching to the best-concerted human arrangements; but I hold that, in our brief span of life, it behoves us to do what in us his[1] to uphold and transmit what we ourselves believe to be the faith once delivered to the Saints. I will not conceal from your Lordship that I felt this obligation the more strongly, from the consideration that the Bishop of Oxford had not only possessed himself (by exchanges effected through previous Chancellors) of the patronage of two of our three parishes, St. Giles's and St. Mary's, – but was at that time negociating (through Lord Campbell) an exchange whereby the only remaining benefice (of St. Lawrence, hitherto in the gift of St. John's College, Oxford) should also come into his hands: and this object was, in fact, soon afterwards effected.

Not willing, therefore, to see my fellow Townsmen, of the Church of England, compelled to lie in a Procrustes' bed I was the more inclined to address myself to this arduous task. The effort has met with no small encouragement, your Lordship will admit, seeing that without public effort, and pending the preliminaries for conveying the site from the Corporation to myself with the assent of the Lords of the Treasury, I was enabled to obtain Subscriptions amounting in my first published list to £5000.

I deeply regret to find, from your Lordship's letter, that any bearing of this end of the County towards the other should have been such as to give umbrage to your Lordship. Very few, I feel sure, if any, of those who have this project at heart have ever entertained such sentiments as those your Lordship has indicated.

On the contrary, in consequence I believe of the absence of the Bishop's favour, who objects in his private capacity to the form of patronage we have adopted, although as being legal it has his official sanction, – And who, acknowledging the interest and importance of the Restoration, wished the patronage to rest with the Incumbents of his own benefices, – I have met with considerable coldness and discouragement from influential persons in these parts.

Under these circumstances I need hardly say that few things would gratify me more than your Lordship's support.

---

1 The original lacks coherence here.

To which I will venture to add that I entertain a sanguine hope that considered in a broader and national point of view, as the restoration of a Solid and beautiful frame of a Church, given by Henry the 8th to the Burgesses of Reading for a Guildhall, and which, by a Grant from Queen Elizabeth, they were empowered to employ for other purposes or to dispose of, – and which for a great many years past has been and is the Borough Bridewell, – it will prove worthy of any investment its supporters may be so kind as to make.

I have to apologise to your Lordship for trespassing upon your attention at so great a length, and have the honour to remain, my Lord,

Your Lordship's obedient humble servant,

W. W. Phelps

Royal Berkshire Archives D/EPB/C95/5
To: The Right Honourable The Earl of Radnor

Reading May 24, 1862.

My Lord,

I beg to return my most cordial and respectful thanks to your Lordship, for a letter received this morning containing a promise of Fifty Pounds towards the Greyfriars Church. The encouragement afforded me by this generous gift is great, and I shall apply myself to the task of raising the remainder of the sum required with increased energy and comfort.

Your Lordship asks me if I think you are doing as much as you ought – a somewhat perplexing question – in reply to which I might, in candour, say that if I saw £100 against your Lordship's name on my list I should not consider it too much; but that the £50 reaches the full requirements, not indeed of my undertaking but of my most grateful content. I am, my Lord,

Your Lordship's obedient humble servant

W.W. Phelps

Royal Berkshire Archives D/EPB/C95/6
To: The Right Honourable The Earl of Radnor

Trinity Parsonage, Reading December 3. 1862

My Lord,

I think your Lordship will be interested in hearing what progress we are making towards the restoration of the Greyfriars' Church in this Town. I have taken the liberty, therefore, of forwarding the last published statement and subscription list.[1]

I am thankful to be able to say that the work of Restoration, which has now been for some time going on, has hitherto given great satisfaction, and fully realized all the anticipations that had been formed of the capabilities of the ruins.

There is every prospect of its being a beautiful and imposing though simple structure, which every one who sees it will be pleased with, at the same time that it supplies a great desideratum, in affording a place of worship, and the

---

1 D/EPB/C95/6a is a copy of Rev W. W. Phelps's printed letter circular dated 26 November 1862, which appeared in the Reading newspapers on 29 November 1862 and is transcribed Document III (i).

Instructions and Comfort of the Gospel of Peace, in a locality of late years becoming populous and hitherto destitute.

I have the honour to remain, my Lord, with much respect and gratitude,

Your obedient humble servant, W.W. Phelps

Royal Berkshire Archives D/EPB/C95/7
To: The Right Honourable The Earl of Radnor
Letterhead showing the Ruins of Grey Friars Church, Reading.

Trinity Parsonage, Reading, June 16. 1863

My Lord,

In reply to the enquiry you do me the honour to make I beg to inform your Lordship that the Restoration of the Greyfriars' Church is not yet completed. Indeed, although the undertaking has certainly met with very encouraging support, it is yet a long way from its completion.

Your Lordship may remember that in my first appeal for public support I stated that Ten Thousand Pounds would be required, viz £7000 for the site and restoration, and £3000 for Endowment. Now that the building has progressed to nearly the completion of all but the internal fittings and I am sufficiently within sight of land to enable me to judge of the whole outlay, I am thankful to be able to say that the above estimate (of £7000) will be found to have been a correct one, and scarcely, if at all, exceeded.

Towards this amount the accompanying list[1] will shew your Lordship that over £6500 has been subscribed, which leaves about £500 still to be raised towards the building.

The Endowment will further be wanting and towards this I have a promise from the Kemp Fund of £1000 Stock on condition of raising £2000 more from private sources. This I fear I shall find an arduous undertaking. But I will confess to your Lordship that in the face of it I cannot suppress an ambition I feel to raise the Endowment to a higher figure, and to say £4000 stock instead of £3000, for the following reason, viz. That if the endowment amounts to £120 per annum, the Ecclesiastical Commissioners will immediately raise it to £150. As, however, the conviction grows upon me of the great importance of this undertaking, which, through God's blessing will, I hope, secure the faithful message of the Gospel to a populous and poor locality, I cherish the hope of ultimate success.

I have not been without some discouragements.

The fact of my own Diocesan's avowed disapproval of the scheme of Trustee Patronage and refusal in any way to contribute to this effort, has buttoned-up the pockets of many in this neighbourhood. Moreover I have failed in my application for a Grant to the Oxford Diocesan Church Building Society, who refuse on the score of the Restoration being <u>in progress</u> when the application came before them. I do not complain, as they could not infringe

---

[1] The accompanying list (D/EPB/C95/7a) is a copy of Rev W. W. Phelps's printed letter circular dated 1 May 1863, which appeared in the Reading newspapers on 2 May 1863, together with the latest Subscribers' List. See Document III (i).

their Rule. But it was unfortunate for me, inasmuch as there never was a moment at which I could have come before them; seeing that it was necessary to commence operations (of demolishing incumbrances, and testing the strength and capabilities of the old building) before the public could be expected to support the project as a feasible one. Moreover I had to possess myself of the whole site by three separate purchases at considerable intervals.

The loss of this Grant carries with it the like refusal from the Incorporated Society. This, your Lordship will see, is a serious matter. In the case of a new Church lately built in the parish of St. Giles in this Town, the Oxford Society granted £400, and the Incorporated £500.

I think your Lordship will be gratified by hearing that, not only is general admiration of the restored Edifice expressed, but that I am able to subjoin the following Testimony of an Eminent Architect, George E. Street, of 51 Rupert Square, London, who on occasion of my application to the Oxford Board stated as follows in his Official Report.

'I have made it my business to inspect it (Grey Friars' Church, Reading) and I am able to report that the work, so far as it had gone, seemed to be exceedingly well and solidly constructed, and to be a faithful Restoration of a very interesting old work'.

I should gladly have spared your Lordship so long a letter, had I known how to be more brief. I have the honour to remain, my Lord,

Your Lordship's faithful humble servant,
W. W. Phelps, Archdeacon of Carlisle

Royal Berkshire Archives D/EPB/C95/8
To: The Right Honourable The Earl of Radnor

Reading June 19. 1863

My Lord,

In reply to your enquiry (which I am sorry I did not gather your Lordship's former letter to convey) I beg to inform your Lordship that Mr. Cust was presented to the Vicarage of St. Mary (not an adjoining parish to my own, but that in which my own district, of Trinity, is situated) by the Bishop of Oxford. I understand him to be a Clergyman of the Bishop's sort, though he is by no means one of extreme views or practices. He was not appointed till the last moment; and not until the benefice had been refused by several of more distinctly high Church repute.

I shall be happy to furnish your Lordship with any further particulars in my power and beg you will believe me to remain

Your Lordship's very obliged and obedient Servant, W. W. Phelps

(iii) Contract for Mason's Work required in the Restoration of the Greyfriars Church Saint Lawrence Reading (1862). Original in the Greyfriars Church Archive

Dated 16th June 1862
Messrs Wheeler to Rev W. W. Phelps

Articles of Agreement
made and entered into this Sixteenth day of June in the Year of our Lord one thousand eight hundred and sixty two Between John Wheeler the Elder John Wheeler the Younger and Samuel Wheeler all of Reading in the County of Berks Builders of the one part and The Reverend William Whitmarsh Phelps of Reading aforesaid Clerk of the other part.
Whereas the said William Whitmarsh Phelps having resolved to restore the Church called the Grey Friars situate on the North side of Friar Street in the Parish of Saint Lawrence Reading aforesaid and having applied for Estimates for the Mason's Work required in the Restoration of the said Church in accordance with the Plans and Specifications prepared by Messieurs Poulton and Woodman of Reading aforesaid his Architects the said John Wheeler the Elder John Wheeler the Younger and Samuel Wheeler have proposed to perform the said Works required by the said Plans and Specifications for the sum of One thousand eight hundred and eighty five pounds upon the terms that they have the materials stated or referred to in the Specification annexed which proposal of the said John Wheeler the Elder John Wheeler the Younger and Samuel Wheeler the said William Whitmarsh Phelps hath agreed to accept on their entering into the present Contract and giving and executing to the said William Whitmarsh Phelps a Bond with one sufficient Surety for the due performance of the said Works
Now therefore these Presents Witness that for and in consideration of the Covenants conditions and agreements hereinafter contained on the part of the said William Whitmarsh Phelps the said John Wheeler the Elder John Wheeler the Younger and Samuel Wheeler do hereby for themselves their heirs executors and administrators covenant promise and agree to and with the said William Whitmarsh Phelps his executors and administrators in manner following that is to say that they the said John Wheeler the Elder John Wheeler the Younger and Samuel Wheeler their heirs executors or administrators shall and will between the day of the date of these Presents and the Twenty fourth day of December next at their own proper costs and charges in all things well and substantially do perform execute and completely finish the said Masons Work required in the restoration of the said Church in all respects contained in the Plans from Number [Blank] to Number [Blank] both inclusive and in such other working drawings as shall from time to time be prepared by the said Messieurs Poulton and Woodman for the execution of the said Mason's Work according to the Specification annexed to these Presents and which Plans and Specifications are respectively signed by the said John Wheeler the Elder John Wheeler the Younger and Samuel Wheeler and the said William Whitmarsh

Phelps for the price or sum of One thousand eight hundred and eighty five Pounds to be paid in the manner hereinafter mentioned

And also that they the said John Wheeler the Elder John Wheeler the Younger and Samuel Wheeler their heirs executors or administrators shall and will at their own proper costs and expenses provide all the materials and things whatsoever which shall or may be necessary proper or expedient for completing and finishing the said Mason's Works and shall and will hire engage and pay all the Workmen labourers and Artificers which shall or may be necessary to be hired engaged and employed in the said Works

And the said John Wheeler the Elder John Wheeler the Younger and Samuel Wheeler do for themselves their heirs executors and administrators further Covenant promise and agree to and with the said William Whitmarsh Phelps his executors and administrators that in case the said John Wheeler the Elder John Wheeler the Younger and Samuel Wheeler shall not complete and finish the said Mason's Works according to the aforesaid Plans and other working drawings as aforesaid and Specification at the time and in manner hereinbefore mentioned then the said John Wheeler the Elder John Wheeler the Younger and Samuel Wheeler their heirs executors and administrators shall and will forfeit and pay unto the said William Whitmarsh Phelps the sum of Three Pounds weekly and every week in respect of the said Mason's Works from and after the said Twenty fourth day of December next until the whole of the said Works shall be fully completed and finished unless the said Messieurs Poulton and Woodman shall by a Certificate in writing under their hands Certify to the said William Whitmarsh Phelps that the said John Wheeler the Elder John Wheeler the Younger and Samuel Wheeler their heirs executors administrators and assigns have all used all possible diligence in performing the said Mason's Works in which case the said William Whitmarsh Phelps hereby agrees to remit and release all claim to the Fine incurred as aforesaid and to enlarge the time for the completion of the said Works (subject nevertheless to the same forfeitures by way of Penalty in case of further breach) as may be agreed on between them.

And the said William Whitmarsh Phelps for himself his heirs executors administrators and assigns for the considerations hereinbefore expressed and on account of the conditions covenants and agreements hereinbefore contained on the part of the said John Wheeler the Elder John Wheeler the Younger and Samuel Wheeler their heirs executors and administrators do hereby Covenant promise and agree to and with the said John Wheeler the Elder John Wheeler the Younger and Samuel Wheeler in manner following, that is to say, that he the said William Whitmarsh Phelps shall and will and truly pay or cause to be paid unto the said John Wheeler the Elder John Wheeler the Younger and Samuel Wheeler their executors or administrators the said sum of One thousand eight hundred and eighty five Pounds whenever the said Messieurs Poulton and Woodman may consider it desirable to give a Certificate to the extent of Seventy five Pounds per Cent upon the actual value of the work done at the time of granting the Certificate and the balance thereof within six months from the completion of the said Mason's Work but subject nevertheless to abatement for any defects in the said Works

And the said parties hereto further agree that all the materials hereinbefore mentioned shall be drawn carried and delivered to and at the site of the said Works without any expense or cost of Carriage or otherwise howsoever to the said William Whitmarsh Phelps his executors and administrators

And it is hereby declared and agreed by and between the said parties hereto that in case the said William Whitmarsh Phelps his executors administrators or assigns shall in writing under the hands of Messieurs Poulton and Woodman require any alteration to be made in the said Specification or Plans or shall direct any more work to be done in or about the said Works than is contained in the said Specification and Plans or shall direct any part of the said Works to be diminished or omitted then and in such case such alterations additions or omissions shall not invalidate this Agreement but the said John Wheeler the Elder John Wheeler the Younger and Samuel Wheeler shall make and execute such Works accordingly and the same alterations additions or omissions shall be valued ascertained and settled by Messieurs Poulton and Woodman unless the said William Whitmarsh Phelps and the said John Wheeler the Elder John Wheeler the Younger and Samuel Wheeler shall fix and agree upon a sum to be paid or allowed for the same and the amount of such valuation or of the sum so fixed and agreed upon shall be paid to the said John Wheeler the Elder John Wheeler the Younger and Samuel Wheeler in addition to the said sum of One thousand eight hundred and eighty five Pounds or deducted therefrom as the case may be but no alteration omission or addition shall be made without the written Order of Messieurs Poulton and Woodman

And it is hereby lastly declared and agreed by and between the said parties hereto that should any thing occur in the execution of the Works which may not be sufficiently particularized either in the Plans future Working drawings or Specification or intended so to be, such omission shall not annul the Contract but the said John Wheeler the Elder John Wheeler the Younger and Samuel Wheeler will be required nevertheless to perform the same conformably with the general tenor and intention of the said Plans future working drawings and Specification as if no omission had occurred

In Witness whereof the said parties to these Presents have hereunto set their hands the day and year first above written

    [Signed] John Wheeler, Samuel Wheeler, John Wheeler Junr.

Witness to the signatures of John Wheeler the Elder John Wheeler the Younger and Samuel Wheeler
    [Signed] J. W. H Davis Clerk to Mr Neale Solicitor Reading

(iv)   Bond for Performance of Contract for Mason's Work required in the Restoration of the Greyfriars Church Reading (1862). Original in the Greyfriars Church Archive.

Dated 16th June 1862
Messrs Wheeler & Mr Charles Ayres to The Rev W. W. Phelps

Know all Men by these Presents that we John Wheeler the Elder John Wheeler the Younger and Samuel Wheeler all of Reading in the County of Berks Builders and Charles Ayres of the same place Coal Merchant are held and firmly bound to the Reverend William Whitmarsh Phelps of Reading aforesaid Clerk in the Penal sum of One thousand eight hundred and eighty five Pounds of good and lawful money of the United Kingdom of Great Britain and Ireland to be paid to the said William Whitmarsh Phelps or to his certain Attorney Successors or assigns for which payment to be well and truly made we jointly bind ourselves our heirs executors and administrators and each of us severally separate and apart from the other of us bindeth himself his heirs executors and administrators firmly by these Presents Sealed with our Seals Dated the Sixteenth day of June in the Year of our Lord one thousand eight hundred and sixty two.
Whereas the above bounden John Wheeler the Elder John Wheeler the Younger and Samuel Wheeler have by Articles of Agreement in writing bearing even date with the above written Bond or Obligation contracted with the above named William Whitmarsh Phelps for the Mason's work required in the Restoration of the Church called the Grey Friars situate in the Parish of Saint Lawrence in Reading aforesaid according to Plans numbered respectively one to [blank] both inclusive and a Specification all which are signed and annexed to the said Articles of Agreement or Contract
And whereas at the time of entering into the said Articles of Agreement or Contract it was stipulated that the said John Wheeler the Elder John Wheeler the Younger and Samuel Wheeler should enter into a Bond with one sufficient Surety for the due performance of their said Contract according to the Plans and Specifications aforesaid and of any other working drawings
Now therefore the condition of the above written Obligation is such that if the above bounden John Wheeler the Elder John Wheeler the Younger and Samuel Wheeler their heirs executors or administrators shall in all things do perform execute and finish in a good and workmanlike manner all and singular the works specified and particularly mentioned or referred to in the said Plans and Specifications and such other working drawings as in the said agreement are stated or referred to and shall and do well and truly observe perform fulfil and keep all and every the Covenants clauses Articles and Agreements in the said hereinbefore in part recited Articles of Agreement or Contract contained then the above written Obligation to be void and of no effect otherwise the same Obligation to be and remain in full force and effect.
Signed sealed and delivered by the said John Wheeler the Elder John Wheeler the Younger, Samuel Wheeler and Charles Ayres in the presence of
[Signed] J. W. H. Davis Clerk to Mr Neale Solicitor Reading

(v) Plans for the Greyfriars Church Chancel (c1910). Originals in the Greyfriars Church Archive.

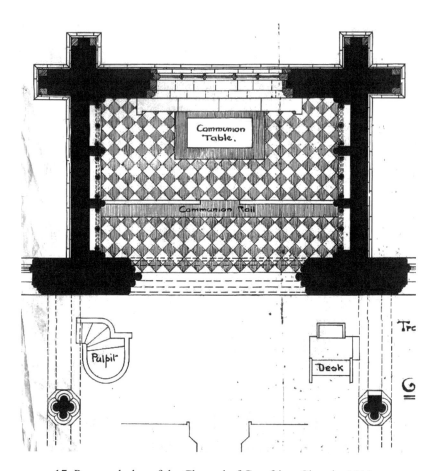

17. Proposed plan of the Chancel of Greyfriars Church c1910.

18. Proposed Chancel – external view of the east end.

These undated plans were drawn up by the architects 'Ravenscroft, Son & Morris of Reading & Milford on Sea, Hants'. This attribution places their creation in the date range 1908–1916.[1] The plans show a shorter chancel than the one in Woodman's sketch of the restored church (see Figure 9), probably in order to encroach less into what was, by the time of these plans, the vicarage garden.

---

1 See entry on William Ravenscroft in Sidney M. Gold, *A Biographical Dictionary of Architects in Reading,* (1999), 146.

(vi) Sentence of Consecration of Greyfriars Church (1863). Original (an attested copy) in the Greyfriars Church Archive.

Dated 2nd December 1863

In the name of God, Amen.
Whereas in and by an humble Petition (bearing date the Twenty eighth day of November last) presented unto Us by the Reverend John Ball, Vicar of the Parish of Saint Lawrence, Reading, in the County of Berks, within Our Diocese, and the Churchwardens and other Inhabitants of the said Parish, it is set forth, That from various causes, the population of Saint Lawrence, Reading, had greatly increased, thereby rendering it essential that additional Church accommodation should be furnished for the use of such of the Inhabitants who were desirous of joining in the public Worship of Almighty God but had hitherto been improvided with the requisite means to enable them to do so.

That in order to meet the requirement the said Petitioners (aided by the liberality of The Venerable William Whitmarsh Phelps, Archdeacon of Carlisle, and others desirous of promoting the Glory of God) had caused a new Church to be erected, the site of which had been duly conveyed to and vested in the Ecclesiastical Commissioners for England and their Successors as hereinafter mentioned.

That by Deed dated the first of August One thousand eight hundred and sixty two made under the authority and for the purposes of the several Statutes commonly known as the Church Building Acts, the said Archdeacon of Carlisle (therein described as The Reverend William Whitmarsh Phelps of Reading) being the owner in fee simple, did (without any valuable consideration) give grant and convey unto the said Ecclesiastical Commissioners All that plot of Land containing thirty perches situate in the said Parish of Saint Lawrence, Reading, bounded on the North and part of the East by Land belonging to Francis Morgan Slocombe Esquire, on part of the South by Friar Street, on the remainder of the South and East by the 'Pigeons' Public House, and on the West by other Land of the said William Whitmarsh Phelps, as the same is more particularly delineated on the Plan in the said Deed. To hold (free from Land tax and Tithe Rent Charge) to the said Ecclesiastical Commissioners and their Successors for the purposes of the said Acts as and for a Site for an intended new Church to be called 'Grey Friars Church', with the surrounding Yard and inclosure and to be devoted when consecrated to Ecclesiastical purposes for ever, by virtue and according to the true intent and meaning of the said several recited Acts.

That the said new Church had been appropriately fitted up and adorned, and was ready to be consecrated and that the part of the said thirty perches of Ground which surrounds the said Church was about to be enclosed with a proper and substantial Fence And that the said Petitioners intended to adopt the requisite measures for procuring a separate Ecclesiastical District to be assigned to the said Church.

And the said Petitioners humbly prayed us as in their said Petition is set forth.
Now We Samuel by Divine Permission Lord Bishop of Oxford being willing to comply with the reasonable and pious prayer of the said Petitioners Do, by

these Presents, by Our Ordinary and Episcopal Authority, separate for the future the said newly erected Church from all common and profane uses, and do consecrate and set apart the same for the Worship of Almighty God, the Administration of the Sacraments, the reading of Prayers, and preaching the Word of God purely and sincerely and for performing all other Religious Ceremonies according to the Liturgy of the United Church of England and Ireland

And We do hereby dedicate the said new Church to Almighty God by the name of Grey Friars which said new Church and the Boundaries thereof are more particularly delineated in the Plan drawn on these Presents.

Saving nevertheless unto Ourself and Our Successors Our Episcopal rights and privileges herein, and saving likewise unto all Bodies politic and corporate and to all persons whomsoever the respective claims to which they or any of them were entitled before the passing of this Our definitive Sentence and final Decree which We make and promulgate by this present writing.

Signed and published in the new Church called Grey Friars at Reading aforesaid this second day of December in the year of our Lord One thousand eight hundred and sixty-three and in the Nineteenth year of our Consecration.
   Samuel Oxon

which I attest
   John M Davenport, Notary Public.

Diocesan Registry, Oxford, 19th September 1873
I certify the foregoing to be a true copy
   [Signed] John M Davenport
   Deputy Registrar of the Diocese of Oxford.

IV. The Early Years of the Parish Church of Greyfriars

(i) Churchwardens of Greyfriars Church Pew Rent Accounts (1864–70). Original in the Greyfriars Church Archive

Messrs John Simonds, Charles Simonds & Co in account with
The Churchwardens of Grey Friars Church Pew Rent Account
Henry Moses Esq MD and W. H. Woodman Esquire

1864

Debit	To	£	s.	d.	Credit	By	£	s.	d.
Mar 11	Maslen[1]	30							
15	Cash	18	15	6					
18	Cash	34	2						
					Apr 18	Cheque book		1	
					30	Barkworth	50		
					30	North[2]	9	8	5
May 13	Maslen	40			May 10	Gas Co.	6	7	
Jun 3	Cash	20							
25	Maslen	7	18						
26	Maslen	30							
					Jul 2	North	7	10	
					13	Barkworth	60		
Aug 8	Maslen	35			Aug 1	Maslen	5	16	6
					16	Gas Co.	1	17	10
Sep 30	Maslen	16	5	6					
Oct 17	Cash	39	4	6	Oct 1	North	7	10	
19	Maslen	35			20	Barkworth	100		
Nov 4	Maslen	30			Nov 2	Maslen	4	1	3
						Balance	83	13	6
		336	5	6			336	5	6

Messrs John Simonds, Charles Simonds & Co in account with
The Grey Friars Churchwardens (Pew Rent Account)
Messrs William Hodges and C. F. Willson (Churchwardens)

1864–5

Debit	To	£	s.	d.	Credit	By	£	s.	d.
Nov 14	Balance of old a/c	83	13	6					
Dec 27	Maslen	11	18						
1865					1865				
					Jan 2	Cheque Bk		2	6
					4	Maslen	3	16	9
Jan 7	Maslen	35			5	North	9	4	7
23	Willson	25	9	8	Jan 5	Woodman	17	2	8

---

1 Mr Maslen collected the Pew Rent from December 1863 to April 1870.
2 Thomas North was the Parish Clerk and Sexton from December 1863 to February 1899.

FROM PRISON TO PARISH CHURCH

Date	To	£	s.	d.	Date	By	£	s.	d.
	Organ Collectn				7	Sheppard	20		
					24	Sheppard	29	15	9
						Bartlett	15		
						Dryland	10		
					26	Reed		18	
					30	Gas Co.	9	11	3
Feb 3	Maslen	35			Feb 23	Smith	5	18	6
					Mar 25	North	8	9	6
Apr 1	Maslen	20	3		Apr 6	Maslen	4	10	
10	Church Expenses	25	9	5	8	Barkworth	50		
					13	Bartlett	5		
11	Maslen	35			22	Wheeler	18	7	3
						Barkworth	30		
May 3	Maslen	30			May 1	Pecover		15	6
					15	Smith	4	18	9
					20	Callas	2	11	3
					27	King	4	4	7
Jun 27	Maslen	14		6	Jun 24	North	8	7	3
Jul 8	Maslen	35			Jul 1	Bartlett	5		
					7	Barkworth	40		
					10	Maslen	3	19	
					11	Willson	2	17	
Aug 1	Maslen	40			Aug 11	Portsmouth	6	5	
14	Church Expenses	24	17	1	21	Gas Co.	10	1	1
					Sep 28	Sundries	1	16	8
					29	Barkworth	60		
						North	8	7	
Oct 3	Maslen	18	3		Oct 2	Ch Book		2	6
					4	Maslen	4	13	3
					5	Bartlett	5		
Nov 2	Maslen	50			Nov 11	Barkworth	18	3	
27	Church Expenses	37	14	2	Dec 1	Wheeler	20		
					4	Woodman	3	5	8
27	Maslen	15			Dec 9	Wheeler	23	7	4
Dec 8	Church Expenses	16	13	6	28	Bartlett	5		
					30	North	9	9	
						Balance	67	1	3
		553	1	10			553	1	10

1866

Debit	To	£	s.	d.	Credit	By	£	s.	d.
Jan 1	Balance	67	1	3	Jan 11	Barkworth	50		
	Cash	16	18			Portsmouth	5	5	
13	Cash	20			17	Sundry bills	10	1	6
19	Maslen	40			19	Maslen	4	1	10
						Callas	9	14	5
Feb 22	Maslen	25			Feb 20	Sundries	3		
					22	Rdg Gas Co	8	12	2
					24	Hodges	2	15	
Mar 28	Maslen	25	15	6	Mar 8	Barkworth	50		
						North	9		
						Bartlett	5		

Date	To	£	s.	d.	Date	By	£	s.	d.
Apr 9	Cash	23	17		Apr 4	Maslen	4	10	9
						Woodman	2	12	6
					5	Barkworth	20		
					20	North	4	2	1
					26	Hunt	2	5	
May 1	Wilson	1	10		May 3	Callas	5	16	3
2	Maslen	40			5	Smith	10	6	4
					24	Small bills	2	10	2
Jun 1	Maslen	25			Jun 12	Barkworth	60		
					21	Bartlett	5		
					27	North	8	13	6
Jul 2	Maslen	16	13		Jul 9	Maslen	4	1	6
16	Collectn	21			19	Sundries	1	17	6
Aug 2	Maslen	40							
22	Collectn for Hospital	20	1	6					
Sep 1	Maslen	30			Sep 1	Ch Bk		2	6
					3	Hospital	20	1	6
					4	Gas bill	12	13	4
					8	Sheppard	15		
					20	Barkworth	60		
Oct 3	Maslen	22	13		Oct 3	North	8	6	
15	Cash	23	19	7	5	Bartlett	5		
					9	Barkworth	28		6
					10	Maslen	4	12	6
Nov 1	Cash	35							
Dec 1	Maslen	25			Dec 27	Barkworth	50		
					28	Bartlett	5		
					31	North	10	7	9
						Balance	10	19	3
		519	8	10			519	8	10

1867

Debit	To	£	s.	d.	Credit	By	£	s.	d.
Jan 1	Balance	10	19	3	Jan 7	Maslen	3	17	6
	Maslen	17	8		12	Sundry bills	4	7	9
14	Church Expenses	20	17		12	Inc Tax & Visitation fees	3	2	8
					14	Grosen	4	3	3
					15	Sheppard	12	17	1
Feb 1	Cash	40							
Mar 4	Maslen	20			Mar 13	Rdg Gas Co	12	9	1
					26	North	9	10	7
						Barkworth	50		
Apr 2	Cash	24	8		Apr 1	Bartlett	5		
15	Church Expenses	21	9	4	11	Atlas Insurance	2	12	6
16	Mr Hawkins		5		12	Income tax	4	6	8
25	Mrs		5		20	Maslen	4	4	5

Date	To	£	s.	d.	Date	By	£	s.	d.
May 3	Carpenter Maslen	40			May 4	Barkworth	34	7	1
					10	Keeley	4	8	
Jun 3	Maslen	20			Jun 24	North	8	9	6
Jul 1	Maslen	12	15	6	Jul 1	Bartlett	6	5	
15	Church Expenses	22	4	1		Barkworth	40		
					8	Maslen	3	12	9
Aug 2	Maslen	50			Aug 22	Wootton	10		
13	Collection for Hospital	25	7	11	23	Gas Co	10	17	3
					26	Barnard	10		
					28	Cheque Bk		2	6
					29	Hospital	25	7	11
Sep 3	Maslen	20			Sep 18	Barkworth	50		
					21	Wootton	7	17	1
						Corps	1		8
						Netherclift	4	14	1
					28	Barnard	3	19	6
Oct 4	Maslen	17		6	Oct 2	Portsmouth	5	5	
	Cash	19	9	7	8	North	8	10	6
					12	Bartlett	6	5	
					16	Maslen	4	7	
Nov 4	Maslen	40							
14	Additional Church Collection	1							
Dec 2	Maslen	20			Dec 17	Barkworth	60		
31	Maslen	12	13		28	Bartlett	6	5	
					30	North	9	11	6
						Balance	18	5	4
		456	2	2			456	2	2

1868

Debit	To	£	s.	d.	Credit	By	£	s.	d.
Jan 1	Balance	18	5	4	Jan 16	Maslen	3	12	6
13	Collection	24	7	1	17	Tax Collector	2	4	3
21	Cash		2						
	Cash		5		21	Netherclift	2	6	11
					27	Gas Co	7	13	8
Feb 3	Maslen	40			Feb 6	Barcham	2	5	
10	Dr Moses repaid	2	7		14	Barkworth	12	13	
Mar 4	Maslen	20			Mar 31	Woodman	2	12	6
						North	10	5	5
Apr 1	Maslen	23	18		Apr 2	Bartlett	6	5	
21	Cash	21	18	9	4	Maslen	4	4	
					11	Wheeler	17	6	1
					13	Barkworth	55	9	4
					30	North	1	10	9
May 2	Maslen	35			May 12	Ch Book		2	6
					18	Income tax	3		5
					19	Barkworth	18	13	1
Jun 2	Maslen	25			Jun 15	Barkworth	50		
					26	North	8	10	9

Debit	To	£	s.	d.	Credit	By	£	s.	d.
					27	Bartlett	6	5	
Jul 1	Maslen	14	3		Jul 17	Maslen	3	14	
16	Wilson	16		5					
Aug 3	Maslen	40			Aug 20	Pope/ Callas	3	10	9
10	Cash - Hospital	28	19	10	21	Hospital	28	19	10
					22	Barkworth	50		
20	Miss Wilson	2							
Sep 4	Maslen	25			Sep 30	North	8	5	
Oct 3	Maslen	21		6	Oct 3	Miller	2	4	
12	Collection	25	3	6	5	Bartlett	6	5	
					6	Maslen	4	6	
						Gas Co	9	16	
					7	Barkworth	25		
Nov 4	Maslen	35							
Dec 5	Maslen	20			Dec 23	Barkworth	50		
31	Maslen	15	8		28	North	9	4	9
					29	Bartlett	6	5	
						Balance	31	7	11
		453	18	5			453	18	5

1869

Debit	To	£	s.	d.	Credit	By	£	s.	d.
Jan 1	Balance	31	7	11	Jan 8	Portsmouth	3	3	8
11	Cash	23	5	4		Barkworth	16	10	
					11	Income Tax	3	4	
					26	Bevington	4	4	
					28	Maslen	3	10	6
Feb 3	Maslen	35			Feb 11	Biggs	4	4	
					12	Waterworks & others		18	
					13	Pecover	4	3	8
					15	Walker	2	2	
					16	Rdg Gas Co	8		
					19	Barkworth	4	13	5
Mar 2	Maslen	30			Mar 29	Ch Book		2	6
Apr 2	Maslen	12	15	6	Apr 1	Woodman	2	12	6
12	Cash	21	2		6	North	10	7	3
					15	Maslen	3	17	9
					20	North	2	14	7
					28	Income Tax	3	4	
May 3	Maslen	35			May 6	Walker	1	9	
					10	Smith	8		
					29	Barkworth	4	4	
						Dist Rate &c	4	10	6
					Jun 29	Campbell	18		
Jul 1	Maslen	38	8		Jul 1	Strickland	10	19	3
12	Cash	17	15	6	2	North	8	7	
31	Fletcher Church Expenses		2	6	9	Maslen	3	13	6
					12	Smith	5	5	
					13	Rdg Gas Co	8	11	8
					29	Bren	8	8	

Date	To	£	s.	d.	Date	By	£	s.	d.
Aug 3	Maslen	40			Aug 16	Hospital	33	6	6
9	Hospital Collection	33	6	6	17	Water Rate	2	4	6
7	Mr & Mrs Sutton	2			31	Bren	8	8	
					Sep 20	Bren	8	8	
Oct 11	Cash	25			Oct 1	Strickland	7	10	
4	Maslen	35		6	16	North	8	10	
					21	Maslen	3	15	
					27	Bren	8	8	
					30	Champ	8	8	6
Nov 11	Maslen	35			Nov 3	Local Board of Health	5		7
					4	Wheeler	5	15	1
					13	Cheque Bk		2	6
					19	Bren	13	8	
					22	Champ & others	3	2	6
					26	Barkworth	100		
						Balance	39	16	10
		415	3	9			415	3	9

1870

Debit	To	£	s.	d.	Credit	By	£	s.	d.
Jan 1	Balance	39	6	10	Jan 5	Strickland	7	10	
10	Cash	20		5	10	North	9	8	2
	Miss Dewe	1			15	Coppen	3		
						Wheeler	1	13	6
4	Maslen	34	15	6	17	Rdg Gas Co	6	16	2
15	Mrs Knox	1			18	Income Tax	4	9	7
						Barkworth	50		
					27	Maslen	3	9	9
Feb 18	Maslen	35							
Apr 2	Maslen	35	18		Apr 1	Strickland	7	10	
11	Cash	20	3		4	North	9	17	4
					5	Jessett	1	18	
					6	Maslen	5	12	9
					12	Walker	2	2	
					18	Atlas Assurance	1	10	
					23	Wheeler	12	19	6
					28	Hart	24	1	1
May 16	Church Mission'y Society	31			May 16	Church Missionary Society	31		
21	Moore	55			26	Champ & others	5	10	9
Jun 8	Moore	7			Jun 6	Mrs Barkworth	1		
13	Coll. C & C Soy	15	8	10	24	Papillon	15	8	4

Date	Item	£	s	d	Date	Item	£	s	d
Jul 11	Quarterly Collectn	22	16	5	Jul 2	Barkworth	60		
					6	North	8	5	
Jun 30	Moore	8	5	6	7	Strickland	7	10	
					13	Barnard	4	18	6
					21	Barkworth	20		
					25	Moore	3	10	3
Aug	Cash	25	10		Aug 4	North	3	4	2
15	Hospital				16	Gas Co	12	4	2
8	Cash	15			19	Hart		16	6
13	Moore	35			29	Hospital	25	10	
Sep 4	Moore	12			Sep 1	Waller &c.	2	13	6
					10	Barkworth	50		
Oct 1	Moore	8			Oct 1	Cheque Bk		2	6
10	Cash	20	18	1	7	Strickland	7	10	
11	Mrs King	1	10		8	North	8	7	9
20	Cash[1]	15	10	8	15	Moore	3	15	
Nov	Cash	50			Nov 16	Grover	2	17	6
26						Sheppard	90	8	2
19	Moore	11							
Oct 22	Moore	13							
Oct 5	Moore	5	3						
15	Moore	20							
Jun 8	Moore[2]								
Oct 15	Stiles		2	6					
Dec 20	Cash	12			Dec 29	Strickland	7	10	
					31	North	10	7	
						Balance	37	11	10
		571	18	9			571	18	9

---

1 This entry has a pencilled note that the deposit is for the Organ Fund. The same note also appears on the following Cash deposit on 20 October, and on the payments to Grover and to Sheppard on November 16.

2 No amount is given. In order to total to the correct amount, it would be 10s. The accounts are rather chaotic at this point in terms of date of entry.

(ii)   Rented and Free Seats in Greyfriars Church (c1880). Original in the Greyfriars Church Archive.

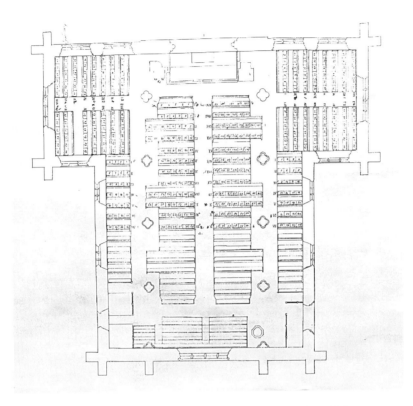

19. Rented and Free Seats in Greyfriars Church c1880.

In this plan of Greyfriars Church, the numbered seats are those allocated to those paying pew rent. The seats that remain are 'free' for anyone to sit in at a service. This plan shows 395 seats allocated, and 172 free.

Although this plan is undated, the position of the organ next to the north door (one of the squares on the bottom left of the plan) means that it was drawn at some date between October 1870, when the organ was first moved there from underneath the west window, and July 1888, by which time it had been moved to the north transept.

(iii) Extract from an Order in Council stating the boundaries of the to be created District of Greyfriars Church (1864). Royal Berkshire Archives D/P97/28/8/4.

27 August 1864

The Consolidated Chapelry of the Grey Friars, Reading, being:
All that portion of the parish of Saint Lawrence, Reading, in the County of Berks, and in the diocese of Oxford, and also that portion of the adjoining parish of Saint Mary, Reading, in the same county and diocese, which are comprised within, and are bounded by, an imaginary line commencing on the boundary which divides the said parishes, at a point in the middle of the Caversham-road, upon the southern side of the bridge which carries the Berkshire and Hampshire branch line of the Great Western Railway over such road; and extending thence eastward along the middle of the fence which forms the southern boundary of the said branch line as far as the south-western corner of the down station of the Great Western Railway aforesaid; and extending thence due southward in a straight line across the road in front of the said station to a point in the middle of the north-eastern end of a certain new road, which leads from the same station to Grey Friars-road; and extending thence south-westward along the middle of such new road to its junction with Grey Friars-road aforesaid; and extending thence, first south-westward, and then southward, along the middle of the last named road to its junction with Friar-street; and extending thence westward along the middle of such street as far as a point opposite to the middle of the north-western end of West-street; and extending thence south-eastward to and along the middle of the last named street to the boundary which again divides the said parishes at a point in the middle of the eastern end of Oxford-street; and extending thence, first westward, and then northward, along the said boundary (following, thereby, first the middle of Oxford-street aforesaid, and then the middle of Thorn-street) as far as a point in the middle of the last-named street opposite to the middle of the eastern end of Chatham-street; and extending thence westward to and along the middle of the last-named street as far as a point opposite to the middle of the southern end of the footway which passes along the front of the cottages and gardens in York-place; and extending thence northward to and along the middle of such footway to the wall, at its northern end, which forms the southern boundary of the gardens and premises in rear of, and belonging to, the houses on the southern side of Welldale-street; and extending thence westward along the middle of such wall to its junction with the fence which forms the eastern boundary of Bedford-gardens; and extending thence northward along the middle of such fence, crossing the western end of Welldale-street aforesaid, to the north-western corner of the garden in the rear of, and belonging to, the western-most house on the northern side of the same street; and extending thence still northward in a straight line to the south-east corner of the wall of the passage at the eastern end of Portland-place; and continuing thence northward along the said wall to its extremity on the south side of Great Knollys-street; and continuing thence in a straight line due north,

across the last-named street, and across certain pasture land, to a point in the middle of the fence which forms the southern boundary of the Berkshire and Hampshire Branch Line of the Great Western Railway as aforesaid; and extending thence eastward along the middle of the last-described fence as far as the first-described point upon the parish boundary in the middle of the Caversham-road as aforesaid, where the said imaginary line commenced.[1]

(iv)   Plan of proposed District of Greyfriars (1864). Royal Berkshire Archives D/QC5/3.

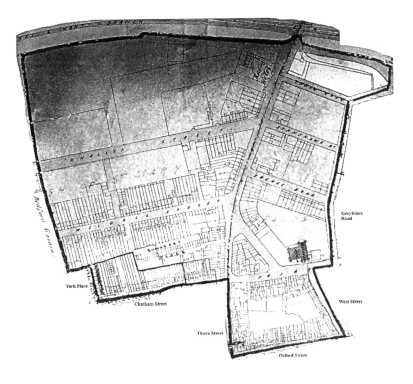

20, District of Greyfriars Church 1864.

Caversham Road separated the parishes of St Mary (to the west) and St Lawrence.

---

1 This also appeared in *The London Gazette* 30 August 1864 page 4221.

(v)   Log Book of Greyfriars Infant School (1865–9). Royal Berkshire Archives R/ES4/1 (Part).

In May 1867, the Greyfriars Infant School split into two Schools, the Senior Infants and the Junior Infants. The entries in this section therefore cover the time before the Infant School was split, and then continues from May 1867 as the record of the Senior Infant School. The records of the Greyfriars Junior Infant School begin in May 1867 and can be found in the following section.

Miss Caroline Willcox was in charge of the Infant School, then the Senior Infant School, until leaving at the end of December 1873.

Grey Friars' Infants' School

January 1865
- 9   School opened. 92 infants admitted in the morning. 34 more, were admitted in the afternoon.
- 10 Rose Evans, aged 12, came as a temporary monitor.
- 11 Slates, pencils, and books arrived. The children were required to purchase the two former.
- 12 I commenced the classification of the children over 6 years of age. The children appear to know very little.
- 13 Mr Barkworth visited the school.

- 16 12 children were admitted.
- 17 The children have acquired a more orderly method of entering and quitting school.
- 18 The monitor is very painstaking, but has yet to learn the art of teaching.
- 19 The attendance of the children is decreasing, in consequence of colds and other ailments.
- 20 The classification of the children completed.

- 23 9 children admitted. Many are still absent from sickness. The rest of the school apparatus arrived.
- 24 Between 60 and 70 children do not know the alphabet.
- 25 Mr and Mrs Barkworth visited the school. Arrival of a 'clock'.
- 26 The children have a very great tendency to 'drawl'.
- 27 Only 55 children in the morning were present, & 25 in the afternoon, in consequence of the inclement weather.

- 30 The 'Timetable' first introduced, and 'Scripture Lessons' commenced. A poor attendance by reason of the weather.
- 31 Mr Barkworth visited the school, and remained during the 'dismissal' of the children.

February 1865
- 1   The Upper Division of the school received an Introductory Lesson on 'Form'. Held an Examination in 'Singing' of the whole school on the gallery.

2	Many of the children are much addicted to cruelty to each other. I had occasion to punish a child, 2½ years, for this fault, by separating him from his companions.
3	The children have been required to buy slate and pencils; several, however, have not yet got them. I have therefore sent written messages to their mothers, requesting them to furnish the requisites.
6	Caroline Cray, aged 14, came (on trial) to assist in teaching. Increase in attendance – 114 present.
7	One of the boys nearly strangled himself by twisting the string of his slate round his neck.
8	The 'order' of the school not so good as before, in consequence of the attendance of about 30 children who were absent during the last ten days.
9	Mr Barkworth brought in a new canvas board for the use of the school. Only one blackboard previously.
10	Rose Evans left school early this morning, in consequence of illness. Children were less orderly than usual.
13	Very wintry day. 83 and 91 children present, respectively.
14	Girls' needlework slightly improving. 1st Object Lesson.
15	Several children absent from colds and chilblains. The Lower Division received their 1st Catechism Lesson.
16	Miss Coles and niece visited the school this morning.
17	73 children present, notwithstanding the weather. Mr and Mrs Barkworth came in and heard the children sing.
20	101 present – 'Coldness of the weather' is one of the reasons assigned for the absence of the children.
21	The elder children, I believe, would improve in simultaneous repetition, were it not for the monotone of the children on the gallery.
22	I find Rose Evans and Caroline Cray remarkably ignorant of common subjects, especially arithmetic: but they are very willing to learn.
23	One child, John Swinny, invariably comes late to school.
24	C. Cray and R. Evans first attempted <u>oral</u> teaching. They succeeded fairly, being unaccustomed to it
27	Several absentees presented themselves. 121 were present in the afternoon. Rose Evans was absent. Her place was supplied by one of the girls from the Girls' School.
28	The numbers were 118 and 123 respectively. R. Evans being still absent, 2 'Girls' supplied her place.

March 1865
1	Being Ash Wednesday, the children were dismissed soon after 3 o'clock. R. Evans absented herself without notice.
2	Mr and Mrs Barkworth visited school in the afternoon. Although very stormy, 116 children were present.

3	115 and 121 children present respectively. Children were rather troublesome, owing to its being Friday, and there being such small accommodation for them.
6	7 admittances. The numbers are increasing, and the inconvenience of a small room is greatly felt.
7	A 'girl' comes every day to teach the 4th class. A permanent monitor has been promised.
8	R. Evans is unable to attend through illness. 2 monitors from the Girls School managed exceedingly well.
9	The 'Lower Division' Girls commenced 'Sewing'. Not more than 3, knew the stitch perfectly.
10	C. Cray attempted to draw a map. She has slightly improved in 'learning by heart'.
13	R. Evans returned to school this morning. 5 more children were admitted.
14	R. Evans has signified her father's intention to remove her from school, in consequence of a renewed pain in her foot. I shall be very sorry to lose her.
15	The 4th class, having no regular teacher, were most troublesome.
16	Miss Coles visited the school this morning, and stayed during one lesson and the 'exercise' of the children. She expressed herself pleased with what she heard and saw.
17	Several of the children have been absent during the latter part of the week through illness, which has lessened the average.
20	Owing to the smallness of the schoolroom, I can only have 4 classes, and have had only 4 registers. Mr Barkworth visited the school this afternoon, and has promised two extra registers, as the number in each class is so large.
21	129 and 125 were present respectively. Several are absent from illness this week.
22	Very stormy: attendance lessened to 122. C. Cray gave a short lesson to the 'Babies' upon the 'Cat'. She is not at her ease in oral teaching.
23	Two of the children were obliged to go home, on account of illness, this afternoon. Ten of the 1st class stayed after school, at their own desire, to work small sums.
24	R. Evans stayed at home from illness. An extra monitor supplied her place. I have heard that a low fever is very prevalent, accounting for the absence of so many little ones.
27	R. Evans has returned to school. 4 children were admitted.
28	The 3rd class have commenced the union of letters into small words. Many of them have learnt the alphabet very quickly, chiefly owing, I think, to the use of pictures.

29 R. Evans was absent from illness. Although a cold wet day, there were present, respectively, 105 and 122. The 1st class took lessons home with them for the first time, which fact greatly delighted them.
30 R. Evans still absent. C. Cray needs to take considerable pains, in order to pass as a Candidate for Pupil Teachership. Her education is merely superficial.
31 122 and 123 present respectively. 5 ladies visited the school this afternoon. The children sang and exercised; 2 ladies stayed during the 'dismissal'.

April 1865
3 R. Evans returned to school this morning, but is still ill with a bad neck. 141 and 137 present respectively.
4 R. Evans was unable to come school this day through illness. 139 and 141 present respectively. The children were unusually quiet this afternoon.
5 136 present in the morning. Mr and Mrs Barkworth visited the school this afternoon: 133 present, although wet, and a 'Band of Hope' Tea meeting to be enjoyed.
6 Miss Wilson and Mrs Moses came to pay the quarterly fees of 3 of the children. Measles has broken out in the neighbourhood of the school.
7 C. Cray has slightly improved in 'map drawing'. R. Evans is absent. 2 daily monitors assist in her place.

10 4 children, absentees for some weeks through illness, returned this morning. Mr, Mrs, Master Barkworth and a young lady visited the school this afternoon. The small schoolroom is unpleasantly hot already.
11 138 and 134 respectively present. Miss Coles came in, in the morning and Mr Barkworth in the afternoon.
12 The discipline of the 3rd class was very good today under Leah Pickett, a monitor from the Girls' School.
13 The children sang all the afternoon, and school broke up for the Easter vacation.

24 23 admittances. 9 children were promoted to the Girls' and Boys' Schools, after which the numbers present in the Infant School were 144 and 151.
25 The children (Upper Division) were very interested in a lesson on the 'Resurrection of the Shunammite's son'; one of their number being 'suddenly' called away from earth. 161 and 159 present respectively. The schoolroom very uncomfortably close.
26 Ellen Capel has assisted this week, and, if suitable, will be a permanent monitor. The children's education suffers greatly from the limited space, and the constant change of teachers.
27 157 and 155, respectively present. The children were very fidgety, especially in the lowest class; owing to the heat of the weather.

28 Mr Barkworth and 2 ladies visited the school this afternoon. We have managed to make a 5th class near the door; but it is very crowded.

May 1865
1. Only 105 and 90 present, respectively, owing to the May 'Cattle Fair'. People afraid to send their little ones.
2. 144 and 116 respectively present. 'The Pleasure Fair' drew away a great many children this afternoon.
3. 142 and 143 children present. Mr and Mrs Barkworth called this afternoon. C. Cray slightly improves in reading.
4. The girls are making a little progress in needlework, but the few 'good' needleworkers have been promoted.
5. C. Cray being ill, her place was supplied by an extra monitor from the Girls' School. The class of boys (about 35 in number) were moderately good.

8. Although the new Infant School room is not completed, we made use of it this afternoon, in order to thin the children, the numbers being respectively 168 and 174.
9. Children still in the new room. C. Cray did not succeed so well as I imagined in instructing the little ones. I fear she did not do her best, preferring to teach older children.
10. It has been a thoroughly wet day; consequently only 79 and 115 were present. The children were all in their old room.
11. A showery day, but 165 present at both attendances. Mr and Mrs Barkworth visited the school today in order to arrange for a gallery in the new schoolroom, which is much needed.
12. 172 and 169 respectively present. In the afternoon, C. Cray was absent on account of ill health: only Ellen Capel assisted by monitors from the Girls' School, to teach.

15. C. Cray has left the school without any previous notice; the work being considered too much for her brain. 156 and 175 respectively present. Ellen Capel, the late monitor has been chosen as future 'Pupil Teacher', in C. Cray's room. Tomorrow a little monitor is expected, to teach until the arrival of an 'assistant' for the Class Room, next Monday. 'Blinds' and 'mantelshelves' first used.
16. Mrs Barkworth paid a visit to the school this morning. 172 and 173 children respectively present.
17. Ellen Capel has received lessons this week; she has been very painstaking. She is striving to pass the examination for the 'End of 1st Year'. Our school door was painted during school hours: consequently, many little ones daubed themselves with it.
18. At present we have to move the children's forms in one corner of the room, for collective lessons; this causes much trouble and, occasionally, confusion, so that we are very anxious for the new gallery.

19	Our class room blinds came down on Monday, and we have been without them ever since. The children were very hot in consequence. 162 and 165 present respectively.
22	Only 150 and 138 present, in consequence of the arrival of a 'circus' in the town. Maria Pocock, our new assistant from the Trinity National School, succeeded very nicely in managing the little ones. Blinds were up.
23	The children 'Marched' for the first time, today. 'Order', in the morning better than usual, especially in E. Capel's class. We sadly want more apparatus in the Class Room.
24	Today we received a new 'ball frame', knitting pins, slates, bell, and blackboard and easel. 176 and 171 present. Mr and Mrs Barkworth visited the school.
25	Only 169 and 156 present respectively: being 'Holy Thursday', and other schools having a holiday, I suspect our children took one. 6 dozen slates have arrived for the use of all the children; hitherto only those have written who have purchased slates. 'Order' improving. 4 Visitors this afternoon.
26	165 and 156 present. The children improve in 'marching'.
29	4 admittances. 178 and 180 present. The playground was first used for the 'babies': but there are very large stones, at present, in it.
30	177 and 178 present. The elder children went into the playground. One boy, Charley Giles, attempted to knit, and has very nearly succeeded.
31	The 'babies' were noisy today, as their teacher was not well enough to look after them, as usual. Miss Coles showed the elder children some work made by the Indians (Canadian) which greatly interested them.

June 1865

1	The attendance throughout the week, at present, has been very regular. 184 and 183 present today. The 3rd and 4th class Girls (beginners this week) will soon work neatly.
2	Although a wet day, there were 171 and 165 children present. Next week (Whitsun) there is a holiday.
12	The school reopened. Several 'tiny' children admitted. 170 and 177 respectively present. The children seemed pleased to return to school, and were tolerably good.
13	Our gallery in the new room was put up, and first used. It is not so large as I imagined it would be, and holds (comfortably) 66 children. 181 and 182 present. Children very much interested in a lesson on the 'Offering of Isaac'.
14	The 'babies' were better behaved today, owing to the energy of the Assistant. The elder children took great pains with their singing this afternoon, and learnt a new 'hymn' and 'song'. I find the gallery very beneficial. 185 and 177 children present. A visitor this afternoon.

15 The 'elder' children have considerably improved in attention during Scripture lesson. We have not yet got pegs for the children's clothes, and find it very inconvenient to use 2 long 'egg' boxes for so many clothes. E. Capel, the intended pupil teacher, is very painstaking and generally satisfactory.

16 4 visitors today: 2, a gentleman and young lady, expressed satisfaction with the school generally. Throughout this week the 'order' in the 'baby' room has improved.

19 164 and 175 children present. A small attendance in consequence of sickness, and the absence of children on visits. E. Capel improves in writing: she has learned to knit today.

20 The children were more troublesome than usual today. The 1st class, however, took more pains with their writing, than ordinarily.

21 It has been exceedingly hot today: only 3 panes and 2 panes of glass respectively, open in both rooms, but, I believe, we are to have more speedily. 4 visitors today; they were pleased with the singing. Ellen Capel gave a little lesson in the 'Class Room' on the 'Cow'. She succeeded very fairly.

22 Mrs Barkworth came in this afternoon, and stayed during dismissal. The children, poor things, were fidgety in consequence of the heat.

23 179 and 173 respectively present. The little 4th class worked industriously in needlework this afternoon.

26 A good attendance today, with 7 new admissions. 183 and 186 respectively present. About 60 sat in the playground to lessons this afternoon, in order to make more room in the Class Room, where all the children remove on Monday afternoons, during the 'Mothers' Working Meeting'.

27 Mr Barkworth visited the school in the afternoon. 3 boys are now learning to knit: many are very anxious to try.

28 A day's holiday because of the Queen's Coronation. [1]

29 A very wet day: only 94 and 103 present. We practised singing in the afternoon.

30 Being still dull, and raining in the afternoon, only 165 and 164 were, respectively, present. Mrs Barkworth brought a lady visitor this afternoon. Our set of desks has just arrived.

July 1865

3 192 and 196 present: the highest numbers we have yet had. The playground has been divested of its stones, and laid with gravel.

4 192 and 191 were respectively present. We are anxiously expecting some sleeping accommodation for the babies, who are very tired these hot afternoons.

5 189 and 192 respectively present. A 4th boy is beginning to knit.

---

1 The anniversary of the coronation of Queen Victoria on 28 June 1838.

6   Mr and Mrs Barkworth called in the afternoon. The elder girls are very anxious to finish a quilt which Miss Coles has brought: they are improving a little in needlework.
7   Mrs Barkworth visited the school at 'morning dismissal'. We are having some clothes pegs put up in the children's porch. 179 and 186 respectively present.

10 A very good attendance in consequence of a 'tea party' in expectation for Thursday. We have 3 more windows open. 201 and 204 present.
11 58 pegs are put up in the 'babies' porch. We have a series of pictures of Scripture lessons.
12 Mrs Barkworth, Master Barkworth, and Miss Hawkins heard the children sing this morning. They have been practising 'Hurrah, Hurrah for England', for tomorrow.
13 The day has proved very wet; so that the tea party is postponed till tomorrow. Only 145 and 177 present.
14 No very particular lessons today. Tickets for the tea party were distributed. The weather proved very fine, and the treat passed off successfully.

17 This afternoon we had the use of both school rooms, as the 'Mothers' meetings' are to be discontinued on account of the interruption to the school work. Mrs and Master Barkworth came to say 'goodbye' before leaving for the country. In addition, we had 3 other visitors. The school treat has had the effect of making the children very noisy today.
18 174 and 148 respectively present. The number was less in the afternoon, in consequence of the Tea Party of the Band of Hope.
19 The children sang a number of hymns very creditably. A young lady visited the school this afternoon.
20 The 'order' at the close of morning school was much improved. 174 and 184 present.
21 Miss Coles visited school in the morning. School has broken up for 4 weeks.

August 1865
21 School re opened. Only 162 and 167 children, respectively, present. The numbers have decreased in consequence of 2 private schools being opened during the holidays. The fever, too, prevails in the neighbourhood.
22 Ventilators have been made at the top and bottom of the rooms, during the holidays. The 'Order' was an improvement on that of yesterday.
23 In consequence of the weather only 126 and 116 were respectively present. The children have not sung as well this week as before the holidays. <u>Faults</u>. <u>Undue loudness</u> and <u>drawling</u>.
24 164 and 162 present. We have received 2 packets of work from ladies, with which the girls are well pleased. The needlework has improved in the last 3 days.

25 The children are very much interested in Natural History Lessons: their lesson, this morning, was upon 'The Bear'.
E. Capel has taken more than ordinary pains this week to write a rounder hand.

28 The two Miss Coles visited the school this afternoon, during the time of recess. Very many of our little ones are absent from sickness just now. Only 171 and 169 present.
29 Increased improvement in needlework. The boys have almost forgotten how to knit during the holidays; dirty hands have been brought with one or 2, until corrected. 176 and 174 present.
30 The children took unusual pains this afternoon to learn the tune of a hymn 'There is sweet rest in heaven'. The first girl learnt to knit.
31 I have sent out 25 notes today after absentees. A little boy, living opposite and an attendant at school, died this morning of fever.

September 1865
1 The answer returned to most of my notes is 'sickness'. 2 or 3 children, however, on account of the long holiday given, have been sent to the private schools before mentioned, and their parents do not like to remove them.

4 The 2 Miss Coles recommenced the taking of the children's clothing money in the Infants' School. Mr Barkworth visited the school this afternoon, having just returned from a tour. 179 and 178 present. W. Webb, a boy who invariably comes late, has appeared early at both attendances today.
5 180 and 178 respectively present. Emily Honeybone, a little girl living next door to the boy mentioned on August 31st, was taken away this morning by the gastric fever. 15 visitors this afternoon, in consequence of a Missionary Meeting being held in the other schools.
6 Having heard that the sister of a little boy still coming to school was supposed to have got the fever, I sent home a note by the boy, wishing him to be kept at home if such were the case. He did not return to school. 181 present both times.
7 I find that Henry Lewer, the boy previously named has got the scarlatina. 3 persons will not send their children to school while the fever is in the neighbourhood. A fresh monitress took the 3rd class today and succeeded very well. 174 present both times.
8 Some of our children have gone 'hopping' with their parents for a few weeks. 173 and 154 present: the extremely hot weather the cause of the decrease.

11 2 children admitted. 6 children came into school immediately after prayer this morning, and one 5 minutes later. The excuses generally are, either, that 'mother couldn't get me ready before' or 'I had to go out for mother'. 3 were late this afternoon.

12   185 and 187 present today. E. Capel showed a slight improvement in 'Parsing' today. The 3rd and 4th Classes, under Monitors, were less orderly than usual.

13   Mrs Barkworth with a lady, and Miss Coles came into school this morning: the two former heard the children sing. Only 170 and 162 present today, in consequence of the Opening of the Exhibition.

14   171 and 162 present. The babies are kept at home in the afternoon, I believe, in consequence of the very hot weather. No late children, this afternoon.

15   We have been busy today putting up some more pictures in the Class Room. Children orderly this afternoon.

18   2 admittances. Only 172 and 168 present. Five more of my most regular children are absent from sickness.

19   172 and 174 respectively present. The children were unusually quick in learning the words of a school song today. They are rather excited, it being 'Fair Week'.

20   171 and 169 present. In writing capital letters, the 1st Class confuse γ and γ, and $\mathcal{U}$ and $\mathcal{U}$, $\mathcal{V}$ they sometimes confuse with $\mathcal{G}$.

21   Very small attendance today; only 138 and 109 present in consequence of the September 'Cattle Fair'.

22   'Pleasure Fair' today. 159 and 107 present. Mrs Barkworth came in school in the morning while the children were at play.

25   Several children, who were out on visits, have returned to school: 180 and 175 present. One child was sent home this morning, for coming to school at ½ past 10 o'clock. 'Bonnet room' first used.

26   The highest attendance since the holidays: 183 and 189 present. A private school has been closed, and some of the children have returned to school.

27   192 and 185 respectively present. Mrs Barkworth and a gentleman visited the school this morning, and Mr Barkworth in the afternoon. A woman wished her little boy to come to school when it was convenient to her, but she did not, at all, wish him to come regularly: I declined the offer.

28   Mrs Barkworth and the 2 Miss Jansons visited the school this morning. They inspected the writing and needlework, and heard the children sing.

29   E. Capel went up as Candidate for Examination to St Giles. Only 166 present in the afternoon, in consequence of there being a holiday at other schools.

October 1865

2   179 and 176 present. Several children have been sent into the country on Saturday and today, so that the attendance is small. Children orderly.

3   [This entry by a different hand]
    Caroline Wilcox 1 C 2 year. [Signed] H. W. Bellavis

4	The children first began to learn 'recitation'. The 1st Class combined writing letters into words. 180 and 158 present.
5	I have commenced Re-classification of the school. 19 boys and 8 girls are destined, respectively for the Boys' and Girls' Schools.
6	18 boys went into the Boys' School, and 6 out of the 8 Girls into the Girls' School. I have retained Willy Champ as his parents thought he was too little to go into the Boys' School.
9	4 children admitted. One girl, 6 years old, has never been to school before. Only 47 in the Class Room: between 20 and 30 children being taken into the School Room.
10	170 and 155 children, respectively, present. We have given all the little girls in the School room, needlework; some of those who have come from the Class Room, however, can hardly manage their needles. Mrs Workman and Miss Coles called.
11	The children now, on account of the departure of our old 1st Class, sing more softly. They are learning a piece for recitation – 'The Bird's Nest'.
12	150 and 153 respectively present. Children very attentive at Scripture Lesson.
13	155 and 150 present, Mrs Barkworth and Miss Coles visited the school this morning.
16	3 children admitted, and put into the 1st Standard. The 'scarlatina' is very prevalent, several children are absent on account of it. One little baby died, this morning, from inflammation.
17	The children were all gathered together in the Class Room this afternoon, in consequence of a Ladies Meeting being held in the School Room. Miss Missen kindly allowed a class of 31 girls to sit at needlework in her school, in order to make room.
18	Practised the children well in singing their old songs: they forget the words of many. First used the New Lesson Book, 'Step by Step' – we used a much more difficult one last year. Very wet this afternoon, but a good attendance.
19	Continued wet weather: only 119 and 116 present. Many of the children suffered from the cold today in the absence of a fire, but, I believe, we are to have one tomorrow.
20	157 and 154 present. The fires were lit for the first time since last winter. Ellen Capel and Maria Pocock each made up the weekly returns of 2 Class Registers.
23	Many more children are away from sickness. I have found that the Lower Division have nearly wasted the time devoted to needlework, in consequence of the neglect of the monitor (not permanent). I therefore take one or two of the little ones occasionally, and instruct them with the Upper Division.

24 I have sent notes after the absentees; 'sickness' is almost the only cause of absence. Gastric fever and scarlatina are prevalent. 158 and 165 present.
25 E. Capel is improving in writing and parsing. The children learnt the tune of 'God bless the Prince of Wales'. 160 and 155 present.
26 A very wet day. 114 and 107 present. First took 'Europe' with E. Capel. This afternoon she gave a lesson to the 1st and 2nd Class Boys on 'Horizontal and Perpendicular lines'. She succeeded fairly.
27 Gave a lesson on the 'Tiger' to the Upper Division. Mr and Mrs Barkworth came in at the close of lessons this afternoon and stayed during 'dismissal'.

30 Only 132 and 141 present, inconsequence of increased illness, and bad weather. Mr Barkworth with two gentlemen called. Girls improve in needlework.
31 Object lesson this morning on 'sponge': children very fond of spelling easy words written on the blackboard. The 4th Class are, at present, more disorderly than any of the others, being chiefly composed of drafts from the baby room.

November 1865
1 E. Capel gave the babies a 'Natural History' lesson on the 'Horse'. The 4th class have been in better order today, under the superintendence of E. Casway.
2 144 and 150 present. Numbers low on account of the wet weather at the beginning of the week. Miss Christy, a District Visitor, came this afternoon, and stayed during Recreation time.
3 148 and 144 present. Maria Pocock is very painstaking in teaching the little ones texts, hymns, and school songs: I practised singing with them this afternoon.

6 4 admittances. 149 and 158 present. A new cupboard has been put up in the School Room. E. Capel was absent this morning from illness – face ache.
7 168 present this morning, the highest number for 3 weeks. Only 150 this afternoon, in consequence of wet. The working Class of Girls is very large now, being constantly augmented from the little 3rd and 4th Classes.
8 164 and 156 present. A box of 'Common Objects' has arrived at last.
9 A very poor attendance, only 116, in consequence of a whole holiday being given to the Boys' and Girls' Schools, about 40 each of Day and Sunday children going to St Lawrence's Church. A half holiday was given in the afternoon.
10 Very good monitors in school today. Children exceedingly good at afternoon dismissal.

13 3 children admitted. 167 and 165 present. 2 children readmitted who had been absent some time from sickness.

14   172 and 169 present. Number increasing in the Baby Room. Mr Barkworth brought in, this afternoon, a little case of children's hymns for the school.
15   168 and 170 present. Some of the children in the Girls' School are, voluntarily, making rag dolls for our babies, we have nearly 40 at present.
16   Mrs Barkworth came in school this morning at the 2nd lesson, and stayed about ½ an hour, noting the work of each class. Archdeacon Phelps visited in the afternoon, and stayed during recreation.
17   A thorough wet day. Only 121 and 125 present. The children answered better than usual at their Scripture Lesson this morning.

20   158 and 177 present. 118 in the School Room the highest number ever present. Children very orderly.
21   I have changed the Baby's Singing Lesson from Friday to Tuesday – the number of children decreasing at the end of the week.
22   Very showery and boisterous day – consequently but few present. Object lesson on 'Glass'.
23   170 and 167 present. The children have learnt a new hymn and song this week. They usually only learn one.
24   The children were exceedingly attentive to their Scripture Lesson on 'The Pharisee and the Publican' and to a Lesson on the 'Elephant'.

27   166 and 175 present. 122 in the School Room this afternoon – 6 admittances.
28   A thorough wet day – only 152 and 146 present. The children in the Class Room learnt the tune 'Weimar' to the Hymn 'Jesus who lived &c'.
29   Mrs Barkworth, Mrs Wigan, and 2 other ladies visited the school this morning, and listened to the children singing. Scripture Lesson: 'Birth of Moses'. Object Lesson 'Ink'.
30   E. Capel gave a lesson on a 'Halfpenny' to the little ones in the Class Room.

December 1865
1   The upper division practised singing (hymns) after Scripture Lesson this morning, in order that the children may better join in the singing on Sunday.

4   176 and 183 present. I have commenced teaching Catechism to the Upper Division: E. Capel has previously done so – she now takes the Lower Division.
5   The children, today, have been much more orderly than yesterday. 179 and 176 present. Nearly all the absentees are away from sickness. 2 children are detained at home on account of the illness of their father from small pox.

6	160 present in the morning – a very wet day. A holiday in the afternoon, in consequence of the 2nd anniversary of the opening of the Church.
7	The worst number, since last winter, in consequence of the weather. Only 93 and 128 present. Children played in the School room for about ½ an hour in the morning, and learned exceedingly quickly in the afternoon, the tune of a hymn and a song.
8	Very low numbers today. Average for the week only 159 – although we have had the highest number present at once since the summer.
11	Only 146 present in the morning. I sent after the absentees. Sickness was the reason assigned for all except 4, who had overslept themselves. In the afternoon, the number increased to 158.
12	Hooping Cough is prevalent now, and the weather is increasingly cold, 163 and 160 present.
13	The children have learnt one round – 'May God bless &c'. Very much inclined to be noisy at afternoon dismissal.
14	Miss Coles called at the end of the morning. 156 and 148 present. E. Capel gave a lesson on 'Honey' to the babies.
15	146 and 132 present. M. J. Collins from the Girls' School has assisted in the babies' room for the last fortnight – having a bad arm and not being considered able to attend her own school.
18	160 and 162 present. Children unruly at times today, in anticipation of Christmas, and a Magic Lantern on Friday.
19	163 and 165 present. Order improved in the 1st and 2nd Classes. Girls trying hard to finish some whitework for Mrs Workman.
20	Rather wet this morning. 150 and 153 present. The children practised some of their old pieces over this afternoon.
21	164 and 163 present. The school has broken up for a fortnight.

Reading Greyfriars' Schools
Summary of the Inspector's Report
on the Infant Schools
1865

The fresh air is admitted cold and raw through [cracks] in walls and windows. This is the case in both Schools and should be corrected. The Babies, 83 present, are in a separate room under a paid Teacher. An additional Teacher should be provided for this room. Another Gallery should be furnished. The present one might be divided, back rails should be added. Toys and some more apparatus introduced. In the upper room there are 113 Children present in four classes under the Mistress and three monitors taken from the Girls' School. The staff is weak. The teaching except in the class under the Mistress imperfect. But she deserves Credit for her exertions in commencing a difficult work.

[Signed] Henry Moses, Secretary.

January 1866

8   Recommencement of school duties. Children unusually noisy, that one would imagine them to have had <u>many</u> weeks' holiday.
9   Mrs and 2 Master Barkworths visited the school this morning, staying nearly one hour and hearing singing. They saw the 'dismissal'.
10 Mr and Mrs Barkworth, myself and Mr Sheppard held a deep consultation respecting the children's beds. Consequence was – my children lost their singing lesson.
11 Very wet day, with small numbers. Our large gallery in the Babies' Room has been made into 2 smaller ones – moveable but very heavy to pull.
12 We have 2 red curtains dividing 2 separate pairs of classes. The children's beds have come, consisting of a little box with mattress and bolster to fit. The appearance of the Class Room is much improved. I think by the change in the gallery.

15 Maria Pocock has been absent today from illness. Her place has been supplied by a young sister, whom, however, I trust will not be required again, as she is so very meddlesome and disposed to quarrel.
16 Maria returned this morning. Order improved today. Natural History on the Bear given by Maria to the 'Babies'.
17 Children learnt the tunes of a new hymn and song very quickly. Lesson to the Upper Division on the 'Apple' – to be concluded next week.
18 The 1st class wrote on their slates the words put on the blackboard yesterday in their lesson on the 'apple'. They were very pleased.
19 The 3 Misses Holt came in this morning ostensibly to see what 'we did' with the children. They stayed about an hour.

22 The Scripture Lesson with E. Capel this morning was very interesting to us, as we had been able to borrow some beautiful illustrations by Kitts, respecting the 'Journeys of the Israelites'. Children were altogether very tiresome today.
23 182 present today – the highest number since the holidays. Leah Pickett has attended from Christmas, as a permanent monitor.
24 190 and 187 present. We now divide the Upper Division into 2 portions for Marching – the 3rd and 4th Classes going into the Babies' Room with E. Capel as superintendent. The 1st and 2nd Classes stay with me.
25 Lesson on the 'Porcupine' given by E. Capel. I gave a Scripture Lesson on 'The Talents' to the 1st 4 classes: they were very pleased with the nice picture of it.
26 Continuation of yesterday's Scripture Lesson: it is such a pleasure to teach them at this daily lesson, especially with the aid of a picture. There is a very good amount of school money this week: £3 has been paid by Miss Wilson for 2 children during the quarter.

29 Very good attendance today. The babies now have their rag dolls to play with: it is very gratifying to see how well they and Maria get on together.

30   The children were very tiresome indeed today. To punish the 1st and 2nd Classes this afternoon, I kept them back to have a whole lesson after the younger ones were gone.
31   Lesson on a 'Wax Candle' to the Upper Division. I must say that the children today have greatly improved in orderly behaviour. Very wet in the afternoon: 185 and 147 present.

February 1866
1   Miss Coles came in this morning, stayed during 'Marching' time and seemed pleased. E. Capel is now learning 'Fractions'.
2   A wet day – 109 and 151 present. The children are learning a little piece for recitation called 'Little children brought to Jesus'.

5   One admittance – a child fit for the Baby Room. 185 and 192 present. 130 in the schoolroom.
6   The highest number since the summer. 197 and 194 present. It has been such a beautiful day that the children have gone out to play.
7   Miss Coles has given me 8 little pinafores to give to those poor children who are without. A. Goding has the first. 187 and 170 present. A wet morning accounted for the discrepancy.
8   181 and 174 present. I am very pleased with the Upper Division at 'Marching' time: they take such pains. All the children, however, are sadly slow lately at learning by heart.
9   A wet day: only 157 and 153 present. Gallery Lesson on the 'Camel' to the Upper Division.

12   Only 172 and 170 present, owing to the 'measles' being prevalent just now. The 3rd and 4th Class Girls have today begun to work in a class by themselves again, since we have Leah Pickett as a permanent monitor.
13   I have heard of more cases of measles today. 168 and 178 present. Boys rather troublesome this afternoon, owing to no permanent monitor for the 3rd Class.
14   Children are learning the 103rd Psalm – Maria has taught the Babies the words and tune of a hymn in addition to the usual weekly one – being quite unexpected – it was quite a surprise.
15   163 and 164 present. The children were very obedient today. 2 boys came in, more than ½ an hour late this afternoon: they staid after school until I went home. I think they will be early tomorrow. One has promised to try. It has been quite their own faults, for they have played on the way.
16   I am sorry to say the two boys mentioned yesterday, came late again today – and were punished in the same way. A wet day, consequently a low attendance. Lesson on the 'Horse and Cow, compared'.

19   Only 148 and 144 present, including 3 admittances. The reason for nearly all the absences is 'measles' or 'colds'.

20 E. Capel absent on account of the sudden death by drowning of her little brother.[1] Mr Barkworth called in the afternoon.
21 No singing in the Babies Room this afternoon as I could not leave the elder children in the charge of temporary monitors. The Upper Division are trying to finish the piece of recitation 'Little children brought to Jesus' by the time their teacher returns.
22 Very good monitor in school today, named Fanny Page. Leah Pickett is taking E. Capel's class, and minds it extremely well.
23 The Upper Division finished the piece of recitation today. Miss Coles called this afternoon. We have heard today that one of our little ones has been burnt to death. The poor child also had the measles.

26 Only 126 and 123 present. E. Capel came back to school, but not to private lessons.
27 A 'tea party' caused the absence of some of the children today. The children were much pleased to recite to their teacher the piece they had learned.
28 The Upper Division of the First Standard commenced today the beginning of a new Reading Book – 'Sequel to Step by Step'. Gave a Gallery lesson this morning on 'Salt'.

March 1866

1 The weather at present is so very cold, that I doubt whether those children who have recovered the measles, dare to venture out. L. Pickett absent this morning on account of the illness of her little baby sister.
2 Very few children today. The boys were very tiresome, however, this afternoon.

5 E. Capel began lessons (early) this morning. 2 boys have returned today, after an absence of 3 or 4 weeks from illness. We have heard today of the death of one of our baby scholars (measles).
6 Another death today. The measles seem increasing. The attendance of the 1st Class is improved; 33 and 34 have been present. The total number of children at school only slightly exceeds 100.
7 So very few babies at school that there was no 'Singing Lesson' in their room. The children were very quiet today.
8 Leah Pickett is now taking the 3rd Class – both that and the 4th require very firm teachers – she manages <u>any</u> class very well; but will be more useful at the 3rd, as they need careful training to prepare them for the 2nd.

---

1 *Reading Mercury* 24 February 1866, 5: Inquest on Tuesday 20 February 1866 at St. Lawrence's Workhouse on Henry Alfred Capel, aged eight years. 'The deceased had been to the British School on Monday morning, and in his dinner-hour he proceeded with two other boys to Bridge-street, and walked along the plank placed across the river basin, when he appeared to be seized with giddiness and fell into the water, which was high and rapid, and he was carried under the bridge. The body was found in the evening in the centre of the stream, at the back of Messrs. Simonds's brewery, Seven Bridges. A verdict of 'Accidental death by drowning', was returned'.

9   The 4th Class this week have gone into the Class Room to lessons. The children have not yet finished learning the 103rd Psalm.

12 1 child, John Wilkins, admitted into the 3rd Class. 114 and 120, respectively present.
13 119 and 117 present. The children less orderly in the morning, than usual.
14 114 and 115 present. Order improved.
15 The working class of girls are busily trying to finish the needlework sent by Mrs Workman. The Upper Division learnt the tune of a new hymn 'I want to be like Jesus'.
16 Mr Barkworth visited the school this afternoon. Girls work finished.

19 155 and 158 present: the School Room is nearly as full as ever – the Babies, also, have attended better. Mr Barkworth called this morning.
20 157 and 150 present. Gave a lesson to the Upper Division on 'Whalebone'. The <u>increase</u> in numbers has caused a <u>decrease of good order</u>.
21 E. Capel gave a lesson to the Babies on 'The Whale'. The Upper Division of the 1st Standard are improving in 'Reading'.
22 Numbers less today. Mr and Mrs Barkworth called in the afternoon, at the Singing Lesson.
23 The 4th Class have been much more orderly, under the charge of Elizabeth Casway.

26 No admittances. 158 and 159 respectively, present. Mr Barkworth called in this afternoon.
27 E. Capel brought in a very nicely written account of 'Christ – as the Good Shepherd'. 159 and 155. The children went out to play this afternoon.
28 152 and 155 present. Practised 2 or 3 hymns with the Babies in the morning. This afternoon the Upper Division practised Singing.
29 The children seem rather riotous today; I suppose because it is the last week before the holidays. They went out to play in the afternoon.

April 1866
 9 Re-opening of school after a week's holidays. 169 and 163, respectively, present. Leah Pickett has obtained a situation as nurse, and has left the school. 2 monitors from the Girls' School have begun on trial today: but we shall want more <u>Pupil Teachers</u>.
10 182 and 174 present. The children are very unruly this week, and the monitors as so very young that they cannot keep them in check.
11 The monitors commenced early lessons this morning. 182 and 162 present. Wet afternoon. Mrs Barkworth called.
12 Took the 4th class to a Writing Lesson this afternoon, to their apparent gratification. 170 and 176 present.
13 Wet afternoon. 179 and 165 present. Mrs Barkworth brought some little handkerchiefs for my children to hem. They are very pleased,

because, when completed, their work is to be sent to the little black children pictures of whom they see on their Missionary Box.

16 A 'circus' took several of our children away from school this afternoon – 190 present in morning.
17 190 and 188 present. Order rather better, but we are sadly in want of teachers. Miss Coles called this afternoon, and looked at the children's needlework, and saw them play.
18 200 and 193, respectively, present. Taught the tune of a hymn to the Babies.
19 Mrs Barkworth called this morning, to talk about the future teaching staff.
20 Order not so good today: the children seemed tired, for the end of the day.

23 Increase of children in the Babies' Room – 72 in the morning, and total 202. Mrs Workman called, to bring some needlework. Only 161 in the afternoon, in consequence of another circus.
24 198 and 194 present. Children more attentive to their Scripture Lesson. Mr Barkworth and Dr Moses came in this afternoon.
25 Conclusion of an Object Lesson on 'Leather'. Mr Barkworth came in and reproved some boys for picking up stones when at play.
26 201 present at both attendances. The children practised Hymn Singing this afternoon.
27 Our gallery is so small, that we have to employ all our small forms in addition, whenever collective lessons are given. Two visitors this afternoon.

30 Two new teachers today – one has never taught before, and the other from first observations, seems too timid to teach. 192 and 199 present.

May 1866
1 Only one teacher today – the other has been so useful at home, that her mother cannot spare her at present. I do not think, however, that she is brisk enough for an Infant teacher. Mrs Barkworth came for more than ½ an hour this morning. Small number on account of the rain and a 'Fair'.
2 Still smaller numbers. Gave a lesson to the Upper Division on India Rubber. Singing with Babies.
3 Kept the first 3 classes in after school to receive their Scripture Lesson, on account of their inattention at the proper time. Sang our nice hymns through this afternoon.
4 The Upper Division marched very carefully this morning. Miss Holt and Mrs Barkworth came into school this afternoon.

7 Mr Barkworth and a gentleman called this afternoon. Another circus this afternoon.

8   200 and 202 present. Emma Pegler, the new teacher, commenced lessons this morning. Children tiresome this afternoon.

9   The order in dismissal is improved: instead of having the children's clothes brought into the schoolroom and held up before them we send the classes to fetch their things from the bonnet room. It is inconvenient on account of the smallness of the room, but we find the plan more quiet and quick.

10   Order improved in the 3rd Class this week. Monitor – Eliza Palmer.

11   E. Capel has now the 1st Class and manages them very well at present. E. Pegler has no idea of teaching, and has not been to school for 2 years.

14   Mr Barkworth came in this morning. E. Capel and E. Pegler take the Boys' and Girls' Class alternate weeks.

15   182 and 191 present. Order bad, in E. Pegler's Class this afternoon.

16   Object lesson on 'Gutta Percha'. Children unusually interested. Mrs Barkworth came in this morning and told me a new teacher would come on trial tomorrow.

17   I think the new teacher promises very well. She has come from St John's School, (Girls).

18   Fewer numbers today. The children have broken up for a week's holiday.

28   School reopened. Several children (absentees from sickness) have returned. 202 and 213 present.

29   217 and 225 present. The Upper Division were arranged in 2 divisions (1st time) for Scripture Lesson. E. Capel taking the 3rd and 4th Classes. The plan answered well, except that it was awkward to move the 1st and 2nd forms. Mrs Barkworth and the Misses Barkworth came in school this morning. Miss Edith brought 2 maps for the Infants.

30   208 and 210 present. The teachers, 6 in number, have made out their Timetables today.

31   The Upper Division have learnt to sing the text 'Suffer little children &c'.

June 1866

1   190 and 201 present. Mrs Barkworth called during the teacher's lessons. Order very defective in E. Pegler's Class this afternoon.

4   212 and 221 present. The order in E. Pegler's Class has slightly improved today.

5   Annie Ford succeeds very well, at present, with her class, and is likewise anxious about her own lessons. 225 and 220 present.

6   221 and 226 present. Gallery lesson on the 'Potato'.

7   Scripture Lesson on the 'Raising of Lazarus'. The Upper Division learnt the tune of Calvary New this afternoon.

8   Mrs Barkworth called this afternoon. The children were particularly good for Friday afternoon.

11 223 and 230 present. E. Pegler certainly manages the Girls' Class much better than the Boys'.
12 A wet day. 219 and 216 present. 'Order' disorderly today, in consequence of the illness of two teachers.
13 Order improved. The Babies in the Class Room sang this afternoon, much better than they have for the last fortnight, I suppose because it was cooler.
14 211 and 206 present. Mr Barkworth called this afternoon. Object Lesson to the Babies on 'Milk'.
15 I find E. Pegler very deficient in Composition, but she is anxious to improve. The girls in the 1st Class find it hard to work evenly with red cotton.

18 Numbers low in consequence of a wet day. 153 and 193 present. Mr Barkworth called.
19 226 and 213 present. E. Pegler was absent this morning from lessons, on account of headache.
20 The Upper Division went out to play in the morning, as well as the afternoon, in consequence of being disappointed the previous day.
21 Maria gave an Object Lesson to the Babies on 'Tin', which they seemed to remember very well. A lady visited the school this afternoon.
22 208 and 205 present. Mr and Mrs Barkworth came in at the commencement of 'dismissal' and stayed throughout.

25 Numbers present: 212 and 224. The taking of the Children's pence, generally makes them riotous on Monday afternoon.
26 It is extremely warm in school. 223 and 226 present. S. Stubbles (4th Standard) learnt a new rule, this morning, in arithmetic.
27 We had quite a storm this afternoon: the rain, stopping the drains, quite flooded the schoolroom: we have never had a more broken afternoon. On the whole, the children were very good. Tomorrow being Coronation Day, there is a holiday.
29 A very small number all day: I suppose because the preceding day's festivities had tired out the mothers and the children.

July 1866
2 Only 184 present in the morning; a storm coming on just at the time for assembling. 218 in the afternoon. E. Capel away from illness.
3 E. Capel is back again, but is still very unwell. The children behaved better this afternoon at the change of lessons, than usual. 201 and 212 present.
4 204 and 216 present. Gallery lesson on the 'Giraffe' this morning. Miss Coles called.
5 E. Capel learnt 'Proportion' this morning. The children were exceedingly good at Singing Lesson.
6 Very showery morning. Mr Sutton just called.

9 212 and 223 present. I have promoted the children today, and the classes are rather large. The Misses Coles stayed upwards of an hour this afternoon, and saw the dismissal.
10 Mr and Miss Missen visited the school this morning. The children are very excited in consequence of the coming tea party.
11 212 and 211 present. Tickets given out for the tea party and school closed for a month.

August 1866
13 Recommencement of school. 206 and 219 present. Misses Coles came to say good bye, as they are leaving Reading. The children were tolerably good.
14 Questioned the Upper Division this morning on various parts of the Book of Genesis, and found they had remembered their lessons pretty well.
15 Put the pictures and texts round the walls. This week the 3rd Class have marched with the Upper Division, in order to give more room in the Class Room.
16 A smaller school today, in consequence of a fire breaking out close to the homes of some of the children, and by which they were prevented from leaving the street, through fear of danger from the unsafe houses. Practised Singing with the Upper Division.
17 The children have been better than expectation all the week, excepting this afternoon, when they were very noisy: it is, however, chiefly the fault of the teachers, in not checking their habit of calling out.

20 3 Admittances. The 3rd Class was taught by a monitor from the Girls' School: its own teacher being absent from indisposition.
21 222 and 215 present. The Babies Room is thinly attended this and last week, owing to the prevalence of Hooping Cough.
22 E. Pegler has been absent all day from illness. She has not seemed at all well lately. The school suffers from the absence of a teacher. Miss Hillier and nieces visited the school this morning.
23 I have told the teachers today that I shall enter cases of lateness in the Log Book – as 2 of them are almost habitually late. The children were more orderly today, in the 2nd Class.
24 A. Ford came in ¼ of an hour late this morning. E. Pegler still away.

27 A small number present this afternoon, owing to a fete in the Forbury Gardens. Children very quiet.
28 A. Ford and E. Pegler late this morning. E. Palmer absent on leave this morning, in consequence of the illness of her mother.
29 A. Ford and E. Pegler late this morning, and the latter this afternoon. Talked seriously to her. A wet day: few children.
30 Mrs Moses visited the schools this morning. Little Fanny Day is going to leave school this week, as she will henceforth live in the country.

31 In both rooms we find the children have forgotten the words of their oldest hymns and songs, so we are teaching no <u>new</u> ones at present.

September 1866
- 3 218 and 212 present. Mrs Barnes wanted to know if her little baby boy could sit in the large room, as he was just 3 years old – and cried to be separated from his brother. Of course it could not be allowed: the children have been very irregular, and school is consequently new.
- 4 Mrs Barkworth paid a short visit at the time of dismissal. Very showery.
- 5 Gave a Gallery Lesson to the 1st and 2nd Classes on 'The Oak'. Mr Barkworth called this afternoon.
- 6 I have taught Nellie Capel 'Compound Proportion' by Cause and Effect. She appeared to manage pretty well.
- 7 The two late teachers have been tolerably punctual this week. The children sang to Mrs Barkworth and a lady visitor this afternoon.

- 10 217 and 220 present. 2 children, absent since the week before the holiday from illness have returned today.
- 11 E. Pegler absent this afternoon – wanted at home. Mr Barkworth came in.
- 12 Mrs Barkworth paid an early visit this morning to tell us the time of the Inspection next month. The children, this afternoon, were noticeably <u>good</u>.
- 13 The children have recommitted to memory their song beginning 'School is begun &c'. Mrs Barkworth visited the school at the Babies' Play Time.
- 14 The monitors are very anxious about their knitting. A. Ford, <u>ill</u> this morning – absent.

- 17 A. Ford still absent with a severe cold. Her class was taken today by Ann Jeffrey, a very indifferent teacher.
- 18 224 and 225 present. Elizabeth Adey took the 3rd Class today, and improved the order.
- 19 Object Lesson on Water to the 1st and 2nd Classes. Mr Barkworth called.
- 20 A. Ford still absent. The 1st Class were kept in to march after the others had gone home this morning.
- 21 Very small number this afternoon, in consequence of the 'Fair'. Mr and Mrs Barkworth called.

- 24 Morning very wet indeed, but 168 present, 204 in the afternoon. A. Ford still absent.
- 25 224 and 215 present. Maria Pocock away through illness, today. Annie Pocock supplied her place. The Baby Room teachers were very energetic and managed very nicely. A. Ford reported herself this afternoon to be better. Mr and Mrs Barkworth called.

26 219 and 218 present. M. Pocock present this morning but absent in the afternoon, and probably will not return this week. Object Lesson to the Upper Division on 'Water'.
27 E. Capel supplied M. Pocock's place today: the deficiency of teachers was felt in the Large Room. 215 and 205 present.
28 The 3 Misses Holt spent the greater part of the morning in school, taking lessons in readiness for Monday. M. Pocock still away.

October 1866
1 Took the school pence previous to leaving the children in the hands of the Misses Holt. Annie Ford occupied her usual place, but the children were very unruly owing to 'morning' affairs.
2 M. Pocock has returned and we have the full complement of teachers. The 2 Baby Room monitors have commenced to give each a Reading Lesson, daily, in the Large Room. S. Stubbles succeeds well with the First Class Girls.
3 Mr Collins called in the morning and amused the children for about 10 minutes. Mrs Barkworth opened the Missionary Boxes this afternoon, and greatly interested the 1st Class.
4 The 3rd Class seem to be settled now that they have their own teacher again. She can <u>teach</u> and in time, I hope to find her valuable.
5 A lady visited the school this morning; and remained during 'Marching' and parts of 2 lessons. The children are recovering from Monday effects.

8 M. Pocock obliged to remain at home today on account of illness. We find our cupboard very small indeed: the teachers today have taken different parts of the room under their charge.
9 222 and 215 present. M. Pocock returned. The 1st Standard are very anxious about the Examination.
10 229 and 218 present. E. Pegler maintains the order of her class better than she did a short time ago.
11 A. Ford stayed at home this afternoon, on account of illness. Her class suffers greatly.
12 Mr Barkworth called this morning. 214 present. Number smaller in the afternoon, on account of the Boys' Holiday

15 2 Monitors from the Girls' School took the 3rd and 4th Classes, while the regular teachers went for Examination. They managed tolerably.
16 [Different handwriting]
Caroline Willcox 4C 1D
Ellen Capel P.T. 1 Yr
[Signed] H. W. Bellavis
17 39 children went into the Girls' and Boys' Schools today and our deficiency of numbers were augmented by 12 children from the Babies' Room.
18 Mrs Barkworth and Miss Lee came and distributed little books to the children.

19 E. Pegler has commenced the keeping of the Register of the 2nd Class. A. Ford still away. E. Capel is taking great pains with her class.

22 A very few children in consequence of the wet. Re-commenced lessons with the teachers.
23 Right glad shall I be when A. Ford returns to school: the order is very unsatisfactory under temporary monitors. 191 and 190 present.
24 Miss Barkworth came this morning, and gave some little books to the Babies.
25 S. Stubbles, 5th Class Teacher, invariably gets her sums correct, and gives great pleasure by her sensible remarks.
26 E. Palmer has been absent today with a headache: she has neglected her duty, in my opinion, this week, for trifling considerations.

29 191 and 201 present. Have rearranged the Teacher's Time Table. M. J. Waugh is dreadfully backward in 'Dictation'.
30 212 and 191 present (a wet afternoon!). A fire in school for the first time this winter. M. J. Waugh is taking a little more pains with the reading of your [sic] class (4th).
31 A. Ford has returned. Miss Christy visited the school this afternoon, and stayed during dismissal. She expressed herself pleased.

November 1866
1 Mrs Barkworth has sent us round some print for pinafores and some nice coloured handkerchiefs for the first Class.
2 205 and 201 present. Mrs Barkworth came in the morning and stayed during 'Recreation'. I gave a Lesson to the 3rd and 4th Classes on 'Chalk'.

5 Mr Barkworth came in this morning. 2 admittances under 4 years of age. 189 and 191.
6 200 and 202 present. The 1st and 2nd Classes are very attentive to the Scripture Lesson. We have arranged today that the 1st and 2nd Class Teachers should each take the Girls for Needlework for a month – as we think both teachers and scholars will be more greatly interested.
7 203 and 202 present. Natural History on 'The Fox' to the Upper Division. Too cold for play today.
8 Mrs Barkworth and 3 or 4 ladies called this morning: Mr Barkworth this afternoon. The Babies' Room not properly dried after cleaning, so we lit a fire.
9 3rd and 4th Classes were very interested in their lesson on 'Salt'. 1st and 2nd Classes kept in to go to their places quietly.

12 205 and 204 present. M. J. Waugh and Annie Ford late at lessons this morning. We have formed the new plan of having the Infant Room Teachers to take turns in taking the lowest Class (4th) in the Senior Room. S. Stubbles has begun today.

13   The illness of her mother has caused E. Pegler to be away, and I do not expect she will attend school at present. Elizabeth Casway, from the Girls' School, managed her class admirably.
14   A lady visitor this afternoon. Lesson to the 1st and 2nd Classes on 'Camphor'. Order in the 4th Class improved today.
15   Two ladies visited the school and stayed nearly all the morning. E. Palmer absent from lessons.
16   Lesson to the 3rd and 4th Classes on 'Wool'. E. Palmer takes the 2nd Class while the temporary monitor goes into the Babies Room.

19   Report arrived. E. Pegler has failed; I am very sorry; she has lately been so very anxious and was getting so very useful. The poor girl's education has been previously much neglected.
20   Mr Barkworth called in the Afternoon to talk over the Report.
21   Annie Ford has taken E. Pegler's place as Second Class Teacher. Gallery Lesson on 'Camphor' concluded.
22   200 and 194 respectively present. Mr Barkworth called during the afternoon's 'Singing Lesson'.
23   Upper Division very dull at Scripture Lesson. Children very anxious about 'needlework'.

26   200 and 195 present. The children were dismissed at 4, in the afternoon – on account of a sale of needlework held by Mrs Barkworth.
27   Books (Reading) arrived, for the use of the 1st Standard. 220 and 218 present.
28   We re-commenced the practice of distributing the clothes to the children, instead of allowing them to fetch them. We found the things damaged on account of the small Cloak room.
29   The teachers took the Singing in the Senior Room this afternoon – and managed very well to teach a difficult tune to the hymn 'Go, when the morning shineth'.
30   Mrs Barkworth spent a great portion of the morning in school. E. Palmer absent from toothache.

December 1866
3   194 and 211 present. Mr Barkworth came in this afternoon. Mrs Moses saw the 'Dismissal'.
4   A wet day but a tolerably good attendance. A. Ford did not manage the Boys in the best way this afternoon.
5   Very small attendance. A holiday in the afternoon on account of a Prayer Meeting being held in the Girls' School Room.
6   E. Palmer absent all day, on account of her mother's illness. The children sang in Classes instead of on the Gallery, because of the darkness in the Afternoon.
7   The children assembled at 1 o'clock in order to be in readiness for a Juvenile Missionary Meeting. Our 1st and 2nd Classes went into the Girls' School.

10   Missionary Boxes opened by Mrs Barkworth in school this afternoon. 195 and 205 present.
11   Wet day. Scripture Lesson on the 'General Work of Jesus'. 194 and 201 present.
12   The Babies learnt the tune of 'Jesus Christ, my Lord and Saviour'.
13   All the children very attentive to their Scripture Lesson – and at their Singing Lesson, the Senior children took great pains.
14   The teachers have had needlework this week, instead of lessons.

17   195 and 201 present. The children unruly at the prospect of a 'Magic Lantern'.
18   Not so many children today. Mr Barkworth called.
19   Mrs and Master Barkworth came this morning. The children are greatly interested in the round 'May God Bless' &c.
20   Hitherto, our fires have been unprotected – Mr Callas came today to take dimensions for 'guards'. School broken up for a fortnight.

Reading Greyfriars Schools
Summary of the Inspector's Report
on the Infant Schools 1866

The Ventilation and warming will be attended to as soon as the funds will allow. Apparatus and playthings have been added in the Baby room. Some of the Classes are very much crowded and another teacher is required in the Seniors' room. The attainments in the first standard are not satisfactory. I attribute this chiefly, if not entirely, to the crowded condition of the room – the want of sufficient agency and the low attainment and rough condition in which the children are when admitted to school.

[Signed] Henry Moses, Secretary

January 1867
7   School re-opened. A very small number in consequence of the weather. One of the waterpipes burst and overflowed the Senior Room – so we were all obliged to occupy the Babies Room.
8   A class of children has been accommodated in the Girls School.
9   We occupied the Galleries of the Senior Room this afternoon. Mr Barkworth called.
10   Very few pence have been paid this week in consequence of the shortness of work.
11   2 fire guards have been made and fitted. Teachers commenced 'Home Lessons'.

14   <u>Cold</u> more severe: only 113 present. Mr and Mrs Barkworth called.
15   The best needleworkers are away, consequently little work is completed.
16   Children are learning a new hymn 'Little hearts pray to Thee'.

17 A 'tea party' in Hosier Street took some of our children this afternoon.
18 Miss Sutton came to give the 1st and 2nd Classes a Scripture Lesson – they were very attentive.

21 Higher numbers (121 and 133) though the weather is still very severe. 3 of the teachers very late this morning, viz. E. Capel, A. Ford, and S. Stubbles.
22 135 and 133 present. E. Capel gave a gallery lesson on 'The Woman of Samaria'.
23 A very small attendance on account of the setting in of a thaw.
24 128 and 135 present. Mrs Barkworth called. The Girls take great pains with needlework, during A. Ford's fortnight in charge of them.
25 128 and 121 present. Miss Sutton gave a Scripture Lesson to the Upper Division on 'The Leper', during which I gave the Lower Division a lesson on 'The Good Shepherd'.

28 192 and 193. The children have come back by wholesale: during the last few weeks several have been ill. Mr Barkworth came in this afternoon.
29 We commenced early lessons this morning. A. Ford came late. M. J. Waugh commenced learning 'Simple Long Division'. 203 and 193 present.
30 201 and 202 present. Mrs and the Misses Barkworth came in this morning, and stayed during 'dismissal'. Mr Barkworth came this afternoon.

31 The children learnt the tune of a new hymn. Teachers had no Home Lessons on account of a Tea Party given by Miss Holt to the Singers.

February 1867
1 The children were very tired today; I suppose because of the closeness of the weather. A young lady visited the school in the afternoon.

4 199 and 202 present. A. Ford absent from lessons in the morning, on account of a broken chilblain.
5 202 and 205 present. An interrupted day: A. Ford absent throughout: Sarah Stubbles in the afternoon on a visit to a sick grandfather.
6 Mrs Moses and Mrs Hayward visited this morning. A smaller attendance.
7 Practised the children in recitation. The Babies learnt a new tune this afternoon.
8 The children have mastered the tune 'Little hearts pray to Thee'. A boy in the 4th Class proved almost incorrigible this afternoon – but he came round after much talking.
11 207 and 224 present. Mr Barkworth came in, and promised us some new Reading Books. The children very unruly because of the great number.

12 Dr Barkworth and Dr Moses came in this afternoon to consult about new galleries.
13 Dr Barkworth called. Object lesson to the Upper Division on Chalk this morning.
14 The Upper Division of the 2nd Class are improving in Reading. The lowest division of the 1st Class are much more dull.
15 Mrs and the Misses Barkworth visited during Dismissal. Children rather good.

18 We have our new galleries, but are minus a curtain, consequently 2 classes remain undivided.
19 224 and 222 present. Dr and Mrs Barkworth called.
20 The children are very interested in a little song they are learning and say it with great zest. The 1st Class are remarkable for their talking.
21 Only 194 this afternoon, a 'Menagerie' taking some away, I believe. M. J. Waugh and E. Capel were absent from lessons this morning, on account of sickness.
22 213 and 203 present. Our new curtains are up and are a great improvement. Mr Barkworth called.

25 218 and 230 present. The Lower Division of the 1st Class have commenced their 2nd Book – First Reading Book. The children went out to play for the 1st time since the autumn.
26 Rather wet. The children unusually tiresome today. The teachers very painstaking at Grammar.
27 The highest Division were very much interested in a lesson on 'The Ostrich'. Mrs Barkworth came into the Babies Room.
28 Scripture Lesson on 'Dives and Lazarus'. Mr and Mrs Barkworth and a Lady visited.

March 1867
1 The new Assistant came on trial today – she managed, as well as might be expected, with strange children.

4 2 or 3 Babies admitted. Dr B. called.
5 216 in the afternoon. The 1st 3 classes learnt a new tune at Marching Time.
6 201 and 211 present. Conclusion of a Lesson to the 1st and 2nd Classes on 'Cork'. Singing with Babies.
7 A very showery day. Natural History to the 3rd and 4th Classes on 'The Ass'. Mrs Barkworth opened the Missionary Boxes – the children helped her to count the money. The Singing Practice (Hymns) was very pleasant; unusual pains.
8 Dr and Mrs Barkworth came in this afternoon. The teachers have been employed this week in pasting pictures, instead of lessons. M. J. Waugh has not succeeded so well with her Class this week.

11 Maria Pocock absent today. E. Capel supplied her place. Annie Ford late.
12 M. Pocock returned, but was unable to teach as she had met with an accident. Very few children on account of the stormy weather.
13 M. Pocock has finally left, for service in a family. Mr and Mrs Barkworth called.
14 Only 71 and 114 present, owing to the severe weather. We practised some of Standard I in a Dictation Lesson.
15 Eliza Palmer possesses great influence over the Babies, and has exerted it <u>well</u> this week. Still a very small attendance.

18 132 and 125 present: an excellent number for the day. E. Palmer absent, with leave. M. Pocock left today. E. Capel in charge of the Babies' Room.
19 A. Ford absent from illness. A monitor from the Girls' School came to teach the 4th Class, while the 4th took the 2nd Class.
20 A higher number today: 146 and 165 present. 3 little girls have commenced 'knitting'.
21 E. Palmer absent from lessons this week. Reason – a severe cold.
22 M. J. Waugh (3rd Class Teacher) is permanent monitor of the 1st Class, during E. Capel's stay in the Babies' Room. A temporary monitor teaches the 3rd Class.

25 Weather very severe again. 204 and 209 present. Mrs Barkworth called after 'Prayers' this afternoon.
26 The children were very good at Scripture Lesson. 3rd and 4th Classes are learning a little Prayer 'Jesus, tender Saviour, &c'.
27 The Babies went out to play for the first time since last summer. Dr Barkworth paid a visit. 148 and 216 present.
28 W. Smither very late this morning – his <u>own</u> fault. Mrs Barkworth came during afternoon Dismissal.
29 A visit, this afternoon, of a stranger lady and gentleman. George Lunnen is extremely forward with 'writing'.

April 1867
1 220 present in the morning – 2 admittances in the Babies Room, and 2 in ours. Harry Burton, a boy who had previously been to no school, is just getting a little into order: he had no idea of it before.
2 216 and 207 present. The Upper Room children went out to play this afternoon. Mrs Barkworth came in.
3 Mrs Barkworth called about the holiday tomorrow. I must mention that M. J. Waugh is the most punctual of the teachers. She is never late except with a very good reason, and that only occasionally.
4 Holiday on account of the marriage of Miss Holt.
5 We promoted 12 boys to the Boys' School, and 9 girls to the Girls' School.

8 Harry Burton is certainly improving but he is lamentably ignorant of good things – knowing nothing of prayer.
9 A very good number: 206 and 218, notwithstanding the promotions. Mrs Moses and the Misses Wilson paid the Quarterly bills for the children's school money.
10 Elizabeth Casway as a temporary monitor from the Girls' School in E. Capel's place, succeeds well.
11 207 and 204. A showery day, so that the children were disappointed of play, but they had 5 minutes talk as a substitute.
12 Miss Sutton complained of Henry Reading's behaviour at her Scripture Lesson. He is always very dull, and I have learnt this evening, that he is slightly deficient in intellect.

15 Mr Barne and Dr Barkworth visited the school this afternoon.
16 Mrs Barkworth and Mr Barne visited this morning and stayed to hear a secular Gallery Lesson to the 1st and 2nd Classes on the 'Eagle'.
17 Not so many children present, being wanted at home to help their mothers in some instances.
18 Broke up for a fortnight inconsequence of the enlargement of the Boys' and Girls' Schools.

May 1867
6 [*This week incorrectly dated as 9th to 13th.*]
   School re-commenced. The new Infant Mistress for the Babies' Room has arrived.
7 Most of the songs and hymns have been forgotten by the children. Mrs Barkworth brought some fresh song books.
8 120 present both times. Our room is too small for comfort and coolness.
9 E. Casway was a good substitute (today) for Sarah Stubbles, who is wanted at home. 118 and 112 present.
10 Harry Burton is more orderly at Prayer Time. Mrs Barkworth and Mrs French came to see the children.

13 120 and 122 present. Mrs Barkworth came in and promised to pay for the 2 Suttons for a few weeks. M. J. Waugh absent from early lessons today, owing to her mother's ill health.
14 Annie Ford knows perfectly how to work her sums, but she invariably gets them wrong at first. I am happy to say, however, that this failure is a grief to her.
15 The highest division of the 1st Class are more backward than I supposed in writing letters. Oral Lesson to the 1st and 2nd Class on the 'Swallow'.
16 A. Ford late this morning. We find it rather close work to march <u>all</u> together in the school room. Parts of 2 Classes have previously marched in the Babies' Room.
17 I reprimanded the teachers on coming late to lessons. Edwin Tubb, an interesting promising child has gone to live at Southampton.

20 124 present this morning. Sarah Stubbles has ceased to be a monitoress; Annie Johnson is on trial in her place.
21 A. Ford takes great pains with her Class, especially in Reading. The Text 'Thus saith the Lord, I know the thoughts &c'. was well remembered.
22 111 present at both attendances. The children went out to play in the afternoon.
23 A. Johnson is scarcely lively enough with the 4th Class. The children are learning 'If I were a Cobbler &c'. Mrs Barkworth called.
24 Henry and Ellen Morley have left the school. Their mother was very sorry to remove them, but their home is now too far off.

27 1 admittance into the 4th Class. 98 and 116 present: it was wet in the morning.
28 116 and 115 present. The children had 'Repetition' instead of 'Marching'.
29 116 and 120 present. Taught the tune of the new song. Children went out to play afterwards.
30 I took the 3rd and 4th Classes to a lesson on 'Sheep'. I find Elizabeth Smith a very intelligent child.
31 Mrs Barkworth opened the Missionary Boxes in school this morning. Miss Sutton came this morning, but did not teach, as the Scripture Lesson was over.

June 1867
3 A small school on account of the weather. E. Capel absent on account of illness. A monitor from the Girls' School (M. J. Moss) supplied her place.
4 E. Capel returned. A. Ford is commencing 'Notes' of Scripture Lessons.
5 Another wet day. The children were very painstaking at their Singing Exercise this afternoon.
6 Mrs Barkworth and Mrs Collins called this morning. Tomorrow and Monday (Whit) were given the children as holidays.

10 Our 1st and 2nd Classes have gone into the Girls' School today, while we have accommodated the Babies: their own room being given up for the use of the Boys.
11 Only 82 and 85 present. The other schools in the town have a week's holiday. Dr Barkworth called.
13 The Infants sent into the Girls' School have been better in 'order' today. The Children went out to play this afternoon.
14 Mr Collins visited this morning. The average attendance this week is good – those that <u>have</u> attended have done so regularly.

17 121 and 114 present. Several children have returned this week. William Huddy and Sarah Herbert have been ill.

18 I shall be very glad when we return to our own schools; for we are so very full of children. Mrs Barkworth and Dr Barkworth visited.
19 One boy was brought to school this morning, after having played the truant for 2 half days. He was punished by staying ¾ of an hour after school and came right enough this afternoon.
20 A stranger lady travelling through Reading called to see the schools. The children sang and recited. She was very pleased.
21 The children have been more disorderly than usual today: we shall be glad to have our own room on Monday.

24 Have our own rooms again. Mrs, Dr and Master Barkworth called: also Mr Collins, and gave a little Scripture Lesson.
25 The children are learning the words of a hymn to sing with the Boys and Girls on the day of the 'Tea Party' – 'Children of the Heavenly King'.
26 1st and 2nd Classes went into the Girls' School, to practise Singing. School has closed for a month. Tickets given out for the Tea Party.

July 1867
29 School re-opened. 7 admittances: only 2 of the children can attempt Reading. Order very good on the whole.
30 A. Johnson wants a little more skill in the management of the 4th Class. A smaller number this afternoon on account of 'Tea Parties'.
31 E. Waugh one of the 1st Standard is improving in Reading. A short time ago there seemed no hope of her. The whole school were more noisy this afternoon on account of the heat.

August 1867
1 The children were promoted this morning: the 1st Class is rather full. M. J. Waugh was obliged to go home this afternoon through indisposition. One of the Girls supplied her place.
2 M. J. Waugh absent all day. E. Casway took the Class, and managed very well. A small number all day, owing to an 'Excursion' from Reading to Weymouth.

5 1 Admittance into the 4th Class. The 1st and 2nd Girls are very deficient in needlework: they have gone backward lately, I have left the care of them to the Teachers.
6 E. Capel absent, owing to bereavement. O. Smith supplied her place. The children marched today very nicely.
7 The children have forgotten most of their hymns and pieces. We have been practising this afternoon.
8 Joseph Salter and George Simmons have very much improved since the holidays. The former is trying to be 'the best boy in the Class'.
9 A. Johnson has kept her Class remarkably well for the last two days: I have scarcely spoken to it. 1st Class very orderly this afternoon.

12	The Rev J. Keeling and Dr Moses visited the school this morning. 110 and 115 present.
13	116 present at both attendances. The children are very listless this week, owing to the extreme heat.
14	A slight accident this afternoon. One boy, accidentally, threw down another (George Wilson) and cut his forehead deeply.
15	A day of showers. 105 present this morning. The needlework is progressing favourably.
16	Miss Sutton came this morning, but the Scripture Lesson had been previously given.
19	No admittances. 114 present this morning. Annie Johnson absent, on leave, this afternoon.
20	The 3rd Class is the smallest in the room since the holidays. M. J. Waugh, however, does not keep it in order lately. She is not firm.
21	2 children (Tagg's) have returned to school today, after a week's absence on account of illness.
22	108 present. The 1st and 2nd Classes were exceedingly attentive at the Scripture Lesson on the Temptation.
23	109 and 116 present. Before Morning Prayers, the children re-learnt one of their hymns.
26	An excellent number today in spite of the wet. E. Capel paid great attention to the needlework this afternoon.
27	Mrs Workman called this morning. A very good attendance.
28	We have discontinued 'Marching' during the warm weather – the Play Ground being used twice a day instead.
29	The 1st Standard are, on the whole, rather <u>dull</u> in learning Writing Letters, especially the small ones.
30	The children are rather excited this afternoon. Mrs Bowyer paid a short visit.

September 1867

2	Mr Barkworth called this afternoon. The children have not brought their money very well today.
3	A wet day. 106 present. Poor little James Butcher has left today until his 2 little sisters have recovered from the scarlet fever.
4	Ellen Chandler is one of the best workers in the 1st Standard, and is the <u>quickest</u>.
5	Dr Barkworth came when the children were at play. Annie Johnson is slightly improving in writing.
6	A 'Circus' drew off some of the children this afternoon. Miss Middleton paid rather a long visit this morning, and Mrs Barkworth came this afternoon.
9	The children have brought their school money better today. The 1st Class take home an easy book (Step by Step) to learn spelling from, every night.

10   120 present at both attendances. Annie Ford is not very capital at 'Composition': she seems rather fearful of attempting a piece of any length.
11   Hannah Sadler invariably puts down <u>small</u> letters for 'capitals'. Children noisy this afternoon.
12   George Simmons is much more improved. He is more obedient than he used to be, and very attentive at Scripture Lesson.
13   I took the 1st Standard to Catechism this afternoon.

16   113 this morning. Dr Barkworth came in. Mrs Barkworth called, and stayed to Prayers.
17   A. Ford still continues to be more punctual. Her class is usually in good order.
18   A. Johnson was very slow, today over her sums – and eventually got them wrong.
19   2 boys, this afternoon, were punished for playing truant. James Butcher has returned.
20   I examined the 1st and 2nd Classes in Scripture this morning. They answered pretty well. Mrs Barkworth came this afternoon, to open the Missionary Box.

23   In consequence of a 'Fair' – the attendance very low – 103 and 64. Mr Barkworth called.
24   110 and 112 present. The children were unusually quiet the first lesson this afternoon.
25   A. Johnson invariably gets her sums wrong lately. Mrs Barkworth called this afternoon and distributed some little Missionary Books.
26   Miss Middleton brought a lady to see the school this morning. They stayed to Dismissal.
27   Miss Sutton gave a Scripture Lesson to the 1st and part of the 2nd Class, while I examined the remainder and the 3rd and 4th Classes.

30   2 admittances: 1 child in the 2nd and the other in the 3rd Class. M. J. Waugh absent on account of 'removal' to another residence.

October 1867
1   A. Ford and A. Johnson have been more accurate in Arithmetic during the last 2 weeks.
2   Alice Chad has greatly improved in Needlework. E. Chandler and D. Waugh are Knitting.
3   Mrs Barkworth called. The Girls, on the whole, answer better than the Boys in Mental Arithmetic.
4   Very cold: the first Fire since last winter. The 3rd Class is invariably the most disorderly in the room lately.

7   103 and 113 present. A wet morning and showery afternoon. Notice given by their mother, of the removal of Edith and Nellie Hamblin. They are going to remove to Weymouth.

8	The children marched this morning, and kept time very well.
9	A half holiday in the afternoon on account of the Pupil Teacher's Examination.
10	Arthur Fry has a bad foot, and consequently is obliged to sit to his lessons. Miss Eaton called.
11	Annie Ford's class, is invariably the most orderly in the room: it is the 2nd in order.
14	No admittances. The 3rd Class were in better order today.
15	George Simmons returned this week, after being absent in the country, for the last 3.
16	John Cheer has made great progress during the last year. He was in the 5th Class in the Babies' Room last October, and is now preparing for promotion to the Boys' School.
17	Dr and Mrs Barkworth paid a short visit this afternoon. The children went out to play both times today.
18	[In different handwriting] 18th Oct/67 Caroline Wilcox 4 Class 1st grade Ellen Capel 2nd year PT Annie Ford 1st year PT [Signed] C. D. duPont, H.M. Inspector
21	Dr and Mrs Barkworth called this morning. A small amount of school money received.
22	Repetition of Texts instead of Scripture Lesson this morning. A half holiday this afternoon.
23	38 children promoted to the other schools; 23 boys and 15 girls. Received 24 from the Junior School.
24	104 present. The children, contrary to their usual habits after promotion, are very orderly.
25	Have paid a great deal of attention to the Marching today.
28	1 Admittance – a child 5 years old: cannot read her letters – A dull day – no play.
29	Secular Lesson: Gallery: on the Giraffe – the children paid great attention. Miss Coles came.
30	Dr and Mrs Barkworth came. The former stayed to see the children exercise, and the latter to Prayers.
31	104 and 103 present. Mrs and the Misses Barkworth called, and saw the 'Dismissal'.

November 1867

1	Miss Sutton gave her usual Scripture Lesson. A wet afternoon: few present.
4	One admittance, Esther Allen, placed in the 3rd Class. Dr Barkworth came in.
5	Mrs Barkworth paid a short visit. The children are taking a greater interest than usual in their 'Marching'.

6   Mrs Barkworth, the Misses Barkworth and 3 young ladies visited this morning and heard some singing.
7   The Upper Division of the First Class are progressing favourably in 'Reading'.
8   E. Capel was absent today through illness: Ann Jeffrey, from the Girls' School, supplied her place.

11 Only 99 present. 'Colds' – 'scarlatina' and 'low fever' are prevalent.
12 The 4th Class Monitress was excused from her midday lesson on account of her mother's indisposition.
13 The children were kept in to correct a mistake in Singing – 'trick-er-ling' for 'trickling'.
14 We have had a supply of materials from London. Some of the children have bought First Standard Books.
15 The 4th Class were restless this afternoon.

18 Dr Barkworth called this morning. Sarah Baton was sent home for back school money and has not since returned.
19 Mrs and the Misses Barkworth with a lady came this morning and saw the 'Dismissal'.
20 There is a great difference between the 1st and 2nd Classes, respecting Scriptural Knowledge. The latter are remarkably quiet, but dense.
21 Did not give a Secular Lesson to the 3rd and 4th Classes this morning, because the apparatus had not been previously prepared.
22 M. J. Waugh was absent today on account of 'a bad eye'. Mrs Barkworth came this afternoon and showed the children an African idol – the God of Medicine.

Reading Greyfriars Schools
Summary of the Inspector's Report
on the Infant Schools 1867

There are two points elicited at this inspection that suggest the existence of some very serious defect in the School management and instruction. They are (a) that out of 70 children over 6 years old, qualified for examination as far as attendances go, only 21 children were presented to Her Majesty's Inspector to be examined – Now of these 70 children only 13 (I am informed) have left the School, hence about 30 children (at least) have been withheld as unfit to pass the Examination of the first class Standard. The second point above alluded to is (b) that in the Senior School there is hardly any difference of age noticeable between the children of the second, third, and fourth classes respectively, and yet many of the oldest children in the fourth and third classes have been in this School since the year 1865, and have (further) attended School well during the past year; Therefore that these children should be in the third and fourth classes reflects seriously upon the general administration and instruction of the School. The head Mistress has perfect control over her School when under Drill, but when a class [is] at lessons the children are unsteady and inattentive. Except in

Writing, the 21 children presented in the first Standard did not pass at all satisfactorily – both the Reading and the Arithmetic give but little evidence of firm or careful teaching.
[Signed] Henry Moses, Secretary

November 1867
25   2 Admittances – both in the 4th Class. Dr Barkworth called.
26   The children in the 1st and 2nd Classes are buying their Reading Books very well.
27   The children in the 3rd Class are far less fidgety under M. J. Waugh than when in the 4th Class.
28   Mrs Barkworth called. The children had a 'run' in the Play Ground this afternoon.
29   Mrs and the Misses Barkworth came this morning, heard the children sing and saw them dismiss.

December 1867
2   A very small number, in consequence of the extreme cold. Children are learning a new song: 'Hop-hop-hop'.
3   Little James Crew, in the 4th Class, dictated the Twice Table for the whole school.
4   A. Johnson absent. Excuse – sickness. E. Giles supplied her place. Mrs Barkworth opened the Missionary Box. A half holiday on account of the anniversary of the opening of the Church.
5   The children are taking great pains to learn the 'Tables' in all the Classes.
6   Mrs Barkworth came in for a short time this afternoon. Taught the tune of 'Hop-hop-&c'.
9   The children are learning the words of the hymn 'I thank the goodness and the grace &c'. A tolerably good attendance.
10   In all classes, there is great anxiety to do well at the monthly Examination held for the 1st time this week.
11   <u>Order</u> in all the classes, very good. Singing in the Afternoon.
12   Examination for the 1st Class – Reading – the <u>best</u> subject. Order very defective.
13   Second Class examined. <u>Order</u> exceedingly good. Subjects, taught during the last month very satisfactory.
16   Third Class examination. Reading, very defective – <u>Elocution</u>, Imperfect. <u>Order</u> – Good.
17   4th Class Examined. Subjects, very fair.
18   School closed for 2 weeks of Christmas Holidays.

January 1868
6   School re-opened. 3 admittances – one boy aged 4 years and 8 months, unable to say or point out the letters.

7   85 and 90 present. Children very tolerable considering they have had a fortnight's run.
8   83 and 92 in attendance: have promoted a few children to higher Classes.
9   A. Ford absent this afternoon on account of her mother's sudden illness. I have sent 2 of her boys into a lower class till Monday on account of their bad behaviour.
10   A. Ford still absent. Olive Smith, from the Girls' School supplied her place. 85 present this afternoon.

13   2 Admittances. The Teaching Staff complete again.
14   M. J. Waugh's sums were all incorrect this morning. I am afraid she is careless.
15   98 and 100 present. Numbers are on the increase. Taught the tune of 'I thank the goodness and the grace'.
16   Numbers respectively 93 and 90. A drizzling rain. Mr Collins called this morning.
17   A very wet afternoon, but 93 present. The numbers have kept up well all the week, considering the weather.

20   Annie Ford was absent today, on account of her illness. 96 and 91 present.
21   Gave the 1st and 2nd Classes an Object Lesson on Glass.
22   98 and 90 present today. Letitia Pope has learned knitting.
23   Annie Ford was late at lessons this morning. E. Capel gave a Lesson to the 3rd and 4th Classes on the Elephant.
24   89 and 87 present. Miss Sutton came in for a short time this morning and heard the children sing.

27   No admittances. 95 and 60 present. A pouring afternoon; therefore the number very good.
28   Conclusion of the lesson on Glass to the 1st and 2nd Classes. M. J. Waugh was a trifle late this morning.
29   It was so bright a day, that the children went out to play this afternoon.
30   I have examined the 1st Class today, and found them considerably improved in order. More creditable writing, too, was presented, being even and well formed.
31   The 2nd Class Examination. Order, less good than before the Holidays. Reading, very imperfect. Mrs Barkworth and Miss Neave called this afternoon.

February 1868
3   The 4th Class have not done their subjects at all well – today. Evidently, they have forgotten the teaching previous to the holidays.
4   The 3rd Class, on the whole, have done better than last month.
5   M. J. Waugh is absent from neuralgia in the face. Dr Barkworth called this afternoon.
6   Mrs Barkworth came for a short time this morning. 95 and 102 present.

7	Miss Sutton gave a Scripture Lesson to the Upper Division. 98 present this afternoon.
10	M. J. Waugh has returned today. The highest numbers since the Holidays – 107 and 103.
11	107 and 111 present. The children marched rather better than usual this morning. A. Johnson is very useful in domestic work about the school.
12	A. Capel and M. Pope are knitting garters.
13	Mrs Barkworth called this morning – 110 present. Some of the 1st Class are greatly improving in Reading.
14	110 present at both attendances. The average of the 2nd Class is slightly the best this week.
17	2 Admittances. 110 present in the morning. The 1st and 2nd Classes were deprived of their play, through naughtiness.
18	E. Capel was late this morning – 10 minutes past 8. The children were very good at Scripture Lesson, and many answered very well.
19	The numbers have been exceedingly good during the last fortnight – hardly any fluctuation. 110 present this afternoon, though wet.
20	We need some new Reading Books very badly. E. Tubb has left for Southampton – I am sorry.
21	Miss Sutton taught in the morning. Miss Neave paid a short visit in the afternoon, in lieu of Mrs Barkworth.
24	113 and 108 present. The children stayed in this afternoon, as the ground was somewhat wet.
25	115 present. A. Ford absent. Her class was very good without her.
26	A. Ford returned. The children have been trying to be very good today. 111 this afternoon.
27	Mrs Barkworth and Miss Neave came this afternoon., to hear the children sing. Miss Sutton will (D.V.) give her Scripture Lesson on Thursday, instead of Friday, during Lent.
28	Dr Barkworth visited the school today.

March 1868

2	113 and 106 present. Dr Barkworth came in the afternoon.
3	A. Johnson absent this afternoon, on account of her mother's illness. C. Giles supplied her place.
4	I have today finished the Examination of the school. Each class has improved – the 3 lowest slightly. The 1st Class, I am glad to say, have made a little progress in everything.
5	Miss Sutton's lesson on the 'Parable of the Sower'. A good attendance.
6	Mrs Barkworth and Miss Neave came and opened the Missionary Box: 3s 0½d.
9	110 and 106 present. Dr Barkworth called this afternoon.

10   Children very interested in their Scripture Lesson on the Parable of the Tares. It being too wet for the children to go out to play, I distributed some little treasures, such as marbles &c.

11   Scripture Lesson on the 'Parable of the Unmerciful Servant'. A wet afternoon.

12   Mrs and the Misses Barkworth came at the end of the afternoon, and saw the Dismissal.

13   The Misses Holt spent the greater part of the morning in school.

16   The children have been rather excited and troublesome today. Dr Barkworth called this afternoon.

17   I am sorry to say that, lately, Annie Ford has been less careful in attending to her own particular duties: minor points have been forgotten, such as, locking the bonnet room door &c.

18   Dr Barkworth called this afternoon. E. Capel gave a lesson to the 3rd and 4th Classes on 'Sugar'.

19   Mrs and the Misses Barkworth spent a long time in school this morning. Too wet for play.

20   109 present – though a wet day. The children have been more than usually troublesome today.

23   2 Admittances: neither can read more than the letters. Only 102 present.

24   Miss Middleton with 2 young ladies, visited the school for a rather long period this morning.

25   The school went on in the usual manner.

26   The teachers are busy finishing some needlework to be sent home at the Easter Vacation.

27   I received 19 children from the Junior Infant Room today – having sent up the same number into the Boys' and Girls' Schools.

30   Letitia and Matilda Pope, 2 of the most promising children, have left, removing entirely from the town.

31   Annie Johnson is acquiring a little more firmness in the management of her class, which, now, is composed of <u>naughty</u> children, to a great extent.

April 1868

1   M. J. Waugh is not managing quite so nicely with her class as she was wont.

2   The Girls cannot work any more before Easter as we have finished our old stock.

3   Dr and Mrs Barkworth called – the latter saw the children march in the Play Ground.

6   A little girl called Ellen Champ admitted into the 2nd Class – formerly she attended St John's Infant School.

7 The children have been very orderly these 2 days, especially considering that it is the 'last week'.
8 Dr and Mrs Barkworth called. A smaller number present.
9 The children dismissed after morning school for the Easter Vacation.

20 School re-opened. A very meagre number, owing to very heavy rain. No fresh admittances.
21 104 present. A brighter day and more orderly children. We have been drilling 'Marching'.
22 98 present, although a wet day. The 2nd Class have been very orderly today.
23 104 present. The children went out to play this afternoon.
24 A wet day, yet 100 and 88 present. The school fees have been tolerably well paid this week.

27 3 New Children have been admitted this morning.
28 103 and 99 respectively present, which, considering the state of the weather and the return after the holidays, is extremely good.
29 Mrs and the Misses Barkworth paid a visit to the School this morning.
30 Kate Sherfield and Elizabeth Goodey came in to teach today: and managed well especially the former, who kept them in good order.

May 1868
1 The numbers were low today on account of the May Fair. Dr Barkworth came while the children were out at play.

4 99 and 104 present. Dr Barkworth called this morning.
5 The children do not sing at all well this week they drawl both words and tune.
6 A large number – 112. Work – as usual.
7 3rd Class Examination. I have been pleased to observe that M. J. Waugh has exerted herself more the last month. Result – more creditable considering the classes have been, in a measure reorganized lately.
8 The 4th Class Examination has not been so satisfactory – but the children are fresh from the Junior Room and have not yet got into our way.

11 No re-admittances, nor fresh children. Dr Barkworth called this morning – and Mrs Moses stayed during afternoon prayers.
12 First Class Examination. The Standard has been lowered this month, in consequence of the children being promoted from the 1st Class. They have acquitted themselves very well, on the whole.
13 The 2nd Class has been very orderly and methodical throughout their Examination today.
14 A. Ford was absent today, on account of illness.
15 A. Ford returned. The school pence, this week, have been rather numerous this week. [sic]

18	102 and 103 present, Miss Paten, a Sunday School Teacher, called this morning.
19	The children did not go out to play, in consequence of the great heat. A. Johnson was absent all day because her mother was ill.
20	109 present. A child admitted, 5 years old, who knows but one or two of the letters.
21	The 2 monitresses, being Singers, left school at 11 o'clock, for Church, as it was Ascension Day.
22	Miss Sutton came as usual. The numbers have been less today – some of our children are ill, and the afternoon was wet.
25	A rather small school today. A slight accident to one child, who cut his head through falling when out to play.
26	Some of the children in the 1st and 2nd Classes are improving in needlework.
27	A very promising child in the 3rd Class has left – his parents moving from the town.
28	The 2nd class exhibits the best order in the room.
29	Miss Sutton absent through indisposition. Mrs Barkworth and Miss Farbrother visited the school.

Whitsun Vacation.

June 1868

8	96 present at the re-opening. One or 2 of the children have the Hooping Cough.
9	E. Capel absent today, through sickness. Martha Mace from the Girls' School supplied her place.
10	Alfred Rolph, in our 1st Standard, has been removed from the school, as his parents were in the parish of St Lawrence.
11	A. Johnson is improving in 'Proportion' sums.
12	Mrs Barkworth called in the afternoon.
15	Dr Barkworth and a gentleman came this afternoon previous to his departure from Reading for the holidays.
16	100 present. I found the 1st Standard deficient in subtracting sums given them mentally and otherwise.
17	M. J. Waugh absent today. The 2nd Class were very attentive and methodical during their Examination.
18	A. Waugh [sic] returned. Her Class is improving slightly in Reading.
19	I was pleased to find on examining the 4th Class that they are more methodical.
22	Josiah Smith, a promising boy, but very delicate and therefore often absent, has returned.
23	The children get into the habit of coming late just now. I sent the Earles home in consequence.

24 Considering it is the Quarter's End – the children have not brought their money well.
25 The Teachers had an interesting Reading lesson this noon.
26 Miss Sutton obtained the children's great attention at her Scripture Lesson.

30 A very small number: a holiday yesterday and the other schools have broken up.

July 1868
1 The children very noisy in coming out of the Play Ground this afternoon.
2 No play this morning, because of the noise of yesterday.
3 Breaking up for the Midsummer Vacation – 4 weeks.

August 1868
3 Re-opening of the school, 97 present at both attendances. 1 Admittance.
4 Many of the children are absent from illness or because in the country.
5 Considering the School Treat is tomorrow, the children are remarkably orderly. Mrs Barkworth and Master Walter paid a short visit.
6 Contrary to usual routine, the children assembled this morning, but separated early to prepare for the afternoon 'Tea Party'.
7 S. Thomas was very disobedient this morning and had to be punished, but ultimately recovered. Babies' Tea Party this afternoon.

10 A good attendance. 1 Admittance.
11 The children answered very well in Scripture. J. Collins is a very quick intelligent boy.
12 102 present. The order in the 4th Class is improving.
13 A wet morning. Some of the younger children are improving in needlework.
14 98 present. Alice Capel is quite a little help in needlework.

17 111 and 109 present, though wet. A. Ford absent from a sore throat.
18 A. Ford still absent   Kate Sherfield from the Girls' School supplied her place.
19 107 present. A. Ford returned. The children learned the tune of 'Musicians all'.
20 C. Casway (2nd Class) under age, is improving greatly in Reading. Only 69 this morning: wet.
21 E. Capel absent for today, through sore throat and hoarseness. This week has been most unsettled.

24 Dr Barkworth, with a lady, came in this afternoon. E. Capel dismissed the school during my temporary absence in the Church-yard.
25 Annie Johnson is obtaining a greater command over her class.

26 Matilda Nash 'cannot be spared' to come to school, very frequently: consequently she is going backward in everything.
27 In reading, many of the 2nd Class children are very deficient.
28 Miss Sutton gave a lesson on 'Daniel in the Lions' den'.

31 109 and 110 present. Louisa Wyatt has returned after illness.

September 1868
1 1st Class Examination. In Catechism, the 2nd answer was very imperfect.
2 The children learnt a chant tune to the words 'Dear Jesus, ever at my side'.
3 The 3rd Class were very methodical during their Examination. Reading somewhat better.
4 The order at the 4th Class Examination was Creditable but the attainments low – owing to so many new and recently absent children having come again.

7 107 present. The intense heat prevents the children from having their full lessons, in a measure.
8 Attendance 110. M. J. Waugh is taking a greater amount of pains with her class than usual.
9 The children learnt the tune of 'March away'.
10 107 present. M. J. Waugh is very careless with her own Arithmetic.
11 Miss Sutton taught. E. Smith (1st Standard) has gone to London until after Xmas.

14 106 present. 1 Admittance (2nd Class) a girl 5.6 at school in London previously.
15 I gave a lesson to the 1st and 2nd Classes on 'Salt'.
16 Dr Barkworth came in this afternoon. Alice Capel shows improvement in Knitting.
17 Miss Middleton paid a visit this morning; the children sang to her.
18 Miss Sutton taught. The attendance this week has been good.

21 The annual 'Fair' is taking place: only 70 present this afternoon.
22 91 and 69 present. Annie Johnson has leave of absence this week.
23 92 in attendance. The children have been fidgety today; I suppose on account of their connection with the 'Fair'.
24 The children learnt the tune of the song 'When mother sends for anything, &c'.
25 A wet day. Miss Sutton did not come in consequence.

28 92 and 104 present. A. Ford absent from school this morning: wanted at home.
29 M. J. Waugh absent today through face ache. A. Johnson returned to school.

30   The 3rd Class have been tolerably orderly without their teacher. 93 present in all.

October 1868
1   Dr Barkworth visited this afternoon.
2   Alfred Watson, a most promising child, has left for a village a few miles off. He has attended the requisite times.

5   A. Ford and A. Johnson absent from 8 to 9 this morning from indisposition.
6   92 and 104 present. The children are learning the words of 'A little bird built, &c'.
7   103 present. Some of the 1st and 2nd Class Girls are very enterprising in work especially Maria Guy and Beatrice Clark.
8   E. Capel absent from sore throat. I took the Class and examined them. They passed very tolerably.
9   Willie Willis (1st Standard boy) has gone in the country, probably for the winter.

12   Beatrice Clark, Alfred Sayer, and one or 2 others have gone for short holidays. Susie Bettridge has returned from London.
13   The Misses Holt paid a visit this morning.
14   106 present. Matilda Nash has returned.
15   Dr and Mrs Barkworth visited this afternoon. The 1st Standard are very anxious to do their best.
16   A circus took away many children this afternoon.

19   Mr Collins (Scripture Reader) took charge of the school this morning, during the Teachers' Examination. Holiday in the afternoon.
20   Annie Johnson has expressed a wish to be a 'Candidate' in E. Capel's room, who leaves at Xmas.
21   M. J. Waugh has finished her needlework.
22   Mrs Barkworth came in while the children were marching.
23   No Miss Sutton this morning. John Herring (First Standard) absent from illness.

26   105 present. Alice Wild and Edward Morley (4th Class) returned after illness.
27   [In different handwriting]
     27th Oct/68
     Caroline Willcox Crtfd. Teacher 4 Class 1 grade
     Ellen Capel P.T. 3rd year
     Annie Ford P.T. 2nd year.
     [Signed] C. D. duPont, H.M. Inspector
28   Dr Barkworth came in. Two First Class Girls from the Girls' School took the 3rd and 4th Classes.
29   24 of my Girls went into the Girls' School this morning: very sorry to lose them.

30   A holiday in honour of the close of the Examination.

November 1868
2   A very unsettled morning: 28 boys promoted and 40 children from the Junior Room admitted.
3   Our school seems quite a new one. 2 more boys sent out. Annie Johnson promoted to the 3rd Class. Mary Jane Waugh at the 4th, as she is going to leave at Xmas.
4   50 children are, at present, in the 1st Standard, and in the 2 first Classes.
5   Mrs Barkworth came in this morning and stayed about an hour.
6   97 present. No Miss Sutton.

9   95 present. 1 admittance from Trinity School (3rd Class).
10   Annie Johnson manages the 3rd Class very tolerably.
11   There is a much greater proportion of girls in the school, at present: e.g., 9 boys in the 1st Class and 21 girls: 12 boys in the 2nd and 18 girls.
12   M. J. Waugh absent from illness. Mrs Barkworth called.
13   Prepared for Miss Sutton, but she was again absent.

16   97 present. Sent after the Absentees – many from illness.
17   An admittance (2nd Class). Mrs Barkworth with 4 other visitors made a long stay.
18   M. J. Waugh absent for this week – continued lumps in her neck.
19   Sent home to Mrs Workman the finished work – handkerchiefs.
20   Did not prepare for Miss Sutton: never came.

23   M. J. Waugh still away. Kate Sherfield from the Girls' School is a capital substitute.
24   90 and 84 present. Dr and Mrs and the Misses Barkworth visited this afternoon.
25   So many of the children are ill either from colds, hooping cough, measles, or scarlatina.
26   Dr Barkworth came in this afternoon.
27   Dr Barkworth brought in the report this afternoon.

30   1 Admittance – a child, 4½ years old, never been to school before, and does not know all her letters.

December 1868
1   The children still away in large numbers.
2   Half holiday this afternoon in consequence of the anniversary of the opening of the Church.
3   Ellen Capel is going to leave Friday 11th. She will be a great loss.
4   Miss Sutton came. There is 30 less average this week than last. The sickness seems to be quite an epidemic.

7   Mrs Barkworth opened the Missionary Box this afternoon – ours contained 2s. 10¾d.
8   67 present. Mrs Barkworth, this afternoon.
9   The children are quite tired and want a holiday.
10 This afternoon the children were able to play.
11 E. Capel has concluded her engagement as Pupil Teacher. We are all very sorry to lose her.

14 We have a new monitress for the 3rd Class – Kate Sherfield. Annie Johnson has been promoted to the 2nd Class and Annie Ford to the 1st.
15 2 boys admitted (1st Standard age) who know only 'a' and 'o' of the Alphabet.
16 Mrs Barkworth paid a short visit.
17 M. J. Waugh, monitress for nearly 3 years, leaves at Xmas.
18 No Miss Sutton came, in consequence of indisposition.

21 The numbers are very small, as the parents know school will be open but for 3 days.
22 A. Ford and A. Johnson succeed as well as can be expected, at present.
23 Broke up this afternoon for 2 weeks.

Reading Greyfriars' Schools
Summary of Inspector's Report on the Infant School 1868

Last year's defects have been largely and very creditably lessened. The accuracy of the first Standard however disappointed me, but the other classes promise well for next year.

Closer attention to class lessons is what the first Standard lack. Drill good. Religious teaching satisfactory. Intelligence improved.

[Signed] Henry Moses, Secretary

January 1869
11 Many old faces back again – but several children are yet far from well.
12 96 present. The children do not seem to have forgotten much in the holidays.
13 We have a monitress on trial at the 4th Class – S. A. Perren.
14 Kate Sherfield does not seem so apt to teach as we before imagined.
15 Dr Barkworth came in this afternoon.

18 [Date incorrectly given as 21st]
    I had occasion to send to Mrs Simmons for some back school money. She came up and promised to pay.
19 S. Perren has considerably improved in her general manner as a teacher, since Xmas.
20 Mrs Barkworth called. We have heard of a girl from Trinity Infant School, who wishes to be a Pupil Teacher but is not likely to meet with a vacancy there.

21 Annie Ford is going to leave, I am very sorry to say. Her parents have left Reading and gone to reside in London.
22 The numbers are reduced again. The average this winter will be very bad.
25 Small numbers again. The reasons, invariably given, are 'ill' – 'colds' – measles, &c.
26 70 present. Scripture Lesson on the 'Prodigal Son'.
27 We are going to try Alice Parsons tomorrow, if she will suit, Kate Sherfield will have to leave. She is very sorry, but really cannot teach the 3rd Class sufficiently.
28 Alice Parsons is very bright and sharp. She succeeded very fairly considering she knew none of our ways, nor the children's names.
29 67 present. The children repeated their texts very nicely this morning.

February 1869
1 80 this morning. We have heard of 2 deaths among our scholars this winter.
2 This is Kate Sherfield's last week at the 3rd Class. I am very glad of it.
3 The children were very listless this afternoon at Singing Lesson.
4 Sarah Perren is a very bad writer, but thoughtful and intelligent, and teaches her children very creditably.
5 Annie Ford dismissed the school this afternoon, in my absence.

8 Alice Parsons installed as permanent monitress of the 3rd Class – to be a Candidate for the Pupil Teacher if she improves in her studies.
9 The 1st Class were very painstaking at their Reading Lesson.
10 3 Misses Holt called this afternoon, and stayed during Recreation.
11 Mrs Barkworth paid rather a longer visit than usual this morning.
12 Our room was required this morning for a meeting, so we were divided – the upper half of the school going into the Girls' School, and the lower into the Junior Room.

15 Our numbers are only slightly increasing.
16 Dr and Mrs Barkworth called.
17 Alice is very backward; never learnt 'Weights and Measures;' knows hardly anything of Scripture, Geography, or Grammar; and spells very indifferently.
18 Some of the Girls are taking extra pains with their needlework, consisting of print and brown pinafores, handkerchiefs, and pieces as specimens of sewing and hemming.
19 Annie Johnson has very greatly improved in her method of setting out her Exercises, since Xmas.

22 87 present. Higher.
23 S. Perren absent from earache and general indisposition: Charlotte Wicks was a substitute.

24 Matilda Smith took the 4th Class today but did not manage it at all well.
25 Sent after the Absentees, and expect a good many back on Monday next.
26 Ellen Ball, monitress today. Very good.

March 1869
1 A great increase – 97. 2 Admittances – one in 3rd and the other in the 4th Class.
2 93 present. Annie Ford absent – illness.
3 Dr Barkworth called this afternoon.
4 Alice is greatly improving in discipline – also with her lessons she takes great pains, being, as I believe, carefully looked after at home.
5 Mrs Barkworth was expected to open the Missionary Boxes, but disappointed. Mrs Workman called.

8 We have heard today of the deaths of 2 of our little ones. The news has made a great impression among the children.
9 Gave a lesson this morning, on the 'Raising of Jairus' daughter'.
10 The children have learnt a new song – 'Hark 'tis the bells'.
11 Examination of the 1st Class. Annie Ford has worked very well with them – and they passed very creditably.
12 Annie Johnson has worked less well. The children were in good order, but not up to the mark.

15 2 children have left: one to reside in the country – the other to go to the Industrial School (where they are clothed) with her sister.
16 3rd Class Examined. Alice has taken great pains; the children and she were strangers to each other 6 weeks ago.
17 The 4th Class have advanced under Sarah Perren's management the last month.
18 Dr Barkworth called.
19 Annie Johnson late this morning.

22 Numbers rather less this week. Dr Barkworth came when the children were at school this afternoon.
23 Mrs Barkworth inspected some of the Girls' work this afternoon.
24 Breaking up for the Easter Holidays.

April 1869
5 Re-opening of school. A very good attendance, and 3 fresh admittances: children under age.
6 New books, slates, &c. have arrived.
7 An influx of children from the Junior Infants' School – 20. Our number was 116.
8 The Teachers have made up their Registers and the Monitresses covered books instead of their regular lessons.

9	A visit this afternoon from Mr and Mrs Campbell (Dr and Mrs Barkworth's substitutes).
12	Alfred Bishop's admittance to the 2nd Class – under 6.
13	Annie Johnson absent through a bad heel – it causes confusion through the school, in some degree.
14	Sarah Perren is not so careful as she ought to be with spelling.
15	Jane Chad is supplying Annie Johnson's place this week.
16	113 is the highest number this week. No play – wet.
19	114 and 112 respectively. Annie Pearson admitted to the 2nd Class. Annie Johnson back again.
20	110 and 113 present. Mrs Workman visited this afternoon.
21	116 in attendance. No play this afternoon as a punishment for disorder.
22	110 present. School money not brought so well this week.
23	Miss Sutton visited his morning, and hopes, next week, to renew her Scripture Lessons.
26	Annie Johnson keeps the 2nd Class in better order. 118 present.
27	Miss Middleton and Miss Sweeting called.
28	Mr Campbell came this afternoon – Annie Johnson has commenced a new garment for needlework.
29	Sarah Perren is not so industrious as she should be with her sewing.
30	Miss Sutton came – taught the 1st and 2nd Classes – and listened afterwards to all the children's repetition.

May 1869

3	Fair Day – yet 115 present this morning and about 80 this afternoon – an improvement.
4	A thoroughly wet day – yet 84 and 83 present.
5	Poor little Maria Guy is ill with the scarlet fever.
6	The children marched indifferently this morning. Miss Middleton called.
7	Miss Sutton came. 103 present.
10	109 present. 2 Londoners admitted – one 5 the other 6.6. I expect the latter is only a visitor.
11	Only a small number this afternoon, in consequence of a 'Review'.
12	Sarah Perren continues to improve in maintaining discipline in her class.
13	The Examinations in the Classes this week have passed off very fairly.
14	The school is closed for a week's holiday.
24	A good attendance. A boy sent home who has a ringworm.
25	Several children are ill. Annie Johnson has commenced her Examination work.
26	Alice Parsons has been rather late at the early morning lesson lately.
27	Many of the girls are steadily improving in needlework.

28 A very wet day, yet 58 and 67 present.

31 Ernest Ball has left the school – he and his sister (who expects to be a monitor there) have gone to St Laurence's.

June 1869
 1 100 present. Sarah Perren has been very careless with her needlework this week.
 2 Mrs Workman opened the Missionary Boxes. Sarah Thomas, 1st Standard, is very willing and useful in any work required.
 3 The 2nd Class are improving in Reading.
 4 96 present. Miss Sutton heard the children repeat their texts this morning.

 7 101 present. A. Ford absent – plea – illness. I'm afraid she stays away for very slight illness.
 8 104 present. Many are still ill.
 9 The children remember their morning texts very nicely.
10 Dr Moses called this morning.
11 No Miss Sutton.

14 Sickness still raging. A small attendance.
15 I shall very much miss Annie Ford after the Midsummer Vacation. Her class is very orderly.
16 Sarah Perren is improving in needlework.
17 Alice Parsons takes great pains with her lessons, but she has not been well grounded previously, so that she often finds many difficulties.
18 A cold and wet day. Miss Sutton absent.

21 Jane Chad has had a short trial as Monitor of the 4th Class, which post she will (D.V.) fill after the holidays.
22 Miss Coles called this morning.
23 We have a new curtain between the 1st and 2nd Classes.
24 Annie Johnson is improving in quickness.
25 Few in attendance.

29 Yesterday was a holiday, being Coronation Day, and but few have appeared today, probably in consequence of the close proximity of the holidays.
30 The teachers have nearly finished their needlework.

July 1869
 1 So few children that the 3rd and 4th Classes have been put together.
 2 Children dismissed for a month.

August 1869
 2 102 present. Many sick ones returned.

3 Numerous admittances, probably because our Tea Party is forthcoming.
4 104 present. Children very noisy.
5 Busy with hanging pictures &c.: children excited.
6 The school very pleased at hearing a letter read, which was sent by Mrs Darkworth.

9 2 Admittances. 102 present.
10 Annie Johnson manages better at the 1st Class than I expected.
11 A Gallery Lesson to the 1st and 2nd Classes on 'The Eagle'.
12 The Girls are commencing fresh work for the Examination. They have, in a great measure, forgotten the way to sew neatly in the holidays.
13 Jane Chad is getting 'at home' with her Class.

16 More admittances 2 – I'm afraid, on account of Thursday's Tea Party.
17 Susie Bettridge has gone to London on a visit for an indefinite period. A good 1st Standard Girl.
18 Alfred Sayer (1st Standard) has removed to Newtown.
19 We dismissed half an hour earlier: a half holiday in the afternoon.
20 Children very tired, and rather few. ½ holiday on account of the Babies' Tea.

23 A good number. Annie Johnson absent on leave.
24 Emily Basdom returned after being absent last week.
25 Mr Bren visited for a short time.
26 Sarah Perren is slightly improving in Writing.
27 George Lunnen, under 6, has removed from the vicinity of the school.

30 Several are absent, but we can scarcely send after them, as the fever is about still.
31 Alice is taking more pains with the Reading of the 2nd Class.

September 1869
1 The children have been learning up some of their old songs. They are greatly delighted with 'Who on our Wall'.
2 Louisa Pike absent on account of having to assist her mother – backward.
3 Mrs Moses, with 2 young ladies, paid a visit this morning, and heard singing and repetition.

6 Dr Moses called, previous to Dismissal.
7 Alice Parsons and Jane Chad late at early lessons this morning.
8 Nellie Willis kept at home during her mother's illness.
9 Willie Hawkins and Henry Woods give A. Johnson a deal of trouble, but she manages them pretty well.
10 Our little blind Jemmy ill is [sic] with inflammation of the eyes &c. We miss him.

13 The Teachers are practising on Examination Papers. Alice had no idea of composition when she came but is now proceeding tolerably. She is very painstaking.
14 E. Basdom absent – in the country. Jesse Pocock sick.
15 The Girls are getting on nicely with their needlework. Mrs Workman opened the Missionary Boxes this afternoon.
16 A showery day: fewer present.
17 103 present.

20 No admittances. 97 present.
21 The 'Fair' is taking our children this week. Only ¾ of a school this afternoon.
22 A still smaller attendance. Nellie Willis returned.
23 Annie Johnson has written her Paper very creditably, and without 1 spelling error.
24 Miss Sutton came in, not to teach, but just to look at the Classes. No play – punishment for bad marching from the Play Ground yesterday.

27 Edward Hamblin returned after 2 or 3 months' absence in the country.
28 Sarah Perren does not manage the 3rd Class so well as she did the 4th. 105 present.
29 A good attendance. Children dismissed until Friday, on account of the Teachers' Examination.

October 1869
1 No Miss Sutton. The Quarterly Accounts sent out.

4 Sent for the absentees – though so young, some of the children are kept at home to assist in the house.
5 Mrs Harries, Whitelands, visited the school.
6 The Girls are getting on with their needlework nicely.
7 The Candidates are keeping their Registers. I cannot say much for their tidiness, but hope better things with the next books.
8 Miss Sutton came while the children were playing this morning, and Miss Middleton in the afternoon.

11 One admittance of a child 8½ years old for 6 months; she is not up to the 1st Standard work.
12 A good number: 112.
13 The Teachers have covered books this morning.
14 Sarah Perren is too fidgety, to obtain perfect order in her Class, as a rule.
15 No play this morning out of doors, as a punishment. 103 only present.

18 A decrease of attendance; sickness is still very prevalent.
19 Ellen Champ and Emily Brown invariably answer the most sensibly during Scripture Lesson.

20 The 1st Standard this year are very irregular compared with previous ones; and others have removed, or are on long visits.
21 Considering the 1st Standard have been under the care of a 2nd and 3rd year Pupil Teacher, Annie Johnson has very firm control over them.
22 Miss Sutton came just before Dismissal and heard one song sung.

25 107 present, but several absent from sickness, among whom is S. A. Jones, a good First Standard Girl.
26 Willie Hawkins, one of the best 1st Standard Boys, ill with fever: he was present on Friday: his little sister ill also. 105 present.
27 Jane Chad works very hard with her class. Dr Moses, with another gentleman, called.
28 40 present in the 1st Standard. Alice Barker away on account of sickness.
29 [In a different hand]
29th Oct/69
Caroline Willcox Certfd Teacher Upper Grade of 4th Class.
[Signed] C. D. DuPont H. M. Inspr.

November 1869
1 Kate Eynott and Louisa Pike returned. A good number.
2 The children are very excited at the prospect of promotion tomorrow.
3 50 children were sent out this morning: 32 into the Girls' and 18 into the Boys' School.
4 I received 30 children from the Junior Room.
5 There is still much sickness. All the 1st and 2nd Classes (at present) with 3 exceptions, are Standard I.

8 2 children have already left from the 2nd Class: Woodley Emery and Alice Wild. They have both left Reading for London.
9 94 present. Marching very good this morning.
10 93 present. We find a difficulty in singing, as ½ the school is totally ignorant of what is known by the other.
11 The 1st Class are almost entirely under Annie Johnson's control. I could never have thought she would manage them so well.
12 The subjects of the Pictures round the room have formed the Scripture Lessons this week.

15 A rainy morning, but a good attendance. A visitor came at the time of Marching.
16 Ellen Box has returned. The 2 Fulbrooks are absent from sickness.
17 The 4th Class is larger than usual this week.
18 Sarah Perren is learning 'Reduction'.
19 The monitresses are taking greater pains with the Order – and the Candidates with the Registers.

22   A wet day. 55 and 83, respectively, present. Dr Barkworth has returned, and was a most welcome visitor this afternoon.
23   92 present. Dr Barkworth called.
24   91 present. The children sang very nicely at their Lesson this afternoon.
25   Mrs Barkworth came this afternoon.
26   85 present. Average 7 less than last week in consequence of Monday's wet.

29   The Report has come! 41 were presented in the 1st Standard: 28 passed in Reading – 34 in Writing – and 35 in Arithmetic.
30   85 and 87 present. Not so many this week in consequence of sickness and poverty.

December 1869
1   The 4th Class attendance is very small.
2   Mrs Barkworth called for a few minutes this afternoon – likewise Dr Barkworth.
3   A small average this week, but the school money more than I expected.

6   Dr Barkworth brought with him this afternoon, a bottle of Condys' Disinfecting Fluid, which has been used.
7   85 and 87 present. A dark afternoon for dismissal.
8   Several children just now are unable to pay their money.
9   The Missionary Box, this afternoon was opened by Mrs Barkworth and the Misses Holt.
10   Average higher than last December despite the sickness.

13   85 present. M. A. Thomas sent home for her school money.
14   Examination of the 1st Class. The subjects for the month had been very fairly mastered.
15   An improvement in the 2nd Class was visible.
16   I was particularly pleased with the Reading of the 3rd Class.
17   The 4th Class showed intelligence and carefulness though 2 of them are very backward.

20   The 2 Fulbrooks have returned after an absence of some weeks through sickness.
21   Mrs Barkworth called this morning and Dr Barkworth in the afternoon.
22   Sent the Quarterly Accounts this morning.
23   School dismissed until January 10th / 70.

Reading Greyfriars Schools
Summary of the Inspectors Report of the Infant School
1869

'The general working tone of this school is now highly satisfactory in all respects...

The accounts should be annually shown to H. M. Inspector...

A. E. Johnson is not old enough to be admitted for less than the full term of five years.'

[Signed] Henry Moses, Secretary

(vi) Log Book of Greyfriars Junior Infant School (1867–9). Royal Berkshire Archives R/ES4/3 (Part)

As stated at the beginning of the previous section, the Infant School, which had opened in January 1865, was split into the Senior Infants and Junior Infants from May 1867. The Junior Infant School was run by Miss Amelia Moody from 6 May 1867 until 25 March 1870.

Grey Friars Junior Infants' School

May 1867
- 6 School recommenced after the Easter holidays, 8 fresh admittances all the children being in the last class.
- 7 A slight improvement in the drill as I have exercised them the greater part of the day.
- 8 I have commenced to classify the children arranging them in 4 classes, there have previously been 3.
- 9 I find I shall require another permanent monitor, an addition to E. Palmer. Annie Johnson is on trial.
- 10 109 and 111 present, Mrs Barkworth and Mrs French visited the School this afternoon.

- 13 The children have very little room to move in. Mr Barkworth called this afternoon. I took the Houlters for lessons and found their attainments were very fair.
- 14 I taught Annie Johnson Practice she seemed to understand it. The children are learning the words of a song; 'How I love to see thee'.
- 15 We have received a supply of school materials slates, pencils, blackboard &c.
- 16 I have allowed them to pick threads from pieces of stuff this afternoon. I find it greatly interests them.
- 17 I find Emily Simmons a very good monitor. She will begin permanently on Monday.

- 20 First used the Admission Book which came last week, 119 present. Mr Barkworth called this afternoon.

- 21 I have refused a child who is only 1 year and 8 months old. The children for their Texts are learning the 23rd Psalm.
- 22 The weather being so cold I have had a fire lighted. The children are improved in the manner of kneeling at Prayer time.
- 23 The Teachers are working from the old Times Table at present; we still have a fire. Mrs Barkworth called this morning and stayed during dismissal.
- 24 Children much improved in going to their different divisions for reading and writing.

- 27 88 and 107 were present. Mrs Barkworth and Miss Christy called this afternoon and stayed to Prayers in which I had to stop in the middle because one of the babies tumbled off of the Form.
- 28 108 and 118 were present, the children are much quieter while their clothes are given out.
- 29 I have had to punish 4 boys for throwing stones in the Playground. Mr Barkworth called this afternoon.
- 30 The first class kept in for bad behaviour and inattention while at their reading lesson.
- 31 I was obliged to give the 3rd class a lesson on the proper way of behaving at Prayer time. Taught Emily Simmonds multiplication of money.

June 1867
- 3 Morning very wet, numbers low, Mrs Barkworth called this afternoon.
- 4 Sarah Perrin came this morning as a permanent Monitor, she is very willing but very thoughtless.
- 5 I have admitted two children today. The children have been very troublesome, especially the 3rd class. They break up today for four days holiday.
- 6 Holiday.

- 10 Numbers are rather low owing to the Holiday and its being a broken week. The Infants are removed from their room to the Senior Infant School, in order to accommodate the boys.
- 11 Sarah Perrin unable to continue as Monitor owing to Home circumstances.
- 12 Children are very disorderly owing to the want of sufficient room.
- 13 Mr Barkworth called this afternoon and found the children out to play in the play ground, where a boy had been throwing stones.

- 16 I had to punish a girl for bad behaviour at Prayer time.
- 17 I began to teach Emily Simmonds how to multiply by numbers above 12 today.
- 18 Louisa Bushnell came this morning on trial as a permanent Monitor.
- 19 Mr Barkworth called this afternoon.
- 20 Several children had to be sent Home for their School money.

24 My children have returned to their own room again as the Boys School is completed. The two Miss Holts and Mr Barkworth called this morning; the 1st and 2nd class were very orderly in having their things given out before dismissal.

25 Lessons as usual. The children are very excited by the School treat which is to be given on Thursday.

26 The school dismissed for four weeks holiday.

July 1867

29 School reopened, I have admitted several children this morning.

30 Children very disorderly indeed, they seem to have forgotten their School songs.

31 The 1st class kept in for bad behaviour while the clothes were given out.

August 1867

1 Eleven children drafted up into Miss Willcox's school.

2 I was obliged to send several children home for their money, even then some returned without it.

5 I have discovered through the Parents that the 2nd class is not properly taught, the Teacher does not appear to [be] sufficiently energetic in her work.

6 Louisa Bushnell seems to try very much with her children, but she cannot succeed in keeping good order.

7 I taught the children a round, 'All good Children' this morning, they like it very much.

8 Lessons as usual, numbers low, owing to the weather being wet.

9 The babies are quieter than they were, and do not so much disturb the order of the School.

12 105 children present this morning. Doctor Moses called this afternoon.

13 Lessons as usual.

14 Children very disorderly at Prayer time, the 1st class kept in to learn their letters.

15 Louisa Bushnell excused from lessons on account of Home duties.

16 I have commenced teaching the children another Text 'Jesus said suffer little children &c'.

19 Weather very hot which makes the children very restless and inattentive.

20 108 children present in the morning and 112 in the afternoon.

21 A little boy fell down and cut his head open this afternoon in the Playground.

22 I gave dictation to Eliza Palmer this morning from the Newspaper and found 9 mistakes in spelling, the paragraph was rather difficult.

23 I found Emily Simmonds improved in teaching her class their letters.

26 The weather stormy, 97 children in the morning and 84 in the afternoon.
27 113 children were present this morning. Emily Simmonds at home ill.
28 The children very much excited today owing to being shown a gold Pencil case which the children of the different Schools, boys, girls and infants are to present to Doctor Barkworth, as well as a vase to his wife on their return Home from the Continent.
29 Louisa Bushnell has taken a half day's holiday on account of her Sister going away from Home.
30 This afternoon the Vase filled with flowers was brought in for the children to see, before being taken to Mrs Barkworth's.

September 1867
2 Mr Barkworth called this afternoon and thanked the children for his present. Numbers were rather high.
3 Some children from the first class were kept in for inattention in doing their exercise.
4 121 children present this morning and 115 this afternoon. Mr Barkworth visited the School.
5 The children have begun to learn a hymn 'Come ye little children &c'.
6 121 children were present this morning and 122 in the afternoon. Miss Middleton visited the School in the morning.

9 Louisa Bushnell did not come to lessons this morning and took a holiday this afternoon.
10 I gave the children in the 1st class a lesson on a 'slate', they did not seem to entirely comprehend it.
11 Eliza Palmer leave from lessons in the morning. I find the 2nd class not much improved with their letters.
12 122 children were present in the morning and 120 in the afternoon.
13 Mrs Barkworth came to see the children this afternoon.

16 The children were rather noisy in changing their lessons today. Miss Holt called this morning.
17 I was obliged to keep the first division of the 1st class after School in order to read, for inattention during the lesson.
18 The 3rd class still have great difficulty in kneeling properly during Prayers. Mr Barkworth called today.
19 I find Louisa Bushnell not much improved in her dictation.
20 Mrs Barkworth opened the Missionary Box this afternoon; children very orderly and attentive during her visit.

23 The numbers are low today on account of the Fair. Mr Barkworth called to see about a broken blind being mended.
24 The children were very quiet during their working time, they seemed to enjoy it very much.
25 Mrs Barkworth came this afternoon to distribute some Missionary Books.

26 Miss Middleton brought a lady to see the Schools, the children sang and exercised during the visit.
27 Miss Sutton visited the School today.

October 1867
1 One boy admitted in the 3rd class. Louisa Bushnell has marked the Register of the 4th class today for the first time.
2 Alfred Watson is improved in his reading, Jesse Allen very careless and inattentive in his reading.
3 The numbers are low today on account of the cold weather.
4 I was obliged to have a fire today for the first time.

7 Mrs Hamden gave notice of her little boy's removal as they are going to leave the Town.
8 Eliza Palmer was absent from lessons this morning owing to her mother's being away from home.
9 The children have had a half holiday today because of the Pupil Teacher's Examination.
10 The order of the third class is improved.
11 I commenced teaching the children a fresh Text today 'The Lord is nigh unto all them &c'. The numbers are low; '84' on account of the wet weather.

14 The numbers are low in consequence of the wet weather. A great many children have come without their money this morning.
15 The children are improved in their Marching, the want of room is a great drawback to them in that respect.
16 I was obliged to punish several children for disobedience and inattention during their exercise. M. A. Thomas returned after an absence of some length.
17 The children seem rather anxious about their Examination. One boy threw stones in the Playground and broke a window.
18 [In different handwriting]
18th Oct/67
Amelia Moody
Probationer's Certificate
[Signed] C. D. DuPont
H. M. Inspector

21 I was very sorry to be unpunctual but in consequence of mistaking the time I was 20 minutes late this morning.
22 Lessons as usual. Mr and Mrs Barkworth called this morning. The children are very much crowded; the morning attendance was 127.
23 I have sent 24 from the 1st class into the Senior Room today and very sorry I was to part with them.
24 I have promoted children from every class, the present 1st class is not very promising as yet.
25 Mrs Barkworth visited this afternoon. Lessons as usual.

28 I have begun to teach the 1st and 2nd class girls needlework. There is only one girl who can work.
29 I find it requires a great deal of patience to teach the little ones how to hold their needles.
30 The order of the room before School begins is not at all satisfactory under the management of Louisa Bushnell.
31 Attendances today are 105 both morning and afternoon. I was obliged to punish several children for bad behaviour during the time I was occupied in taking one or two of the girls individually for work.

November 1867
1 Mr and Mrs Barkworth visited the School today and I am sorry to say the children were very disorderly during the visit.

4 Mr Barkworth came this morning just as the children had finished Marching. They are improved in that respect, I think in consequence of marking time in their class.
5 The three monitors came late this morning and did not apologise for doing so, I was obliged therefore to show them their error both in regard to manners and punctuality.
6 Mrs Barkworth, the Misses Barkworth and three young Ladies visited the School this morning to hear the children sing and exercise.
7 The second class disorderly, owing to the carelessness of the Teacher.
8 I examined the third class in Reading and found Emily Simmonds has been trying her best with her children.

11 I read some rules which I have composed for the regulation of those who take upon themselves weekly, the order of the room, children &c.
12 The numbers are very low owing to sickness being so prevalent and the coldness of the weather.
13 Eliza Palmer broke the rule today of talking with Louisa Bushnell during school hours.
14 Lessons as usual, two children sent Home for their School pence.
15 Miss Sutton came this morning and the children repeated to her the 23rd Psalm and sang a hymn.

18 One admittance today the child was placed in the 4th class. Mr Barkworth called to read the Inspector's Report.
19 The room begins to assume a much more orderly aspect since the observance of the 'rules'.
20 The children are improved in their 'Marching'; Eliza Palmer late for early lessons.
21 Lessons as usual. The numbers are still low.
22 Miss Sutton gave the 1st and 2nd class a lesson on the 'Birth of Christ'.

25 Four admittances were made this morning and Willy Huddy returned after an absence of several weeks.
26 The numbers are increased, the attendances today were 98 and 99, morning and afternoon.
27 Eliza Palmer very late for early lessons, in consequence of seeing her Aunt off by the Train.
28 Lessons as usual. Mrs Barkworth visited the School in the afternoon.

Greyfriars Junior Infants' School
Summary of the Inspector's Report
1867

In the Junior Room the new Mistress gives good promise of success. Her class lessons are careful and earnest and she has her children steadily under control during lessons. She has, however, placed herself at a disadvantage in her work by treating her first class boys as a distinct class separate from her first class girls, though their attainments are about the same, and so in her 2nd class, thus making four classes out of children who by their attainments constitute only two classes.
[Signed] Henry Moses, Secretary

November 1867
29 Lessons as usual. Numbers low.

December 1867
2 The 1st class kept in to exercise. Mr Barkworth called this morning.
3 There are only 4 babies in the 4th class on account of the weather.
4 The children are learning an account of the Birth of Christ from Luke II.
5 The second class kept in to learn their Bible verses.
6 I had to send several children Home for their School pence today, and then some returned without it.

9 The numbers are low, Louisa Bushnell is improved in her needlework.
10 I gave Mary Ann Jones a lesson on 'the way to hold and put in the needle' this afternoon.
11 The 1st class has learnt three verses from Luke II.
12 Eliza Palmer excused till ¼ past 9 o'clock in the morning.
13 Miss Sutton visited the School this morning and gave the children a Lesson on the 'Birth of Christ in connection with Xmas'.

16 Mr Barkworth called this morning. I find several of the children are sick and many will not return to School till the Spring.
17 The numbers are very low on account of the severe weather.
18 The children received a bun and a Book each from Mrs Barkworth. We break up for the Xmas vacation and return to our duties January 8th [sic], 1868.

January 1868

6 [This day and the following two weeks are incorrectly numbered 8th to 19th January.]
School reopened, the weather very unfavourable.
7 The numbers are very low indeed, 57 were present this morning and 49 this afternoon.
8 Lessons as usual. The children are rather disorderly, the effect of the holidays.
9 I have begun to teach them 'The North wind does blow'.
10 Mr Barkworth called this morning.

13 There are a great many ill and some of the Parents are obliged to keep their children at Home for want of the means to pay their School Pence.
14 Emily Simmons has begun to learn Addition of 'Weights and Measures'.
15 I gave Louisa Bushnell about eight lines of dictation and found 13 mistakes in spelling.
16 Louisa Bushnell excused from early Lessons.
17 Mrs Barkworth called today; 61 children present in the morning, and 59 in the afternoon.

20 The attendances were 63 and 73 today. I sent after the absentees and found sickness and the weather the principal cause of our low numbers.
21 I examined the 2nd Class in reading and found them much improved.
22 Louisa Bushnell leave from School in the afternoon. Eliza Palmer more correct in her Arithmetic than she was.
23 Mr Barkworth called today. The numbers are still low.
24 Miss Sutton called today but did not stay to give the children a Scripture Lesson.

27 I admitted a child 2 years old into the fourth Class. Eliza Palmer is improved in the repetition of her lessons.
28 I have begun to teach the children a Spring Song 'I'm a pretty little thing'.
29 Mrs Barkworth visited the School today. Emily Simmons, three mistakes in her dictation in spelling.
30 The children are not so orderly as I could wish in the change of their lessons. Mr Barkworth visited the School this afternoon.
31 Mrs Barkworth brought a Lady to see the School but the children had gone into the Playground. Miss Sutton came this morning and gave a Scripture lesson on the circumstances of the Child Jesus being taken into Egypt.

February 1868

3 I admitted a boy into the 3rd class today. Many of those children who were kept at Home on account of sickness have returned.

4	Sarah Sherwood in the 1st Class was very disobedient and obstinate today. The Tidyness of the room is not at all satisfactory. Mrs Barkworth called today.
5	Lessons as usual.
6	The order of the room is not at all good before Prayers in the morning, the teachers leave their classes too much.
7	Miss Sutton visited the School and gave a Scripture lesson. Several children were punished for bad behaviour during her visit.
10	The numbers are still increasing with the fine weather. Mrs Barkworth visited the School this afternoon.
11	Louisa Bushnell is absent on account of sickness. The children are learning the tune of their first Spring Song.
12	The 1st Class kept in, on account of 'disorderly sitting' while receiving their clothes.
13	The 3rd Class disturbs the order of the room by its bad order and discipline.
14	Miss Sutton came this morning and told the children about a little boy whose leg was broken in the play ground, through being pushed down by another boy and warned them never to be rough in their play.
17	Two children were admitted this morning and several returned after an absence of several months.
18	Eliza Palmer absent through sickness. The numbers are much higher than they were.
19	Three children were kept in today to read owing to their inattention during that lesson.
20	Louisa Bushnell's dictation was marked 'fair', the mistakes in spelling were less than in the preceding week.
21	Miss Sutton came this morning and gave the children a Scripture Lesson, they were on the whole rather attentive.
24	Mr Barkworth visited the School today, the numbers are increasing.
25	Eliza Palmer had 6 mistakes in her dictation this morning. The 3rd Class detained after twelve for a repetition of their morning 'Reading lesson'.
26	Miss Sutton visited the School today to give notice that through Lent her lessons would be given on 'Thursdays' instead of 'Fridays'.
27	The children repeated the Hymn they have finished learning ('Jesus when He left the sky') to Miss Sutton.
28	Lessons as usual. Mrs Barkworth called today.

March 1868

2	Several children have been admitted today, the children seem very disorderly through being interrupted by the crying of the fresh-comers in the 4th Class.
3	Two children were punished today for disobedience. I think it will be a lesson to the whole School.

4   The 3rd Class is improved in discipline under the care of Emily Simmons.
5   Miss Sutton visited today and heard the children sing some Hymns.
6   My 1st Class is improved in their writing with the exception of a few who do not attend regularly and are careless.

9   Sarah Sherwood quite refractory through being sent out of her class for punishment.
10 The marching today was very indifferent indeed, the children did not keep their steps together well.
11 Doctor Barkworth called today and was pleased with the increase of attendance.
12 Miss Sutton gave the children a Scripture Lesson on the 'Lost piece of Silver' this morning.
13 Mrs Barkworth and a Lady visited the School this afternoon and brought a Pocket handkerchief to be hemmed.

16 The children have begun to learn Psalm cxxi today, they seem very anxious to say it nicely.
17 Mrs Barkworth called this afternoon. The 1st and 2nd Class boys were very talkative during their writing lesson and consequently had to write after School.
18 Matilda Pope in the 1st Class finished her third piece of hemming this afternoon, it is much neater than the last.
19 Miss Sutton came and gave her Bible lesson this morning, the children were on the whole attentive.
20 Lessons as usual.

23 I admitted 6 children this morning. Miss Holt came and saw the children dismissed.
24 The marching this morning was much better, it was done with more spirit than it is generally.
25 Doctor Barkworth called this afternoon. There were present 109 in the morning and 105 in the afternoon.
26 Miss Sutton came and took her lesson, the children in the 4 Class were rather troublesome during her visit.
27 I have sent 21 children up to Miss Willcox's School, and therefore have promoted children from every class.

30 I allowed my Teachers to <u>write</u> their Scripture this morning and found all were not capable of doing so.
31 The children are rather anxious about their promotion into the Senior Infant School now.

April 1868
1   The children from the 1st and 2nd Class who were fit for promotion have been examined in reading by E. Palmer and myself and we found them on the whole pretty fair.

2 The order of the School is very creditable.
3 I am very pleased with Emily Simmonds' needlework, it is neat, regular and quickly done.

6 I have admitted several children today and have been obliged to refuse two who were too old.
7 Doctor Barkworth called today, he was pleased with numbers of the children.
8 Lessons as usual. The children are rather excited with the idea of breaking up for the Easter holidays.
9 The children were dismissed this morning, to return to School on April 20th.

20 The numbers are very good considering the School has been closed for ten days and a half.
21 I took the 2nd Class for reading and found it required to learn the Alphabet, so many of the children being unacquainted with their letters.
22 The 3rd Class is very disorderly, and consequently disturbs the whole School.
23 Joseph Rolph is rather sharp at figures, he answered the test in the 1st Class this morning.
24 Miss Sutton came this morning, and being rather late the children were out for Recreation.

27 Several admittances were made this morning. I sent after the absentees and found a great many were at home on account of sickness.
28 Louisa Bushnell's lessons imperfect, and therefore returned as the[y] frequently are.
29 The 2nd Class children are very restless and inattentive while exercising.
30 I gave my Teachers a lesson on Numeration this morning, E. Palmer seems to understand it, but it required some patience to make the principles of it simple and plain to E. Simmonds and L. Bushnell.

May 1868
1 Miss Sutton gave a Scripture lesson today to the 1st and 2nd Classes on the history of 'Joseph'.

4 Five admittances were made today. The whole School punished by not going into the Playground this afternoon owing to their not being orderly at their work.
5 Alice Chandler has begun to hem a Handkerchief this afternoon, she is the best sewer in the 1st Class, since the departure of the children who were promoted to Miss Willcox's School.
6 Louisa Bushnell's dictation very discreditable to her this morning, she had 17 mistakes in spelling.
7 Doctor Barkworth called this morning. Lessons as usual.

8   Miss Sutton called today and gave her lesson by continuing 'The History of Joseph'.

11 I admitted some more children this morning, most of them did not know their letters.
12 E. Palmer was late for morning lessons. The 'marching' is improving.
13 The children have learnt a new Hymn 'When for some little insult given &c'. I taught them the tune to it this morning.
14 Doctor Barkworth visited the School today. The second class was kept after School this afternoon for bad behaviour in Prayer time.
15 Miss Sutton visited the School but did not stay to give her lesson as usual.

18 Miss Holt saw the children dismissed today. Several of the absentees are at Home with bad coughs.
19 Mrs Barkworth and the Misses Barkworth came to hear the children sing, and were very pleased with them.
20 I have examined the 1st Class individually in Reading and Writing and I find several of the fresh children are very backward indeed.
21 Doctor Barkworth came this afternoon and expressed his satisfaction with regard to the number of attendance, that in the morning being 109 and the afternoon 107.
22 Miss Sutton called as usual and gave a Scripture lesson.

25 The hooping cough seems to be increasing, one child was sent home with it today.
26 Clement Curtis was punished today for inattention and talking in lesson time.
27 Lessons as usual.
28 The 2nd Class is improved in its order during change of lessons.
29 Miss Sutton absent through not being well. Miss Farbrother with Mrs Barkworth visited the School.
    Whitsun Holidays.

June 1868
8   107 were present on the reopening of the School. Seven admittances were made this morning.
9   E. Palmer absent part of the morning owing to her further illness.
10 Joseph Rolph has left the School for St Laurence's as his Parents reside in that Parish.
11 Lessons as usual.
12 Mrs Barkworth called this afternoon.

15 Doctor Barkworth brought a gentleman with him this afternoon, he came for the last time before leaving Reading for the holidays.
16 The 1st class was examined this morning in their Arithmetic and was found to have improved.

17   E. Simmons received instruction in division of Weights and Measures this morning which seems to be understood by her.

18   E. Palmer took the children this morning for Exercise and I was pleased with the order maintained by her during the time.

19   The children learnt the tune today of the School song 'Will you walk into my Parlour &c'.

22   Kate Atwood the most promising girl in the 1st Class was punished today for disobedience to her Teacher.

23   A mother came this morning to enquire about a hat which was lost and could not be found.

24   I have sent several children home for their School money it being the End of the quarter.

25   Lessons as usual.

26   Miss Sutton came too late for the Scripture lessons.

30   The children are very unsettled in consequence of the holiday yesterday.

July 1868

1   E. Palmer absent since Friday, this is her last week at School owing to Home circumstances.

2   E. Simmonds not quite capable of keeping the 2nd Class in order. Sarah Kendall a girl of 13 years has been trying for the last two days to keep the 1st Class in order but has entirely failed owing to a want of discipline.

3   We break up today for the Midsummer Vacation 4 weeks.

Midsummer Holidays

August 1868

3   The School re-opened with only one Teacher E. Simmonds, the consequence being great disorder at change of lessons &c.

4   Still no chance of an increase of teachers Louisa Bushnell not being likely to return owing to ill health.

5   Doctor Barkworth called this afternoon.

6   The children dismissed at 11 o'clock owing to the School treat of the older children.

7   The treat for my own School today. The behaviour was on the whole good.

10   The attendance good, several returned from being absent through sickness.

11   I am labouring under great difficulties for want of proper teaching power.

12   E. Simmonds keeps the 2nd Class in better order than she did formerly.

13   Ellen Robinson from the Girls School seems to get on very well with her class, I hope she will be able to come as a monitor.

14 Lessons as usual.

17 Several children were admitted today. Elizabeth Parsons came this morning, she is to stay a week on trial as a Teacher.
18 E. Robinson a very promising girl as a monitor, she will make a good disciplinarian.
19 The 1st Class not at all in good order, I am afraid E. Parsons cannot control such young children, she seems to lack the power of commanding their attention.
20 Lessons as usual. Numbers are low owing to the wet weather.
21 Numbers are higher today. I am going to give E. Parsons another week's trial, she is slightly improved in discipline.

24 Two admittances were made today. Three children returned after being absent through sickness. Doctor Barkworth visited the School today.
25 I taught E. Robinson 'Compound Multiplication', she did two sums afterwards correctly.
26 Doctor Barkworth's visit today was short. The order of the children seems improved, compared with that after their return from the Midsummer holidays.
27 Doctor Barkworth visited the School this afternoon. I took the boys of the 1st Class for reading this afternoon, they do not get on as fast as the girls.
28 Miss Sutton came this morning and gave the 1st and 2nd Classes a Scripture lesson. I taught E. Simmonds 'Long Division of Weights and Measures' today, she seems to find it rather difficult.

31 E. Parsons improves in the discipline of her class.

September 1868
1 Emily Pike takes great interest in her reading.
2 The children are obliged to re-learn their School songs, they have just finished 'A little bird built &c'.
3 A girl in the 1st Class obliged to be sent Home through falling down and playing roughly in the Playground.
4 Miss Sutton visited and gave a Scripture lesson.

7 E. Simmon's [sic] lessons returned because they were not properly learnt.
8 I gave E. Simmons 'dictation'; there were four mistakes in spelling.
9 I examined the 2nd Class in reading and found that the reading lessons had not been thoroughly taught, as there were several very deficient in their Reading.
10 E. Robinson sums were very imperfectly done this morning.
11 Miss Sutton came and gave her Scripture lesson, the children were very restless during her visit.

14 The numbers are not so high today, owing to the cold weather. Earnest [sic] Ball asked to be re-admitted after going to St Laurence's School.
15 Doctor Barkworth visited the School this afternoon. E. Parsons at home because of sickness.
16 Emily Pike improves in Reading and writing in the 1st Class.
17 I find great difficulty in keeping order, in consequence of the increase in the number of Babies.
18 I have taught the children the Text; 'My little children let us not love in word &c'. and tried to make them understand the meaning of it. Miss Sutton heard the children say 'Texts' as she thought they were too tired for a lesson.

21 The annual Fair being held today, many of the children are absent. Willie Dormer's jacket cannot be found.
22 Ellen Robinson brought all her sums incorrect this morning. E. Simmons' Dictation was very neatly written.
23 The children in the 2nd Class marched very nicely this morning.
24 The 3rd Class was very disorderly this morning in returning from the Playground.
25 I have every reason to believe that Willie Dormer's jacket was abstracted from the Bonnet room on Monday.

28 Three Admittances were made this morning. E. Parsons absent from morning lessons.
29 I examined the 2nd Class today in Reading, they are on the whole improved, but the Teacher still has to acquire method and steadiness in giving her lessons.
30 The children had to return to the Playground again this morning in consequence of the disorderly manner of several of the children in coming into School.

October 1868
1 Doctor Barkworth called this afternoon. Kate Atwood finished a Pocket handkerchief, the work in it is very fair for a child of her age.
2 Miss Sutton came this morning and gave a Scripture lesson on 'Samuel the child'.

5 The numbers very high today. There are three children who have attended the requisite number of 'Times' cannot be found in consequence of removing from their residences.
6 The writing in the 1st Class is not at all satisfactory, the Boys especially are idle.
7 Today I taught the children the tune of 'Hop, hop, hop', they appear to enjoy it very much indeed.
8 The 1st Class improves in Arithmetic. L. North, Emily Pike, E. Emmens are particularly bright at it.

9	The children are learning the text 'The eyes of the Lord are in every place &c'. I think it is needed, as they seem to forget it when their Teacher's eye is <u>not</u> on them.
12	The numbers are still higher this week; 129 in the morning and 127 in the afternoon.
13	The Misses Holt visited the School this morning just at the conclusion of the reading lessons, so they declined to hear the children sing.
14	The Teachers are doing Examination Papers this week on their different subjects, that of E. Simmons looks very neat.
15	Doctor and Mrs Barkworth visited the School this afternoon.
16	Miss Sutton came this morning but did not give a lesson as the children were in the Playground.
19	A half holiday was given today on account of the Pupil Teacher's Examination.
20	I examined the 2nd Class in Reading and found they were not so fluent as they should be.
21	The 3rd Class was disorderly today during the time of dismissal.
22	The children appear very anxious to do well at their Examinations, Mrs Barkworth called today.
23	Herbert Coles is particularly bright at Arithmetic. The morning was wet so Miss Sutton did not come.
26	The children are not so orderly as they generally are, owing to the excitement of tomorrow.
27	[Different handwriting] 27th Oct/68 Amelia Moody Probationer 2nd Year [Signed] C. duPont, H. M. Inspector
28	The numbers are rather high today. I am going to send the whole of the 1st Class up to the Senior Infant School.
29	Lessons as usual.
30	Holiday in honour of the Examinations.

November 1868

2	The children are promoted from every class. I find the original 2nd Class not so backward as that of last year.
3	I devoted a great deal of time to drilling and exercise this morning, the 2nd Class requires it.
4	The children are learning the verses from St Luke II respecting the birth of Christ.
5	I punished a child for bad behaviour in Prayer time today.
6	Miss Sutton visited the School today.
9	The numbers are much lower today, many of the children have measles and Hooping cough.
10	I am teaching the children 'Before the bright sun rises over the hill' with the actions.

11 Dr Barkworth visited the School.
12 The 1st Class is improving in their reading.
13 The School pence is very low this week.

16 The measles seem very prevalent among the children, there are several fresh cases found today.
17 Lessons as usual.
18 Mrs Barkworth visited the School today.
19 Elizabeth Parsons begins to learn Vulgar Fractions this morning.
20 [*Incorrectly dated as 18th.*]
   I sent after some School pence this morning but not got it.

23 [*This week incorrectly dated 21st to 24th.*]
   The 'marking time' is not at all satisfactory in the 2nd Class.
24 Dr Barkworth visited the School this afternoon.
25 Kate Jones is very dull and backward with holding her needle.
26 Willie Styles was punished for disobedience to his Teacher today.
27 Miss Sutton visited the School this morning.

30 Lessons as usual.

December 1868
1 Numbers are very low, fresh cases of measles in many families.
2 A half holiday is given today in honour of the Anniversary of the opening of 'Grey Friars' Church'.
3 The weather is very damp and unsuitable for young children to attend School.
4 The second class not at [all] orderly in their manner of leaving School during dismissal.

7 One little Boy in the 3rd Class is dangerously ill with the scarlet fever.
8 There are several children who can repeat correctly the verses from St Luke II.10–14.
9 There are fresh cases of measles found among the children. Charlotte Barkshire is very ill and not expected to live.
10 Lessons as usual.
11 Miss Sutton visited the School today for a few minutes.

14 I examined the 2nd Class in Reading and found it has improved under the management of E. Parsons.
15 Mrs Barkworth visited the School this afternoon.
16 The 3rd Class is very noisy today owing to the inattention of the Teacher.
17 Lessons as usual.
18 Miss Sutton discontinues her visits on account of ill health.

21 The numbers are still very low in consequence of sickness.
22 Little Willie Chadd is dead, he died of Scarlett Fever.

23 Lessons as usual. I have dismissed the children for the Xmas Holidays.

Reading Greyfriars Schools
Summary of the Inspector's Report on the Junior Infants School 1868.

In the junior room all is going on quite satisfactorily. Larger and plainer Reading cards are required.
[Signed] Henry Moses, Secretary

January 1869
- 11 We begin School today. The numbers are increased. This afternoon each child received from Mrs Barkworth some useful article of clothing, a toy, orange and Bun. The mistress received a very nice Crossover[1] kindly made by Mrs Barkworth.
- 12 The children are rather excited from the consequence of their Xmas Treat.
- 13 Lessons as usual. E. Parsons is getting on with her Arithmetic, she is very accurate.
- 14 Doctor Barkworth called today.
- 15 Those children who have returned after sickness are extremely restless and disorderly.
- 18 I have sent after several absent children and I find many are still sick.
- 19 I am teaching the children the Text The Blood of Jesus Christ &c.
- 20 The 'Marching' this morning was very indifferent and the singing was also faint.
- 21 I find the children have forgotten their School songs.
- 22 Lessons as usual.
- 25 The numbers are rather higher today, but there are several absent through illness.
- 26 I examined the 2nd Class in Reading and found them thorough and precise in what they know and also in discipline.
- 27 Lessons as usual. Dr Barkworth visited the School.
- 28 The Marching today was not satisfactory.
- 29 Mrs Barkworth visited the School today. Ellen Robinson's lessons very imperfectly learnt.

February 1869
- 2 Anne Bedbury in the 2nd Class is in a Consumption, she is very ill indeed.
- 3 Emily Simmonds Dictation was very badly written this morning and 15 errors in spelling.
- 4 The order of the children before Prayers is not at all satisfactory under the management of Marion Parsons.
- 5 Lessons as usual.
- 6 Doctor Barkworth visited the School today.

---

1 A wrap worn around the shoulders and crossed in front.

9   The whole School was kept in this afternoon for being disorderly before grace.
10 M. Parson's Scripture was very well written.
11 Miss Holt visited the School and was very pleased with the Needlework.
12 The 1st Class does not go to their places properly and orderly, the Teacher is too anxious about it, and consequently the children get frightened and don't know where to go.
13 Lessons as usual.

15 Two admittances were made this morning. E. Robinson's lessons were again imperfect.
16 I have taught the children the Tune to 'I love little Pussy'. They are also learning the Hymn 'Poor and Needy'.
17 The 3rd Class very disorderly at Prayer time.
18 Doctor Barkworth visited the School this afternoon. M. Parson's Map of England from memory was very satisfactory.
19 Lessons as usual.

22 The numbers are steadily increasing with the fine weather. Anne Bedbury died yesterday, as the Bell was tolling for Church.
23 The two Holders are to leave us at the end of the week, they are leaving Reading.
24 Lessons as usual.
25 Dr Barkworth visited the School this afternoon.
26 Mrs Barkworth visited the School. The children went into the Play ground this afternoon.

March 1869
1   83 children were present this morning. Miss Holt called.
2   M. Parsons improves in the management and discipline of her class.
3   The children in the 3rd Class are very idle during drill, not being kept to it by their Teacher.
4   Doctor Barkworth visited the School this afternoon.
5   Lessons as usual. The children seem restless and tired.

8   The Attendance today is better than last week, but illness and want of means are still the cause of many being absent.
9   Mrs Barkworth called this afternoon with another Lady. The children sang and exercised.
10 Sarah Anne Barton and Ellen Lunnen are hemming Pocket handkerchiefs very neatly considering their age.
11 I am teaching my children the Song 'Little Bird with bosom red'.
12 The 'Marching' was much better this morning.

15 E. Robinson's Scripture and Catechism was so imperfect that I was obliged to return her Lessons.

16 Lessons as usual.
17 Doctor Barkworth called this afternoon.
18 M. Parson's Grammar requires a great deal <u>more</u> judgment and thought.
19 The 1st class improves with their Reading and Arithmetic. Mrs Barkworth called today.
22 Doctor Barkworth called, while the children were in the Playground.
23 The children are very much improved in the order of the School routine.
24 Today the School is closed for the Easter Holidays.

Easter Holidays

April 1869
5 Four Admittances were made today.
6 Doctor, Mrs Barkworth and Family leaves Reading today for six months, in order to restore Doctor Barkworth's health.
7 I promoted 20 children from the 1st Class, to the Senior Infant School today.
8 We have to begin at <u>the</u> beginning again for the children in the 2nd Class are not at all up to their work, consequently the School does not work in order and discipline.
9 The Revd C. Campbell and Mrs Campbell called this afternoon, the Clergyman who is to do duty in the place of Dr Barkworth.

12 Two Admittances were made today and two children sent to try school for the first time.
13 E. Robinson's Dictation very badly written.
14 I have to take the whole School from their Lessons from drill and discipline.
15 The weather is very warm, it makes the children listless.
16 Sent two children home for their School pence and the Parents say. 'it was sent on Monday'.

19 Two Admittances were made today. The children have been obliged to have 'Drill' instead of their 'usual Lessons'.
20 There is an improvement in the Drill, and order of the 1st Class. Mrs Workman called, the children sung; 'See the little busy Bee'.
21 I gave the two first Classes a Lesson on the Crucifixion of Our Lord to show how His blood was shed in order that our hearts might be washed and made clean from sin; they repeated the Texts 'Create in me a clean heart, &c'. and 'The blood of Jesus Christ His Son &c'. 87 children were present.
22 The order in the 2nd and 3rd Classes is better today. The children on the whole are more quiet and orderly than they have been, since their return from the Easter Vacation.
23 I find the school money has been brought much better this week, than in many of those preceding it. Miss Sutton came this morning.

26 92 Children present in the morning. I had to punish John Jeffreys for direct disobedience to myself.
27 Arthur Ellis in the 2nd Class died this morning at ½ past 3 o'clock, of Scarlet Fever, he was at School only a week ago, I told the children about it this morning, instead of a Scripture Lesson. Miss Middleton and another Lady visited the School and were pleased with their singing.
28 Marion Parsons had leave from Lessons on account of her Mother being ill.
29 The 1st Class is very inattentive and not at all thorough in their 'reading' for the last fortnight.
30 Miss Sutton visited the School today, she gave a Scripture Lesson, and the children repeated Texts to her; she was very much pleased with the order of the School.

May 1869
 3 The Spring Pleasure Fair is held in Reading today, consequently the numbers are low.
 4 The numbers still lower today, owing to the weather being so wet.
 5 I examined the 2nd Class in Arithmetic, Reading and Writing, they were all satisfactory except the Reading.
 6 Thomas Guy is absent, on account of his Sister having Scarlet Fever.
 7 Miss Sutton came this morning and gave the children a Lesson on 'Our Father which art in heaven'. M. Parsons absent from morning Lessons on account of illness.
10 I have sent after the Absentees and find a great many at Home through illness; F. Price has the Scarlet Fever.
11 The numbers are low today owing to a Review being held near Reading.
12 I am sorry to say that E. Robinson has been copying the answers to her sums.
13 I have finished teaching the children today their number of Texts, which they usually say in the morning after Prayers.
14 Lessons as usual. The children are dismissed today for a week's holiday in consequence of Whitsuntide.

Whitsun Holidays

24 Four Admittances were made this morning. A little Boy fell down in the Playground and cut his forehead, but it was not anything serious.
25 I took the first Class Girls for 'Reading' and found two or three children very backward.
26 I have finished teaching this morning the Text; 'Suffer little Children to come unto me'.
27 Lessons as usual.

28 I was obliged to be absent from School through indisposition. The numbers were very low owing to the wet weather.

31 Three Admittances were made today.

June 1869
1 The numbers are a little higher today. E. Simmon's [sic] dictation was written without a mistake this morning.
2 I am teaching the children the Text, 'Children obey your Parents'.
3 The Missionary Box was opened today by Mrs Workman.
4 Miss Sutton gave the children a Lesson on the Birth of Christ this morning.

7 Four admissions were made this morning. The girls in the 1st Class are improved in their 'Reading'.
8 Marion Parsons absent this afternoon through illness.
9 M. Parsons is still absent. E. Robinson was hurried in her repetition of Scripture this morning.
10 Doctor Moses called this morning. M. Parsons has returned to her duties today.
11 I have sent after several children's school pence but have not succeeded in getting it. E. Robinson excused from learning her Geography on account of Home duties.

14 Three Admittances were made today. Lessons as usual.
15 The Babies which are freshly admitted disturb the School very much with their crying.
16 The Revd C. Campbell visited the School today, all but the Girls sewing class were in the Playground.
17 Mary Anne Thomas in the 1st Class is very ill. The numbers are low today owing to the stormy weather.
18 The weather is still cold and wet. The children were kept in this morning for being disorderly during the change of lessons.

21 The weather seems to keep many of the children at Home. Lessons as usual.
22 Mrs Holt called to tell me that her little boy Edward Holt in the 2nd Class has died in Salisbury of Diphtheria about three weeks ago.
23 Lessons as usual.
24 The 1st Class was kept in for inattention during their reading Lesson.

28 Holiday in consequence of the Queen's 'Coronation Day'.
29 The numbers are very low indeed on account of the Holiday at the beginning of the week.
30 The two 'Woods' (boys in the 1st and 2nd Classes) are absent through illness. They have the 'Chicken's Pox'.

July 1869
1 Lessons as usual.
2 The children are dismissed today for our month's holiday.

The Midsummer Holidays

August 1869
2 School re-opened today. Fourteen children were admitted this morning.
3 The children in the 4th Class are perfectly distracting, they prevent all order and quiet in the School.
4 I was obliged to send one Baby home, it could not be pacified, consequently it disturbed the whole School.
5 The children have forgotten their School songs as well as their letters. E. Robinson was absent without leave from this morning's lessons.
6 Lessons as usual, the children are still very disorderly except the 1st Class, that has been a little better today.

9 Three more admittances were made this morning. E. Robinson again absent from lessons on account of Home duties.
10 Mrs Workman visited the School this morning with two young Ladies and the children sung a Hymn.
11 The 1st Class kept in to read. The 3rd Class disorderly at Prayer time.
12 Bertha Jennings in the 3rd Class is dead. She died of fever. 103 present this morning.
13 The numbers are very low today owing to the wet weather and the G.W.R. excursion to Weymouth.

16 Five admittances were made this morning, the numbers are much higher today, owing to the Tea Party on Friday I suppose. E. Robinson was absent from this morning's Lessons without leave.
17 The children are very idle today.
18 The I and II Classes were sent back to the Playground this morning owing to the disorder in which they returned to their places.
19 The children had a half holiday today owing to the School Treat.
20 My children (the Junior Infant School) drank Tea in the Girls' School this afternoon and after a game of play, and each child receiving a Toy and a Bun, they were dismissed.

23 Two admittances were made this morning and Sarah Anne Hawkins returned after an absence of more than a year.
24 The 1st Class was kept in [*illegible*] for general inattention during the Lessons.
25 The children are going through all their Hymns and School songs for repetition which they had forgotten during their holidays.
26 Lessons as usual.
27 E. Robinson again absent from Lessons on account of Tooth-ache.

30 The children are very disorderly today in the 3rd Class, so much so, that they disturb the whole School.
31 I examined the 1st Class in 'Reading', and found the children individually were not thorough in what they knew.

September 1869
1 The writing is not good in many cases, owing to the irregularity of the children.
2 The 2nd Class on the whole is not in its attainment so bright as it should be, but I think it may be traced to most of the children being rather young for the class.
3 Mrs Moses with two young Ladies, visited the School this morning and heard the children sing and do their exercises.

14 I have returned to my duties again, after being absent from School a week through illness.
15 E. Parsons seems to have kept the School in good order during my absence, judging by the discipline which prevails at present.
16 The weather is very wet and windy, the numbers consequently are rather low.
17 The weather is still very unfavourable for the School.

20 The children have finished learning 'I think when I read that sweet story of old', but they do not yet sing it nicely.
21 E. Robinson absent from morning Lessons. E. [*Illegible surname*] and [*Illegible name*] in the 1st Class read very distinctly and accurately for their age.
22 E. Robinson again absent from Lessons and no home Lessons learnt on the previous morning.
23 E. Parsons' Examination Paper looks neater than usual, she seems to be taking pains with it.
24 Miss Sutton visited the School this morning and heard the children repeat their Texts.

27 One child brought to be admitted on Trial.
28 E. Simmond's Dictation was not so well written this morning as it might have been.
29 I examined the 2nd Class in 'Arithmetic' and cannot say much in favour of its thoroughness, owing perhaps to the children being those who have been in School a short time.
30 Holiday in consequence of the Pupil Teacher's Examination.

October 1869
1 Mrs Barkworth came in this morning and surprised me, just as I was giving the children 'Texts'.

4	Fannie Earles in the 3rd Class died on Friday last of Scarlet Fever, she was at School on Tuesday last.
5	The children are learning to repeat the Hymn 'Jesus high in glory'.
6	E. Simmond's composition this morning was not as carefully done as it might have been.
7	The 1st Class Boys were kept in to write copies as did not do them in school time.
8	Lessons as usual.
11	[*This week incorrectly dated 10th to 14th.*] E. Simmonds is absent till Thursday morning, in order to pay a visit to Aldermaston.
12	The numbers are still low, many being absent through sickness and the weather.
13	The 2nd Class had to be sent back to the Playground for not marching into School <u>on the lines</u>.
14	Thomas Smart has lost a Shawl in School, it has been put on in a mistake and has not been returned.
15	Miss Sutton did not come today as expected. The 1st Class boys were lazy in their Reading.
18	The numbers are very low owing to the wet weather. One child was admitted into the 1st Class this morning.
19	Willie Styles very disobedient and troublesome.
20	Kate Jones 'a girl of the 1st Class' died on Sunday last of Scarlet Fever.
21	The numbers are low this week in consequence of the wet, cold weather.
22	Miss Sutton called today just as the children were being dismissed.
25	Two children were brought to be admitted on trial. Miss Holt saw the School dismissed in the morning.
26	E. Simmond's Scripture on her Examination Paper is very satisfactory.
27	Doctor Moses visited the School this morning for a short time with another Gentleman.
28	The children are very excited today, and get tired over their lessons, they have had rather a longer time for play than usual, in order to refresh them for tomorrow.
29	[In different handwriting] 29th Octr/69 Amelia Moody Certf Teacher upper Grade 4th Class Marion E. Parsons P.T. 1st year [Signed] C. D. DuPont

November 1869

1	M. Parsons absent today on account of illness. I had no Teachers this morning in consequence of the Examination in the Girls' School.

2   I have prepared my 1st Class to be promoted to the Senior Infants School tomorrow. It is very trying to lose them, just as they are getting intelligent.
3   33 children were sent up to the Senior Infant School this morning, some of them were very unwilling to go.
4   I rearranged my Classes, promoting children from every Class.
5   Holiday in honour of the Examination.

8   I have admitted one child this morning into the 3rd Class.
9   Fred Ward is very ill in the 1st Class it is not yet decided whether it is fever.
10 The children of the 2nd require a great deal of training in the way of going to their places on the Gallery.
11 Weather very cold consequently numbers are low.
12 The School pence is very low this week.

15 The numbers are rather low today owing to the wet weather.
16 The second Class is not at all orderly in the process of marching to their places &c., and the 1st Class does not set them a good example in that respect.
17 I taught Marion Parsons 'Proportion' this morning, she worked two sums fractionaly [sic]) and I found them correct.
18 [*Incorrectly dated 19th.*]
    M. Parsons absent by leave from quarter to eleven in order to see the Doctor this morning.
19 [*Incorrectly dated 20th.*]
    Dr Barkworth and Family returned to Reading today, the children have been expecting to see them.

22 Extremely wet today consequently only 27 Children present.
23 Dr Barkworth called this afternoon, the numbers are still low owing to the weather and sickness.
24 John Jeffreys in the 1st Class was very obstinate and disobedient, I was obliged to give him the cane.
25 Dr Barkworth called this afternoon, and Mrs Barkworth, just as the children were being dismissed.
26 E. Robinson excused from Lessons on account of feeling unwell.

29 A very wet day, therefore the numbers are very low. The Government Report has arrived.
30 E. Robinson absent from Lessons after being absent the preceding day.

December 1869
1   Emily Simmonds getting on fairly with her Arithmetic, she is learning Fractions for the 7th Standard.
2   Mrs Barkworth called this afternoon before we had said 'Grace'. Dr Barkworth called later in the afternoon.
3   Marion Parsons is improving in her Needlework.

6   Dr Barkworth called this afternoon and gave me some disinfecting fluid to purify the air of the School-room.
7   The numbers are a little higher today. The 1st Class is not nearly as orderly as it might be, owing to the discipline being lax.
8   Lessons as usual. Mrs Barkworth with the Misses Holt called in the afternoon.
9   Dr Barkworth called today.
10 Miss Sutton came just as the School was being dismissed from morning Lessons.

13 Marion Parsons improves in Map drawing, she is practising France now.
14 Dr, Mrs Barkworth and another Lady visited the School this afternoon and heard them sing some Rounds.
15 Lessons as usual. Three 1st Class Boys were kept in for being irreverent in Prayer time.
16 The afternoon is very wet. Numbers are lower than in the morning.
17 I have sent several children after their School pence and some have not returned.

20 The 1st Class was kept in for disorder.
21 Dr Barkworth and Mrs Barkworth visited the School.
22 E. Simmonds desires to become a Pupil teacher.
23 We dismiss the children today for their Xmas holidays. School reopens on January 10th/70.

Reading Greyfriars' Schools
Summary of the Inspector's Report – Infant Schools
1869

The general working tone of this School is now highly satisfactory in all respects.
[Signed] Henry Moses, Secretary

(vii)   Annual Letter addressed to the Congregation and Parishioners of Greyfriars, Reading, by their Pastor (1868). Original in the Greyfriars Church Archive.

'I must work the works of Him that sent me, while it is day; the night cometh, when no man can work'. – John ix,4.
Reading: Printed by J. Macauley, 113, Broad Street.
1868

[p. 3]
To the Congregation and Parishioners of the Grey Friars, Reading.

My Dear Friends,
Since I last addressed you, another year has passed, and we are all by so much nearer to that moment, when the relation of Pastor and People shall have ceased forever. The flight of time, and the deaths which are perpetually occurring make this fact increasingly real. Would that in every case it were equally influential! The circumstances however of the present age are sufficiently significant, and everything leads us to conclude that we are on the verge of a momentous crisis, beset with perplexities and agitations, to which, the coming of the Son of Man affords the only adequate solution. While to every reflecting person this thought will be one of peculiar solemnity, the remembrance of so many obligations incurred, and so little realized, must weigh with special intensity upon the minds of those who have been appointed as 'Messengers, Watchmen, and Stewards of the Lord, to teach and to premonish, to feed and provide for the Lord's family; to seek for Christ's sheep that are dispersed abroad in the midst of this naughty world, that they may be saved through Christ forever'. By the side of an ideal so truly exalted, the highest evidence of ministerial fidelity fades into insignificance, and we can only abase ourselves to the dust, exclaiming with the great Apostle, 'Who is sufficient for these things?'

[p. 4]
Yet amidst these and other causes of humiliation, I would fain hope that I have not shunned to declare unto you the whole counsel of God, even that Gospel, which is 'the power of God unto salvation to everyone that believeth'.

It has been my desire to contribute to your spiritual good in whatever way I feel to be likely to promote that object. To this end, I have from time to time procured the assistance of ministers and other friends who have had experience in the Mission field, and in the course of the past year several interesting accounts have been given of the progress of God's work in Heathen lands. I have urged your attendance at the meetings of our Religious societies and on other special occasions in connection with the defence and confirmation of the Gospel, while in our ordinary Parochial agencies, abundant scope has been provided for the encouragement of all who are disposed to employ themselves for the good of their fellow creatures. And were we to judge from such indications as Church Collections, (which are considerably higher than those of the preceding year) we might conclude that there had been a proportionate increase of that 'faith which worketh by love'. Such in a measure, I believe to be the case. At the same time it should be remembered, that the true prosperity of a congregation is to be determined, not by the question of numerical strength, or by the mere reputation for liberality, so much as by the consistent walk and conversation of its members. I would indulge the hope that this character may be ascribed to many amongst you, and that in an age unprecedented for religious confusion, you are 'shining as lights in the midst of a crooked and perverse nation', uninfluenced by that worldly conformity, which is not more grievous to the Spirit of God than it is injurious to the interests of the soul. Against this confusion

[p. 5]
in all its forms – whether it be the overlaying of Gospel simplicity with ceremonial observances, or the removal of that line of demarcation which separates the service of God from that of the world – I have always endeavoured to raise my voice, nor have I seen anything in the practical development of these errors, which convinces me that I have taken too strong a view of the dangers, with which they are fraught. Let us never forget that 'Strait is the gate and narrow is the way which leadeth unto life, and few there be that find it!'

Last year I adverted to the scanty attendance at the Devotional Meeting on Saturday Evenings. It is therefore with great thankfulness, that I am able to announce a decided improvement on that head. Our Sabbath and week day Services are also well attended, which is the more satisfactory from the conviction, that nothing beyond the simplest mode of administration has ever been attempted. Our Schools have been greatly enlarged, and are now both in numbers and attainment not unworthy of consideration. May they long be permitted to exercise a beneficial influence upon the rising generation! At page 11 you will find a statement, which has already appeared in the local papers, and to which I invite the attention of those, who have not yet given any contribution.

I cannot conclude, without an allusion to the removal of the late Archdeacon Phelps, who in God's Providence was permitted to be the chief instrument in erecting that beautiful Edifice, in which it is our privilege to worship. We hope shortly to set up a tablet to his memory, which apart from private acknowledgment, may perpetuate the recollection of an effort, designed for the Glory of God and the Salvation of Immortal Souls. That these objects may be abundantly realised is the prayer of

Your affectionate Pastor,
S. M. Barkworth
Reading, May 1868.

[p. 6]
LIST OF VISITORS AND THEIR DISTRICTS.

Boyer, Mrs	Somerset Place (part of)
Bramwell, Miss	Stanshawe Road, Tudor Street
Budd, Miss	Vachel Road (south side)
Christie, Miss	Warren Place
Eaton, Miss	Bloomfield, Marlborough, and York Terraces
Fletcher, Mrs	Chatham Street (part of north side), Hope Place, part of Lower Thorn Street (west)
Goulding, Mrs	Lower Thorn Street (east), Caversham Road (east)
Hayward, Mrs	Oxford Street (north) from West Street to Thorn Street, including Ball, Oxford, and North Courts
Hale, Mrs	Part of Great Knollys Street, Caversham Road (west), Podmore Cottages

Holt, the Misses	Weldale Street (south)
Moses, Mrs	Weldale Street (part of north side), North Street
Middleton, Miss	Chatham Street (Part of north side)
Philbrick, the Misses	Weldale Street (part of north side), Weldale Place
Phelps, Miss	West Street (west), Friars Place
Tanner, Miss	York Place, Chatham Street (part of north side), Chatham Court
Workman, Mrs	Chatham Place
Wheeler, Miss	Java Place and Gladstone Place
Weightman, Mrs	Part of Somerset Place, Lower Thorn Street, and Weldale Street
Waller, Mrs	Thorn Street (east), Thorn Court
Wainhouse, Miss	Osborne Terrace, Grey Friars Road (west)

[p. 7]
NATIONAL AND INFANT SCHOOLS.

It is a pleasure to be able to note a marked improvement in all the above during the past year. H. M. Inspectors' Report in October last was decidedly favourable, especially of the Boys' and Girls' Schools; also, of the Junior Department of the Infant School, now under the care of Miss Moody, a Certificated Mistress from Cheltenham. Should any desire to ascertain for themselves the efficiency of these Schools, visitors will be always welcome. The numbers are as follows;

DAY SCHOOLS.

SCHOOL	NO. ON REGISTER	AVERAGE ATTENDANCE
Boys	175	156
Girls	148	107
Senior Infants	123	106
Junior Infants	114	102
Total	560	471

SUNDAY SCHOOLS

SCHOOL	NO. ON REGISTER	AVERAGE ATTENDANCE	
		Morning	Afternoon
Boys	210	122	128
Girls	165	105	122
Infants	168	123	131
Total	543	350	381

Teachers' Meetings are continued every alternate Thursday, at 8pm, and all are invited to attend.

On Sundays a Bible Class for Young Men is held in the Mission Room, at 9.30am and at 2.30pm. One for Servants and for any Young Women who like to join, at 3.30pm, in the Infant School.

The Working Parties are as before, that for our own Poor, at 4pm, on the *last Tuesday* in the month, and the Juvenile Missionary Gathering, at 2.30pm, on the *first Thursday*.

[p. 8]
Instead of meeting in the Evening, the School Children work every alternate Friday afternoon for Missionary Objects, whilst interesting accounts are read to them.

We thankfully believe that Mr Collins continues to labour faithfully though quietly amongst our poor, and that his Mission Room Services are valued by many.

The Mothers' Meetings are carried on every Monday, at 2.30pm, in the Mission Room, and at 7.30pm in the Girls' School Room.

The Dorcas Sale is still held in the Infant School on Monday Afternoons, at 4pm. The small number of Purchasers is a cause for regret but must be attributed to the extreme poverty of the Parish. Ladies might materially assist, by becoming Purchasers on behalf of the Poor.

The Grey Friars Infants' Friend Society, under Mrs Workman's kind management, has proved a valuable addition to our Charities. The need for the formation of a Society for the Relief of our Aged Poor is much felt, but no plans for meeting it have yet been formed.

CHURCH MISSIONARY ASSOCIATION.

COLLECTIONS AFTER QUARTERLY LECTURES.

	£	s.	d.
April 10	1	11	3
June 11	2	13	0
September 20	9	8	5
December 17	1	15	6
	£15	8	2
Miss Batchelour's Box		4	1½

[p. 9]
It is earnestly hoped that those members of the congregation who are not already subscribers to this good cause, will at once become so, or else apply for a Box, which will afford the opportunity of giving to God according as he has prospered them, and also of collecting the offerings of others.

The Grey Friars Juvenile Association has contributed £18 10s. 6¾d. during the past year.

The School Boxes contained the following amounts, £3 of which have been forwarded to Umritzur, for the child in the Orphanage, supported by our Sunday School Children and their Teachers:

		£	s.	d.
Sunday School,	Boys	1	19	10¾
	Girls	3	16	11¼

		£	s.	d.
	Infants		18	1
	Teachers	2	9	2
	Bible Class	1	7	11
Day School,	Boys		6	3¼
	Girls		9	0½
	Infants (senior department)		7	9½
	Infants (junior department)		3	4
		£11	18	5¼

[p. 10]

SACREMENTAL ALMS.
1867.

RECEIVED.	£	s.	d.	PAID.	£	s.	d.
Offertory Collections	62	4	11½	In small sums	13	6	9½
Private Communions	2	16	0	Payment of Dorcas Work	3	2	9
Box at Church Door		8	6	Meat	16	3	7
				Grocery	13	7	7
				Bread	3	0	8
				Wine and Stout	3	16	0
				Coals	3	12	6
				Blankets	2	13	4
				Flannel	2	2	3
				Tracts	3	0	0
				Balance in hand	1	4	0
	£65	9	5½		£65	9	5½

COLLECTIONS IN GREY FRIARS CHURCH.
1867.

		£	s.	d.
January 13	Church Expenses	20	17	0
February 10	Schools	24	17	2
March 10	Society for Promoting Christianity amongst the Jews	22	9	2
April 14	Church Expenses	21	19	4
May 19	Church Missionary Society	45	7	7
June 16	Colonial and Continental Church Society	25	16	7
July 14	Church Expenses	22	4	1
August 11	Berks Hospital	25	7	11
September 8	Irish Church Missions	19	5	8
October 2	Reading Protestant Association	14	19	10
October 13	Church Expenses	20	9	7
November 17	Church Pastoral Aid Society	33	9	1
December 4	Grey Friars Mission	12	19	3
December 25	East London Relief Fund	6	4	9
		£316	7	0

[p. 11]

GREY FRIARS SCHOOL ENLARGEMENT FUND.
TREASURER'S ACCOUNT, 1867.

Dr.	£	s.	d.	Cr.	£	s.	d.
To Donations	626	10	0	By Purchase of Ground	275	0	0
To National Schools Annual Account of	15	12	5	By Messrs Wheeler	407	6	1
To Balance due to Treasurer	40	3	8				
	£682	6	1		£682	6	1

S.M. BARKWORTH, *Treasurer*.

NATIONAL SCHOOLS.
TREASURER'S ACCOUNT for the year ending September, 1867.

Dr.	£	s.	d.	Cr.	£	s.	d.
To Annual Subscriptions and Donations	74	8	6	By Balance due to Treasurer, 1866	92	7	7
To School Pence	68	7	0	By Master's Salary	99	12	0
To Government Grant	67	12	0	By Mistress' Salary	60	0	0
To Part of Collection after Sermons	16	14	11	By Payment of Pupil Teachers and Monitors	27	12	6
To Sale of School property &c.	7	14	5	By Stationery, Books and Maps	20	0	8
To Balance of first Building Fund	77	8	8	By Repairs &c.	14	17	4
To Balance due to Treasurer	33	8	3	By Fuel and Gas	6	7	3
				By New Desks	9	8	6
				By Cleaning Rooms and Sundries	7	1	11
				By Insurance and Local Taxes	8	6	0
	£345	13	9		£345	13	9

H. MOSES, *Treasurer*.

[p. 12]

INFANT SCHOOLS.
TREASURER'S ACCOUNT for the year ending September, 1867.

Dr.	£	s.	d.	Cr.	£	s.	d.
To Annual Subscriptions	31	2	6	By Balance due to Treasurer	10	12	7
To School Pence	45	2	5	By Mistresses' Salaries	82	19	4
To Government Grant	65	19	8				

Dr.	£	s.	d.	Cr.	£	s.	d.
To Part of Collection after Sermons	9	0	0	By Payment of Assistants	24	1	6
To Sale of School Property		5	0	By Stationery and Books	10	0	0
				By School Repairs and Alterations	5	0	0
				By Fuel and Gas	6	7	3
				By Cleaning Rooms and Sundries	10	0	0
				By Balance in hand	2	8	11
	£151	9	7		£151	9	7

H. MOSES, *Treasurer*.

SUNDAY SCHOOL.
TREASURER'S ACCOUNT, 1867.

Dr.	£	s.	d.	Cr.	£	s.	d.
To Balance in hand	30	19	10	By Bills for Clothing	65	15	2
To Annual Subscriptions	32	6	6	By New Forms	1	7	0
				By Books for Lending	4	4	0
To Children's Deposits	53	1	9	By Bibles and Testaments	1	14	0
To Interest in Savings' Bank	1	10	2	By Reward Books &c.	6	16	0
				By Sunday School Institute	1	11	6
				By Catechisms and Hymn Books		8	0
				By Missionary Maps		5	0
				By Repairing Pictures		6	5
				By Printing Club Cards		16	0
				By Repayment of Deposits	1	17	11
				By Balance in hand	32	17	3
	£117	18	3		£117	18	3

M. J. HOLT, *Treasurer*.

[p. 13]

BOOT CLUB.
TREASURER'S ACCOUNT, 1867.

Dr.	£	s.	d.	Cr.	£	s.	d.
To Balance in hand	7	18	11	By Bills for 198 pairs of Boots	55	11	6
To Subscriptions and Donations	19	8	0	By Repayment of Deposits		13	11½
To Children's Deposits	28	18	6½				
	£56	5	5½		£56	5	5½

E. HOLT, *Treasurer*.

GREY FRIARS MISSION FUND.
TREASURER'S ACCOUNT, 1867.

Dr.	£	s.	d.	Cr.	£	s.	d.
To Balance in hand	46	12	6	By Scripture Reader's Salary	65	0	0
To Rent of Shed	2	0	0	By Rent of House	16	0	0
To Donations & Annual Subscriptions	74	6	0	By Coals	6	13	0
				By Gas	2	0	2
To Collection after Sermon	12	19	3	By Callas	1	13	0
				By Poor Rate	2	3	9
				By District Rate	1	14	2
				By Water Rate	1	1	6
				By Sundries		6	0
				By Balance in hand	39	6	2
	£135	17	9		£135	17	9

S. M. BARKWORTH, *Treasurer.*

-----o-----

GREY FRIARS INFANTS' FRIEND SOCIETY.
TREASURER'S ACCOUNT, 1867.

Dr.	£	s.	d.	Cr.	£	s.	d.
To Annual Subscriptions	19	15	0	By Materials for supply of Boxes &c.	20	6	10
To Donation	5	0	0	By Balance in hand	4	8	2
	£24	15	0		£24	15	0

E. BARKWORTH, *Treasurer.*

[p. 14]

MOTHERS' MEETING CLOTHING FUND.
TREASURER'S ACCOUNT, 1867.

RECEIVED	£	s.	d.	PAID	£	s.	d.
Balance in hand	3	15	1	Articles Purchased	52	4	5½
Mothers' Deposits	39	16	4	Balance in hand	2	15	5½
Subscriptions	11	8	6				
	£54	19	11		£54	19	11

C. WORKMAN, *Treasurer.*

DORCAS FUND.
TREASURER'S ACCOUNT, 1867.

Dr.	£	s.	d.	Cr.	£	s.	d.
To Balance in hand	1	14	3	By Bills for Calico, Print, & Flannel	17	15	9½
To Subscriptions and Donations	11	12	6	By Balance in hand	11	13	6
To Weekly Deposits	16	2	6½				
	£29	9	3½		£29	9	3½

E. BARKWORTH, *Treasurer*.

SUNDAY SCHOOL MISSIONARY WORKING FUND.
TREASURER'S ACCOUNT, 1867.

RECEIVED	£	s.	d.	PAID	£	s.	d.
Subscriptions	6	16	6	Articles Purchased	5	16	4
				Balance in hand	1	0	2
	£6	16	6		£6	16	6

C. WORKMAN, *Treasurer*.

[p. 15]

GREY FRIARS CHURCH
THE CHURCHWARDENS ACCOUNT
from 16th April, 1867, to 4th April, 1868.

Dr.	£	s.	d.	Cr.	£	s.	d.
To Cash by 3 Quarterly Collections*	67	2	9	By Pew Opener's Salary	25	0	0
				By Bell Ringers	5	0	0
To Balance paid by Incumbent	60	15	4	By Organist	25	0	0
				By Organ Blower	3	0	0
				By Lamplighter		18	0
				By Gas Company	18	10	11
				By Coals and Wood	14	8	6
				By Five new Lamps and Taps for Church Yard Gates, &c.	12	9	2
				By Repairs to Windows, and Glass Doors, Guttering, and Stack Pipes	4	17	11
				By Holland Blinds for North Transept	5	5	0
				By Floor Cloth, &c., for New Vestry	3	4	1
				By Fire Insurance	2	12	6
				By Water Rate		10	0
				By Tuning Organ		15	0

	By Repairs to Church Gates, Fencing, &c.	1	10	0
	By Care of Church Yard	1	7	0
	By Sundry Small Accounts	3	10	0
£127 18 1		£127	18	1

W. HODGES & C. F. WILLSON, Churchwardens.

* It will be seen that the 4th Quarterly Collection has not been received in time for insertion here.

[p. 16-20]

LIST OF SUBSCRIPTIONS AND DONATIONS TO THE GREY FRIARS PAROCHIAL CHARITIES

Subscribers are particularly requested to notice, that Subscriptions on behalf of the Day Schools and the Boot Club are always *paid in advance*, so that those kindly given in October 1867, will not be acknowledged till the next Report, when their expenditure will be accounted for at the same time.

First Half of the Table:

	School Enlargement Fund £ s. d.	National Schools £ s. d.	Infant Schools £ s. d.	Sunday School £ s. d.	Boot Club £ s. d.
Allaway, Mr	3 3 0	1 1 0	1 1 0	1 1 0	2 6
Alsop, Mrs		2 6		2 6	1 0
Anderson, Mr		1 1 0			
Barkworth, Rev Dr	300 0 0	5 0 0	2 10 0	1 1 0	3 10 6
Barkworth, Mrs S. M.		5 0 0	2 10 0	1 1 0	10 6
Barkworth, Mrs (senior)		10 0 0			
Barkworth, H., Esq	25 0 0				
Barkworth, T., Esq	5 0 0				
Ball, Mrs George	3 0 0	10 6	5 6	5 0	5 0
Boyer, Mrs	2 0 0	10 6	10 6		5 0
Bosisto, Mrs		2 0			2 6
Barnard, Mrs			1 6	2 6	
Boyle, Hon. R.	5 0 0				
C. S. B.		5 0			
Coles, the Misses		1 0 0	10 0		5 0
Christie, Miss		1 1 0		5 0	3 0
Carpenter, Mrs		5 0	5 0		
Claxson, Miss		5 0		5 0	2 6
Canney, Mrs		4 0		1 0	3 0
Callas, Mr		2 6		2 6	2 6
Champ, Mrs		5 0	5 0		
Carter, Mrs (the late)		5 0			

Cosburn, Mr	5 0	2 0			
Davis, Mr					2 6
Drummond, Mrs	10 0			5 0	
Dewe, The Misses	10 0 0	1 1 0		1 1 0	3 0
Disney, R., Esq		5 0		5 0	2 6
Dryland, R. C., Esq		1 1 0	10 6		2 6
Dryland, Mrs					
Dobbyn, Miss					1 0
Day, Mr		2 6			1 0
Eaton, Mrs	1 0 0			10 0	
Friend, A	5 0	2 6			
Fulbrook, S., Esq	5 0 0	5 0	5 0	10 6	
Farbrother, Miss		2 6			
Fletcher, Admiral	3 0 0				
Fletcher, Mrs J. V.		10 0	10 0	5 0	1 0
Ford, Miss				3 0	
Goulding, Mrs		5 0		2 6	
Goulding, Mrs W.			5 0	2 6	
Goddard, Mr		2 0	2 0	2 6	1 0
Green, Miss	5 0 0				
Gadesden, A. W., Esq	5 0 0				
Holt, Rev R. F.		1 1 0		10 6	
Holt, the Misses					10 0
Holliday, Mr		10 6			
Harris, T., Esq	5 0 0	1 0 0			
Harris, Mrs			1 0 0	10 0	2 6
Harris, Miss		5 0			1 0
Hand, Mrs	10 0	2 6	2 6		2 6
Hobbs, Mr		2 0			
Hobbs, Miss S.					3 0
Horlock, Mrs		1 0			
Howes, Mrs				2 6	1 0
Heelas, Mr D.		7 6	2 6	7 0	3 0
Hillier, the Misses		10 0	5 0		1 0
Hawkins, Mrs B.	2 0 0	10 0		10 0	10 0
Hawkins, Mrs		2 6	2 6		
Hawkins, Miss M. A.	10 6	2 6	2 6	2 6	2 6
Hoyle, G. W., Esq				5 0	3 0
Hodges, Mr	1 1 0	10 0		2 6	1 6
Heading, Mr		2 6		2 6	
Hayward, J., Esq	5 0 0	10 0	10 0	5 0	2 6
Henderson, Mrs John		5 0	5 0		1 0
Ivey, Mr		5 0		2 6	2 6
Janson, A., Esq	10 0 0				
Janson, Miss	10 0 0				
Jones, Mrs		5 0			1 0
Jennings, Mr					1 0
Jessett, Mr		2 0		1 0	1 0
Knox, Mrs H. Carnegie		3 0 0	2 0 0	1 0 0	10 0
King, Mrs		10 0	5 0		
King, Mr					
Knott, Mr		2 6			
Keft, Mr		2 6	2 6	2 6	2 6

Name	£ s d	£ s d	£ s d	£ s d	£ s d
Keeley, Miss		2 6		2 6	
Lanfear, C., Esq	1 0 0	10 0		10 0	2 6
Lanfear, Miss		10 0		10 0	2 6
Lovejoy, Mr			1 1 0		
Malthus, Miss					10 6
Macaulay, Mrs		2 6			2 6
Moses, H., Esq. M.D.		1 1 0		5 0	
Moses, Mrs	5 0 0	1 1 0	10 6	5 0	3 0
Maslen, Mr	5 0	5 0			
Maslen, Mrs				5 0	
Morris, Mrs		1 1 0	5 0	5 0	3 0
Neale, Miss	15 0 0	2 2 0	1 1 0	1 1 0	2 6
Nicholas, J., Esq	3 0 0	1 1 0			
Neale, W., Esq		1 1 0		10 6	
Outen, Miss	5 5 0	5 0	5 0	5 0	3 0
Phelps, Miss				10 0	
Pitcher, Mrs					
Palmer, the Misses		10 6			2 0
Pell, Miss				10 6	3 0
Piggott, Mrs	5 0 0	2 6		2 6	
Philbrick, the Misses		10 0		7 6	2 6
Povey, Miss		5 0		5 0	3 0
Parker, Mrs		5 0		5 0	1 0 0
Paice, Mr		2 6			2 6
Poulton, Mrs		10 6	10 6		
Pecover, Mrs		1 0			1 0
Reed, Mr		10 0	5 0		3 0
Sutton, M. H., Esq	50 0 0	2 10 0	2 10 0	5 0 0	1 0 0
Sutton, Mrs M.				1 0 0	
Sutton, A., Esq	10 0 0				
Sutton, Miss E,		10 0		5 0	2 6
Slocombe, W., Esq		1 1 0	10 6		
Sowdon, T. F., Esq	10 0 0	1 1 0	1 1 0	10 0	3 0
Snare, Mrs		2 6			3 0
Sheriffe, Miss	5 0 0				
Sharp, Mr		2 0		3 0	3 0
Smith, Mrs W. C.		2 6	5 0		
Smith, Mrs		2 6	2 6	2 6	
Smith, Mrs C. S.		6			
Smith, Miss				2 0	
Simonds, John, Esq	10 0 0	2 2 0	1 1 0		
Simonds, Mrs C.	3 0 0				
Sherwood, Mr H.		5 0			
Sherwood, Mr W.		5 0			
Sheppard, Mrs		5 6	5 0	5 0	6 0
Southey, Mrs		6 0			
Thorpe, Mrs		10 6		5 0	5 0
Thank Offering	1 0 0				
Tatem, Miss		10 0	10 0	10 0	5 0
Tanner, Miss	5 0 0	10 0		10 0	3 0
Tanner, Mr		5 0			
Wilson, the Misses	60 0 0	5 0 0	5 0 0	2 2 0	2 2 0
Woodman, Mrs					

Name	£ s. d.	£ s. d.	£ s. d.	£ s. d.	£ s. d.
Workman, J. W., Esq	20 0 0	2 0 0	1 0 0		
Workman, Mrs				1 0 0	1 5 0
Wilkins, Mrs		2 6		2 6	
Willson, Mr	3 3 0	10 0	5 0	2 6	3 0
Willson, Mrs					
Wheeler, Messrs	5 0 0				
Wheeler, Mrs S.		5 0	2 6	2 6	2 6
Wheeler, Miss		2 6			
Wainhouse, the Misses		2 6		2 6	
Wellsteed, Moores, Co.		10 0		10 6	
Webb, Mrs R.	2 2 0	1 1 0		1 1 0	3 0
Waller, Mrs		2 6	2 6	2 6	2 6
Woods, Mrs		5 0		5 0	2 0
Weightman, Mrs		5 0		1 6	1 0
Wellman, Mr				5 0	
Wickes, Mrs			1 0		
Willats, Mr	10 6				
Wooton, Mr		5 0			
£	626 10 0	74 8 6	31 2 6	32 6 6	19 8 0

[Second half of the Table]

	Mothers' Meeting Clothing Fund	Mission Fund	Dorcas Fund	Infants' Friend	School Missionary Working Fund
	£ s. d.	£ s. d.	£ s. d.	£ s. d.	£ s. d.
Allaway, Mr					
Alsop, Mrs					
Anderson, Mr					
Barkworth, Rev Dr				2 2 0	
Barkworth, Mrs S. M.	1 1 0			2 2 0	
Barkworth, Mrs (snr)					
Barkworth, H., Esq					
Barkworth, T., Esq					
Ball, Mrs George	2 6				
Boyer, Mrs					
Bosisto, Mrs					
Barnard, Mrs					
Boyle, Hon. R.					
C. S. B.					
Coles, the Misses					
Christie, Miss					
Carpenter, Mrs					
Claxson, Miss			10 0		
Canney, Mrs					
Callas, Mr					
Champ, Mrs				6 0	
Carter, Mrs (the late)					
Cosburn, Mr					
Davis, Mr					

Drummond, Mrs						
Dewe, The Misses		1 0 0			10 6	
Disney, R., Esq						
Dryland, R. C., Esq						
Dryland, Mrs					6 0	
Dobbyn, Miss						
Day, Mr						
Eaton, Mrs	10 0	10 0		10 0	10 0	
Friend, A						
Fulbrook, S., Esq						
Farbrother, Miss						
Fletcher, Admiral						
Fletcher, Mrs J. V.	3 0				4 0	
Ford, Miss						
Goulding, Mrs						
Goulding, Mrs W.					6 0	
Goddard, Mr						
Green, Miss						
Gadesden, A. W., Esq						
Holt, Rev R. F.						
Holt, the Misses						
Holliday, Mr						
Harris, T., Esq						
Harris, Mrs	10 0	10 0				5 0
Harris, Miss						
Hand, Mrs						
Hobbs, Mr						
Hobbs, Miss S.						
Horlock, Mrs						
Howes, Mrs						
Heelas, Mr D.						
Hillier, the Misses						
Hawkins, Mrs B.					10 6	1 0 0
Hawkins, Mrs						
Hawkins, Miss M. A.	5 0			5 0		
Hoyle, G. W., Esq						
Hodges, Mr						
Heading, Mr						
Hayward, J., Esq						2 6
Henderson, Mrs John						
Ivey, Mr						
Janson, A., Esq						
Janson, Miss						
Jones, Mrs						
Jennings, Mr						
Jessett, Mr						
Knox Mrs H Carnegie	1 0 0	1 0 0		1 0 0	1 1 0	
King, Mrs			1 0 0		10 6	
King, Mr					10 6	
Knott, Mr						
Keft, Mr						
Keeley, Miss						
Lanfear, C., Esq						

Lanfear, Miss																	
Lovejoy, Mr																	
Malthus, Miss													10	6			
Macaulay, Mrs													6	0			
Moses, H., Esq. M.D.					1	1	0										
Moses, Mrs	10	0										1	1	0			
Maslen, Mr																	
Maslen, Mrs																	
Morris, Mrs					1	0	0						10	6			
Neale, Miss	10	0		20	0	0									1	0	0
Nicholas, J., Esq																	
Neale, W., Esq																	
Outen, Miss																	
Phelps, Miss	5	0			5	0			5	0			5	0			
Pitcher, Mrs													10	6			
Palmer, the Misses																	
Pell, Miss																	
Piggott, Mrs																	
Philbrick, the Misses																	
Povey, Miss																	
Parker, Mrs								1	0	0							
Paice, Mr																	
Poulton, Mrs																	
Pecover, Mrs																	
Reed, Mr																	
Sutton, M. H., Esq	1	0	0	20	0	0						5	0	0	1	0	0
Sutton, Mrs M.	1	0	0	1	0	0		4	0	0		1	1	0			
Sutton, A., Esq	2	2	0	5	0	0											
Sutton, Miss E,																	
Slocombe, W., Esq																	
Sowdon, T. F., Esq																	
Snare, Mrs																	
Sheriffe, Miss																	
Sharp, Mr																	
Smith, Mrs W. C.																	
Smith, Mrs																	
Smith, Mrs C. S.																	
Smith, Miss																	
Simonds, John, Esq																	
Simonds, Mrs C.																	
Sherwood, Mr H.																	
Sherwood, Mr W.																	
Sheppard, Mrs																	
Southey, Mrs																	
Thorpe, Mrs																	
Thank Offering																	
Tatem, Miss													6	0			
Tanner, Miss								10	0				10	6			
Tanner, Mr																	
Wilson, the Misses	2	0	0	20	0	0						4	4	0	2	0	0
Woodman, Mrs									5	0							
Workman, J. W., Esq																	
Workman, Mrs					2	0	0	2	2	0			10	6	1	1	0

	£ s d	£ s d	£ s d	£ s d	£ s d
Wilkins, Mrs					
Willson, Mr					
Willson, Mrs					3 0
Wheeler, Messrs					
Wheeler, Mrs S.				10 6	
Wheeler, Miss					
Wainhouse, Misses			10 0		
Wellsteed, Moores					
Webb, Mrs R.	10 0				5 0
Waller, Mrs			10 0	10 6	
Woods, Mrs					
Weightman, Mrs					
Wellman, Mr			5 6		
Wickes, Mrs					
Willats, Mr					
Wooton, Mr					
£	11 8 6	74 6 0	11 12 6	24 15 0	6 16 6

[Back Cover]

THE SERVICES AT GREY FRIARS CHURCH are ON SUNDAYS At 11am and 6.30pm and ON WEDNESDAYS At 7pm.
The Holy Communion Is administered on the First Sunday in the Month, after the Morning Service, and on the Third Sunday in the Month at 8am.
Baptisms Are administered on the Last Sunday in the Month at 3pm.
The Church is now Licensed for the Solemnization of Marriages.
A Meeting for Prayer Is held on Saturdays at 7.30pm.

(viii) 'Son, Remember'. A sermon preached at Greyfriars Church on 21 May 1865. Copy in the Greyfriars Church Archive.

'Son, Remember'.
A Sermon preached at Grey Friars Church, Reading, on Sunday Evening, May 21, 1865, by the Rev S. M. Barkworth, M.A.
of Worcester College, Oxford, Incumbent.

Printed by Request. The profits, if any, will be devoted to the Charitable Institutions of the District.

Reading
Printed and Sold by T. Barcham, 89, Broad St.
1865

[p. 2]
NOTE.
   This Discourse is published in deference to the wishes of some members of the Congregation, but against the judgement of the Author. He trusts, however,

that what was received with deep attention, may in this way promote the spiritual good of those to whom it was addressed. This consideration alone induces him to give a more permanent form to statements, which have nothing to recommend them, beyond the importance of the subject to which they relate. Reading, June 1st, 1865

[p. 3]

A SERMON.
LUKE XVI. 25.
'And Abraham said, Son, Remember!'

Although it forms no part of the divine purpose to minister to mere excitement, yet the Word of God may be regarded as the source of every impression calculated to arouse and actuate the heart. And very frequently the most striking effect is produced through the most ordinary appliances. Our Lord is sparing of outward manifestations. A single word or look suffices to awaken a train of thought, and acts as a key to a most important position. And though we may not characterise the language of scripture as ironical, yet it is not too much to say, that there are occasions in which it conveys the most withering rebuke, and makes the sinner the instrument of his own condemnation. An instance of this moral retaliation occurs in the words of our text. It would appear as if the guilt of this character was heightened by the assertion of a claim, which his earthly life had repudiated. No doubt this was not the first time that he had called Abraham his father, and had pleaded the supposed privilege of a godly connection as an excuse for carelessness and impenitence. It was meet that the vanity of this plea should be exposed, and how could this be done more effectually, than by adopting that relation which was the ground of confidence.

'*Thou hast appealed to me as a Father, though thou wert none of mine*'. I have but to address thee in corresponding terms, and the history of thy sad disobedience rises up with terrible distinctness. Ah! brethren, there is fuel in the breast of man which only needs one spark of Divine wrath to kindle an eternal flame. And of all the torments reserved for the ungodly, none will exceed the sting of an

[p. 4]

awakened memory. This then will form the main subject of discourse, and may it please God to direct the word to the conviction of the sinner, and to the quickening of every true believer. May it confirm the declaration, that '*Not everyone that saith unto me, Lord, Lord, shall enter into the kingdom of heaven, but he that doeth the will of my Father which is in heaven*'.

Our text contains:–

      I.   AN AWFULLY IMPORTANT TRUTH.
      II.   A MOST CONSTRAINING ADMONITION.

1. THE TRUTH WHICH IS SO AWFULLY IMPORTANT MAY BE THUS STATED.

Forgetfulness in time, is followed by *recollection in eternity*. For when it is said, '*Son, remember*', there is a manifest allusion to a long period of unconcern. This was the grand difference between the two characters described in this parable – the one *remembered*, and the other *forgot*. The same distinction still exists between the children of God, and the children of the world, and though at first sight this view may seem inadequate, yet it will account for the salvation or the perdition of every member of the human race.

It is in the nature of man to forget. I do not confine the term to its strictly literal sense – for many of the sons and daughters of men are as remarkable for the power of memory, as God's people are deficient in that most valuable faculty. But this is a mere question of natural gifts, for which we are in no way responsible, except so far as they are used or abused. The forgetfulness with which we are chargeable, relates to the character and ways of God; that melancholy indifference to the things which belong to our peace – that insidious lethargy which steals over the immortal soul, and gradually destroys all spiritual emotion. In the largest sense, all Sin is forgetfulness. It is the insensibility of the mind to the claims of infinite Holiness, and above all, the deadness of the heart to the unspeakable gift of a Saviour's blood, the uncontrollable enmity to all that is holy, spiritual, and divine. Ignorance on these points is natural to man, but alas! it becomes more than second nature in all who are not recovered by Redeeming Grace. The word contains no heavier charge against a man than this, *he forgets God*; and at the last day nothing more will be required to seal His eternal doom!

[p. 5]

I am led to lay such stress upon this point, from the conviction that the most momentous issues are involved in the most apparently trivial circumstances! How great is the number of those who listen to the preaching of the Word! How various the impressions made upon them, and yet how few the instances in which the seed is brought to good effect. Men in general think it enough that their approbation has been elicited, or that their interest has been engaged, or their fears aroused, or that some course of action has been suggested to which they were previously insensible. Nay, they may go so far as to admit the application of certain statements to themselves, but, in the majority of cases, there the matter ends. There is no attempt to gather up the fragments, no effort to reduce their convictions to practice, no earnest prayer that the word of God may remain with them, and that the law of God may be written and engraven on the tablets of the heart. The fact is, brethren, in the majority of cases Divine truth comes in at one ear, and goes out at another. Men hear, and then they forget. They believe after a fashion, but they do not change. 'They fear the Lord, but they serve their own Gods', and if any excuse for this negligence is required, it is considered sufficient to plead the infirmities of nature. A good intention, but a feeble principle; a disposition to obey, but a want of power to accomplish. So that by degrees, a condition which ought to excite the most lively alarm, is regarded as the merest necessity. Men go on from week to week, and from year to year, first remembering and then forgetting, presenting every variety of religious appearance, but bringing forth no fruit unto perfection – always learning, and never able to come to the knowledge of the truth.

May I not appeal to your consciences in support of these statements? Is there not this perpetual tendency to let slip the things that you have heard? and more than that, to regard this tendency as a pardonable weakness!

Perhaps some of you have been under strong convictions, and have been almost persuaded to seek redemption through His blood, the forgiveness of sins. The way of eternal life has been so plainly marked. The favour of God set forth in such attractive terms. The love of Christ has appeared the one thing needful, and under this impulse, you have determined to cast in your lot with the people of God.

[p. 6]
Yet where are you at this moment? Can you identify yourselves with the same beings who were once possessed by such strong and ardent feeling? Can you point to the practical effect of any one of those impressions, which seemed to have taken such hold upon you? No! your goodness is as 'a morning cloud, and as the early dew it goeth away'. No trace survives of that wondrous impulse, which seemed destined to carry all before it.

And of those who are in some degree moved by Divine Grace, may we not enquire – Are not you alive to this dangerous liability? Do you not behold 'another law warring against the law of your mind', and bringing you into captivity to the law of sin, which is in your members? Is there not a perpetual disposition to attach importance to the things which are seen – a lingering of heart amidst the cares and pursuits of this life – an inclination to postpone eternal subjects to a future consideration? There is no Christian, however eminent, who will not admit that such is the tendency of the mind. Where God is concerned, forgetfulness is the order or our being; for while '*the Bridegroom tarried, they all slumbered and slept*'.

But will this state continue? Is forgetfulness in time, to be succeeded by eternal oblivion? Far otherwise. The words of our text indicate a condition in which conscience resumes its power, *frees* itself from the restraints of which it has been fettered, and vindicates the sentence of eternal Judgment. *'Son, remember!'*

There are seasons in our present experience, when these words ring in our ears, when the days that are past rise up before us, and the sins of youth come back to our thoughts with all the freshness of yesterday. That first great transgression opening the way to a course of crime, from which we date the loss of friends, of health, and reputation. The chain may be long and winding, but it comes back to one circumstance which gave the tone and direction to our life. Was it not thus with the Patriarchs, when standing before that mysterious stranger? In that distant land there was nothing to remind them of their former doings. But conscience was at work, and no lapse of time, or change of scene, can affect its resistless action. '*We are verily guilty concerning our Brother, in that we saw the anguish of His soul, when he besought us, and we would not hear, therefore is this distress come upon us*'. And, brethren, the pressure of

[p. 7]
immediate misery, frequently brings to light those instances in which we have been forgetful of God, and of our own souls; instances in which we have neglected the precious opportunities of receiving and declaring the truth, when we have *'forborne to deliver them that were drawn unto death*;' when we have failed in the manifestation of a meek and Christian Spirit – yea, when we have been the occasions of leading others into sin. God awakens the conscience, and makes it discharge its office, and then the arrows of Divine conviction penetrate the joints of the harness. '*Son, Remember*'. Recall the season of early training, when the sweet influences of home and kindred were at their height, when the Word of God possessed a power, which at least restrained thee from open transgression; and then recall the moment when thou didst give heed to the voice of the charmer, when the thought of sin ripened into desire, and desire led on to actual fulfilment. Henceforward, trace those days in which pleasure and pain were so strangely mingled, when stray conviction struggled with the love of sin, but finally yielded to a stronger influence. Remember from whence thou art fallen, and repent, and do thy first works, lest a worse thing come upon thee. Happy is it, brethren, if even from thence you are led to seek the Lord! He stirs your memory that He may reach your heart – and through the shadows that beset the awakened mind, He would bring in the light of pardoning mercy. Oh, be not disobedient to the heavenly vision – but yield yourselves to Him, before that day, when the heavens shall be brass to your prayers – and He who now reasons with you, shall pronounce your irrevocable doom.

But again, the scene passes from time to eternity, and then what do these words imply? It is no longer the remonstrance of the Spirit to a wandering sinner – no longer the intimation that God waiteth to be gracious – but the announcement of a fixed, unalterable state, of which, the most painful element, will be the consciousness, that perdition was self procured – *Son, Remember*. The course which you adopted, was that of your own deliberate choice, and your end is according to your work. You had the same opportunities of hearing and knowing the truth as others. Your earthly lot was one of prosperity, or it was one of adversity – over this you may have had no control. But your eternal condition has

[p. 8]
been formed by yourselves – it is the natural result of those principles which you thought fit to adopt, and you reap just what you have sown. *Son, Remember*. Those things which you would not heed in life, must be the subjects of your consideration throughout eternity! The evil passions which you would not restrain in a day of grace, are now to spend their fury upon you. You preferred the pleasures of sin to the Cross of Christ, and now you shall eat of your own way, and be filled with your own devices. Oh, brethren, a fearful retribution is preparing for the sinner through those circumstances which minister to his present enjoyment. The '*worm that dieth not*', even now rears its head – and '*the fire that is not quenched*', gathers its first spark from the unlawful desires of the heart. And it will form the highest punishment, to trace the inseparable connection between a life of self-pleasing, and an eternity of woe. *Son, Remember*! Ponder those occasions in which you yielded yourselves

to the pleasures of the flesh, and of the mind: carnal pursuits or intellectual enjoyment. You now see, that though in the eyes of men, the one is disgraceful and the other honourable, yet both are equally remote from the knowledge of God. The profligate inherits eternal corruption. Human reason terminates in the blackness of darkness for ever. You would not believe when it would have been your highest happiness to have done so. You are compelled to believe where no advantage shall ever attend the miserable acknowledgment.

From a consideration of such an awful character, we gladly turn to:–

II. THE CONSTRAINING ADMONITION WHICH THE TEXT ENFORCES.
There is an appeal to nominal Christians on the ground of their profession. Son or daughter – thou that makest thy boast of God, as a Father, and of Christ as a Saviour – thou that hast a form of knowledge and of the truth – what evidence hast thou of thy heavenly adoption? Brethren, does the Spirit witness with your spirits, that you are the Children of God, and heirs of eternal life? Is there anything in your conduct by which men may take knowledge of you, that you have been with Jesus – any token whereby you may assure your hearts before Him – any delightful interchange of thought and feeling to mark the connection between yourselves and the Throne of Grace? If not, I beseech you to enquire whether the plea of affinity will not

[p. 9]
aggravate your present disobedience, and your future doom.

No delusion is greater, or more fatal in its consequences than this – Many surname themselves by the name of Christian, to whom He will profess, '*I never knew you, depart from me, ye workers of iniquity*'. Awake to the solemn fact that all are not Israel, who are of Israel; that the sons of God are they who are led by the Spirit, and that no amount of outward privileges can make a man a Christian, or atone for a wrong state of heart. *Seek* to know God as He is revealed in the face of Jesus Christ; *seek* to change the outward relation of nature and providence, for the vital bond of Redeeming Grace – strive to realize 'that death unto sin and new birth unto righteousness', apart from which, the highest religious profession, is as sounding brass and a tinkling cymbal. The Spirit of God is the Author of this work – The Saviour's Blood, the ground of its efficiency – the obedience of man, the evidence of its operation. Vindicate your profession by a service inspired and sustained by Divine Grace. This is the one great test. 'He that saith He abideth in Him, ought himself also so to walk, even as he walked'. It is also the one great security, the pledge of present and eternal acceptance. 'For whosoever shall do the will of my Father which is in heaven, the same is my brother, and my sister, and my mother'.

Furthermore – *the text enforces the importance of attention upon all who are, and all who would become the Children of God. Son, Remember* – In the affairs of this life, there is no hope of success, where there is no application, and the first principles of science must be acquired as the condition of advancement. The rule holds good in reference to that knowledge wherein standeth our eternal life. The present is not the age of miracles. God works by means, and if men will not give heed to instruction, they cannot expect the seed to take root in their hearts! Are any now complaining that they derive no benefit from the Word of God, that it leaves them much as it finds them. Then let me ask – Do you make any effort to retain the Word – do you receive it as a message from God to your own soul – do you pray over it – do you strive to apply it to your own case, and seek for grace to follow it out to its practical issue? I do not say that it is necessary to recollect every sentence of a discourse – but there should be some effort to retain the substance – to apprehend

[p. 10]
the main topic of consideration – to place it, so to speak, in a niche by itself – separate and distinct from other associations. And where there is no such effort, men stand self condemned – as triflers with the most solemn interests – chargeable with rejecting an instrumentality, which God has specially blessed to the conversion of souls – Nor is it any excuse to plead, as some do, the perpetual recurrence of the same subject. How often is it said, 'we hear nothing else but the fall of man – the necessity of a new heart and a right spirit – the power and influence of faith. A little variation would be desirable, or at least, the modification of those extreme statements, which present the Gospel in so ungenial an aspect'. Might we not reply – Have you yet acquired this elementary knowledge? Have you beheld yourselves as guilty, ruined creatures? Have you any saving experience of that transition from death unto life, without which, no man can see God? If not, can you be reminded too often of your one woeful want? Can you be urged too strongly to seek those things which belong to your peace? Can you be warned too plainly of the hopeless condition of those who think to meet their Lord, without having on the wedding garment? Such indeed is the weakness of the human mind – so unfavourable are we to any gracious influence – so deeply rooted in prejudices and self-love, that we require the continual repetition of the same truths. Here a little, and there a little – line upon line – and precept upon precept; and well indeed will it be, if from all we have read, and heard and felt, we collect one beam to enlighten our darkness – gain one spot of ground, whereon we may rest our weary souls.[1]

Furthermore – *The subject suggests the duty of close personal examination.* The powers of memory are strengthened by the exercise of reflection; and where can reflection be so profitably employed, as upon the instincts and tendencies of our nature, especially where these have been the occasions of sin. Acquaintance with the heart cannot be neglected without the most serious injury. If you have any experience of the power of sin, if you are alive to the influence of some peculiar snare, you are called upon to be most minute and particular in your dealings with it. You must watch every rising movement with sacred anxiety, protect the avenues of thought and

[p. 11]
feeling with unremitting care. And for this purpose, recollection is indispensable. You are to revive the remembrance of sin, not indeed that you may dwell upon it with unhallowed interest, or weave the thread of frivolity or defilement, but simply in self defence, that you may detect the giant forms of

---

1 [*Footnote in the original.*] See Cecil's Original Thoughts.

evil when clad in friendly garb. You will recall the condition of mind and body which are most favourable to the incursion of hurtful lusts, the circumstances which are most obstructive to faith, most depressing to Christian love, and most discouraging to the maintenance of a spiritual frame.

'*Son, Remember*' what HAS been the issue of this course, what is the invariable tendency of such habits. What is the *real motive* that underlies this particular action. Remember how often you have had reason to bewail your want of circumspection how much ground you have lost through weak compliance, how many sorrows have sprung up to rebuke your secret love of sin. And do you think that any alteration has taken place, that a difference of outward form can affect the character of that abominable thing which God hates, or that any strength of mind on your part, can enable you to resist the fiery darts of the wicked one? No, brethren we are never safe, but when with a humbling recollection of our past weakness, we are 'asking our way to Zion, with our faces thitherwards'. Never do we give such advantage to Satan, as when we remain in contented ignorance of his devices. Dread nothing so much as this fatal insensibility; while *you* are sleeping, SIN is gathering strength, and every occasion which passes unheeded, is the standing point of a fresh attack, which will not cease until you are laid prostrate at the feet of your great adversary. Beloved friends, look to yourselves, and at the same time look to Jesus – exclaiming, 'who can tell how oft he offendeth'. 'Cleanse thou me from secret faults; hold up my goings in thy paths, that my footsteps slip not'.

FINALLY. *There is a word of deep and blessed encouragement.* As they who forget now, shall be reminded hereafter, so they who exercise themselves in the things of God, shall attain to a condition where everything delightful shall be remembered, and everything painful be banished for ever.

This Life is our season of preparation for another state of existence. The gracious discipline we realize here below, is the pledge of a

[p. 12]
blissful experience in the world to come. Memory will then retrace those scenes of conflict which have issued in perfect peace. Moments spent in communion with an unseen Saviour, will be succeeded by the revelation of his glory. Sorrow and sighing shall flee away – or if remembered, shall exist as the subject of adoring gratitude; bringing into clearer view the brightness by which they are eclipsed; just as the rain drops sparkle in that sun, which soon absorbs them into himself. The question for each of us to-night is this – Will you remember now, in order that you may forget; or will you encourage a dream, from which you must awake to shame and everlasting contempt. Brethren, hesitate not to prefer a state of present discipline, with the assurance of future happiness, to those pleasures of sin which are only for a season, and which expose the soul to eternal pain and misery. 'Sorrow endureth for a night, but joy cometh in the morning'. 'Be thou faithful unto death, and I will give thee the Crown of Life!'

T. BARCHAM, MACHINE PRINTER, READING.

(ix) Permission for the Solemnization of Marriages at Greyfriars Church (1866). Original in the Greyfriars Church Archive.

Dated 25 January 1866

Samuel, by Divine Permission Lord Bishop of Oxford,
To all whom it may concern, Greeting.
Whereas a new Church having, under the authorities and provisions of the several Acts of Parliament commonly known as the 'Church Building Acts', been built and endowed at Reading in the County of Berks within Our Diocese, the same was, on the Second of December One thousand eight hundred and sixty three, consecrated by the name of 'Grey Friars': And whereas by an Order of the Queen in Council of the Twenty seventh day of August One thousand eight hundred and sixty four a District was assigned to the said new Church to be called 'The Consolidated Chapelry of Grey Friars, Reading', and the limits of the same District were duly defined: And whereas the respective consents of the Patrons and Incumbents of the said District Church of Grey Friars, Reading, have been duly obtained in writing under their hands and seals for the publication of Banns and the solemnization of Marriages within the same: Now We, therefore in exercised and execution of every power and authority enabling Us in this behalf, Do hereby give and grant Our full Licence and Authority that Banns of Marriage shall be hereafter published, and that Marriages shall be

[p. 2]
hereafter solemnized in the said District Church, for the convenience and accommodation of the Inhabitants residing within the District assigned to the same Church by the Order in Council aforesaid wherein it is called 'The Consolidated Chapelry of the Grey Friars, Reading'.
Given under Our hand and Episcopal Seal this twenty fifth day of January in the year of our Lord One thousand eight hundred and sixty six and in the twenty first year of Our Consecration.
[Signed] S Oxon

(x) Greyfriars Church Minutes of Vestry Meetings from April 1869. Original book in the Greyfriars Church Archive.

[Inside Cover]
This Book contains Notes of the Yearly Vestry Meetings, and of such occasional meetings of the Churchwardens and Sidesmen as it may be deemed desirable to record.

[p. 1]

Grey Friars Church
29 April 1869
Meeting this day in Vestry
Dr Barkworth presided.

Present William Hodges elected by him as his church Warden.
Present Mr William Allaway proposed Mr Champ.
Present Mr Keft seconded.
Present Mr Champ.
Present Mr Pierce who entered after Meeting broke up.

William Hodges, signed by order of Dr Barkworth.

Note – This and the two following leaves are the only Minutes of all the Vestry Meetings held from the date of the Consecration of Greyfriars' Church, Wednesday December 2nd 1863.

[On two pages]

Grey Friars
10th April 1871
Meeting this day in the Vestry
Dr Barkworth presided.

Mr W. Hodges having intimated his desire to be relived of the office of Churchwarden it was decided to accept his resignation and after a vote of thanks to Mr Hodges for his kind and efficient superintendence of the duties for the last 6 years it was proposed by Dr Barkworth that Mr C. F. Willson be elected as his successor. Mr Hodges seconded this proposition.
    Mr Hodges then proposed and Dr Barkworth [seconded] the nomination of Mr Champ as the representative of the Parish. This then carried unanimous[ly], The meeting separated with a vote of thanks to the Vicar.

S. M. Barkworth DD
Vicar of Grey Friars.

(xi)   Licence of non-Residence for 1869. Original in the Greyfriars Church Archive

Vicarage of Grey Friars, Reading, Berks
Diocese of Oxford.
Copy of Rev Dr S. M. Barkworth's Licence of Non-Residence.
Under 1 and 2 Vic. c.106 – Sec. 43, &c.

Samuel by Divine permission, Lord Bishop of Oxford,

To our beloved in Christ, Shadwell Morley Barkworth, Clerk in Holy Orders, D.D., Vicar of Grey Friars, Reading, in the County of Berks, within our Diocese
Greeting.
We do hereby license you to be absent from your said Benefice until the Thirty-first day of December One Thousand Eight Hundred and Sixty nine on account of illness and incapacity of Body, you having provided for the duties of your Benefice to Our satisfaction.

Given under our Hand this Thirtieth day of December in the year of our Lord one thousand eight hundred and sixty eight.

N.B. The Act directs that a Copy of the Licence shall be transmitted by the Incumbent to the Churchwardens within one month from the granting thereof, to be by them deposited in the Parish Chest; and that a Copy of the same shall be produced by the Churchwardens and publicly read at the Visitation of the Archdeacon.

(xii)   Correspondence and Accounts for moving the Pulpit and Reading Desk (1872). Originals in the Greyfriars Church Archive.

1. Letter:
25 January 1872.
From John M Davenport, Oxford Diocesan Secretary.
To the Rev Dr Barkworth, Vicar of Greyfriars Church.

Oxford

Dear Sir,
   If you can be certain there will be no opposition to the proposed removal of the Pulpit and Desk, I should not incur the expense of a Faculty. If otherwise, please to write again to
   Yours very truly,
   [Signed] John M Davenport

2. Letter
11 Jun 1872.
From Rev Dr S. M. Barkworth, Vicar of Greyfriars Church.
To Mr C. F. Willson, Churchwarden, Greyfriars Church.

Walthamstow

Dear Mr Willson,
   Having had time to consider the subject of the Pulpit and Reading Desk, I write a few lines to say that perhaps it might be well for you to issue a notice to the Seat holders with a view to the adoption of some plan which might render

the performance of the Service in Grey Friars Church somewhat less burdensome than must be the case, while things remain as they are.

Should such a meeting take place I should wish it to be said that

(1) <u>Under no circumstances</u> could I ever again read the prayers, or preach a Sermon, in the Desk or Pulpit, as at present located – <u>I have suffered more than anyone can possibly conceive</u> of the strain consequent upon the great distance which lies between the Minister and the People in both their positions – especially the latter – and am not disposed to incur a repetition of what I have endured.

(2) Should the majority of the seat holders entertain this view of the question, I should suggest that a plan, which I understood was to be prepared by Messrs Wheeler, be submitted to their inspection, and that they be invited – should the plan be approved – to carry out the same, <u>without any expense to myself</u> which after all that I have done, I think I ought not to be asked to incur, and should decline to partake of the same.

(3) It should be borne in mind that in the event of their removal taking place the Pulpit must be very considerably lowered as the height is altogether not of character with the structure of the Church and contributes in no small degree to the inconvenience of the Preacher. – The Pulpit should also be brought forward as much as possible – I should say <u>beyond</u> the Communion rail, otherwise no real benefit will be secured – in this case the front of the pew on each side should be removed and then there will be no difficulty as to a passage. I lay the more stress on this because it would be a pity when the plan had been adopted that it should fail that of due utility in consequence of any consideration of <u>mere look</u>.

(3) [sic] It would be essential before commencing operation to have the <u>Bishop's permission</u> – or a <u>faculty</u> either of which will be sufficient to protect the Churchwardens from foolish and vexatious opposition, though as Mr Davenport's letter informs us, such an expedient is not <u>generally necessary</u>.

(4) Supposing that the plan be not approved, and it be determined of the majority, that things are to remain as at present I beg to say that I have made arrangements for my own personal convenience by the contemplation of a desk in the front of the Communion table, at which it is my intention to read the Service and also to preach – and about which I have already communicated my views to Mr Sheppard, who will receive instructions to carry them out should the verdict of the meeting be unfavourable to my interests.

I am sorry to appear desirous of any change in arrangements, which were no doubt conceived with the best intentions – But the value of anything can only be known of by experience – and mine has taught me that <u>in these two respects</u> a decided mistake has been made. I shall be glad to hear from you as to how you proceed in this matter and with the prayer that the Divine Blessing may rest upon the congregation and on him who now supplies my deficiency.

I remain yours most truly,
S. M. Barkworth

3. Draft letter to seat holders, Greyfriars Church

Dear Sir,
    A vestry meeting will be held at Grey Friars school room on Thursday evening next to take into consideration what steps shall be taken respecting the alteration of the Pulpit &c.
    Your attendance on this occasion is particularly requested.

4. Letter
19 Jun 1872.
From Rev Dr S. M. Barkworth, Vicar of Grey Friars Church.
To Mr C. F. Willson, Churchwarden, Grey Friars Church.

                      Harrow House, Clifton Gardens, Folkestone
Dear Mr Willson,
    I shall be glad to hear what has resulted from the meeting (supposing it to have taken place) which I suggested to you a few days ago.
    The issue of this would in some degree tend to determine my general course of action.
    I expect to be here about a fortnight longer (or perhaps 10 days) – so that you will know where to direct to, if you have aught to communicate. <u>After</u> that date, I will write again, should I not have heard from you.
    Meanwhile, I am yours most faithfully,
    [Signed] S. M. Barkworth.

I hear that Dr Ellis complains of the situation of the Pulpit – which I cannot wonder at.

5. Letter
26 Jun 1872
From John Henderson, Seat holder, Grey Friars Church.
To Mr C. F. Willson, Churchwarden, Grey Friars Church.
                              4, Prospect Terrace, Reading
Dear Sir,
    I shall not be in Reading tomorrow so will be unable to attend the Vestry Meeting.
    If we are able to secure sittings sufficiently near for Mrs Henderson <u>to hear</u>, it is a matter of very little consequence to me where the Pulpit is placed, and I shall be glad to assist in promoting any improvements that may be considered desirable.
    I am dear Sir,
    Yours very truly,
    [Signed] John Henderson

6. GREY FRIARS CHURCH ACCOUNT FOR ALTERING PULPIT, &c.

Cr.	£	s.	d.	Dr.	£	s.	d.
M. H. Sutton, Esq.	5	0	0	Messrs Wheeler			
The Hon R. Boyle	3	0	0	Brothers'			
The Misses Wilson	2	0	0	Account	21	0	0
Mr Weightman	1	1	0				
Admiral Fletcher	1	0	0				
Mr S. Wheeler	1	0	0				
The Misses Holt	1	0	0				
Mr Allaway		10	6				
Mr Parsons		10	6				
Mr C. F. Willson		10	6				
Mr Champ		10	6				
Mrs Boyer		10	0				
Dr Workman		10	0				
Dr Moses		10	0				
Mr Geo. Ball		10	0				
Mr Flanagan		10	0				
Dr Woodhouse		10	0				
Miss Dewe		7	6				
Miss Wheeler		5	0				
Mrs Geo. Ball		5	0				
Mrs Piggott		5	0				
Mr N.		4	6				
Mr Smith		2	6				
Mr Cork		2	6				
Mr North		2	6				
Miss Claxton		2	6				
	£21	0	0		£21	0	0

We have great pleasure in forwarding the above Account to Subscribers.
Yours faithfully,
C. F. Willson & H. Champ, Churchwardens

Appendix 1:

List of the Reading Borough Bridewell Keepers from the late 18th Century until the Bridewell's closure in March 1862[1]

1778 to 1786	Joseph Clack
1789 to 1806	John Shaylor
1810 to 1818	Henry Simpson
1818 to 1827	William Paradice
1827 to 1832	John Warburton
1832 to 1860	John Readings
1860 to 1862	Charles Hardiman

Appendix 2:

Greyfriars Church Personnel during the first vicar's incumbency, from December 1863 to October 1874

Trustees:
August 1862 to March 1866
- Rev John Ball
- Rev Peter French
- John Neale
- Rev William Whitmarsh Phelps
- John Simonds

March 1866 to May 1875
- Rev Peter French
- Rev Edmund Hollond
- Ven. William Whitmarsh Phelps[2]
- John Simonds
- James Morgan Strachan

Vicar: Rev Dr Shadwell Morley Barkworth

Mission Room Scripture Reader: Mr Charles Collins

---

1 The end dates of Clack and Shaylor are uncertain, as is the start date of Simpson. The dates given are substantiated dates of them being Keepers of the Bridewell. Shaylor was temporary Bridewell Keeper from October 1789 to October 1791, at which date he was appointed to the role.

2 The Ven W. W. Phelps died on 22 June 1867 in Appleby, Westmorland, but his place as a Trustee of Greyfriars Church was not reassigned until May 1875.

Churchwardens:

December 1863 to November 1864	Dr Henry Moses
	Mr William H. Woodman
November 1864 to April 1868	Mr Charles F. Willson
	Mr William Hodges
April 1868 to April 1871	Mr Henry Champ
	Mr William Hodges
April 1871 to April 1881	Mr Henry Champ
	Mr Charles F. Willson

Parish Clerk and Sexton: Mr Thomas North

Organist
    July 1869 to October 1871   Mr W. H. Strickland
    October 1871 to February 1875   Mr John. H. Stark

Bell ringer   Mr Charles Swain

Pew Rent Collector
    December 1863 to April 1870   Mr Maslen
    April 1870 to beyond 1900   Mr William Moore

Head Masters and Mistresses of Greyfriars Schools (where known):

Infants School (to May 1867)
    January 1864 to May 1867   Miss Caroline Willcox

Junior Infant School (from May 1867)
    May 1867 to March 1870   Miss Amelia Moody
    March 1870 to December 1872   Miss Maria Millen
    January 1873 to August 1873   [Name not known]
    August 1873 to April 1874   Miss Marianne Eliza Spillard
    April 1874 to 1888   Miss Eliza Coo

Senior Infant School (from May 1867)
    May 1867 to December 1873   Miss Caroline Willcox
    January 1874 to ?   Miss A. F. Hickmott

National Schools:
    Girls
    January 1864 to September 1875   Miss Agnes Missen
    Boys
    January 1864 to December 1895   Mr William Moore

Index

Abery, Thomas 134
Abingdon xvi, 11, 12, 25, 181
  Berkshire Quarter Sessions of Peace at xvi, 11, 12, 25
  House of Correction at 11, 12
Abraham, Miss 173
Accountant xxvi
  General 42, 44, 46, 50, 52, 54, 55, 114, 120, 123, 127
Acts of Parliament
  1 & 2 Victoria Cap.106 sec.43 315
  1 & 2 Victoria Cap.107 162, 162 n4
  2 & 3 Victoria Cap.40 (Local) xxxi n6, 2, 40, 44, 49, 50, 54, 56, 60, 62, 63, 66, 67, 69, 72, 111, 112, 114, 116-119, 121, 122, 127
  3 George IV Cap.72 162, 162 n3
  5 & 6 William IV Cap.76 sec.94 49, 51, 54, 60, 61, 69, 81, 82, 120-122
  8 & 9 Victoria Cap.70 152, 153, 162, 162 n5
  9 George III Cap.16 66
  11 & 12 Victoria 153
  12 George I Cap.32 53, 120
  12 George II Cap.24 120
  12 & 13 Victoria 122
  19 & 20 Victoria Cap.55 162, 162 n6
  22 George III 11, 12
  23 Victoria Cap.16 112, 114
  31 Henry VIII xxix n4
  58 George III Cap.45 162, 162 n1
  59 George III Cap.134 162, 162 n2
  Church Building Acts 152, 153, 162, 196, 314
  Municipal Corporations Mortgages &c. Act 1860 35, 44, 63, 64, 67
  Reading Corporation Markets Act 1853 56, 78
Adams, Mrs 173
Adey, Elizabeth 230
Agg, Edith 90, 109
Aitcheson, D. 173
Aldermaston 288
Alexander,
  Mrs 173
  Thomas 134
  Widow 133
Alfrey, R. 173
Allaway, William 300, 303, 315, 319
Allen,
  Esther 243
  Jesse 268
Alleston & Co 112
Alliston, John 54, 70-74, 129
Allsop, Mr 173
Allum, John xlvii
Alsop, Mrs 300, 303
Ambleside 174
Anderson, Mr 300, 303
Andrewes, Charles xxxvi n7, 33-35
Andrews,
  J. P. xvi
  Rev C. 173
Annesley, Martin 15, 16
Annual rent of £22 xxviii, 2, 50-56, 60, 61, 66-68, 70-73, 120-122
Appleby 172, 320 n2
Architect xxvi, xxxv, xxxvi, xxxvi n8, xxxviii, 172, 189, 190, 195
Ardley 177
Aston, Sir Arthur xiv

Atherton, Nathan 74
Atlas Assurance / Insurance 200, 203
Attorney xxvi, 73, 109, 129, 150, 193
  General 67
  Power of 143
Atwood, Kate 276, 278
Augmentation Court of the Crown 2
Aust, John xxxvii, xxxviii
Austwick,
  Ann 135
  Harwood 135-138, 141, 151, 173
  Lancelot 130, 131, 135-137, 140, 141, 151
  Mary Ann 135, 136
Aylmer, Col 173
Ayres, Charles 193
Back-to-Back Housing xxvi, xlvii
Bacon,
  Basil 73
  Lt Charles Basil 74
Bailey,
  Goody xii
  John 173
Baker xxvi, xlvii
Ball,
  Ellen 257
  Earnest 259, 278
  George 173, 319
  James 174
  John 132
  Miss 173
  Mrs George 173, 300, 303, 319
  Rev John xxiii, xxxiii, xxxiii n3, xxxix, xl, 152-156, 165, 165 n1, 167, 170, 173, 186, 196, 320
Ball Court xxv n5, 292
Ballard, John xiii, 9
Banbury, W. 174
Band of Hope 211, 215

Bank of England xxxii, 44, 46, 50, 52-55, 111, 112, 114-116, 118, 120, 121, 123, 127
Barcham, T. xlvii, 174, 201, 306, 313
Barfoote, Johan 9
Baring, Henry 50, 56, 72, 121, 129
Barker, Alice 262
Barkshire, Charlotte 280
Barkworth
  Adela Catherine xli n2
  Alfred William xli
  Constance Helena xli n2
  Edith Marion xli, xli n2, 227
  Ellen Gertrude xli n1
  Emma Louisa xli, xli n2
  H. 300, 303
  John xli
  Master 211, 215, 234, 240
  Masters 222
  Miss 232
  Mrs (see also Ellen Jansen) xlix, 203, 258, 260, 267, 270, 281, 283, 298, 299, 300, 303
  death xlix
  memorial xlix, l
  opening Missionary Box 231, 234, 236, 239, 242, 245, 247, 255, 257, 263, 267
  visiting Schools 208, 209, 211-215, 217-220, 222, 225-228, 230-245, 246-251, 253-257, 263-265, 267-273, 275, 279-283, 287, 289, 290
  Mrs (senior) 300, 303
  Reginald Edward xli n1
  Rev Dr Shadwell Morley xli, xlii, xlvii-l, 258, 267, 292, 296, 298, 300, 303, 306, 315-318, 320
  appointment at Greyfriars xli
  career before Greyfriars xli
  children xli

D.D. xlv n1, xlix
death xlix
ill health xlviii, 283, 316
income 198-204
  pew rent xlii, xlii n2, 165, 167, 205
  Queen Anne's Bounty xlii
leave of absence in 1869 xlviii, 283, 289, 315, 316
marriage xli
memorials xlix, l
moving the pulpit and reading desk xlviii, 316-318
preacher xlii, xlvii, xlix, 306, 317
public subscription for Schools xlii
purchase of land for Schools xlv, xlviii
resignation xlviii, xlix
sermon xlii, xlvii, 306-313, 317
vestry meetings 314
vicarage (Trinity Lodge) xlii
visiting Schools 208-217, 219, 220, 222, 224-228, 230-257, 263-266, 267-283, 289, 290
T. 300, 303
The Misses 227, 235, 236, 243-245, 248, 249, 254, 269, 275
Walter Theodore xli, xli n2, 251
Barnard, 201, 204
  Mrs 300, 303
Barne, Mr 238
Barnes,
  John 15, 15 n3
  Mrs 230
Barrett, Mr Alderman 28
Bartle, Miss 174
Bartlett, 199-202
  W.R. 173
Barton, Sarah Anne 282
Basdom, Emily 260, 261

Basildon, 90, 175
Baster, Mrs 174
Batchelour, Miss 294
Bath 176
Batho, Japhet 14
Bato, Mr 174
Baton, Sarah 244
Battel Manor 133
Bazett,
  Col 174
  R. Y. 174
Bear 216, 222
  Inn xxii, 31
Beazley, Widow 132
Bedbury, Anne 281, 282
Beddome, R. B. 174
Bedford, J. 174
Bedford
  Gardens 206, 207
  Row 139
Beesley, Robert xvii
Bell, Rev C. D. 174
Bellavis, H. W. 217, 231
Bennet, Jos. H. 174
Bent, Robert xii
Benyon, Richard (aka Fellowes) M.P. 68, 174
  mortgage of Council property xxix, 56-60, 78-80, 130
Berkley, David 13
Berkshire Chronicle xxxv n1, xxxv n3, xxxvii n1, xxxviii n1, xlvii n2, xlviii, xlix n1, 166, 184 n1
Berkshire, County of xviii, xxvi
  bridewell built 1786 xiii, xvi, 81
  gaol, old (Castle Street) xiii, xvi, 7
  gaol (built in 1793) xvi, xvii, 23-27
  gaol (built in 1844) 37, 40, 62
  Justices of the Peace xiii, xiv, 11, 13, 62
  commission to inspect House

of Correction xvi, 11-13
Quarter Sessions xvi, 3-5, 7, 8,
   11-14, 21, 23-28,
 at Abingdon xvi, 11, 12, 25
 at Newbury 3, 8, 25
 at/for Reading 23-28
Bettridge, Susie 252, 260
Bevan, R. C. L. 174
Bevington 202
Bickham, Charles Curry xxxi, 47,
   48, 59, 62, 63
 lease of Pigeons xxxi, 47, 59, 62,
   63, 75, 79, 83-90, 93, 97, 99,
   105, 106, 124, 126
 mortgage 95-99, 109
 sale of share of Castle Street
   Brewery xxxi, 89, 90, 95, 99
Big Ben xxxvi
Biggs 202
Billing,
 John xx, xxi
 R. 16
Binfield, Miss xl, 174
Binney, Miss 174
Bishop, Alfred 258
Blackwell,
 Councillor 41
 Mr 174
Blagrave 32
Blaise Castle 176
Blake, William 15
Blakiston, Sir Matthew 174
Blandy,
 John Jackson xxix, xxx,
   xxxii n1, 27, 28, 41, 65, 77,
   80-82, 84, 89, 111, 113,
   115-118, 127, 130, 174
 William xxii, xxvii, 15, 30, 36,
   39-43, 61, 142-144, 147, 151
Blandy
 & Hawkins, brewers 62
 Shop 21
Blatch, Rev James 174
Bloomfield Terrace 292

Blount, Michael xvii
Blunnon, James 20
Blyth, James 174
Bonney, William 20
Boorne, James 30, 32, 37, 38,
   41-43, 127, 130, 174
Boot maker xxvi
Bosisto, Mrs 300, 303
Bouverie, Hon P. P., M.P. 174
Bowes, John 10
Bowyer, Mrs 241
Box, Ellen 262
Boyer, Mrs 292, 300, 303, 319
Boyle,
 Hon. R. 300, 303, 319
 Mary 15, 15 n1
Bracher, R. 174
Bradenham 91, 99, 105
Bradley, R. jun. 174
Brain, Mr Councillor 34
Bramwell, Miss 292
Bray 3, 4
Bren, Mr 202, 203, 260
Brewer, Sampson 15
Bricklayer xx
Bridewell
 Borough or Town xv-xx,
   xxii-xxv, xxvii-xxix, xxxiii,
   xxxvii, 13-15, 15 n2, 16, 17,
   19, 20, 22-25, 29, 32-46, 48,
   58, 61-67, 70, 74-82, 85, 116,
   118, 124, 128, 148, 164, 166,
   167, 170, 187, 320
 calendar of prisoners xvi,
   13-15
 carpentry work on 16
 description xv, xviii-10, 23, 25
 escapes from xv, xvii
 extra cells added xix, xxiii, 34
 hundredth part of knight's fee
   etc. xxviii, 1, 2, 66, 77
 inspection visits by
   Borough Committee 23, 24
   Committee of the Society for

the Improvement of Prison
  Discipline xix
Howard, John xv, xvi n1
Neild, James xviii, xviii n1,
  xx n1
three Justices of Peace xvi,
  11-13
improvements xx, xxiii, 81
irons on prisoners xviii, 17-19
keeper, xv, xvii, xviii, xx,
  13-16, 35, 58, 61, 62, 81, 82,
  320
  Clack, Joseph xv, 13-16, 320
  Dunt, Henry xv, 10, 11
  Hardiman, Charles 35, 320
  Paradice, William 320
  Readings, John xx, xxix, 35,
    80, 81, 320
  Shaylor (Shailor), John xvii,
    xviii, xxx, xxx n2, 47, 77,
    82, 85, 133, 320
  Simpson, Henry 20 n1, 320
  Warburton, John 320
keeper's house xx, xxii, xxvii,
  xxix, xxx, xxxii, xxxiii,
  xxxv, xxxvii, 29, 36, 45, 47,
  58, 62, 63, 65-67, 75, 80-82,
  128
  demolition xxxvii
  proof of Title xxix, 66, 67
  purchase, xxvii, xxxii, xxxiii,
    43, 45, 62, 65, 75
  rebuilt xvii, xxx, 82, 85
  statutory declaration of
    John Jackson Blandy xxix,
      48, 66, 67, 81, 82
    John Readings xxix, 80
land to west (Weedon estate)
  xxiv, xxxiii, xxxiv, xlii
matron xx, 35, 61
medicines prescribed xix, 22
privy xx, 124 n2
purchase by Rev W. W. Phelps
  xxvii, xxviii, xxxi-xxxiii,
  43-46, 58, 62, 64, 74, 75,
  123, 127, 167
annual rent of £22
  encumbrance xxix, 2, 70-73
Lords Commissioners,
  approval of xxix, 36, 43,
  123, 124, 126, 128
release from mortgage xxix, 59,
  60, 78-80
repairs xvii, xx, 32, 33
roof removed xvii
straw xv, xviii, xix, 21
subsistence of prisoners xiii,
  xv, xviii, 10, 20
water xv, xviii, xix, xx, xx n1
well xviii, xx n1
whipping xvi, 14, 15 n1, 15 n3,
  15 n4
whitesmith work on 17
County
  opened in 1793 xvi, xvii
Bridge Street xxii, 224 n1
Brighton 175
Briscoe, The Misses 174
British Archaeological
  Association xx, xxi
British School 224 n1
Broad Street xlvii, 290, 306
Brocklesby, George 110
Brooke, S. B. 174
Bros,
  Thomas (the elder) 54, 70-74,
    129
  Thomas (the younger) xxviii, 50,
    54-6, 61, 68, 70-73, 121, 129
Broughton Poggs xxxvi
Brown,
  Emily 261
  J. D. 174
  Mr Alderman 30, 32, 38, 39
  The Misses 174
  W. 172
Browne, Thomas 9
Buckingham, County of 91, 99,

105, 110
Budd, Miss 292
Builder (also see The Builder)
  xiv, xxv, 172, 190, 193
Bulley (see Ring, Bulley & Co.)
  Mr xviii
  Rev Dr 174
Bunny, Major 174
Burfoot, Mrs H. 174
Burrows, Benjamin 133
Burton, Harry 237, 238
Burton upon Trent xxiii, xxiii n2, 152
Bushnell,
  James 15
  Louisa 265-272, 274, 276
Butcher, James 241, 242
Butler,
  Councillor 36, 46
  C. J. 174
Caen stone xxxviii
Callas, Mr 199, 200, 202, 234, 298, 300, 303
Calvert, Charles William 89, 99, 101-108, 110
Campbell,
  Lord 186
  Mrs 258, 283
  Rev Colin xlviii, 202, 258, 283, 285
Campsiding 42, 42 n1
Canney, Mrs 300, 303
Capel,
  Alice 247, 251, 252
  Ellen (Nellie) 211-214, 216-225, 227, 228, 230-232, 235-241, 243, 244, 246-248, 250, 251, 253-255
  Henry Alfred 224 n1
Carlisle, 105, 171
  Archdeacon of (see Rev W. W. Phelps) xxiii, xxiv, xxxviii, 105, 170, 189, 196
  Bishop of 174

Diocese of xxiv
House (see Trinity
  Lodge/Parsonage) xlii
Carpenter xiv, xviii, xx, xxvi, xxxv, xxxvi, xlvii, 16, 21, 172
  Mrs 201, 300, 303
Carter,
  Mr W. 174
  Mrs 300, 303
Carus, Rev Canon 174
Casky, John 10
Castle Street xvi
  Brewery xxxi, 83, 89, 95, 99
Casway,
  C. 251
  Elizabeth 219, 225, 233, 238, 240
Cattle Fair xliv, 212, 217
Caversham 178, 180
  Bridge 51
  Chapel 51
  Road xi, xxiv, xxv, xxxvi n4, xlv, xlvii, 133, 134, 137, 165, 168, 206, 207, 292
Cerate 22
Chad,
  Alice 242
  Jane 258, 260, 262
Chadd, Willie 280
Chalk, James J. 157, 158
Chamberlain, Thomas 15
Champ
  Ellen 248, 261
  Henry 203, 315, 319, 321
  Mrs 174, 300, 303
  Willy 218
Champion, Thomas 145
Chancery,
  Court of 32, 40-44, 46, 50, 52, 54, 55, 62, 111, 120, 123, 127
  Oath in 81, 82
Chandler,
  Alice 274
  Ellen 241, 242

Charles II, charter of 70
Charwoman xxvi
Chatham
　Court xxv n5, 293
　Place xxv, xxv n5, 293
　Street xxvi, xlvi, 206, 207, 292, 293
Cheapside xxvi
Cheer, John 243
Chelsea xli
Cheltenham 89, 90, 95, 97, 293
Cherry, Rev H. C. 174
Chessall, Miss 174
Chesterman, James 20
Chieveley 178, 180
Chilcote, Mrs 174
Chisman, George 95
Christie (Christy), Miss 219, 232, 265, 292, 300, 303
Christopher, Rev A. M. 174
Church Missionary Society 203, 295
Church Pastoral Aid Society 295
Circus xliv, 213, 226, 241, 253
Civil War xiv, xv
Clack, Joseph xv, 13-16, 320
Clark,
　Beatrice 253
　James 132
　Mr Councillor 33, 39
　Rev H. 174
　Rev W. 174
Claxson, Miss 300, 303
Claxton, Miss 319
Clayton,
　Edward xiii
　James 14
　Margaret xiii
　William xiii
Clement, Richard 13
Clutton, Mrs 174
Coal 21, 35, 295, 298, 299
　Merchant 193
Cobham, Alexander 13, 77

Coles,
　Herbert 279
　Miss 175, 209-211, 213, 215, 217, 218, 221, 223, 224, 226, 228, 243, 259
　The Misses 175, 216, 229, 300, 303
Collier (Collyer),
　Map (plan) xvii, xxx, xxx n1, 46, 81, 85
　William 82
Collins,
　Charles xlvi, xlvii, 231, 239, 240, 246, 253, 294, 320
　Ferdinando xvi, 11
　Henry 110
　J. 251
　Mary Jane 221
　Mrs Charles 239
Colonial and Continental Church Society 295
Compigne, Alfred 95
Connop, Rev John 175
Coo, Miss E. 321
Cookesley,
　Mrs 175
　Rev Dr 175
Cookham (Cookeham) 3, 4
Cooper,
　Jane 11
　Lewis (Councillor/Mayor) xxxix, 30, 32, 39, 41
　Messrs L. & W. 175
Copeland, John 15
Copland, The Misses 175
Coppen 203
Cork, Mr 319
Corkhouse, xi n6
Corn Exchange 39
Corps 201
Cosburn, Mr 301, 303
Cottrell, Mr 26
Coulthard, Rev R. 175
Coventry friary xxxvi n6

Cowan, C., M.D. 175
Cowlard, Mrs 175
Cowper, R. 175
Cowslade, Messrs 175
Cray, Caroline xliv, 209-212
Creed, Henry 152
Cresswell, Susan 137
Crew, James 245
Croasdaile, Mrs 175
Crocket, Jos. 175
Cuddesdon College xl
Culverlands 181
Cumberland 105
Currie, Miss 175
Curties, Thomas Grint 55
Curtis, Clement 275
Cusack, Rev E. 175
Cust, Rev Arthur Perceval Purey xxxix, xl, xlii n1, 175, 189
Dalby,
  Alice 133
  Edward 133
  Elizabeth 133
  John 133, 134
Dan, Suzan xiii
Darter, Councillor/Alderman William Silver 30, 32, 33, 36, 175
Davenport, John M. xlviii, 155, 156, 172, 197, 316, 317
Davies,
  James [or Davis] 92, 105, 106
  Mr 175
Davis,
  J. W. H. 156, 192, 193
  James [see Davies] 105
  Mr 301, 303
Dawson, John xii, xiii, 9
Day,
  Fanny 229
  Mr 301, 304
  Thomas 21
Dean, Samuel 133
Deane,
  Henry 13, 15, 81
  John 13
  Matthias xxx, 46, 81, 83-85
  R. 175
  Samuel 134
  Thomas 81
Den of thieves xl
Dentist xxvi
Dewe,
  Miss 203, 319
  The Misses 175, 301, 304
Dilwyn, Mrs 175
Disney, R. 301, 304
Dissolution xi, 1, 65
Dixon,
  Mr 175
  Mrs 175
Dobbyn, Miss 301, 304
Dod, Miss 175
Dodd, Grantham Robert 90, 109
Dolman, William 9
Domestic servant xxvi
Dorking 99, 105
Dormer, Willie 278
Dorset, The Misses 175
Downing,
  Elizabeth 134, 134
  William 134
Downshire, Marquis of 175
Down's Syndrome xli
Drake, W. R. 175
Dress maker xxvi
Drummond, Mrs 301, 304
Dryland
  Mrs 301, 304
  Robert C. 82, 171, 175, 199, 301, 304
Ducket, William 14
Duke Street Bridge (see High Bridge)
Dunbar, Sir William 119, 127, 128
Dunlop, Mr 175
Dunn, John 20

Dunt, Henry xv, 10, 11
DuPont, C. D. 243, 253, 262, 268, 279, 288
Durell, Rev T. V. 175
Eales, Daniel 13
Earles,
  Fannie 288
  the 250
Earley Court 119, 128
East, William 15
East London Relief Fund 295
Easton, C. 175
Eaton,
  Miss 243, 292
  Mrs 301, 304
Ebenezer Place xxv n5
Ecclesiastical Commissioners xxxiv, 153, 156-159, 162, 163, 188, 196
Edgar, John 14
Eliot, W. 175
Elizabeth I
  Charter for Reading in 1560 (letters patent) xi, xi n8, xii, xiii, xxviii, xxx, xxxi, 2, 46, 50-52, 54, 56, 61, 62, 65-70, 72, 112, 114, 119, 121, 129, 187
  Queen of England 2, 46, 50, 51, 67, 70
Elliott,
  Mrs 175
  Rev E. B. 175
Ellis,
  Arthur 284
  Dr 318
Else, Mary 20
Elwes, John 11
Emery, Woodley 262
Emmens, E. 278
Englefield,
  Estate xxix
  House 56, 57, 78
  Sir Francis 51

Estcourt, Rt Hon T. S. 175
Evangelical xxxiii, 186
Evans, Rose xliii, 208-211
Exall, Alderman 38
Eynott, Kate 262
Eyre,
  Rev F. J. 175
  Sarah 137
Faculty xlviii, xlviii n2, 316, 317
Fair xliv, 51, 212, 217, 226, 230, 242, 249, 252, 258, 261, 267, 278, 284
Farbrother, Miss 250, 275, 301, 304
Farley, William 15
Farnham 135, 136
Farrow, E. L. 175
Farrowe, Wydow 9
Fearnley, Councillor 46
Fearnside, T. R. 77
Fellowes, Richard (see Benyon)
Fenton, Miss 175
Ferguson, W. H. 175
Fernhill 176
Fete 229
Fillensor,
  John 14
  Ralph 14
Filleul, Rev P. 175
Fire Insurance Office 48, 87
Fisher,
  Jane 175
  Miss C. S. 176
  Mrs (of Basildon) 175
  R. (jun.) 175
  R. (sen.) 175
  W. 175
Fisher Row 17 n1
Fitzgerald v Champnoys 115
Flanagan, Mr 176, 319
Fletcher
  Admiral J. V. 202, 301, 304, 319
  Miss 176
  Mrs J. V. 176, 292, 301, 304

Thomas 14
Folkestone 318
Forbury xiii, xvi, 32, 51, 164, 229
Ford,
  Annie 227, 229-233, 235, 237-239, 242, 243, 246-249, 251-253, 255-257, 259
  Miss 301, 304
Fosbery, Rev Thomas Vincent xxxix, xl, xlii n1
Fostern (see Vastern)
France, Rev Thomas 176
Franciscan (also see Minor Brothers) xi, xi n4, xx, xxxvi, xxxvi n6, 1, 2
French,
  Mrs Penelope (see Valpy) 238, 264
  Rev Peter xxiii, xxiii n2, xxvii, xxxiii, xxxix, 152-154, 156, 165, 167, 170, 176, 320
  Rev Thomas Valpy xxiii n2
Friar Street (see Fryer Street) xi, xiii, xxiv, xxvi, xxvii n1, xxviii, xxxi n2, xxxii n3, xxxiii n4, xxxiv, xlvi n1, xlviii, 46, 47, 58, 59, 63, 75, 78-80, 83, 85, 86, 89, 90, 92, 95, 97, 99, 104-106, 112, 113, 115, 117, 118, 124, 126, 128, 130, 133, 136, 137, 139, 140, 144, 148, 150, 152, 153, 158, 162, 190, 196, 206
Friars (see Minor Brothers)
Friars Place xxxvi n4, 293
Friary xi, xi n4, xii, xiv, xx, xxi, 1, 2
  additional land xi
  British Archaeological Association visit xx, xxi
  burial under east wall xxxviii
  chapter house xi
  cloister xi, xxxvi
  closure/dissolution in 1538 xi, xi n2, 1, 65

  Coventry's transepts xxxvi n6
  disposal by Henry VIII xi, 1
  dormitory xi
  foundation xi
  history xi n4
  infirmary xi
  kitchens xi
  popular for burial xxxviii
  refectory xi
  remains xi, xx
  warden's house xi
Frowd,
  Miss 176
  Miss Ann 176
  Miss Sarah Thaine 176
  Miss Susan 176
  Rev Dr 176
  Rev Edward 176
Fry, Arthur 243
Fryer(s) Street (see Friar Street) 133, 134, 134
Fryers 133
  Garden 134
  Ground 134
Fulbrook (Fullbrook),
  S. 156, 171, 176, 301, 304
  the two 262, 263
Fulker, Barba 10
Fulkes, Mr 32
Fuller,
  Joseph 176
  Sarah 14
Furnell, John Mitchell 136-139, 141, 151
Gadesden, A. W. 301, 304
Gaol (Gaole)
  Borough (see Bridewell, Borough or Town)
  County (see Berkshire County Gaol)
Gardner (Gardener),
  James Agg 89, 90, 95, 97-99, 109
  John 95-97, 109

Mary 89, 90, 95, 97-99, 109
Garrard, Mr 28
Gas
  allowance 35
  Co 198-204, 298, 299
  fitting 172
Gay, George 176
Gazette (The London) 69, 207 n1
George, Mrs 176
Giles,
  Charley 213
  C. 247
  E. 245
Gilliat,
  A. 176
  J. S. 176
  Mrs 176
Gladstone Place 293
Glazier xx, 172
Gleed, Rev G. 176
Gloucester,
  County of 89, 95, 97
  Terrace 136
Glover,
  Jacob 14
  John 14
  William 9
Goddard,
  Mr 301, 304
  Mrs G. A. 176
Goding, A. 223
Goldsmid, Sir F., M.P. 176
Goodey, Elizabeth 249
Goodhart, Rev C. J. 176
Gordon, Sir H. Percy 176
Gosling, J. 176
Goulding,
  Mrs 292, 301, 304
  Mrs W. 301, 304
Graham, Thomas 176
Grant, John 13
Great James Street 139
Great Knollys Street xxv, xxv n2, 206, 292

Great Western Hotel xl
Green, Miss 176, 301, 304
Gregg, Rev J. R. 176
Gregory, Swarbreck 55
Greyfriars Church xi, xiv, xxi,
  xxiii, xxviii, xxxv, xxxix,
  xl-xliii, xlvi-l, 58, 60, 62, 65,
  75, 76, 79, 105, 118, 124, 126,
  139, 146, 148, 153, 156,
  163-171, 173, 182, 184-188,
  190, 193, 194, 196-198,
  205-207, 290, 306, 314-316,
  318, 320
  Archive 46, 65, 70, 74, 77, 78,
    80, 81, 85, 89, 95, 99, 105, 111,
    118, 128, 139, 146, 152, 156,
    162, 164, 190, 193, 194, 196,
    198, 205, 290, 306, 314-316
  baptisms xlvi, xlvii, 172, 306
  Barkworth memorial xlix, l
  bell
    ringer 299, 321
    turret xxxviii
  bible class xlvi, 293, 295
  body and side aisles 1-3, 62,
    65-67
  chancel xxxvi, 195
    arch xxxviii, 171
    brick exterior, instead of flint
      xxxvi
    plan 194
  churchwarden xlviii, 198,
    314-319, 321
    election xlvii
    named
      Henry Champ 315, 319, 321
      William Hodges xlvii, 198,
        300, 315, 321
      Dr Henry Moses xlvii, 198,
        321
      Charles F. Willson xlvii, 198,
        300, 315, 316, 318, 319, 321
      William H. Woodman xlvii,
        198, 321

pew rent accounts xlii, 198
communion
  cloth 178
  plate 178
consecration xxxvi n1, xxxviii,
    xxxix, xlvii, 68, 76, 105, 114,
    152-154, 163, 171, 172, 175,
    196, 314, 315
  fees 172
  sentence of xl, 196, 197
conveyance to Phelps xxxv, 105,
    118, 128, 166, 167
district xlii, xlvii, 153, 169,
    196, 206, 207, 314
  visitors xlv, 219, 292
Dorcas Society xlv, xlvi, 294,
    295, 299, 303
east wall xxxvi, xxxviii, 171
  accident xxxvii
  skeleton xxxviii
endowment xxxv, xxxix, xlii, 62,
    165-170, 173, 183, 188
Estate xxv, xxxii n3, 67, 130,
    139, 145, 146
  bowling alley 130, 134
fire insurance 299
font xxxviii, 181
harmonium xxxviii
incumbent xxxv, xli, xlii, xlvii,
    xlviii
Infants' Friend Society 294, 298,
    303
Juvenile Missionary Gathering/
    Association xlvi, 233, 294, 294
lamplighter 299
marriages xlvii, 172, 306, 314
mission fund 295, 298, 303
Mission Room xlvi, xlvii, 293,
    294, 320
Mothers' meetings xlv, xlvi,
    214, 215, 294
  clothing fund 298, 303
nave xi, xvii, xxix, xxxvi, 2
organ xxxviii, xlix, 205

blower 299
fund 199, 204 n1
tuning 299
organists 299, 321
parish (also see Greyfriars
    Church / district) xxv
parish clerk and sexton
    179, 198 n2, 321
parish population xxiv-xxvi
pew xxxviii, xl
  opener's salary 299
  rent xlii, xlii n2, 198, 205
  rent collector 198 n1, 321
porch inside south door xlviii
prayer meeting xlvi, 233, 306
pulpit xxxviii, xlviii, 182,
    316-318
reading desk xxxviii, xl, xlviii,
    180, 316
reasons for purchase
  accommodation for public
    worship xxiv, 164, 167, 169
  increase in population xxiv,
    xxv, xl, 164, 166, 167, 169,
    170, 186
reredos xlix
restoration xxiii, xxiv, xxvii,
    xxvii n1, xxxi n4, xxxiii,
    xxxv-xxxix, xl, 62, 119, 164,
    165-173, 182, 184-190, 193
roof xxxviii
Scripture Reader (see Charles
    Collins)
services xxxix, xl, xlii, xlvi, xlix,
    292, 306, 317, 317
Sunday School xlii, xliii, xlv,
    xlvi, 293, 294, 297, 300
  missionary fund 299, 303
  teacher 250, 295
transept xxxii, xxxvi, xxxviii
  Coventry friary xxxvi n6
  north xxxii, xxxvi, xlviii, 146,
    171, 205, 299
  south xiii, xxvii n3, xxxiv

transfer of ownership to Ecclesiastical Commissioners xxxiv, 153, 156-159, 162, 163, 196
trustees xxxiii, xxxv, xli, xlvii, 154-156, 165, 167, 170, 183, 186, 188, 320, 320 n2
vestry xxxii, xlviii, 146, 299, 315
  meeting xlvii, 314, 315, 318
west window xx, xxi, xxxvii, xxxviii, 205
window glass (church glass) xxxviii, 150
Greyfriars House xxxii
Greyfriars Road xxxv, xxxvi n4, 140, 206, 207, 293
Greyfriars Schools xxxiv, xlii, xliii, xlv, 292, 295
  blinds 212, 213
  boot club xlv, 297, 300
  Boys' School xlii-xlv, 211, 218, 219, 231, 237, 238, 243, 248, 262, 266, 293, 295, 321
  burnt to death, pupil 224
  consumption (tuberculosis) xliv, xliv n1, 281
  cost to attend xliii
  curriculum xliv
    alphabet 208, 210, 254, 255, 274
    arithmetic xliv, 209, 228, 242, 245, 252, 263, 265, 271, 275, 278, 279, 281, 283, 284, 287, 289
    catechism xliv, 209, 220, 242, 252, 282
    dictation 232, 237, 266, 267, 271, 272, 274, 277, 278, 281, 283, 285, 287
    dismissal 208, 211, 214, 215, 219, 221, 222, 227-230, 232, 233, 235-237, 242-244, 248, 260, 262, 263, 265, 266, 279, 280
    drill xliv, 244, 249, 255, 264, 279, 282, 283
    form 208
    grammar 236, 256, 283
    knitting xliv, 213, 214, 216, 230, 237, 242, 246, 247, 252
    maps, map drawing 210, 211, 227, 282, 290
    marching xliv, 213, 222, 223, 226, 230, 231, 236, 239, 241, 243, 247-249, 253, 258, 261, 262, 268, 269, 273, 275, 278, 281, 282, 288, 289
    natural history xliv, 210, 214, 216, 219, 220, 222, 223, 225, 228, 230, 232, 236, 238, 239, 243, 246, 260
    needlework xliv, 209, 212, 214-219, 225, 226, 232-235, 240-242, 248, 250, 251, 253, 256, 258, 259, 261, 269, 270, 273, 274, 280, 282, 289
    object lesson xliv, 209, 219, 220, 223, 224, 226-228, 230-233, 236, 246, 248, 252
    prayers 216, 237, 238, 241-243, 249, 265-267, 272, 275, 279, 281, 282, 284, 286, 290
    reading xliv, 224, 225, 231-233, 236, 239-241, 244-247, 250-252, 256, 259, 260, 263, 265, 267-269, 271-275, 277-281, 283-285, 287, 288
    reciting texts xliv, 219, 223, 224, 243, 256, 259, 265, 266, 268, 269, 278, 283, 284, 287
    science xliv
    scripture xliv, 208, 211, 213-215, 218, 220, 222, 226, 227, 229, 232-244, 247, 248, 251, 252, 255-258, 261, 262,

269-278, 282, 284, 285
sewing 210, 256, 258, 260, 274, 285
singing xliv, 208, 209, 211, 213-229, 230, 233-236, 238-241, 244-247, 249, 251, 252, 256, 257, 260, 262, 263, 264, 266-269, 271-273, 275-279, 281-284, 286-288, 290
writing xliv, 214, 217-219, 225, 237, 238, 241, 245, 246, 260, 263, 265, 273, 275, 278, 278, 284, 287
death of a pupil xliv, xliv n1, 211, 216, 217, 224, 256, 257, 280, 282, 284, 285, 286, 288
diphtheria xliv n1, 285
Enlargement Fund 296, 300
gallery xliii, 208, 209, 212, 213, 221-224, 226-228, 230, 233-236, 238, 243, 260, 289
gastric fever 216, 219
Girls' School xlii-xlvi, 209-212, 218-221, 225, 229, 231, 233, 234, 237-240, 244, 246, 248, 250, 251, 253, 254, 256, 262, 276, 286, 288, 293, 294, 295, 321
hooping (whooping) cough xliv, 221, 229, 250, 254, 275, 279
hopping xliv, 216
Infant (School) xlii-xliv, xlvi, 208, 211, 212, 216, 221, 227, 232, 234, 238, 244, 255, 264, 290, 296, 300, 321
Inspector's Report Summary 221, 234, 244, 255, 264, 270, 281, 290, 293
Junior Infant School xliv, xlv, 208, 243, 248, 249, 254, 256, 257, 262, 264, 270, 281, 286, 293, 295, 321
magic lantern 221, 234

measles xliv, xliv n1, 211, 223, 224, 254, 256, 279, 280
missionary box 226, 231, 234, 236, 239, 242, 245, 247, 255, 257, 259, 261, 263, 267, 285
Mixed Junior School xliv
monitor/monitress xliii, 208, 210-212, 216-219, 221-225, 227, 229-233, 237-239, 244, 250, 255-257, 259, 262, 264, 265, 269, 276, 277, 296
National xliii, 293, 296, 300, 321
opening xliii
playground 213, 214, 241, 245, 248, 251, 262, 265, 266, 268, 271, 272, 274, 277-279, 282-286, 288
ringworm 258
scarlet fever (scarlatina) xliv, xliv n1, 216, 218, 219, 241, 244, 254, 258, 280, 284, 288
school pence/money xliv, 222, 228, 231, 234, 238, 241, 243, 244, 249, 251, 255, 258, 263, 265, 266, 268-271, 276, 280, 283, 285, 289, 290, 296
Senior Infant School xliv, xlv, 244, 264, 265, 268, 273, 279, 283, 289, 293, 295, 321
small pox 220
soup kitchen xliii
tea party 211, 215, 224, 229, 235, 240, 251, 260, 286
treat 215, 251, 266, 276, 281, 286
Grosen 200
Grove, The 133
Grover, 204, 204 n1
  Ann 20, 21
Guildhall (Gyldehawle, Hall) xi, xii, 1-3, 11, 19, 47, 85,187
Gun Street xxxvi
Gundry, John Worthy 14

Gunter, Nicholas 4
Guy,
  Maria 253, 258
  Thomas 284
Haden of Trowbridge xxxvi
Haines, Thomas 14, 15
Halcomb, Miss 176
Hale, Mrs 292
Hall (see Guildhall)
Halligan, Thomas 128
Hamblin,
  Edith 242
  Edward 261
  Nellie 242
Hamden, Mrs 268
Hamilton, George A. 44, 45, 64
Hampshire xxvi, 195, 206, 207
Hand, Mrs 301, 304
Handcock, John 13
Hardiman, Charles 35, 320
Hare Hatch Lodge 182
Harford, S. 176
Harries, Mrs 261
Harrington Mrs 176
Harris,
  John 13
  Miss 301, 304
  Mr Alderman 30-32, 35
  Mrs T. 176, 301, 304
  Thomas 176, 301, 304
Harrison, Miss 176
Harrow 175
  School xxiii n4
Hart 203, 204
Harwood, Isabella 137
Haslam, James 176
Hatchard, Rev T. D. 176
Havell, John 17, 17 n1, 19, 21
Hawkes,
  Henry 24, 89, 176
  J. G. 31
Hawkins, 200
  Blandy &, brewers 62
  Miss M. A. 177, 215, 301, 304
  Mrs B. 177, 301, 304
  Mrs (senior) 176, 301, 304
  Sarah Anne 286
  Thomas xxxi, 176
    lease of Pigeons xxxi, xxxi n3, 89, 90, 99
    mortgage with Rickfords xxxi, 90, 93, 94, 99, 101, 106, 109
    purchase from Charles Curry Bickham xxxi, 89, 90, 95, 99, 109
    purchase from heirs of Thomas Rickford xxxi, 89, 91-94, 99, 106, 109
    sale of lease of Pigeons to Phelps 105-110
  Willie 260, 262
Hayes, Rev Sir J. 177
Hayling Island 136
Hayward,
  Johnson 177, 301, 304
  Mrs 235, 292
Head
  Master xxiii n2, xliv, 321
  Mistress xliv, 244, 321
Heading, Mr 301, 304
Hedges, Francis 15
Heelas,
  Messrs 177
  D. 301, 304
Henderson,
  John 318
  Mrs John 301, 304, 318
Henry VIII, King of England xi, 2, 65
  charter (letters patent) for Reading 1542 xi, xi n5, xi n7, xxviii, xxix, 1-3, 44, 65, 67, 68, 114, 187
  dissolution of monasteries xi
  grant to Robert Stanshawe xxix, xxix n4, 1, 2, 65
Hepinstal, Miss 177
Herbert, Sarah 239

Hern 115
Herring, John 253
Herringham, Mrs 177
Hewett, Robert (Councillor, Mayor) 41, 44, 177
Hewitt,
  A. T. 177
  Charles 90, 92, 105, 106
  F. 177
  Rev A. 177
  Thomas 177
Hewlings (chimney sweep) 21
Heycock,
  Joseph 130, 131, 133
  Mary 131
Hickmott, Miss A. F. 321
Higgs,
  Holland Thomas 132, 133
  Mrs 177
Highbury Grange 178
High Bridge (Duke Street Bridge) xvi, xxii, 15 n2, 32, 39
  House xxii, xxvii, xxviii, xxxii, 30, 32, 38-46, 61-64, 111, 116
High church xxxiii, 189
High Wycombe 181
Hill,
  Frances 131, 132
  Joseph 130, 131, 135, 141, 151
  Prospect 136
  Theodosia 131, 132
  William 9
Hillier,
  Miss 229
  The Misses 301, 304
Hind, Miss 177
Hinde, Giles 3, 4
Hindon xxiii n4
Hobbs,
  Miss S. 301, 304
  Mr 301, 304
  William 91, 109
Hobby, Thomas 134
Hoddle, W. 123, 127

Hodges, William xlvii, 177, 198, 199, 300, 301, 304, 315, 321
Holders, the two 282
Holding,
  Miss 177
  Rev John 177
  The Misses 177
Holland Blinds 299
Holliday, Mr 301, 304
Hollond, Rev Edmund 165 n1, 177, 320
Holme Park 179
Holt,
  Edward 285
  E. 297
  Miss 226, 235, 237, 267, 273, 275, 282, 288
  Mrs 285
  M. J. 297
  Rev R. F. 301, 304
  The Misses 222, 231, 248, 253, 256, 263, 266, 279, 290, 293, 301, 304, 319
Holy Trinity Church,
  Burton upon Trent xxiii, xxiii n2, 152
  Reading (see Trinity Church)
Home Fast 133, 137
Honeybone, Emily 216
Hope Place xxv n5, 292
Hopkins, Rev W. T. 177
Horlock, Mrs 301, 304
Hosier Street 235
Hospital
  in Greyfriars building xii, xiii, xiv
  Normansfield xli
  Royal Berkshire xxxvii, 200-204, 295
Houlters 264
Houlton, Thomas 16
Hounslow, J. W. 177
House of Correction (Borough) xii-xvi, 3-9, 11-13, 20, 58, 62,

75-77, 79, 124, 128
  during Civil War xiv, xv
  governor xii, 5-7
  inspecting xvi, 11, 12
  irons on prisoners 5
  keeper xii, xiii, xiv, 9, 20
    Ballard, John xiii, 9
    Clayton, William xiii
    Dawson, John xii, xiii
    Remnant, John xiii
    Simpson, Henry (William) 20, 20 n1, 320
    Tubb, Henry xiii, xiv
    Woodes, William xiv
  keeper's house xiii, xiv
    provision xiii
    removing Mrs Clayton xiii
    salary xiii
    Tubb and Woodes sharing xiv
  management of xii, xiii, 3-8
  marshal 4, 5
  matron xiii
  repairs xiv
  set up xii
  straw 5
  subsistence of prisoners xiii
  use by the County xiii, xiv, 3, 4, 81
  whipping at 3, 6-8
House of Correction (County)
  built in 1786 xiii, 23-25
  governor xvii
  use by the Borough 23
Howard,
  Benjamin 20
  John xv, 11
  Rev J. F. 177
Howe, John 74
Howell, Mrs 177
Howes,
  R. 177
  Mrs 301, 304
Howman, Rev G. E. 177
Hoyle, G. W. 301, 304

Huddy, William 239, 270
Hughes,
  Francis 137
  H. 177
Hughes Hughes,
  W. (jun) 177
  W. (sen) 177
Huish, Mr 177
Hull xli
Hulme, Rev George xxiv, 185
Hundleby, George 74
Hunt 200
Hunter, Sir Paul 177
Hyde Park 136
Income Tax 200-203
Industrial School 257
Inner Distribution Road xxvi
Inner Temple 50, 70
Ireland 11, 126, 153, 155, 170, 175, 193, 197
Irish Church Missions 295
Ironmonger, 172
  Sarah 20
Ivey, Mr 301, 304
James, Rev John 177
James I, King of England 3, 4, 8
Janaway, Joseph 10
Jansen, Ellen (see Mrs Barkworth) xli
Janson,
  A. 301, 304
  Miss 301, 304
  The Misses 217
Java Place 293
Jeffrey, Ann 230, 244
Jeffreys, John 284, 289
Jemmy, blind 260
Jennings,
  Bertha 286
  Mr 301, 304
  R. 177
Jersey 175
Jessett, Mr 203, 301, 304
Johnson, 115

Annie E. 239-242, 245, 247, 248, 250-262, 264
Bathsheba 14
Joseph 177
Johnstone, Captain 177
Joiner xxvi
Jones,
   Elizabeth 14
   Kate 280, 288
   Mary Ann 270
   Mrs 301, 304
   S. A. 262
Jumper, Thomas (see Haines) 14
Keating, Hon Mr Justice 177
Keeley,
   Miss 302, 304
   Mrs 177
   W. 177, 201
Keeling, Rev J. 241
Keft, Mr 301, 304, 315
Kemble, Mrs H. 177
Kemp Fund 188
Kendall, Sarah 276
Kennard, Rev R. R. 177
Kennet, River xxii
Key, Dowager Lady 177
Kindersley, Sir Richard Torin 102, 103
King, 199
   Ann 15
   Isaac 100
   Isaac (2) 110
   Maria Golding 100
   Mr 301, 304
   Mrs 173, 177, 204, 301, 304
King Street xxvii n2, 156
Kingsclere 177
Kingston 21
Knapp, Mr 81
Knight,
   John 135, 136-138, 141, 151
   Roger xii
Knott, Mr 301, 304
Knox, Mrs H. Carnegie 203, 301, 304
Labourer xxvi, 13, 191
Lackley, Ann 21
Lahore, Bishop of xxiii n2
Lake, G. H. 177
Land Tax xxviii, xxix, 77, 134, 136, 138, 141, 163, 196
Lanfear
   C. 302, 304
   Miss 177, 302, 304
Langdon-Down, Dr John Haydon xli
Langley, Rev John 177
Laundress xxvi
Laurie, G. 177
Law, J. H. 156
Le Grice, Henry 130, 131
Leach, Mr Councillor 31
Leaver, William 20, 21
Lee,
   John 176, 177
   Miss 231
Leicester, County of 130
Lennox, Lord Arthur 50, 56, 72, 121, 129
Levett, Mrs 178
Lewer, Henry 216
Lewis,
   Herbert 95
   Robert 14
Lincolns Inn 115, 130, 135
Lind, Mrs 178
Link Saint Mary Bourne 90
Little Orte 51
Lock-ups xxii, 29-33, 35, 61, 62
Lodge, James 178
London xxxvi, xl, 48, 50, 87, 110, 111, 127, 156, 158, 159, 161, 189, 244, 252, 253, 256, 258, 260, 262, 295
   & County Bank 170, 178
   Banks 168
   Bridewell xv
   City of 70, 90, 99, 105

Lords Commissioners (also see
  Lords of the Treasury) 35, 40,
  43, 45, 49, 50, 52-56, 60, 61,
  64, 72, 74, 76, 78, 116, 119,
  120-124, 126, 127, 128-130
  approval of Bridewell etc sale
    xxix, 35, 40, 43, 119, 122-124
  regarding the Pigeons issue 116
  responses to Corporation 43, 45,
    64
Lords of the Treasury (also see
  Lords Commissioners) 37, 40,
  41, 44-46, 61, 62, 68, 111-115,
  117, 118, 122, 123, 166, 186
Loveden, Edward Loveden 11
Lovejoy,
  G. 178
  Mr 302, 305
  Samuel 21
Lower Thorn Street xxv, 292, 293
Lumbert, Miss 178
Lunnen,
  Ellen 282
  George 237, 260
Lush, Miss 178
Maberley, Miss 178
Macaulay, Mrs 302, 305
Macauley, J, 290
Mace, Martha 250
Magistrates' Offices / Chambers
  xxii, xxviii, 30-32, 37, 39, 41,
  62
Maine, Rev Lewin George
  xlii n1
Maitland,
  Mrs Fuller 178
  W. Fuller 178
Major, Rev Dr 178
Malthus, Miss 302, 305
Mangling trousers xxvi
Mansfield, John 13, 14
Mapledurham xvii
Market Place 31
Marlborough Terrace 292

Marlow,
  Emma xlvii
  Harry Frank xlvii
  Thomas xlvii
Marsh,
  Rev Dr William 178
  Sir Charles 77
  Rev William 132
Martin, Sir H. 178
Mary, Queen of England
  Letters Patent 51
Maslen,
  Mr 198, 198 n1, 199-203, 302,
    305, 321
  Mrs 302, 305
Mason (see Stone mason)
Masters, Captain 178
Mathers, Miss 178
Mathews,
  John 178
  J. 178
  Miss 178
Matthews, Miss 178
Mattingley, The Misses 178
Maule, J. 28
May
  Mrs 178
  Walter 178
  William 10
Mayers, Miss 178
McMurdo,
  E. L. 178
  Miss 178
Menagerie 236
Merewether, Henry Alworth 25
Micklem, Edward 138, 139, 141,
  145, 151
Middle Row xxii, 31
Middlesex xxvi, 70, 130, 136
  Royal East Middlesex Militia
    74
Middleton, Miss 241, 242, 248,
  252, 258, 261, 267, 268, 284,
  293

Midwinter, W. 178
Milford on Sea 195
Mill Lane 39, 41
Millen, Maria 321
Miller 202
Minor Brothers / Friars (also see Franciscan) 1, 2, 65
Missen,
　Agnes xliv, 218, 321
　Miss 229
　Mr 229
Mitchell. Miss 178
Monck,
　Councillor John Bligh 29, 30, 33
　John Berkeley 23
　Miss 178
　Mrs 178
Montressor, Major 178
Moody, Amelia xliv, 264, 268, 279, 288, 293, 321
Moore,
　Rev E. 178
　William xliv, 203, 204, 321
Morgan, Rev James 13
Morley,
　Edward 253
　Ellen 239
　Henry 239
Morrell, Rev R. P. 178
Morris, Mrs J. T. 178, 302, 305
Morse, Peter 10
Mortimer,
　Rev Dr 178
　Thomas Hill 130, 131, 135, 141, 151
Moses,
　Dr Henry xlvii, 201, 221, 226, 234, 236, 241, 245, 255, 259, 260, 262, 264, 266, 270, 281, 285, 288, 290, 296, 297, 302, 305, 319, 321
　Dr W. 178
　Mrs 211, 229, 233, 235, 238, 249, 260, 287, 293, 302, 305

Moss, M. J. 239
Mount, W. 178
Mullins, Edward 139, 141, 143-147, 151
Mundy, Mrs 178
Munvile James 10
Murray, Miss Scott 178
Myddleton, Miss 178
Nash, Matilda 252, 253
Nashe, Johan 9
Neal, Mary xlvii
Neale,
　John xxvii, xxvii n1, xxxii-xxxiv, xxxii n1, xlvi n1, 65, 112, 113, 115, 117, 118, 128, 147, 149, 152-154, 156-163, 165, 165 n2, 167, 170, 178, 192, 193, 320
　John (2) 15
　Mary xlvi, xlvi n1, xlvii n1, 178, 302, 305
　W. 302, 305
Neave, Miss 247
Needlewoman xxvi
Neild, James xviii, 8 n39, xx n1
Netherclift 201
Neville,
　Hon Mirabel J. 178
　Richard 134
Newberry, Giles 133, 134
Newbury (Newbery, Newberry) 3, 5-8, 25
　Mary 14
　Thomas 14
Newtown 260
Nicholas, J. L. 178, 302, 305
Nicholls, Miss 179
Nind, Rev P. H. 179
Nixon, The Misses 179
Nokes, James 15
North,
　L. 278
　Thomas 198, 198 n2, 199-204, 319, 321

North
  Court xxv n5, 292
  Street xxv, 293
Northampton, William Marquis of 51
Office of Land Revenue Records and Inrolments xxviii, 77
Orte land 51
Osborne Terrace 293
Outen, Miss 302, 305
Over, John 10
Oxford, 155, 156, 316
  Bishop of, xxxiii, xxxix, xl, xlvii, 66, 152, 155, 156, 160, 167, 183, 184, 186, 188, 189, 196
  Wilberforce, Rt Rev Samuel xxxiii, xxxix, 152, 153, 156, 196, 197, 314, 315
  Diocesan Church Building Society 173, 188
  Diocesan Secretary/Deputy Registrar,
    Davenport, John M. xlviii, 155, 156, 172, 197, 316, 317
  Diocese of xxxiv n2, xl, 162, 196, 197, 206, 314, 315
  English Dictionary 42 n1
  St Peter-le-Bailey Church xli
  University of,
    Corpus Christi College xxiii n4
    Magdalen College 174
    St John's College 186
    Worcester College xli, 306
Oxford
  Court xxv n5, 292
  Road xxiii, 168
  Street xlvii, 206, 207, 292
Oxfordshire xxvi, xxxvi
Packer, Joseph xvi, 15, 15 n2
Page,
  Fanny 224
  Francis 13
Paice, Mr 302, 305

Pain, William 10
Painter xx
Palmer,
  Eliza 227, 229, 232, 233, 237, 264, 266-276
  George xxii, 29, 31, 32, 179
  R. (Robert) of Holme Park 179
  The Misses 302, 305
Papillon, Major 179, 203
Paradice, William 320
Parker, Mrs 302, 305
Parliamentarian xiv
Parratt, J. E. T. 179
Parry, John 14
Parsons,
  Alice 256-261
  Marion Elizabeth 277, 278, 280-285, 287-290
  Mr 319
Paten, Miss 250
Patey,
  James 11, 12
  John 133
Patronage xxxiii
  Greyfriars Church xxxiii, 152, 154, 155, 165, 167, 170, 184, 186, 188, 314
  St Giles's Church xxxiii, 186
  St Laurence's Church xxxiii, 153, 167, 183, 186
  St Mary's Church xxxiii, 186
  Trinity Church 185
Payn, Dept Clerk of Peace 12
Payne, Rev W. 179
Pears, Rev Dr 179
Pearson, Annie 258
Peasemore 181
Pechell, Mrs 179
Peck, John 34
Pecover,
  Mr 179, 199, 202
  Mrs 302, 305
Peel, F. 45, 116
Pegler, Emma 227-233

Peircy, Sarah 10
Pell, Miss 179, 302, 305
Penyson, William 51
Perfect, Robert 179
Perren, Sarah A. 255-262
Perrin, Sarah 265
Perrot, Mr 179
Perry, John 15
Phelps,
  Miss Ann 179, 293, 302, 305
  Mrs 179
  Rev H. H. 179
  Rev John 179
  Rev William Whitmarsh xxii,
    xxiv, xxvii-xxix, xxxi-xxxv,
    xxxvii-xl, xlii, xlviii, 29, 36-
    46, 58, 62, 64, 65, 70, 74,
    76-82, 89, 105-119, 122-130,
    147-150, 152-154, 156, 158,
    162, 163, 165-172, 179,
    182-184, 187-193, 196, 220,
    292, 320, 320 n2
    agrees purchase price of
      bridewell etc xxvii, 39, 41, 42
    Archdeacon of Carlisle xxiii,
      xxiv, xxxviii, 105, 170, 179,
      189, 196, 220
    birth and early career xxiii n4
    chaplain in Carlisle xxiv
    circulars xxxiii, xxxv, 164,
      166-171
    contribution to lowering roads
      near church xxxviii, 172
    conveyance of bridewell etc
      xxxv, 46, 118, 122, 123, 128
    curate of
      St Laurence xxiii
      Sonning xxiii
      Sulhamstead xxiv
    death 292, 320 n2
    decided on purchase of
      Greyfriars xxiii
    first ten subscriptions of £100
      xxiii, xxvii
    offer to purchase Bridewell etc
      xxvii, 36
    purchase of
      bridewell xxvii, xxviii,
        xxxii, xxxiii, 43-46, 58, 62,
        64, 74, 75, 78, 79, 123, 124,
        127
      bridewell keeper's house
        xxxii, xxxiii, 43-46, 58, 63,
        65, 75, 124, 127
      land to the north xxxii, xxxiii,
        167
      land to the west xxiv, xxxiii,
        164, 165, 167, 168
      lease of Pigeons xxxi, xxxii,
        xxxiv, 89, 105-110, 125, 167
      Pigeons xxix, xxxi-xxxiii,
        43-46, 59, 64, 65, 111-116,
        127
      strip of land to the north xxxii,
        xlvii, 146, 148, 150
    resignation from Trinity
      Church xxiv
    subscription list for Greyfriars
      Church xxiii, xxvii, xxxvii,
      xxxviii, 164-166, 167,
      167 n1, 168-170, 172, 173,
      184, 184 n1, 186, 187
    transfer of ownership of
      Greyfriars Church and land to
      the Ecclesiastical
      Commissioners xxxiv, 153,
      156-159, 162, 163, 196
    trustee of Greyfriars Church
      xxxiii, xxxv, xli, 154-156,
      165, 167, 170, 320, 320 n2
    vicar (earlier perpetual curate)
      Trinity Church xxiii, xxiv
  Rev W. W. (Punjab) 179
Philbrick, The Misses 293, 302,
  305
Phillips,
  Councillor 32
  G. 179

J. M. 26, 27
Pickett, Leah 211, 222-225
Pidgeon,
  C. 179
  J. 179
Pierce, Mr 315
Piercy, Rev Peter 179
Pigeons public house xiii, xxii,
  xxvii, xxx-xxxv, 2, 29, 36, 38,
  40, 43-47, 59, 60, 62-70, 74,
  75, 78-86, 89, 90, 92, 95, 97,
  99, 104-106, 111, 112,
  114-117, 124, 126, 128, 162,
  172, 196
  lease xxx, xxxi, xxxi n2, xxxii,
    xxxiii, xxxiv, 38, 46, 47, 59,
    62, 63, 66, 69, 75, 79, 81,
    83-86, 89, 90, 92, 95, 97, 99,
    104-106, 124-126, 167, 172
  no proof of Title xxix
  purchase xxix, xxxi, xxxii,
    xxxiii, 43, 45, 46, 59, 62, 64,
    74, 75, 111, 112
  rebuilding in 1790 xxx, 82
  Schedule of buildings xxxi, 2,
    40, 49, 63, 66, 67, 69, 112,
    114, 115, 119
  Three Pigeons xxxi n1, 63, 126
Piggott,
  Mrs 302, 305, 319
  Sarah 10
Pike,
  Emily 277, 278
  J. 179
  Louisa 260, 262
Pine Apple public house xlvi
Pink, Mary 10
Pinnorck, Hannah 10
Pitcher, Mrs 302, 305
Pleasure Fair xliv, 212, 217, 284
Plumber xx, xxxv
Plumptre, J. P. 179
Pocock,
  Annie 230
  Jesse 261
  Maria 213, 218, 219, 222, 223,
    230, 231, 237
Pococke, Jerome, xii
Podmore Cottages 292
Police Station xxii, 30-32, 37, 42,
  61
Poole, Mr 31
Poore, Robert 13
Pope, 202
  John 20, 21
  Letitia 246, 248
  Matilda 247, 248, 273
Portland Place 206
Portsmouth 199, 201, 202
Pottman(s) Brook 133, 134, 137
Poulton,
  Charles 132, 133
  Mr 81
  Mrs 302, 305
Poulton & Woodman xxxv,
  190-192
Povey, Miss 302, 305
Powell, Ann 20
Powney, Penyston 12, 13
Powys, Hon & Rev A. L. P. P.
  179
Pratt, Miss 179
Prerogative Court of Canterbury
  91, 101, 136, 145
Preston, Samuel 127, 179
Preston & Ley 110
Price, F. 284
Pring, Mr 179
Pringle, Alexander 50, 56, 72,
  121, 129
Prior Court 181
Procrustes' bed 186
Prospect
  Hill 136
  Terrace 138
Pryor, Barnard 10
Punjab 179, 181
Purvis, Captain 179

Puttrell, Miss 179
Pye, Henry James 11
Quarter Sessions xvi, xx, 3, 7, 8, 11-13, 23-28
Queen Anne's Bounty, Office of xlii
Quentery, Miss 179
Radnor, Rt Hon Earl of xxxiii n1, xxxv, 25 n95, 179, 182-185, 187-189
Railway xi, xxvi
  Bridge (Caversham Road) xxv
  Great Western 206, 207, 286
Raimondi, Miss 179
Raine, Miss C. 179
Randall, Ven Archdeacon xxxix, xl
Ravenscraft, Alce 11
Ravenscroft
  Son & Morris 195
  William 195 n1
Rawlence, Mrs 179
Read, Widow 134
Read, (Reade), James 20, 21
Reading xxi, xxvi, xxxv, xxxvi, xliv, 80, 81, 229
  Abbey 51
  grant to friars in 1233 xi
  grant to friars in 1285 xi
  Hospitium xii
  ruins xxi
  Civil War occupation xiv, xv
  Corporation (Mayor and Burgesses)
    agreeing to buy High Bridge House 39, 41, 42
    annual rent of £22 xxviii, 2, 50-56, 60, 66-68, 70-73
    Borough Quarter Sessions xx, 23-28
    Borough Surveyor 30, 32-34, 36-38
    fire engine 37, 42
    Local Board of Health xxv, 203
    lowering roads near Greyfriars Church xxxviii, 172
    mortgage to Richard Fellowes/Benyon xxix, 56-60, 78-80, 130
    move to new Guildhall by 1543 xi
    move to new Guildhall in 1578 xi, xii
    non-payment of Knight's Fee etc. xxviii, 66, 67, 77
    payment of Knight's fee etc 1, 2
    Pigeons purchase price issues 40, 44, 116
    Police Buildings xxii, xxiii, xxvii, xxviii, xxxii, 32-35, 37, 39, 41-44, 111, 112
    Recorder 25, 111
    removal of new cells from Bridewell 37, 38, 41, 42, 58, 75, 79, 124
    valuation of Bridewell etc. 38, 62
    Watch Committee 29, 35
  Jobcentre xxvi
  Mayors, named
    Andrewes, Charles J., 33, 34
    Annesley, Martin 15, 16
    Boorne, James 37, 38, 41-43, 127
    Cooper, Lewis xxxix
    Deane, Henry 13, 15
    Gunter, Nicholas 4
    Hawkes, Henry 24, 89
    Hewett, Robert 44
    Palmer, George xxii, 29, 31, 32, 179
    Simonds, H. A. 35
    Turner, Richard xi, xi n6
    White, Edward Skeate 13
  Mercury xv, xv n4, xvi n5, xvii n1, xx n3, xx n5, xxv n4, xxxv n1, xxxv n3, xxxvii n1,

xxxviii n1, xl n2, xlvii,
xlvii n2, xlvii n8, 15 n1, 15 n2,
15 n3, 171, 224 n1
Protestant Association 295
School (Free School) xxiii n2,
49, 112, 119, 121
Town Clerk xxix, xxx, xxxii,
xxxii n1, 24, 25-28, 34-36, 39,
41-45, 48, 49, 55, 65-67, 73,
77, 80-82, 84, 87, 89, 111,
113-118, 122, 127, 130
Reading, Henry 238
Readings,
  Elizabeth xx
  John xx, xxix, 35, 80, 81, 320
Reed, A. 179, 199, 302, 305
Regent Place xxv
Remnant, John xii, xiii
Repton 179
Richerson, Jane xix n1, 20, 21
Rickford
  Hannah Maria xxxi, 89, 91-94,
  99-110
  Thomas xxxi, 47, 48, 59, 62, 63,
  75
    death xxxi, 92, 99, 101
    lease of Pigeons xxxi, 47, 59,
    62, 63, 75, 79, 83-89, 93, 99,
    105, 106, 124, 126
    will 91, 92, 94, 99, 101, 102
  Thomas Parker (Captain) xxxi,
  89, 91-94, 99-106, 109, 110
Ring, Bulley & Co. 22
Roberts, Mrs 179
Robinson,
  Ellen 276-278, 281-287, 289
  Rev Dr 180
  Rev J. E. 180
  Wydow 9
Rolph,
  Alfred 250
  Joseph 274, 275
Row, William 180
Royal Berkshire Archives xv

D/ELV/O17 11
D/EPB/C95/1 182
D/EPB/C95/1a 164, 182 n1
D/EPB/C95/2 182
D/EPB/C95/3 184
D/EPB/C95/3a 166, 184 n1
D/EPB/C95/4 185
D/EPB/C95/5 187
D/EPB/C95/6 187
D/EPB/C95/6a 167, 187 n1
D/EPB/C95/7 188
D/EPB/C95/7a 169, 188 n1
D/EPB/C95/8 189
D/P97/28/8/4 206
D/P163/1/1 xlvii n4
D/P163/1/5 xlvii n6
D/QC5/3 207
Q/SO/5 12
R/AC1/1/24 xvii n3, xxx n1
R/AC1/1/25 20 n1
R/AC1/1/26 83
R/AC1/2/1 23 n1
R/AC1/2/4 29
R/AS2/4 xxv n3
R/AT3/25/10 xi n6
R/D49/1/1 130
R/D142/3/18 xxv n4
R/ES4/1 208
R/ES4/3 264
R/FZ2/23/8 xiv n2
R/FZ2/24/4 xii n3
R/FZ2/31/21 xv n2, xv n3, 10
R/FZ2/31/41 xv n2
R/FZ2/37/1 xv n2
R/FZ2/37/14 xv n2
R/FZ2/38/6 16
R/FZ2/40/18 xv n2
R/FZ2/41/8 xv n2
R/FZ2/43/6 xv n2, 20
R/FZ2/43/32 22
R/FZ2/45/6 19
R/FZ2/45/7 17
R/FZ2/46/25 xv n2
R/FZ2/46/40 xv n2

R/FZ2/47/3 xv n2
R/FZ2/48/10 xv n2
R/FZ2/48/13 xv n2
R/FZ2/50/7 xv n2
R/FZ2/55/1 xv n2
R/FZ2/55/13 xv n2
R/FZ2/56/45 xv n2
R/FZ2/57/23 xv n2
R/FZ2/62/13 84
R/IC1/6 1
R/IC1/8 2
R/JQ1/10A/1 13
R/JQ1/10A/2 13
R/JQ1/10A/3 14
R/JQ1/10A/4 15
R/JQ1/19 23
R/Z3/13 9
R/Z8/1 3
R/Z8/2 8
R/Z8/5 xiv n1
R/Z8/7 xv n1
Royal East Middlesex Militia 74
Royalist xiv
Rudall, William 111, 113-115, 117
Ruddock, Messrs 180
Russell,
  Lord John xx n4, 26-28
  William 55, 127
Russell Street xxiii n2
Sackville Street xxv n4
Saddington 130
Sadler, Hannah 242
Saint (St) Giles's
  parish 13-15, 189
  patronage xxxiii, 186
  vicar xxxix, xlii, xlii n1
Saint (St) James Church,
  Westminster 130
Saint (St) John's
  Girls' School 227
  Infant School 248
Saint (St) Jude's Church, Chelsea
  xli

Saint (St) Laurence's
  (Lawrence's)
  Church in Appleby, 172
  Church in Reading xii, xxi, 152, 153, 219
  churchwardens 196
  Curate of, xxiii, 6
  parish of, xxvii, xxxi n2,
    xxxiv n2, 6, 14-16, 47, 77, 83,
    85, 86, 90, 92, 97, 104, 106,
    124, 128, 130, 133, 134, 137,
    139, 140, 145, 146, 152-154,
    156-159, 161, 162, 186, 190,
    193, 196, 206, 207, 250, 275
  patron(age) of xxxiii, 153, 167, 183, 186
  school 259, 275, 278
  vicar of xxiii, xxxix, xlii, xlii n1,
    152, 153, 155, 156, 167, 169,
    186, 196
  Workhouse xxvi, 224 n1
Saint (St) Mary's
  Butts xxii, xxxvi
  Church xxi
  parish xxvii, 14, 185, 206, 207
  patronage of xxxiii, 186
  vicar of xxxix, xlii, xlii n1, 169, 186, 189
Saint (St) Peter-le-Bailey Church,
  Oxford xli
Salisbury 285
Salmon,
  F. 180
  W. 180
Salter, Joseph 240
Saul, Mrs 180
Saunders, Hannah 10
Savile Row 130
Savory, J. 180
Sawyer, C. 180
Sayer, Alfred 253, 260
Scholar xxvi, 224, 232, 256
Scotford, Sarah 10
Searle, Thomas xlvii n1

Sellar, A. 180
Sellwood, R. 180
Selwyn,
　Rev E. 180
　Rev E. J. 180
Seven Bridges 224 n1
Shackel, W. 180
Shaile, Richard 14
Shailor (see Shaylor)
Sharp,
　Granville 30
　Mr 302, 305
Shaylor (Shailor),
　John xvii, xviii, xxx, 95, 77, 82, 85, 133, 320
　William 132
Sheepshanks, Miss 180
Sheppard,
　Ambrose xxxvi, xxxvi n4, 180, 199, 200, 204, 204 n1, 222, 317
　Mrs H. 180, 302, 305
Sherfield, Kate 249, 251, 254-256
Sheriffe, Miss 302, 305
Sherwood,
　H. 302, 305
　Mrs R. 180
　R. 180
　Sarah 272, 273
　W. 180, 302, 305
Shinfield (Shinefield) 185
Shoemaker xx, xxvi, 14
Shuter, Mrs T. A. 180
Siege of Reading xiv
Simmons,
　Charles 13
　Emily (see Simmonds)
　George 240, 242, 243
　Mrs 255
Simonds,
　B. 19
　Henry 42
　Henry Adolphus (Councillor, Mayor) 30, 32, 35

H. & G. Simonds Brewery 224 n1
　John xxvii, xxvii n2, xxxiii, 152-154, 156, 165, 167, 170, 180, 302, 305, 320
　John & Charles, Bank xxvii n2, 166, 170, 198
　Miss 180
　Mrs Charles 180, 302, 305
Simmonds (Simmons), Emily 264-267, 269, 271, 273, 274, 276-279, 281, 285, 287-290
Simpson
　Henry 20 n1, 320
　William 20, 20 n1, 21
Skye, Thomas 14
Slaughter, John 132
Slocombe,
　Francis Morgan xxxii, xxxiii, xxxvi n7, 42, 139-152, 162, 172, 196
　W. 180, 302, 305
Smart, Thomas 288
Smith, 199, 200, 202
　C. W. 180
　Dr R. P. 180
　Elizabeth 239, 252
　Jason 180
　Josiah 250
　J. S. 180
　Matilda 257
　Miss 302, 305
　Mr 319
　Mrs 302, 305
　Mrs Bailey 180
　Mrs C. S. 302, 305
　Mrs W. C. 302, 305
　Olive 240, 246
　S. 180
　Thomas 132
Smither, W. 237
Snare, Mrs 302, 305
Snowdon, T. F. 180
Society for Promoting

Christianity amongst the Jews 295
Somerset Place xxv n5, xxvi, xlvii, 292, 293
Sonning xxiii
Soole,
  Laura (see Laura Sutton)
  Rev Seymour Henry xxvii n3
Southampton 90, 91, 99, 136, 238, 247
Southey, Mrs 302, 305
Southwold xli
Sowdon, T. F. 302, 305
Soy, C. & C. 203
Speenhamland 3, 4, 6
Spillard, Marianne Eliza 321
Spokes,
  James (jun.) 20
  James (sen.) 20
  P. 180
Sprague,
  T. 180
  T. B. 180
St Maur, Lady Henrietta 180
Stafford, County of 152
Stamp, Hannah 16
Stanshawe, Robert xxix, xxix n4, 1, 2, 65, 66
Stanshawe Road xxv, xxv n4, 292
Star Lane xxii
Stark, John H. 321
Statutory Declaration by
  John Jackson Blandy xxix, 48, 66, 67, 81
  John Readings xxix, 80
  William Blandy 144, 151
Stephens,
  Charles 57, 119, 123, 126-128
  Mrs 180
  William 95, 135-138, 141, 151
Stephens, Blandy & Co, bankers, 166, 170, 180
Stevens,
  Miss 180
  W. 180
Steward, Mr Councillor 33, 36
Stewart,
  Alice 14
  Duncan 180
Stiles 204
Stirling, Rev C. 180
Stokes, D. 180
Stone, Mrs 180
Stone mason xxvi, xxxv, xxxvi, xxxvi n2, xxxvi n3, xxxvii, 190, 191, 193
Strachan,
  James Morgan 320
  Miss 180
Strahern, J. M. 165 n2
Strange, W. 180
Straw xv, xviii, xix, 5, 21
Street, George E. 189
Strickland, W. H. 202-204, 321
Strong,
  George 137
  George Simmonds xlv, 146
Stuart, Clarence E. 180
Stubbles, Sarah 228, 231, 232, 235, 238, 239
Styles,
  T. V. 181
  Willie 280, 288
Suffolk xli
Sulhamstead xxiv
Sun Fire Insurance 48, 87
Surgeon xviii, xxvi, 21, 142, 144, 151
Surrey 99, 105, 135, 136
Sutton, 238
  A. 181, 302, 305
  Laura (m. Rev S. H. Soole) xxvii n3
  Martin Hope xxvii, xxvii n3, 181, 203, 228, 302, 305, 319
    Memorial Hall xxvii n3
    memorial in Greyfriars church xxvii n3

Messrs 181
Miss 235, 238, 239, 241-243,
  246, 247, 250-255, 258, 259,
  261, 262, 268, 269-280,
  283 285, 287, 288, 290
Miss E. 302, 305
Mrs M. H. 203, 302, 305
& Sons xxvii n3
Swain, Charles 321
Swallow, James 15
Sweeting, Miss 258
Swinny, John 209
Symes, John xii
Szlarska, Madame 181
Tagg's children 241
Tailor xxvi
Tanner,
  Jonathan 95
  Miss 181, 293, 302, 305
  Miss M. 181
  Mr 302, 305
Tatem, Miss 302, 305
Taylor,
  Mr Councillor 30, 32, 44
  J. 181
  J. O. 181
  William 13
  Teacher xxvi, xlvi, 210, 213, 221,
    224, 226-238, 240, 248, 251,
    253, 255, 257, 259, 261, 265,
    266, 269, 272-274, 276, 277,
    278-280, 282, 288, 293
  Certified xliii, 231, 253, 262,
    288
  Examination of 231, 253, 261,
    268, 279, 287
  Head (see Head Master, Head
    Mistress) xliii, xliv
  Probationary xliv
  Pupil (P.T.) xliv, 211, 212, 214,
    225, 243, 253, 255, 256, 262,
    279, 287, 288, 290, 296
  Sunday School 250, 295
  Trinity Church Boys' School
    181
Teddington xli
Terry,
  Miss 181
  W. 181
Thane, William 132
Theale 3, 4
The Builder xxi n1
The National Archives xxv n2
Thomas,
  Mary Anne 263, 268, 285
  Sarah 251, 259
Thompson, Rev Sir H. 181
Thorn (see Lower Thorn Street)
  Court xxv n5, 293
  Street xxvi, 206, 207, 292, 293
Thorne, George xii
Thorp, Joseph 13
Thorpe, Mrs 302, 305
Thoyts, M. G. 181
Three Pigeons (see Pigeons)
  xxxi n1, 63, 126
Thwaites, A. 181
Tilehurst 136
Tiler xxxv, xxxvi
Tilleard, Richard 11
Tite, W. M.P. 181
Town Hall 1, 32, 49, 122
Tramper 14
Trench, Rev F. 181
Trendell, J. 181
Trimmer, William 137
Trinity
  Church xxiii, xlii, 62, 152, 185
    Boys' School 181
    district 189
    Infant School 255
    National School 213, 254
  Lodge/Parsonage (see Carlisle
    House) xlii, 41, 166, 168-170,
    183, 187, 188
  Place xli
Tristram, T. H., D.C.L. 181
Trowbridge, Haden of xxxvi

Trustees of the Birkenhead Docks
v. Laird 115
Tubb,
 Edwin 238, 247
 Henry xiii, xiv
 Mrs 181
Tucker,
 Rev John 181
 Thomas 21
Tudor Road (Street) xxv, 292
Tull,
 H. 181
 Mrs 181
Turner,
 Lord 114
 Richard xi, xi n6
 Thomas 20
Tutbury Castle 174
Twysden, Rev T. 181
Tyndale,
 George Booth 130, 131,
  134-138, 141, 151
 Rev T. 181
Tyrrell, John 135, 136
Uhthoff, G. 181
Umritzur 294
Underwood, James 10
Upper Clapton 70
Urmston, Mrs H. Brabazon 181
Usborne Miss E. 181
Vachel,
 Dorothy 134
 Thomas 134
Vachel Road xi, xxv, 292
Valpy,
 Capt., R.N. 181
 Mrs 181
 Mrs G. 176, 181
 Penelope (see Mrs Penelope
  French) xxiii n2
 Rev Dr Richard xxiii n2
 Rev Gabriel 181
 Rev Julius 181
 Thomas Valpy French xxiii n2

Vanheythuson, Major 181
Vansittart, George 13
Vastern (Fostern) Meadow 133,
 134, 137
Vincent, Widow 132
Vines,
 Charles 181
 Edward 91, 99-101
Wainhouse,
 Miss 293
 The Misses 303, 306
Waldegrave, Hon & Rt Rev
 Samuel, 174
Walford, Mr Alderman 33, 36
Walker, 202, 203
 Charles 20, 21
Wallace, John 15, 15 n3
Waller,
 Mrs 293, 303, 306
 R. W. 181, 204
Wallington, Joseph 15
Walter
 Jacob 15
 John, M. P. 181
Walthamstow xli, 316
Wantage 3
Warburton, John 320
Ward, Fred 289
Wardell, Miss 181
Warner,
 John Warner & Sons xxxvi
 Thomas 15, 16
Warren Place xxv n5, xxvi, xlvii,
 292
Wasey, Miss 181
Washerwoman xxvi
Water Rate 202, 203, 298, 299
Watson,
 Alfred 253, 268
 Thomas 13
Waugh,
 D. prayer
 E. 240
 Mary Jane 232, 235-238,

240-242, 244-250, 252-255
Webb,
  Grace 16
  John 16
  Mary 137
  Mrs R. 181, 303, 306
  R. T. 181
  W. 216
Weedon,
  estate xxiv
  John xxxii n3, 130, 138-145, 151, 165
  Mrs Sarah xxiv, xxv, xxxiii, 145-147, 151, 172, 181
Weightman,
  Mr 319
  Mrs 293, 303, 306
Weldale (Welldale)
  Place 293
  Street xxv, xxvi, 206, 293
Wellman, Mr 303, 306
Wells,
  Councillor Dr 29, 30, 32-34
  John 34
Wellsteed, Moores, Co. 303, 306
Wentworth, William 132
Westmerland, Robert xiv, xiv n2
Westminster 2, 48, 51, 87, 130
West Street xlvii, 206, 207, 292, 293
  Hall xlii
Weymouth 240, 242, 286
Whaley, W. J. 127
Wheeler,
  John (elder) xxxvi, 190-193
  John (younger) xxxvi, 190-193
  Messrs Wheeler Brothers xxxv-xxxvii, 181, 190, 193, 199, 201, 203, 296, 303, 306, 317, 319
  Miss 293, 303, 306, 319
  Miss 181
  Mrs S. 303, 306
  Samuel xxxvi, xxxvi n1,
190-193, 319
Whitaker (Whittaker), Alfred Hanbury 65, 112, 115
White,
  Edward Skeate 13
  James 21
  Lieutenant Colonel Luke 119, 127, 128
  Mary 14
  William 21
White, Borrett & White 158, 159, 161, 162
Whitehall 26-28
  Place 156-159, 161, 162
Whitelands 261
Whitesmith xviii, 17, 17 n1, 21
Wickes, Mrs 303, 306
Wicks, Charlotte 256
Wigfield, Mrs 181
Wilberforce, Rt Rev Samuel xxxiii, xxxix, 152, 153, 156, 196, 197, 314, 315
Wild,
  Alice 253, 262
  Martha 15
Wilder,
  F. 182
  Rev Henry 12
  Rev John 182
Wilkins,
  John 225
  Mrs 303, 306
Willats, Mr 303, 306
Willcox (Wilcox), Caroline xliii, xliv, 208, 217, 231, 243, 253, 262, 266, 273, 274, 321
Williams
  Deacon & Co 170
  family (Greyfriars missionaries) xxxvi n1
  George 47, 63, 83, 86, 90, 92, 97, 105, 106, 126
  Samuel 14
Willis,

Nellie 260, 261
William 13
Willie 253
Willis, Percival & Co 170
Wills, John 89, 99, 101-108, 110
Willson
  Charles F. xlvii, 181, 198, 300, 303, 306, 315, 316, 318, 319, 321
  Mrs 182, 303, 306
Wilson, 200, 202
  Alfred 182
  Col Samuel 182
  C. Lea 182
  Ford 182
  George 241
  Miss 202, 211, 222
  Rev Canon 182
  Robert 47, 86, 90, 92, 97, 105, 106
  The Misses 182, 238, 302, 305, 319
Wilton xxiii n4
Wiltshire xxiii n4, xxvi
Winche, Richard xii
Winchester xx
Wood, Mrs 182
Woodford, Rev J. R. xl
Woodhouse, Dr R. T. 182, 319
Woodley,
  Francis 13
  T. 182
Woodman,
  Miss 182
  Mrs 302, 305
  Poulton & Woodman xxxv, 190-192
  William H. xxxvi, xlii, xlvii, 38, 182, 195, 198-202, 321
Woods,
  Henry 260
  Mrs 303, 306
  The two 285
Wooton, Mr 303, 306

Wootton, W. 182, 201
Workman,
  C. 298, 299
  Dr 319
  John W. 182, 303, 305
  Mrs 218, 221, 225, 226, 241, 254, 257-259, 261, 283, 285, 286, 293, 294, 303, 305
  Mrs J. 182
  Mrs W. R. 182
  Thomas Skeete 142-145, 151
Worthington, Miss 182
Wyatt, Louisa 252
Wyndham v. Rickford 102, 103
Yateley 180
Yield Hall (see Guildhall) xi, xi n6
York
  Place xxv n5, 206, 207, 293
  Terrace 292
Young,
  Miss 182
  William 21
Young Men's Association 182

Berkshire Record Society: volumes in print

Berkshire Glebe Terriers, 1634, ed. Ian Mortimer (1995)

Berkshire Probate Accounts, 1583-1712, ed. Ian Mortimer (1997)

Enclosure in Berkshire, 1485-1885, ed. Ross Wordie (1998)

Reading Gild Accounts, 1357-1516, ed. Cecil Slade (2 vols, 1999-2000)

Accounts of the Kendrick Charity Workhouse, Newbury, 1627-1641, ed. Christine Jackson (2001)

Berkshire Nonconformist Meeting House Registrations, 1689-1852, ed. Lisa Spurrier (2 vols, 2002-3)

Thames Navigation Commission Minutes, 1771-1790, ed. Jeremy Sims (2 vols, 2004-5)

The Diocese Books of Samuel Wilberforce, 1845 and 1854, ed. Ronald and Margaret Pugh (2006)

Berkshire Religious Census, 1851, ed. Kate Tiller (2007)

Berkshire Archdeaconry Probate Records, 1480-1652: Index, ed. Pat Naylor (3 vols, 2008-9)

Diaries and Correspondence of Robert Lee of Binfield, 1736-1744, ed. Harry Leonard (2010)

Reading St Laurence Churchwardens' Accounts, 1498-1570, ed. Joan Dils (2 vols, 2011-12)

The Church Inspection Notebook of Archdeacon James Randall, 1855-1873, and other Records, ed. Sabina Sutherland (2013)

Newbury to Chilton Pond Turnpike Records, 1766-1791, ed. Jeremy Sims (2014)

Berkshire Feet of Fines, 1307-1509, ed. Margaret Yates (2 vols, 2015-16)

Reading Abbey Records: a New Miscellany, ed. Brian Kemp (2018)

Berkshire Schools in the Eighteenth Century, ed. Sue Clifford (2019)

Hungerford Overseers' Accounts, 1655-1834, ed. Peter Durrant (2021)

Tudor Windsor, ed. David Lewis (2022)

Medicine and Society in Late Eighteenth-Century Berkshire: The Commonplace Book of William Savory of Brightwalton and Newbury, ed. Stuart Eagles (2024)

Greyfriars, Reading: From Prison to Parish Church, ed. Malcolm Summers (2024)

To order volumes, and to join the Society, please use the links on the website www.berkshirerecordsociety.org.uk. Postal enquiries to the Berkshire Record Society, c/o Royal Berkshire Archives, 9 Coley Avenue, Reading, Berkshire RG1 6AF.